British Armored Car in Jerusalem, March 1948

UNDER THE COVER OF WAR

As long as memory is alive . . . hope in our return is alive.
Hamdi Muhammad Matar, Qaluniya village

PALESTINIAN FAMILY FROM BAYT SAHUR VILLAGE

UNDER THE COVER OF WAR

The Zionist Expulsion of the Palestinians

ROSEMARIE M. ESBER

Arabicus Books & Media

First U.S. Edition

For information about permission to reproduce selections from this book, write to
Permissions, Arabicus Books & Media, LLC
P.O. Box 320092, Alexandria, VA 22320

Cover art and book design by Alex McDonald, VPI

Library of Congress Cataloging-in-Publication Data

Esber, Rosemarie M.
Under the cover of war : the Zionist expulsion of the Palestinians / Rosemarie M.
Esber. -- 1st ed.
p. cm.
Summary: "Under the Cover of War presents a critical examination of the last six
months of the British Palestine mandate, November 1947 to mid-May 1948. Unpublished
military and diplomatic sources and new, original refugee interviews support the Palestinians account of their Nakba (catastrophe)"--Provided by publisher.
Includes bibliographical references and index.
ISBN 978-0-9815131-7-1 (alk. paper)
1. Palestine--History--1929-1948. 2. Jewish-Arab relations--20th century. 3. Jews--
Palestine--History--20th century. 4. Jews--Palestine--Politics and government--20th
century. 5. Arabs--Palestine--History--20th century. 6. Arabs--Palestine--Politics and
government--20th century. 7. Palestine--Politics and government--1917-1948. 8. Great
Britain--Politics and government--20th century. 9. Refugees, Palestinian Arab--History--
20th century. 10. Zionism--Palestine--History--20th century. I. Title.

DS126.E764 2008
956.94'04--dc22

2008014389

Arabicus Books & Media, LLC
P.O. Box 320092, Alexandria, VA 22320
www.arabicusbooks.com

Printed in the United States of America
2 3 4 5 6 7 8 9 0

Not only did they drive us out of our villages and cities,
but also from the habitations of men.

Badr Shakir al-Sayyab, *Caravan of the Wretched*

PALESTINIAN REFUGEE MOTHER AND CHILD NEAR JERUSALEM, 1948

To those forced from their homelands, abused,
neglected, and abandoned; and,

To my family and friends for your constant
encouragement, support, and love,

I dedicate this book.

PHOTOGRAPHS

Front cover: Palestinian boy holding his sister, Lebanon, 1948
Back cover: Haganah forces attacking Palestinian village near
al-Ramla, 1948

Maps

CONTENTS

ACKNOWLEDGMENTS

This book began as a quest to understand the root causes of the Arab-Israeli conflict. It could not have been completed without the unwavering support of my extended family, friends, and the staff of many institutions.

I would like to thank the staff of numerous archives, including the British National Archives, the Friends Service Committee in London, the American Friends Service Committee in Philadelphia, St. Antony's Middle East Center, the Imperial War Museum, the U.S. National Archives, and the United Nations. I am also grateful to the librarians of the School of Oriental and African Studies, University of London; Georgetown University Special Collections; George Washington University; the Middle East Institute; and the Library of Congress, especially the prints and photographs division.

A grant from the Council of American Overseas Research Centers (CAORC) enabled my oral history research in Jordan and Lebanon. The CAORC director, Mary Ellen Lane, was especially supportive of this project. The Hashemite Kingdom of Jordan's Department of Palestinian Affairs granted permission for research in the Palestinian refugee camps. My research in Jordan and Lebanon was facilitated by CAORC's Amman office, by Le Centre d'Etudes et de Recherches sur le Moyen-Orient Contemporain (CERMOC), and by the Jordanian Women's Union. Afaf al-Jabiri was singularly helpful in facilitating field research in the refugee camps throughout Jordan.

Many other individuals supported my field research. Oroub El-Abed facilitated my research in Lebanon and Jordan. Ibtisam al-Khalil, with the National Institute of Social Care and Vocational Training located in the ʿAyn al-Hilwa refugee camp, assisted in collecting interviews in Lebanon. CERMOC in Beirut was a welcoming research base.

I am also indebted to my parents Mary and Edward, and my aunts Rose Marie and Margaret, for their support. I want to thank Mary Ann, Edward, and Mark Esber, Rouane Itani, Patricia Lee, Patrick Marroum, Alixa Naff, Marguerite Nakhoul, Amy Thomas, and Tahani Sharé for their editorial, linguistic, and logistical assistance.

I am grateful to Alex McDonald for his dedication to the design and production of this book and to Kate Mertes for preparing the index.

A number of colleagues read prior versions of the manuscript and provided invaluable comments, including Tancred Bradshaw, Matthew Hogan, Alex Martin, Khalid Al-Saif, Emad Shahin, Paula Simmons, David Sowd, and Lynn Simarski.

I am deeply indebted to all the Palestinian refugees who entrusted me with their experiences and shared their traumatic memories. They understand the importance of history and of never forgetting. I will never forget them.

Rosemarie M. Esber
May 2008

ABBREVIATIONS

AACI	Anglo-American Committee of Inquiry
ACP	Aharon Cohen Papers
AEC	Arab Emergency Committee
AFSC	American Friends Service Committee Archive
AHC	Arab Higher Committee
AHE	Arab Higher Executive
AIR	Air Ministry
ALA	Arab Liberation Army
ANC	Arab National Committee
BGA	Ben-Gurion Research Center, Sde Boker
BMEO	British Middle East Office
CAB	Cabinet Office Papers
CIA	Central Intelligence Agency
CID	Criminal Investigation Division
CO	Colonial Office Papers
COS	Chief of Staff
CP	Sir Alan Cunningham Papers
CZA	Central Zionist Archives
DAG	Departmental Archives Groups
DEFE	U.K. Ministry of Defense
DBG–YH	David Ben-Gurion's Yoman Hamilhama, 1948-1949 (The War Diary)
EMP	Elizabeth Monroe Papers
FBIS	Foreign Broadcast Intelligence Service
FO	Foreign Office Papers
FM	Foreign Ministry (Israel)
FP	W. V. Fuller Papers
FRUS	Foreign Relations of the United States
GLP	Sir John Glubb Papers
GOC	General Officer Commanding
GP	Sir Henry Gurney Papers
GSC	General Staff Counsel
GSI	General Staff Intelligence
HA	Haganah Archives
HHA	Hashomer Hatzair Archive
HIS-AD	Haganah Intelligence Service – Arab Department

HQ	Headquarters
ICP	Israeli Communist Party Papers
IDF	Israeli Defense Force
IDFA	Israel Defense Forces and Defense Ministry Archives
ISA	Israeli State Archives
IZL	Irgun Zva'i Leumi (National Military Organization, or the Irgun)
JEM	Jerusalem East Mission Papers
JI IZL	Jabotinsky Institute, IZL Papers
JM	Justice Ministry Papers
KMA	Kibbutz Meuhad Archives
KMA-PA	Kibbutz Meuhad Palmach Archives
LA	Labor Archives
LPA	Labor Party (Mapai) Archives
LCP	Larry Collins Papers
LHI	Lohamei Herut Yisrael (Freedom Fighters of Israel, or Stern Gang)
MAM	Israel Minority Affairs Ministry Papers
MELF	Middle East Land Forces
MP	Miss Dorothy Blanche Morgan
NACP	U.S. National Archives at College Park, Maryland
NP	Lieutenant Colonel C. R. W. Norman Papers
OC	Officer Commanding
PP	General Sir Harold English Pyman
PRO	Public Records Office
QHR	Quarterly Historical Report
RAF	Royal Air Force
SP	Lieutenant General Hugh Stockwell Papers
STH	Sefer Toldot Hahaganah (History of the Haganah)
TJFF	Transjordan Frontier Force
TNA	The National Archives of the United Kingdom
TT	Thames Television
WO	War Office Papers
YND	Yosef Nahmani Diary
UNPC	U.N. Palestine Commission
UNSCOP	U.N. Special Committee on Palestine

A CROWD IN CAIRO PROTESTING THE U.N. RESOLUTION
TO PARTITION PALESTINE, DECEMBER 1947

INTRODUCTION

The defeat of the Arabs in Palestine is no simple setback or light, passing evil.
It is a disaster in every sense of the word.

Constantine K. Zurayk, *The Meaning of the Disaster*

The transformation of the great mass of Palestinian Arab society into refugees is a saga of betrayal, human suffering, and violent dispossession. Zionist Jewish settlers expelled the indigenous Palestinian Arabs[1] from their ancestral lands during the 1948 Palestine war. The escalating violence in Palestine from November 1947 to mid-May 1948 resulted in the Palestinians' loss of lives, homes, lands, and livelihoods— and the beginning of the Arab-Israeli conflict. Subsequent regional wars have been deeply rooted in the Palestinians' forced displacement, the destruction of their society, and the seizure of Arab lands during the establishment of the State of Israel in 1948. International repercussions of the Arab-Israeli conflict continue to affect global stability.

This book does not tell the story of the creation of *all* the Palestinian refugees or the entire history of the ongoing Arab-Israeli conflict. Rather, it focuses on the final six months of the British Palestine mandate, which coincides with the civil war phase of the Palestinian-Zionist[2] conflict. This study aims to improve understanding of a period that determined the outcome of the 1948 war: the creation of a Jewish state and of stateless Palestinians.

The final months of Britain's rule over Palestine were perhaps more decisive—and certainly more violent—than the preceding three decades of colonial rule. The country quickly degenerated into civil war as Britain abandoned the Holy Land to its mutually hostile Arab and Jewish inhabitants. The political leadership of the *yishuv*, the minority Jewish community, seized the initiative to determine Palestine's fate. Zionists sought with single-minded determination to establish a Jewish state in mandate Palestine, while the Palestinian Arabs, the majority community, tried with varying degrees of ability and commitment to prevent that outcome. The fragmented Palestinian leadership (weakly supported by Arab neighbors with questionable motives and competence) proved incapable against its more sophisticated and better prepared Zionist opponents.

Random acts of violence by Arabs and Jews followed the November 1947 U.N. resolution supporting the partition of Palestine and quickly escalated into full-blown civil war. The six months of intercommunal violence initiated and shaped the removal of the Palestinian population. During the civil war period, Zionist Jewish military organizations forced more than 400,000 Palestinian Arab inhabitants from their homes in about 225 villages, towns, and cities in Palestine.

From mid-May 1948 through early 1949, an interstate war—partly provoked by the Zionist depredations against Palestinian civilians—raged between the newly declared State of Israel and neighboring Arab countries. During these eight months, Israeli armed forces drove approximately 400,000 more Palestinians from their homes and lands, depopulating another 306 towns and villages. Israeli forces seized 78 percent of mandate Palestine during the 1948 war. Dispossessed and dispersed in the region and worldwide, the Palestinians have been prevented by Israel from returning to their homes and lands since 1948.

In the six decades since the 1948 war, the government of Israel has used various techniques to continue its policy of subjugating the Palestinian Arab population under its control and seizing additional Arab land. Sanctioned methods include violence, anti-Arab legislation, confiscation, isolation, deprivation, and harassment by Israeli settlers, whose impunity the state protects.

Although the existence of Palestinian refugees is acknowledged by the international community, the causes of the Palestinians' displacement, and its crucial beginnings in late 1947 and early 1948, are less well known. The Palestinian narrative of profound fear and enduring loss is frequently distorted in the telling, and often dismissed when told, even by scholars who have consulted Israeli archives that corroborate the Palestinians' victimization. This book recounts that story in verifiable detail.

I refer extensively to unpublished materials to describe the early period of Palestinian Arab displacement. Two primary sources proved essential to reconstructing this critical history. The first is my original collection of over 130 oral testimonies from Palestinian refugees who witnessed and were victims of the civil war. The second primary source is documentation from the U.S., British, and U.N. archives, particularly underutilized military records. The documentary record is mutually supportive of and corroborated by the oral testimonies of refugees. I review all of these sources against a broad array of secondary Israeli historical studies that are based on archival sources.

Palestinian oral accounts and narratives are essential not only for a comprehensive detailed factual account of this period but also from a moral perspective to understand historical events from all sides. Palestinians refer to the dispersal of the population and the destruction of their culture and society in 1948 as *al-Nakba* (the catastrophe or disaster). The *Nakba* is the Palestinians' own story of tragedy and loss, and they are the most credible source to tell it.

The expulsion of Palestine's Arabs is a historic injustice. The people of nearly an entire nation were driven from homes and native lands that their ancestors had inhabited for centuries. An estimated eighty-four percent of the Palestinians expelled were children under 15, pregnant girls and women, nursing mothers, people over 60, and the infirm. In modern terminology, such wholesale population removal is called "ethnic cleansing."[3]

Since 1948, Palestinians and Israelis have vehemently debated the causes that led to the Palestinians' displacement, each side blaming the other. Palestinians generally contend that they were intentionally forced from their homeland by Zionist Jewish settlers who wished to seize their land for a Jewish state. Israelis typically have assigned responsibility for the Palestinians' displacement to several factors—alleged evacuation orders issued by Arab leaders, the "spontaneous" and "natural" consequences of a bitterly fought war, and the Arab states' aggressive military measures intended, Israelis argue, to prevent the establishment of the Jewish state.

In fact, the Palestinian version of events is far closer to the truth. By including the Palestinians' own narrative along with British, American, and other contemporary written and oral accounts (including available prestate and early state Israeli records) the full story emerges, definitively revealing Israeli claims of innocence in the Palestinian population's displacement to be false.

The Palestinian refugee oral testimony combined with the documentary record confirms that Palestinian Arab displacement during the civil war period was primarily the result of the deliberate and systematic use of force against Arab civilian population centers by Zionist military organizations. Zionist forces engaged in intensifying threats and violence against civilians, with the purpose of depopulating Palestine of its majority non-Jewish inhabitants. This aggression was unleashed during the first period of the 1948 war.

Another ill-studied aspect of the early period that enabled the Palestinians' expulsion was the rationale and behavior of the British government as it relinquished the mandate and abandoned Palestine to its fate. How and why British withdrawal policy contributed to the Palestinians' forced displacement is also explained in this book. British policy, indifferent to consequences not affecting British interests, played a decisive role in the flow of events leading to the creation of the Palestinian refugees. Britain's "hands-off" policy resulted in a power vacuum that enabled Zionist military forces—under the cover of war and unimpeded by the threat of military intervention by the British or the Arab states—to begin forcibly intimidating the Palestinian Arabs to leave their homes during the mandate's final six months.

The British withdrawal from Palestine left an enduring problem for the international community (one that the United States should strive to avoid duplicating when it prepares to extricate its forces from Iraq). Unless the outstanding issues of 1948—most important among them the fate of the Palestinian refugees—are resolved, prospects for regional and world peace will remain bleak.

An enduring and just solution is possible if it is based on international law, human rights, and a thorough understanding of the roots of the Arab-Israeli conflict. This book seeks to contribute to that understanding. A peaceful resolution of the dispute should be based on the restoration of the legal and human rights of the Palestinians and the redress of injustices wrought in 1948 and after.

***

1. Palestinian Arabs are now referred to simply as "Palestinians."

2. The term *Zionist* refers to the yishuv's political aspiration of establishing a Jewish state in Palestine. The term also refers to the prestate Zionist fighting units and groups that would become the armed forces of the newborn state of Israel in May 1948. The term *Israeli* refers to the citizens of the new state and apparatus after the state's declaration.

3. The forcible deportation of a population is defined as a crime against humanity under the statutes of both the International Criminal Court and the International Criminal Tribunal for the Former Yugoslavia. In 1992, the U.N. General Assembly condemned ethnic cleansing and racial hatred in Resolution 47/80.

PALESTINIANS FROM HAIFA FLEEING ZIONIST
BOMBARDMENT, APRIL 1948

I

The Creation of Palestinian Refugees
A Historical Perspective

Hundreds of thousands of Arabs who will be evicted from Palestine . . .
will grow up to hate us.

Aharon Zisling, Israeli minister of agriculture, June 1948

The existence of Palestinian refugees remains an unresolved griev-
ance at the heart of the Arab-Israeli conflict and a major obstacle
to Middle East and world peace. The crux of the conflict is the
establishment of a Jewish state in Palestine, the Zionists' forced displacement and dispossession of the Palestinians from their homeland, and the
subjugation of Palestinians who remained in what became the State of
Israel in 1948, as well as those in the West Bank, East Jerusalem, and the
Gaza Strip, which Israel occupied in 1967.

Palestinian Arabs have struggled since the late nineteenth century to
retain their homeland and to prevent their displacement by Zionist settlers. After World War I, European Jewish settlers, with British approval
and protection, converged on the majority Arab country in great numbers
with the intention of transforming Palestine into a Jewish state. While
Britain still held the Palestine mandate, the Zionists succeeded in that
endeavor during the civil war, the first period of the 1948 war, before it
broadened into the regional Arab-Israeli War.

The conflict's human costs have been high, unbalanced, and are still
mounting. The British estimated the population of mandate Palestine at
1,320,000 Arabs and 640,000 Jews in May 1948.[1] In the 1948 war alone,

the *yishuv*, or prestate Jewish settlement in Palestine, suffered 6,000 dead, nearly 1 percent of the community, and thousands were injured. After European Jewry was decimated by the Holocaust, the additional Jewish lives lost to establish the Jewish state were particularly wrenching to the yishuv.

The Palestinian Arab losses are harder to calculate, if not impossible. With no Palestinian government and a wide dispersion of the population during and after the war, no accurate casualty records were created. Palestinian Arab society and culture were shattered in 1948, and an estimated 20,000 Palestinians died during the war, about 1.5 percent of the Palestinian Arab population. The number of Palestinians injured remains unknown.[2] Thousands of others, particularly children and the elderly, died as a result of the refugees' living conditions. A British Red Cross officer reported in 1949 that one refugee camp had 4 percent deaths per month.[3]

The great mass of Palestinians became refugees during the 1948 Arab-Israeli war. Zionist militias expelled approximately 800,000 indigenous Arabs from their homes and lands in Palestine. W. de St. Aubin, delegate of the League of Red Cross Societies to the Middle East, placed the number of refugees at closer to one million based on registration for relief.[4] An American Red Cross official estimated that pregnant and nursing mothers, children under 15, adults over 60, and the infirm composed 84 percent of Palestinian refugees by October 1948. A U.N. refugee expert supported this estimate.[5] The vast majority of Palestinians forced into exile were defenseless noncombatant civilians. Only a small percentage of refugees were able-bodied men; the rest were dependents and broken family groups, which had lost their men.[6]

Approximately 250,000 Palestinians who were driven from their homes lived in the area designated as the Jewish state in the U.N. partition plan. All others, about 69 percent, were expelled from areas designated as the Palestinian Arab state, in violation of the partition resolution.[7]

The 1948 Arab-Israeli war opened a conflict that continues to rage throughout the region and to cause worldwide repercussions. Since Israel was established during the 1948 war, many other wars have been fought to reassert or reverse the new realities. The 1956 Suez Crisis was precipitated by Britain, France, and Israel, which together attacked Egypt, ostensibly because Egypt had nationalized the Suez Canal and closed it to Israeli shipping. Israel initiated the 1967 war (Six Days' War)—purportedly fearing an imminent Egyptian invasion—with a preemptive strike against Egypt and Syria. In six days, Israel defeated Egypt, Jordan, and Syria and captured and occupied additional territory from each country, including the remaining parts of historical Palestine: the West Bank (and East Jerusalem) from Jordan, the Gaza Strip, as well as the Sinai Peninsula from Egypt, and the Golan Heights from Syria. Approximately 100,000 more Palestinians were forced from their homes by Israeli Defense Forces (IDF) and some 200,000 Jordanians, Syrians, and Egyptians were displaced from the occupied areas.[8]

From 1969 through 1970, hostilities continued between Israel and Egypt (the War of Attrition). Egypt initiated the war in an attempt to reclaim the Sinai with the support of the Soviet Union and the Palestinian Liberation Organization (PLO). During the 1973 war, Egypt again attempted to reclaim the Sinai Peninsula—and Syria the Golan Heights—from Israel. The end of the war opened the way for peace talks between Egypt and Israel.

Since the late 1960s, Israel has been in almost continuous conflict with Lebanon, its northern neighbor, which hosts an estimated 100,000 Palestinian Arabs displaced during the 1948 Arab-Israeli War. The refugees destabilized Lebanon's delicate sectarian balance and provided recruits for PLO military operations. Israeli forces raided Lebanon in 1968 and 1973 in response to cross-border attacks by Palestinian guerrillas. In 1978, Israel invaded south Lebanon up to the Litani River in an attempt to push the PLO from south Lebanon. An estimated 14,000 Lebanese and Palestinian civilians were killed in the fighting. Ongoing PLO guerrilla incursions and attacks in northern Israel resulted in Israel's 1982 invasion of Lebanon. Israeli forces bombarded Beirut, occupied southern Lebanon, and enabled allied Lebanese Christian militias to massacre hundreds of civilian Palestinians in the Sabra and Shatila refugee camps on the outskirts of Beirut.

Israel continued its occupation of southern Lebanon until 2000, when Hizballah[9] (the Party of God) paramilitary forces drove Israeli occupying forces from Lebanon. Hostilities on the border continued until the 2006 Lebanon War, which was allegedly sparked by Hizballah's abducting two Israeli soldiers and killing three others. In response, Israel invaded Lebanon and battled Hizballah paramilitary forces in southern Lebanon and northern Israel.

LEBANON

Safad

SYRIA

Acre

Haifa

Tiberias

Nazareth

Baysan

Jinin

River Jordan

Tulkarm

Nablus

Jaffa

MEDITERRANEAN SEA

Ramallah

Al-Ramla

Jerusalem

Gaza

Hebron

Dead Sea

Beersheba

EGYPT

0 10 20 30 40 50

Kilometers

TRANSJORDAN

Mandate Palestine Subdistricts and Capitals 1947-48

Israeli bombardment severely damaged the infrastructure of Lebanon and further traumatized the war-weary population. Over one million Lebanese civilians were displaced; 1,000 Lebanese, mostly civilians, were killed, and thousands were injured; while 123 Israelis were killed, 300,000–500,000 were displaced, and Hizballah rocket attacks damaged infrastructure in northern Israel. Just before a U.N.-brokered cease-fire in August 2006, Israel dropped millions of unexploded cluster bombs on Lebanon, which continue to maim and kill Lebanese civilians. Israel's bombing of the Jiyyeh power station released about 15,000 tons of heavy fuel oil (more than 4 million gallons) into the Mediterranean, damaging the ecosystem and creating a long-term environmental disaster for countries bordering the sea. Another 25,000 tons of oil from the power plant burned, spewing a black cloud into the air which rained toxic oil downwind.[10]

While Palestinians who remained on their lands endure second-class status as Arab citizens of the State of Israel, those Palestinians living in the occupied West Bank, East Jerusalem, and the Gaza Strip bear the daily deprivations and humiliations of military occupation. Two major popular *intifadas* (uprisings) have erupted against Israeli occupation since 1967. The first began in the Palestinian refugee camp of Jabalia in 1987 and spread throughout the occupied territories, lasting until 1993. The Palestinians employed civil disobedience, boycotts, and strikes, but it was the stone-throwing youths pitted against the military might of the IDF that focused international attention on Israel's occupation. The second intifada, known as the al-Aqsa Intifada, began in 2000 and officially has not ended. The IDF and armed Jewish settlers in the occupied territories have attempted to suppress these uprisings with brutal force. Palestinian civilians are killed or injured almost daily, and economic and humanitarian conditions in the territories are abysmal.

The Arab states' animosity toward Israel is rooted in the injustice inflicted by Zionists on the Palestinians during the 1948 war: the expulsion of the native Palestinian Arab population, the illegal seizure of their private property, and the continued expansion of the State of Israel on Arab land. Authoritarian Arab regimes have exploited the nearly unceasing state of tension or outright war in the Middle East to maintain power and stifle social and political development. Host governments view Palestinian refugees as a social, economic, and political burden, as well as a destabilizing factor in and a security risk to their countries. In most Arab states, the Palestinians are treated as second-class citizens or foreigners, and they are given little chance to become permanent residents. The conflict has also contributed to the economic underdevelopment of the region and has had a negative impact on the global economy.

The cost of the Palestinian-Israeli conflict to U.S. taxpayers alone is $3 trillion since World War II.[11] But the cost of the conflict to the United States has not been simply monetary. The United States has suffered incalculable human losses also. U.S. peacekeepers, soldiers, diplomats, journalists, businesspeople, students, and tourists count among the casualties of the Middle East conflict. U.S. influence and prestige also continue to suffer from ill-advised foreign policies. The people of the region living under oppressive regimes view U.S. influence and actions as complicit in sustaining the conflict. These perceptions have contributed to the rise in Islamic militancy, acts of terrorism, and anti-Western sentiment, particularly anti-Americanism. The intensity of hostility toward the United States was most spectacularly demonstrated by the 2001 terrorist attacks on the World Trade Center, the Pentagon, and in Pennsylvania. The 2003 U.S. invasion and occupation of Iraq is seen by most in the Middle East as synonymous with Israel's occupation and oppression of the Palestinian people. Both are viewed as imperialist attempts to destroy Arab societies and alienate the people from their land and resources. Many Arabs link the current region-wide conflict to the 1948 war, and they believe that a resolution to the overall Middle East conflict must also justly redress the Palestinian-Israeli conflict.

Context and History of the 1948 War

The competing historical narratives of 1948 are summed up in evocative terminology. The 1948 Arab-Israeli War is known to Israelis as "the War of Independence." For Palestinians, the war is *al-Nakba*, the "catastrophe" or "disaster." It is also known as the first Arab-Israeli War, the 1948 Palestine war, or simply "the 1948 war." The words "independence" and "catastrophe" succinctly reflect the terminology of victor and vanquished. The Zionists established the Jewish State of Israel in approximately 78 percent of mandate Palestine, while 90 percent of Palestine's indigenous Arabs in the overtaken areas were expelled from their homes and dispersed throughout the Middle East.[12]

The 1948 war took place over two distinct periods: the "civil war" fought between Jewish and Arab armed groups within Palestine's borders from November 29, 1947, through May 15, 1948, as the British were withdrawing from mandate Palestine; and the "multistate conflict" fought after May 15, 1948 (the date British rule over Palestine officially terminated) between the newly declared State of Israel and Iraq, Syria, Lebanon, Egypt, Saudi Arabia, and Transjordan, each of which dispatched army contingents into the territory of the former mandate Palestine.

Understanding the unfolding civil war is essential to comprehending how the Palestinian refugees were created. The decisions and strategies employed by each protagonist during that critical chaotic period created the conditions that spurred the Palestinian exodus and thereby also helped determine the final outcome of the 1948 war. The Palestinian historian Walid Khalidi argued in 1986 that "in many ways the civil war was the more crucial and certainly the more devastating to the Palestinians. The civil war ended with the establishment of the state of Israel but also with the virtual destruction of the Palestinian community. . . . If the history of the regular war needs to be *rewritten*, the history of the *civil* war has still to be written."[13]

The Palestinian historical narrative has been echoed to some extent by Israeli scholars, chiefly by the generation of Israeli "new historians." They include Simha Flapan, Benny Morris, Ilan Pappé, Tom Segev, and Avi Shlaim. These Israeli historians have reexamined the history of 1948 and the early years of the State of Israel using contemporary archival sources. They challenge the official narrative about the founding of Israel and expose many of the "historical truths" as propaganda, such as: the Zionists welcomed the partition of Palestine; the Arabs were militarily superior to Zionist forces; the Palestinian Arabs were encouraged by their leaders to leave and fled despite Jewish leaders' efforts to convince them to stay; the Arabs rejected partition and launched war; and Israel extended its hand in peace after the war but Arab leaders did not respond.

Nonetheless, in some cases, the new historians' excessive or even exclusive reliance on Israeli archives has limited their narratives and conclusions. And, as Avi Shlaim has noted, the "new" histories questioning official Zionist and Israeli history are not new at all. Palestinian, Arab, Israeli, and Western writers had advanced many of the arguments central to the new histories long ago (including the Palestinian viewpoint regarding the creation of the Palestinian refugees), but their work received little attention.[14]

Palestinian perspectives on the war critical of Israel have remained relatively absent from historical discourse. Indeed, Palestinian recollections are sometimes dismissed out of hand or deemed of limited worth for a number of reasons, especially the lack of corroborative documentary evidence and an intrinsic prejudice against the use of oral evidence. Nonetheless, a historical narrative of the 1948 war, and particularly the refugee question, remains patently incomplete without the perspective of the refugees.

This book incorporates Palestinians' personal recollections of the civil war into the examination of their displacement. Some 130 new refugee interviews, along with previously recorded testimonies, are included. The Palestinians' experience of displacement and exile is *their* story. By telling the story in their own voices, this book reveals a Palestinian narrative long absent from history.

How the Palestinians Became Refugees in 1948: Historical Arguments

Until the late 1980s, historical literature on the creation of the Palestinian refugees fell into two ideological camps: pro-Zionist and pro-Palestinian. Pro-Zionists have claimed that the Palestinian Arabs left in 1947–49 in response to orders from Arab leaders, or (as a concession mostly from the Israeli "new historians" and as a result of their research) the refugees were a "spontaneous" and "natural" consequence of war.[15] Pro-Palestinians have argued that the Arabs were expelled according to a premeditated Zionist plan.

In the early and mid-1980s, new evidence became available that illuminated the decision making and events of the 1948 war. Britain's and Israel's declassification of a large body of documents enabled researchers to review a wealth of contemporary sources and thereby draw more nuanced and accurate conclusions about the war and the creation of the refugees during its course.

Some of the pertinent 1948 records remain secret, however. The IDF papers are still partly classified, including the larger part of the Haganah (HA) Intelligence Service *(Shai)* reports.[16] The Haganah and the Israel State

Archives (ISA) "continue to keep sealed" certain sensitive documentation, according to Benny Morris.[17] Among the documents and sections that remain secret are those that "contain evidence of atrocities committed by Israeli soldiers against Palestinian civilians" during the 1948 war, or those which "record high-level discussions among Israeli cabinet ministers about the need to expel the Arab populations," according to Tom Segev.[18]

During the 2001 Israeli-Palestinian peace negotiations, at Morris's request, classified minutes and testimonies from 1948, which had been retained by the ISA and the IDF archives, were about to be declassified by Justice Minister Yossi Beilin. The Israeli journalist Aluf Ben reported that these records would have revealed the "expulsion and massacre of the Arabs that was carried out by the Israeli Defense Forces during the war of independence."[19] The decision to declassify the documents was rescinded under pressure from the state archivist Evyatar Friesel and the Israeli defense establishment. They claimed the files were "liable to damage the State's foreign relations."[20]

Nevertheless, the declassification of a great many contemporary records in the mid-1980s changed the debate about 1948. The opening of the Israeli archives was the decisive factor in the rise of the Israeli new historians and their ability to examine and write about the founding and early years of Israel based on contemporary documents. As a result, the history of 1948 developed into a vitriolic debate between "old" versus "new" Israeli academic circles, as well as between pro-Zionist and pro-Palestinian camps.

The changes are best viewed in the context of the controversy over what caused the Palestinian Arabs to abandon their homes. The debate was initiated immediately after the refugee situation began in early 1948. Palestinians and pro-Palestinian sources consistently have attributed the exodus to a well-organized and preconceived Zionist plan to drive the Arabs out of Palestine through intimidation, expulsion, and terror—"the substitution of one people for another by force of arms."[21] According to this argument, the 1948 war was fundamentally different from most other wars, in which civilians flee their homes to escape the fighting but return after the cessation of hostilities. The Palestinian American historian Rashid Khalidi has summed up the consistent Palestinian position on the causes of the Arab exodus: "Their flight was . . . the desired outcome of a process which began early in this century, when a nationalist movement in the classical 19th century tradition selected an Asian land for its colonial activities, established itself step-by-step with Great Power assistance, and fought to overcome the resistance of the indigenous population."[22]

This position was argued at the United Nations as early as 1951. In a study of the Palestinian refugees submitted to the U.N. General Assembly, the Palestinian scholar Fayez Sayegh argued that the Israelis had carried out a premeditated expulsion of the Palestinians. He identified a number of factors to support his argument: "The shifting international scene and the attainment of a recognized juridical status by the Jewish State, together with the growing imbalance of Zionist and Arab military potential in favor of the former—rendered the circumstances favorable for launching the long awaited Zionist campaign for the forcible and violent displacement of the Palestinian Arabs."[23]

After the 1948 war, Israeli leaders accepted no responsibility for the Palestinian exodus (and officially still do not). They denied all suggestions that a "transfer" of the Arabs was planned and then executed. According to Israeli leaders, the Palestinian exodus was the practical and moral result of Palestinian Arabs' and the neighboring Arab states' waging war in defiance of the international community. Israeli Foreign Minister Moshe Sharett (Shertok) stated the moral case in a July 30, 1948, letter to the United Nations.

> The Arab mass flight from Israel and Israel-occupied territory is the direct effect of Arab aggression from outside. Justifying their invasion, the Arab governments claimed that they responded to a call for rescue addressed to them by the Palestine Arabs. The plain fact, however, is that but for the intervention of the Arab states, there would have been an overwhelming measure of local Arab acquiescence in the establishment of the State of Israel, and by now peace and reasonable prosperity would have reigned throughout the territory to the enjoyment of Jews and Arabs alike.[24]

Additionally, Israeli spokespersons have at times argued that Arab leaders ordered the Palestinian Arabs to evacuate their homes in Jewish-controlled areas in order to embarrass the Jews in the international community, to justify the planned Arab invasion of May 15, 1948, and to clear the way for the invading Arab armies. The validity of the "Arab orders" argument has been challenged, most particularly by the research of Walid Khalidi, Erskine Childers, and Benny Morris, each from a different ideological perspective.

Indeed, contemporary official statements indicate that the "Arab evacuation orders" argument is not tenable. Moshe Sharett himself stated that "the war brought in its wake a mass exodus, mostly spontaneous, resulting in great suffering."[25] His observation that the exodus was "mostly spontaneous" implicitly concedes that it was not the result of any organized Arab general evacuation policy.

Israel's first prime minister, David Ben-Gurion, presented his government's official "Arab orders" argument on October 11, 1961, in the Knesset: "The Arabs' exit from Palestine . . . began immediately after the U.N. Resolution, from the areas earmarked for the Jewish state. And we have explicit documents testifying that they left Palestine following instructions by the Arab leaders, with the mufti at their head, under the assumption that the invasion of the Arab armies at the expiration of the mandate [would] destroy the Jewish state and push all the Jews into the sea, dead or alive."[26]

According to Walid Khalidi, the Israeli allegation that specific Arab radio broadcasts ordered the Palestinian Arabs to leave the country was not mentioned by the Israelis until 1949. Realizing the political problem posed by the miserable conditions of the Palestinian Arab refugees, the new Israeli state sought to cast blame for the refugees' plight on Arab leaders, Khalidi asserts. Under the auspices of the Israel Information Center in New York, Joseph B. Schechtman, a pro-Zionist American, alleged in a two-page pamphlet in 1949 that the Arab Higher Committee (AHC) urged the Palestinian civilians to leave their homes in order to clear the way for the invading Arab armies.[27]

Relying on Israeli archival documents, the Palestinian British historian Nur Masalha has shown that Schechtman had been working for the Israeli Cabinet's 1948 "Transfer Committee." The committee's goal was to develop plans for Palestinian Arab depopulation. The Israeli government tasked Schechtman (the author of two books on European population transfer) with collecting material and carrying out further study for the Transfer Committee on Palestinian resettlement in Iraq. Schechtman would become "the single most influential propagator of the Zionist myth of voluntary exodus in 1948," Masalha argues.[28]

Working independently to investigate the Israeli allegation of Arab radio-ordered evacuation, Walid Khalidi and the Irish journalist and broadcaster Erskine Childers reviewed the Israeli claims. Khalidi examined the British Broadcasting Corporation (BBC) *Summary of World Broadcasts* (SWB), U.S. Foreign Broadcast Information Service (FBIS) files, and three major Arab newspapers without finding any evidence to support Israeli government claims that Arab leaders ordered Palestinians to leave their homes.[29] Childers examined official Israeli statements about the Arab exodus and found that "no primary evidence of evacuation orders was ever produced."[30] He requested the "explicit documents" from the Israeli government but reported that he never received them. Childers also examined Arab radio broadcasts, which the BBC had monitored throughout 1948. He concluded that "there was not a single order, or appeal, or suggestion about evacuation from Palestine from any Arab radio station, inside or outside Palestine, in 1948. There *is* repeated monitored record of Arab appeals, even flat orders, to civilians of Palestine *to stay put*."[31] My own review of the FBIS files, interviews with Palestinian Arab refugees, and archival research affirm previous findings—that no contemporary evidence shows that Arab leaders issued general evacuation orders to the Arab population in Palestine.

Israeli Prime Minister Ben-Gurion also attributed the Palestinian exodus to a "domino effect." He contended that the sight of fleeing refugees encouraged neighbors to follow them. Palestinian testimony and contemporary documents, which this book examines in detail, show that in the overwhelming majority of cases, Arab villagers and townspeople remained in their homes until Zionist forces threatened attack or attacked. Only after the fighting intensified, and particularly in April 1948 after Zionist forces massacred more than 100 civilians in Dayr Yasin village (a figure exaggerated to 254 at the time by Zionist war propaganda), did many men begin to escort their wives, children, and elderly to safety in other villages or outlying areas. In fewer cases, a general state of fear and panic did cause Palestinian Arabs to leave their villages before an actual attack.[32] But the "domino effect," insofar as it occurred, was usually precipitated and encouraged by Zionist terrorist or military operations, as this book will describe.

On the pro-Palestinian side, scholars have drawn definitive conclusions but with limited evidence. The Palestinian historian Nafez Nazzal is a notable example. In 1974, he completed his groundbreaking study of the Palestinian Arab exodus from the northern Galilee region for his doctoral dissertation. Nazzal's research utilized first-hand accounts from

Palestinian Arab participants and witnesses to the 1948 war, as well as documentary evidence, to reconstruct the exodus from the Galilee. (His study included the Galilee's northern subdistricts of Safad, Acre, Haifa, Nazareth, Tiberias, and Baysan.) Nazzal concluded that "in view of the ideology, proclaimed intentions, and actions of the Zionist movement in Palestine, and after an examination of the evidence presented . . . no other conclusion is possible than that the Arabs of Galilee—and indeed all the Palestinians made refugees by the 1947–49 fighting—left their homes as victims of a conscious and willful Zionist policy."[33]

Nazzal cites Zionist terrorism, rumors, psychological pressure and panic, siege, direct attacks on civilians, and direct expulsions as the reasons for the Palestinian exodus from the Galilee. Nazzal's work, which predated the declassification of key British, Israeli, and U.S. documents, did not insist on the premeditation or preplanning of Zionist policy, only that the policy was "conscious and wilful." His conclusions relied heavily on interviews with Palestinian Arab civilians and participants in the war. Because Nazzal did not examine events of the 1948 war throughout the country, his generalized conclusions about the Palestinian Arab exodus, especially in the civil war period, were necessarily tentative, as he did not have access to the contemporary documentary record. Ultimately, as we will see, that record would back up his conclusions.

The academic theory of "natural" or "spontaneous" flight derives primarily from pro-Zionist sources, often echoing Israeli official spokespersons. In one of the first in-depth studies of the origins of the Palestinian refugees, *A Political Study of the Arab-Jewish Conflict: The Arab Refugee Problem (A Case Study)*, published in 1959, the Israeli Rony Gabbay offered the academic practical case complementing the moral case offered by Moshe Sharett: "The Arab refugee problem, as any other refugee problem, was a natural consequence of the insecure and precarious wartime conditions."[34]

It is highly debatable that massive refugee problems are "natural consequences of insecure and precarious wartime conditions." Numerous large-scale wartime displacements—the Armenians and Greeks from Turkey, the ethnic groups of modern Yugoslavia, the American Indian removal, the Germans from postwar Czechoslovakia, the Tartars of Crimea, and post–World War II Jewish displaced persons—were most clearly not natural results of generalized war conditions.

Gabbay conceded that the tragedy of the Palestinian refugees was unusual in "its extent and magnitude" because "in less than six months almost 70% of the Arab population of Palestine deserted their homes and fled in distress." Gabbay writes that while there were many reasons for the exodus, "the Arab exodus was never a determined policy, planned and executed for its own sake—at least not in the early stages of the flight. It was rather a spontaneous reaction to the calamitous development of those days of 1948."[35] Gabbay argued that the refugees were a "spontaneous reaction" and a "natural consequence" of war. While refugees are a consequence of war, Gabbay did not offer direct evidence that the Palestinian Arab refugees' flight was spontaneous or otherwise prove that the remarkably high 90 percent refugee rate, reached by the end of the war, was a "natural consequence" of it. His conclusion that the Arab exodus was not a determined policy "at least not in the early stages of the flight" implies that he had entertained the possibility that a determined policy existed at some point.

Gabbay appears to have pioneered the idea that population displacement occurred in different phases. He postulated three phases to show "the development of the problem and to determine its causes." These were (1) December 1947 to March 1948; (2) April to May 15, 1948; and (3) the period following May 15, 1948.[36]

Gabbay's theory is flawed. In the first phase, he wrote, "there was no sign of any mass exodus or wholesale evacuation," and "the Arab community as a whole felt itself quite stable and well prepared to meet the future with success." This is incorrect, for as I will show, by the end of Gabbay's first phase, displacement had already commenced and Palestinian Arabs were demonstrably anxious and uncertain of their future. Before April 1948, Zionist attacks had forced Palestinian Arabs to leave 26 villages throughout the country, 12 percent of the total number of Arab locales that would be depopulated by the mandate's end. Furthermore, as British withdrawal from Palestine proceeded over this time, anxiety and pessimism spread among the Palestinian Arab population in response to escalating Zionist attacks and atrocities, which terrified the Palestinians into evacuating.

Gabbay also writes that the Palestinian Arabs' departure from April to May 15 "cannot be attributed to any specific reason. . . . Rather, the exodus was the result of many diverse elements—psychological, military and political—which combined together to produce this phenomena [sic]."[37] In fact, Palestinian refugee testimonies and other sources confirm that from April to May 15, 1948, the threat of British intervention to prevent Zionist military action was dissipating, and credible reports of pervasive and large-scale atrocities against Arabs were circulating. Without a deterrent, Zionist forces greatly expanded the systematic practice of intimidating Palestinian Arabs into abandoning their lands through direct attack and terror, including massacres and other means of psychological warfare.

Nearly 30 years later, Benny Morris investigated the causes of the Palestinians' displacement. In his 1987 book, *The Birth of the Palestinian Refugee Problem, 1947–1949*, Morris made extensive use of declassified Israeli, British, U.S., and U.N. archival sources, and private papers. He cites Gabbay's research as the only other work that dealt with the subject of Palestinian refugees in a "relatively serious manner." Although Morris considers Gabbay's work pioneering, he also calls it "premature" in that Gabbay had almost no access to contemporary documents. In spite of his own extensive archival research, Morris concludes his study in words that reflect Gabbay's: "The Palestinian refugee problem was born of war, not by design, Jewish or Arab. It was largely a by-product of Arab and Jewish fears and of the protracted, bitter fighting that characterized the first Israeli-Arab war; in smaller part, it was the deliberate creation of Jewish and Arab military commanders and politicians."[38] His conclusion, echoing Gabbay's non-archival and interview-free research, for the most part evades the conclusions his own data should have compelled.

Many of Morris's critics praise his research yet criticize his conclusions. Nur Masalha argues, based on the whole set of evidence Morris cites, that "while it is true that military history is full of scorched earth tactics and expulsions to clear the theater of war, it is difficult—in light of the systematic nature of the 'clearing out' operations and the sheer magnitude of the exodus (not to mention the careful efforts to prevent the return of the refugees)—not to see a policy at work."[39]

In a 1990 follow-up, *1948 and After: Israel and the Palestinians*, Morris introduces a variation of his "born of war, not by design" conclusion, stating that "what occurred in 1948 lies somewhere in between the Jewish 'robber state' and the 'Arab orders' explanations."[40] Norman Finkelstein, an anti-Zionist American Jewish scholar, argues that although Morris "shatters one of the most enduring myths about the origins of the Israeli-Arab conflict," he merely substitutes a "new myth, one of the 'happy median,'" which is "scarcely more credible" than the old myth.[41]

Morris's ultimate conclusion as to what created the Palestinian refugees in 1948 remains confusing and contradictory. In 2002, he stated in *Crimes of War* that the Palestinian Arab depopulation was a "form of ethnic cleansing." This assertion seems to concur with his other statements to the *Guardian*, in which he speculated that the Middle East would be "a healthier, less violent place" if Ben-Gurion had engineered "a comprehensive rather than a partial transfer in 1948."[42] But Morris appears to have reversed himself again in the 2004 revision of his original work, titled *The Birth of the Palestinian Refugee Problem Revisited*. In it, he explicitly reaffirms his main conclusion that the Palestinian Arab refugees were essentially a product of the "war and not design, Jewish or Arab."[43]

The American researcher Michael Palumbo's conclusions, which were based on the documentary record and oral history, reflect those of Masalha and Nazzal. He wrote in his *The Palestinian Catastrophe: The 1948 Expulsion of a People from Their Homeland* that the Palestinian exodus was a "human tragedy" as well as a historical controversy. Thus, he turned to a new source to reflect the human experience: recollections of Palestinian Arab refugees. Palumbo found one of the "most remarkable aspects" of his research to be "the consistent accuracy of these Palestinian memoirs in the light of American, United Nations, Israeli, British, and other non-Arab sources. . . . Frequently, poorly educated Arab peasants recall facts that are substantiated by recently available archive documents. There is also verification for the testimony of many Israelis who have spoken honestly about the expulsion of Arabs in 1948."[44]

Palumbo states that most of the sources he consulted made clear that the refugees left their homes as the result of Zionist "terror and psychological warfare." While he acknowledges the importance of other factors in the Palestinian Arabs' exodus, including the early flight of their military and political leaders, the lack of cooperation and leadership among Arab factions, and the Dayr Yasin massacre, Palumbo nonetheless contends that "no amount of pseudo-academic argument about an 'irrational panic syndrome' or the 'loss of community infra-structure' can obscure the fact that most Palestinians did not leave their homes until their town or village was invaded by an Israeli army that subjected them to a reign of terror."[45]

Palumbo's conclusions, as this book shows in fuller detail, are more accurate than those of Morris. Although attributing the Palestinian Arabs' exodus to "invasion" simplifies the diversity of violent intimidation employed and feared, Palumbo's contention that Palestinian Arabs remained in their homes until targeted by Zionist violence or psychological intimidation is correct. He is also correct in his assessment of an ideological root to the forced depopulation. Palumbo views the expulsion of the Palestinian Arabs as "the fulfillment of the destiny that was implicit in Zionism from the very beginning."[46]

On the more policy-oriented question of Zionist planning, Walid Khalidi takes issue with Morris's conclusion that there was no premeditated expulsion plan. Khalidi asserts that the Haganah operational "Plan D" implemented in March and April 1948 was the Zionist plan to expel the Palestinians.[47] Morris views it instead as a military program geared to achieving military ends. Furthermore, Morris considers Plan D to be marginally important because the Arabs fled before expulsion orders became necessary. In contrast to Morris, Ilan Pappé, another Israeli "new" historian, views Plan D in much the way that Khalidi does: "Plan D was, in many ways, just what Khalidi claims it was—a master plan for the expulsion of as many Palestinians as possible."[48] Pappé argues in *The Ethnic Cleansing of Palestine* that "the Zionist movement did not wage a war that 'tragically but inevitably' led to the expulsion of 'parts of' the indigenous population." He asserts that the main goal of the war was the ethnic cleansing of all of Palestine, which the Zionists "coveted for [their] new state."[49]

Nur Masalha, in *The Expulsion of the Palestinians: The Concept of "Transfer" in Zionist Political Thought, 1882–1948*, states that although Plan D "was not a blueprint for the expulsion of the Arabs, [the plan] was anchored in the politico-ideological concept of transfer and provided the operative policy in the field."[50] It is clear from internal Zionist discussion and instructions, Masalha argues, that the Jewish Agency leader David Ben-Gurion had decided "it would be better that as few a number as possible of Arabs would remain in the territory of the [Jewish] state."[51] Although Morris's discussion of Plan D echoes Masalha's assertion that the plan provided operational justification for acts of depopulation, Morris does not address the issue of ideological underpinnings in his own comprehensive conclusion.[52]

Morris's work on the refugee issue was considered a breakthrough by many pro-Palestinians. His research, relying on many declassified Israeli primary sources, fundamentally challenged the established Israeli argument that the Palestinian refugees resulted from a voluntary mass migration or were prompted by orders from Arab leaders. Israeli documents that Morris presented confirmed that Zionist forces did indeed expel Palestinian Arabs from villages and towns, and that massacres did occur at the hands of the Zionists. He also confirmed the findings of Childers and Khalidi that Arab leaders gave no blanket order for Palestinian Arabs to leave their homes.[53]

Somewhat ironically, pro-Zionist historians criticize Morris for not using more Arab sources in his study.[54] Morris stated in his book that Arab state papers for this period have not been opened to Israeli or Arab researchers by their governments. His critics may be offering more polemics than analysis; they should know that researchers have little or no access to such records.[55] Morris maintains that he tried to compensate for a lack of available documentary Arab material—and still integrate the Arab side of the story—by culling from Zionist intelligence reports and from British and American diplomatic dispatches. As a result, however, he reports on and analyzes events primarily from the official Israeli, British, and U.S. government viewpoints. He includes little direct Palestinian Arab experience in his study, except for intermittent references to Nafez Nazzal's oral history work.

In response to criticism, Morris questions whether the addition of the Palestinian Arab viewpoint would have altered his main conclusions on the causes of the Palestinian exodus.[56] But he formulated his conclusions on Palestinian Arabs' motivations and decision making with scant direct investigation into their viewpoint, while also dismissing the obvious importance of their perspective out of hand. So his methodology must be deemed fundamentally insufficient and his findings inconclusive.

The General Debate about 1948

The advent of Israel's new historians has created yet another controversy about 1948. That is the debate between pro-Zionist scholars, who hold to traditional official Zionist history about Israel's creation, and those who champion the new history by professional Israeli historians working with contemporary archives, but who still typically do not inform their perspectives with direct Arab sources. The debate has sparked vitriolic criticism and rejoinder in articles, books, and conferences. The Israeli human rights activist and writer Israel Shahak has observed that "from the moment of their appearance on the scene, the 'new historians' were subjected to relentless abuse, often resembling witch-hunts."[57]

Morris, in particular, has been roundly criticized, not only by the Israeli public at large, but perhaps even more acrimoniously by other Israeli historians.[58] Critics of the new historians frequently bypass issues of historical accuracy and hurl accusations of political disloyalty. They charge new historians with besmirching Zionism and the State of Israel, sympathizing excessively with the Palestinians, and providing supporting evidence for the Palestinian enemy. Critics fear an alteration in public opinion, as well as the new historians' potential influence on world opinion. In reply, Morris argues that "Israel is now strong and established enough to take the truth about the circumstances of its conception, a truth, incidentally, by no means more bloody, dastardly, or base than that of most nations in times of great upheaval and revolution (and such was 1948)."[59]

In spite of the controversial nature of Morris's work in Israel, his conclusions are gradually and tentatively being acknowledged by segments of the academic community and the general public, including elements in the former Labor government. For instance, Israeli Acting Minister of Foreign Affairs Shlomo Ben-Ami echoed Morris's "happy median" conclusion almost verbatim in a statement at the 55th General Assembly of the United Nations on September 18, 2000: "Clearly, the Palestinian refugees were victims of the Arab-Israeli conflict. Israel, however, can assume neither political nor moral responsibility for this tragedy that was the direct result of the all-out onslaught against reborn Israel launched by the Arab armies in 1948. The Palestinian refugee problem was born as the land was bisected by the sword, not by design, Jewish or Arab. It was largely the inevitable by-product of Arab and Jewish fears and the protracted bitter fighting."[60] As Ben-Ami illustrates here, the growing acceptance of Morris's work by current Israeli officials has not led to the acceptance of any responsibility for the Palestinian refugees.

The reasons for eschewing responsibility have a bearing beyond the historical debate. The issue of how the refugee problem was created has fundamental political consequences for the State of Israel, which helps explain why the debate falls along political lines and often is expressed in political terms. As Pappé has argued, "The sweeping loyalty to a position of denial [of expulsion] in Israel is not just a case of court historians faithful to Zionist ideology. There is an overall tendency to deny that there ever was an expulsion—with many insisting that there was just a flight. This denial is driven by an apprehension . . . of facing the Palestinian demand for the 'right of return.'"[61]

This book contributes to a better understanding of the 1948 Arab-Israeli war by incorporating the Palestinian viewpoint into the framework of contemporary perspectives found in the documentary and other records. As a result, a more precise narrative explains the causes of the Palestinian Arab exodus from its inception in the 1947–48 civil war period.

This research strongly supports, if not conclusively demonstrates, that the creation of the Palestinian Arab refugees began in the convergence of a chaotic civil conflict, British inaction to suppress the escalating violence, and the Jewish Agency's seizure of the opportunity presented by the cover of war to effect long-held aims of political Zionism: the establishment of a Jewish state in Palestine with a population practically devoid of non-Jews. This was done by employing systematic and violent intimidation to drive out the native Palestinian Arab civilian population, which consisted largely of disempowered women, children, and elderly people incapable of resisting.

♒

1. S. G. Thicknesse, *Arab Refugees: A Survey of Resettlement Possibilities* (London: Royal Institute of International Affairs, 1949), 1. The 1948 Arab population figures cited for villages, towns, and urban areas are derived from *Palestine 1948: Fifty Years after al-Nakba—The Towns and Villages Depopulated by the Zionist Invasion of 1948* (map), in Salman H. Abu-Sitta, *The Palestinian Nakba, 1948: The Register of Depopulated Localities in Palestine* (London: Palestine Return Centre, 1998). Abu-Sitta estimates a 3.8% natural Palestinian Arab population growth based on the mandatory government's 1944 census statistics.
2. Ibid., 6n3, cites U.N. Information Center, London, "United Nations Relief for Palestine Refugees" (February 4, 1949), which lists refugee deaths in the Gaza area during December 1948 at 120 per night, which was reportedly exceptional. The 20,000 figure allowed for natural mortality rates and for deaths during the fighting.
3. GLP, Suggested Partition Frontiers in Palestine, refugee mortality [Commander of the Arab Legion, Brigadier General Sir John Glubb Pasha], n.d.
4. W. de St. Aubin, "Peace and Refugees in the Middle East," *Middle East Journal* 3.3 (1949): 251. St. Aubin did emergency relief work for the American Red Cross from 1943 until 1948 when he was appointed delegate of the League of Red Cross Societies to the Middle East. Soon after, he became a special consultant on humanitarian affairs on the staff of Count Bernadotte, U.N. mediator for Palestine. St. Aubin wrote that Palestinian refugees were distributed as follows: Lebanon, 130,000; Syria, 85,000; Transjordan, 95,000; Palestine North and East, 400,000; Gaza area, 225,000; Israel, 50,000; and Iraq, Egypt, etc., 15,000.

5. Thicknesse, *Arab Refugees*, n. 1, U.N. Information Center. William L. Gower of the American Red Cross provided this estimate, which was supported by the U.N. refugee expert Sir Raphael Cilento (10n2).

6. Ibid., 10–11.

7. GLP, Suggested Partition Frontiers in Palestine [Glubb].

8. Fred J. Khouri, *The Arab Israeli Dilemma* (Syracuse: Syracuse University Press, 1968), 149.

9. Hizballah is a Shi'a Islamic organization founded during the Lebanese civil war.

10. The Geneva Conventions and the International Criminal Court statute prohibit nations at war from intentionally inflicting unnecessary environmental damage.

11. Thomas R. Stauffer, "The Cost of Conflict in the Middle East: What the U.S. Has Spent," *Middle East Policy* 10.1 (2003): 45–102. Stauffer estimates costs from 1956–2000 in 2002 dollars.

12. John Ruedy, "Dynamics of Land Alienation," and Janet L. Abu-Lughod, "The Demographic Transformation of Palestine," in *The Transformation of Palestine: Essays on the Origin and Development of the Arab-Israeli Conflict*, ed. Ibrahim Abu-Lughod (Evanston: Northwestern University Press, 1971), 119 and 160–61.

13. Walid Khalidi, "The Arab Perspective," in *The End of the Palestine Mandate*, ed. William Roger Louis and Robert W. Stookey (Austin: University of Texas, 1986), 132.

14. Avi Shlaim, "The Debate about 1948," *International Journal of Middle East Studies* 27.3 (1995): 289.

15. DAG 13/3.1.0:1, S 0158, Foreign Minister of Israel to U.N. Mediator, July 30, 1948.

16. According to Benny Morris, almost all the Israeli Foreign Ministry's archives from 1948 to 1957, as well as documents from other ministries, including the prime minister's office, have been declassified. He asserts that in the past decade and a half, the Israel State Archives have declassified almost all of the Israeli cabinet protocols for 1948–49, and additional IDF and Haganah documents have been declassified as well, including IDF operational and intelligence material from 1948; Morris, *1948 and After: Israel and the Palestinians* (Oxford, U.K.: Clarendon, 1990), 7. See also Haim Levenberg, *The Military Preparations of the Arab Community in Palestine, 1945–1948* (London: Frank Cass, 1993), ix.

17. Benny Morris, *The Birth of the Palestinian Refugee Problem Revisited* (Cambridge: Cambridge University Press, 2004), 5.

18. Tom Segev, *1949: The First Israelis* (New York: Owl, 1998), vii.

19. Aluf Ben, "This Is How the Records of 1948 Were Almost Made Public," *Ha'aretz*, February 16, 2001, trans. Elia Zureik.

20. Ibid.

21. Rashid Khalidi, foreword to Nafez Nazzal, *The Palestinian Exodus from Galilee, 1948* (Beirut: Institute for Palestine Studies, 1978), ix.

22. Ibid.

23. Fayez A. Sayegh, *The Palestine Refugees* (Washington, D.C.: Amara, 1952), 9.

24. DAG 13/3.1.0:1, S 0158, Foreign Minister of Israel to U.N. Mediator, July 30, 1948.

25. Ibid.

26. Ilan Pappé, "Were They Expelled?" in *The Palestinian Exodus, 1948–1998*, ed. Ghada Karmi and Eugene Cotran (Reading, U.K.: Ithaca, 1999), 39; Erskine B. Childers, "The Other Exodus," *Spectator*, May 12, 1961, 672–75.

27. Joseph B. Schechtman, *The Arab Refugee Problem* (New York: Philosophical Library, 1952).

28. Nur Masalha, "From Propaganda to Scholarship: Dr. Joseph Schechtman and the Origins of Israeli Polemics on the Palestinian Refugees," *Holy Land Studies* 2.2 (2004): 188–97.

29. Walid Khalidi, "Why Did the Palestinians Leave?" *Middle East Forum* 35.7(s1959): 21–24.

30. Childers, "Other Exodus."

31. Ibid.

32. Abu-Sitta, *Palestinian Nakba,* 9. The names of Arab villages are transliterated in various ways, e.g., Dayr Yasin also appears as Deir Yassin.

33. Nazzal, *Palestinian Exodus,* 105.

34. Rony Gabbay, *A Political Study of the Arab-Jewish Conflict: The Arab Refugee Problem (A Case Study)* (Geneva: E. Droz; Paris: Minard, 1959), 54.

35. Ibid.

36. Ibid.

37. Ibid.

38. Benny Morris, *The Birth of the Palestinian Refugee Problem, 1947-1949* (Cambridge: Cambridge University Press, 1987), 286.

39. Nur Masalha, *The Expulsion of the Palestinians: The Concept of "Transfer" in Zionist Political Thought, 1882-1948* (Washington, D.C.: Institute for Palestine Studies, 1992), 180.

40. Morris, *1948 and After,* 17.

41. Ibid.

42. Benny Morris in *Crimes of War: The Book,* see www.crimesofwar.org/thebook/arab-israeli-war. html; and Morris, "A New Exodus for the Middle East?" *Guardian,* October 3, 2002.

43. Morris, *Birth Revisited,* 588.

44. Michael Palumbo, *The Palestinian Catastrophe: The 1948 Expulsion of a People from Their Homeland* (London: Quartet, 1989), xviii.

45. Ibid.

46. Ibid., xix.

47. Walid Khalidi, "Plan Dalet: Master Plan for the Conquest of Palestine," *Journal of Palestine Studies* 18.69 (1988): 22–28.

48. Ilan Pappé, *The Making of the Arab-Israeli Conflict, 1947–51* (London: I. B. Tauris, 1992), 94.

49. Ilan Pappé, *The Ethnic Cleansing of Palestine* (Oxford, U.K.: Oneworld, 2006), xvi.

50. Masalha, *Expulsion of the Palestinians,* 178.

51. Michael Bar-Zohar, *Ben-Gurion: A Political Biography* (Hebrew), vol. 2 (Tel Aviv: Am Oved, 1977), 703; cited in Masalha, *Expulsion of the Palestinians,* 178.

52. Morris, *Birth,* 62–63.

53. Ibid., 30.

54. Shlaim, "Debate about 1948"; Morris, *1948 and After,* 40.

55. Morris, *1948 and After,* 42. Morris first made this assertion in *Birth,* 1. See also Shlaim, "Debate about 1948," 290; and Avram Sela, "Arab Historiography of the 1948 War," in *New Perspectives on Israeli History: The Early Years of the State,* ed. Laurence J. Silberstein (New York: New University Press, 1991).

56. "Benny Morris," *Ha'aretz,* April 23 and May 1, 1992; cited in Shlaim, "Debate about 1948," 296.

57. Israel Shahak, The New Israeli Historians and 1948, February 12, 1995, www.soci.niu. edu/~phildept/Kabitan/Morris/html.

58. Ibid. See also Shabtai Teveth, "The Palestine Arab Refugee Problem and Its Origins," *Middle Eastern Studies* 26.2 (1990): 220–26; and Efraim Karsh, *Fabricating Israeli History: The "New Historians"* (London: Frank Cass, 1997).

59. Benny Morris, "The Eel and History: A Reply to Shabtai Teveth," *Tikkun* 5.1 (1989): 20.

60. Statement by Acting Minister of Foreign Affairs Shlomo Ben-Ami at the General Debate of the 55th General Assembly of the United Nations, September 18, 2000. Israeli Ministry of Foreign Affairs, www.israelmfa.gov. The bibliography about Arab refugees posted on the Israeli Ministry of Foreign Affairs website of May 3, 1999, included Rony Gabbay's work (and Schechtman's tract) but not Benny Morris's study. See www.mfa.gov.il/MFA/Foreign%20Relations/Israels%20

Foreign%Relations%20since%201947/1947-1974/Israel-s%20Foreign%20Relations%20201947-1974-%20Selected%20bib.

61. Pappé, "Were They Expelled?" 38. The Palestinians' right of return to their original homes, subject to their desire to live at peace with their neighbors, and the right to compensation is recognized by U.N. General Assembly Resolution 194 adopted in December 1948, and by the Universal Declaration of Human Rights, Article 13. Israel's admission to the United Nations was in fact conditioned on its willingness to abide by Resolution 194, which called for the refugees' repatriation and compensation. See General Assembly Resolution 273, May 11, 1949.

*ZIONIST BOMB ATTACK IN JERUSALEM THAT KILLED
14 AND INJURED MANY CIVILIANS, JANUARY 1948*

II

Mandate Palestine
Prelude to War and Displacement

The wisdom of Israel is now the wisdom of war, nothing else.

David Ben-Gurion, Jewish Agency chairman, January 1948

The 1948 war was a half century in the making. The conflict took root and developed between August 1897 (when the first Zionist Congress adopted the goal of creating a home for the Jewish people in Palestine) and November 1947 (when the U.N. General Assembly recommended the partition of Palestine). From the very beginning, it became apparent to many observers that the interests of the Arab majority and the colonizing Jewish minority in Palestine would prove irreconcilable. Zionists openly expressed their ambitions for Jews to become the ruling and majority population through massive organized immigration. Many advocated dispossession of most indigenous Arabs. These stated goals rapidly precipitated ethnic conflict.

Both Jewish nationalism, manifested as political Zionism, and Arab nationalism, emerging in various forms in different locations, grew dramatically in the late nineteenth and early twentieth century. Facilitated by British policy, Eastern and Central European Jews began to immigrate to Palestine in great numbers during this period, compelled primarily by anti-Semitic oppression at home and the Zionist ideal of national rebirth. The Zionists sought to establish an independent Jewish state in Palestine, while Arab nationalists sought ethnic political unity and independence from Ottoman (Turkish) rule over the Middle East.

To enlist Arab and Jewish support during World War I, the British government made ill-defined promises to the different parties: first to the Arabs, in the 1915 and 1916 McMahon-Hussein correspondence, and then to the Jews in the 1917 Balfour Declaration. These commitments lent support to the two groups' respective but clashing national aspirations in Palestine. Britain's policy created a dilemma over Palestine's future that would prove unsolvable during its rule.

For the Zionists, the Balfour Declaration affirmed Jewish claims in Palestine as a right. For the Arabs of Palestine, it represented an external usurpation of the 90 percent Arab majority's right to self-determination. For the British, it came to be viewed as a monumental foreign-policy blunder and "a striking contradiction" of publicly declared principles supporting the Arabs' rights to self-determination.[1] In terms of historic development, the declaration would prove, as U.S. military intelligence eventually summarized it, "the opening wedge for the establishment of a Jewish state in Palestine."[2]

Further complicating the question of Palestine were French aspirations in the Levant. British and French counterparts discussed the matter informally in 1915 and colluded to divide Ottoman-controlled lands between them. May 1916 saw the ratification of the Sykes-Picot Agreement (named for its principal British and French negotiators), which defined postwar areas of direct and indirect British and French control in Arab lands and southeast Turkey.[3]

The Allies' victory in World War I set a new course for Palestine's history. British forces entered and occupied Palestine in 1917 and placed it under military administration. The Balfour Declaration endorsed as British policy the establishment of a "national home" for the Jewish people in Palestine, subject to the proviso that "nothing shall be done which may prejudice the civil and religious rights of existing non-Jewish communities in Palestine."

Modern Middle East history would be determined for the following decades by the major powers and their colonial interests. The Arab territories of the defeated Ottoman Empire were entrusted to the Allied nations, specifically Britain and France, and administered as mandates according to the decisions of the newly established, European-dominated League of Nations.[4] Mandates for Syria and Lebanon were assigned to France. Control of Iraq was given to Britain. Despite Palestinian Arab opposition, the Palestine mandate was also allotted to Britain in 1920. The mandate's principal obligations included securing the Jewish national home, developing self-governing institutions, and safeguarding the civil and religious rights of all of Palestine's inhabitants. The largest territorial portion of the original Palestine mandate would be severed in 1922 to form the state of Transjordan, today known as the Hashemite Kingdom of Jordan. In the remainder of the Palestine mandate west of the Jordan River—the biblical Holy Land—direct British rule would continue.[5]

Palestinian Arabs opposed the Balfour Declaration and the mandate.[6] The King-Crane Commission, dispatched to Palestine by U.S. president Woodrow Wilson, confirmed that opposition and indicated the reasons for it. The commission warned the 1919 Paris Peace Conference that "anti-Zionist feeling" in Palestine was "intense and not lightly to be flouted." The commission also determined that the founding of a Jewish state could not be accomplished "without the gravest trespass upon the civil and religious rights" of the indigenous Arab population. The British military believed that violence was inevitable. No British officer believed that the "Zionist program could be carried out except by force of arms."[7]

Zionist designs for population change were seen as the core of the burgeoning conflict. The King-Crane Commission, the first of many commissions to Palestine, reported that Jewish colonists were anticipating a "radical transformation of the country" and "looked forward to a practically complete dispossession of the present non-Jewish inhabitants of Palestine, by various forms of purchase."[8] Chaim Weizmann, a native of Russia and the Zionist representative to the peace conference, announced that the Zionist Organization's intentions for the Jewish national home were to "build up gradually a nationality which would be as Jewish as the French nation was French and the British nation British. Later on, when the Jews formed the large majority, they would be ripe to establish such a Government as would answer to the state of the development of the country and to their ideals."[9] The contrasting aims, aggravated by local incidents, would lead to outbreaks of violence.

Politics and social conditions in the two communities varied. Two major political camps emerged in the Palestinian Arab community over the course of the mandate. Each camp was dominated by one of two notable Jerusalem families, the al-Husaynis and the Nashashibis. Despite their differences over the control of political offices and tactics of national expression, the Arab parties shared the objective of an independent Palestine, which would ensure the civil and religious rights of the existing Jewish minority but end Jewish immigration and the mandate itself.

The Jewish Agency for Palestine, an official body established by the Palestine mandate in 1928, represented the Jewish settlement in Palestine. That institution came to be led by David Ben-Gurion, acting through the socialist-nationalist Mapai party (the Land of Israel Worker's Party, or "Labor" party). A right-wing "Revisionist" faction dissented from the agency and called for a Jewish state over all of Palestine and the retention of Transjordan in a final Jewish state. As the Jewish population grew with immigrants from around the world, the Jewish Agency formed more state-like institutions, including an underground army. The Revisionists operated their own insurgent cell-groups and guerrilla militias noted for terrorist actions.

Palestinian Arabs began to express their anti-Zionism violently, particularly when they felt that the British failed to address their fears and demands. The first major anti-Zionist outbreak occurred in response to the League of Nation's decision in favor of the British mandate. Arabs in Jerusalem rioted in April 1920. A British military commission determined that the violence was provoked by unfulfilled promises of independence, a belief that the Balfour Declaration (now incorporated into the mandate's charter) implicitly denied Arab rights to self-determination, and Arab fears that a Jewish national home in Palestine would result in a great increase in Jewish immigration, leading to the Arabs' economic and political subjection.[10]

A year later in May 1921, Arabs rioted in Jaffa in response to an upsurge in Jewish immigration. The rioting spread spontaneously to Jewish rural settlements. The Jewish leadership suggested that the riots were "artificially stimulated" by the *effendi*, or upper class, but the Haycraft Commission attributed Arab violence to generalized economic and political grievances due to Jewish immigration. Arabs clearly understood that "Jewish predominance was envisaged not only by extremists but also by the responsible representatives of Zionism."[11] Winston Churchill, then secretary of state for the colonies, attempted to placate Arab fears by stating in a 1922 white paper that Jewish immigration should not exceed the "economic absorptive capacity" of Palestine.[12] Churchill did not envision self-government for the Arabs in the foreseeable future. Rather, the British government "favored quiet and, in essence, inaction as the prudent policy," a position which endured throughout the mandate period.[13]

The vexing issues of Zionist land purchases and immigration continued to fan anti-Zionism, and religious sensitivities increased hostilities. In September 1928, when observant Jews attempted to separate men from women during prayer at the Western Wall in the Old City of Jerusalem, Arab nationalists viewed the action as flouting the Arabs' traditional control over the area, which was held by Islamic trust. Communal sensitivities were revived and expressed in the following year's disturbances. Hundreds of young Jews demonstrated in August 1929 at the Western Wall, provocatively raising the Zionist flag and singing "Hatikva," the Zionist anthem. Soon after, Arab mobs and armed bands killed 133 Jews and injured another 232 throughout Palestine, notably in the established Jewish communities of Hebron, Jaffa, Jerusalem, and Safad. British troops and police seeking to quell the violence killed a reported 116 Arabs and wounded 232.[14]

British Repression of the Arab Rebellion for Independence

Although British commissions linked Arab grievances to Jewish immigration and land alienation, the British government failed to fundamentally address either these issues or Arab complaints about the absence of majority rule. Meanwhile, Zionist organizations were steadily acquiring land and increasing the Jewish population in Palestine. Because Britain officially supported the development of the Jewish national home and functioned as the established government, Arab violent opposition was aimed first at the British and then at the *yishuv*, the Jewish community in Palestine. The British described the Arab violence as "offensive" rather than defensive, because it was designed to frustrate the Jewish political land settlement officially supported by the British.

Arab economic distress induced by absentee landlords selling their lands, evictions of peasant farmers, and a Jewish economy closed to Arab laborers was nevertheless recognized by the British Hope-Simpson Commission of 1930. "There was no room" for a single additional Jewish settler if the Arab villagers' standard of life "was to remain at its existing level," the commission reported.[15] Far from stopping Jewish immigration, however, the British government reaffirmed that only "economic absorptive capacity" should limit it. Jewish immigration into Palestine soon shot up by 217 percent, spurred on by a recrudescence of anti-Semitism in Poland and particularly by the founding of the Third Reich in 1933.[16] This arrival in Palestine of so many of Europe's endangered Jews occurred during a global depression, which drove most developed nations to limit immigration to their own countries. The Arabs protested that Jewish immigration and land sales violated the mandate's commitment to safeguard Arab rights.

These developments, combined with the death of the Syrian-born Muslim religious teacher and social reformer Shaykh 'Iz al-Din al-Qassam, killed in action against British security forces in 1935, ignited the Palestinian Arab revolt for independence in 1936. The rebellion became known as the Great Revolt. Arab towns and large villages established national committees to provide local leadership. Arab cadres formed the Arab Higher Committee (AHC) with the Mufti of Jerusalem, Haj Amin al-Husayni, as its president. In 1921 the British appointed him as grand mufti (the Muslim religious scholar who interprets Islamic law), further enhancing his prestige.

The rebellion took the form of strikes and outright revolt against British rule and Jewish settlement. Rebels assaulted Jews and destroyed their property, sniped at settlements, and sabotaged British installations. By mid-August 1936, the Zionist leadership began participating in an armed response, further developing the structure of Zionist paramilitary units. More than 1,000 Arabs died during the six-month revolt in 1936, mostly in fighting with British forces. The rebellion aroused in the external Arab world for the first time "not merely sympathy with the Palestinian Arabs but strong feelings of antipathy towards Zionism."[17]

A British commission was again dispatched in late 1936 to investigate the recurring Arab unrest. In 1937, the Royal (Peel) Commission recommended terminating the mandate and partitioning the country into a Jewish state, consisting of the Galilee and the coastal plain, and an Arab state (which might be merged with Transjordan), to include the generally poorer remainder of Palestine. The British were to retain a mandate enclave that included the holy places in and around Jerusalem.

One component of the plan was particularly ominous for Palestinian Arabs: the concept of "population transfer" advocated by British and Zionist officials. The commission recommended the compulsory relocation of approximately 200,000 Arabs from the proposed Jewish area to the Arab area. In response, the AHC rejected partition, demanded the independence of Palestine, and resumed the rebellion.

Zionist parties were sharply divided on partition, but the principal leadership favored the plan. On population removal, the position of the Jewish Agency chief, David Ben-Gurion, was unequivocal: "I support compulsory transfer. I do not see anything immoral in it." Speaking at a Jewish Agency executive meeting on June 12, 1938, he described its advantages, noting that "with compulsory transfer we [would] have vast areas." Ben-Gurion believed that "removing the Arabs from our midst . . . will not be achievable easily (and perhaps [not] at all) after the [Jewish] state is established. . . . This thing [transfer] must be done now." The first crucial step, he believed, was "*conditioning ourselves for its implementation.*"[18] For Ben-Gurion, two necessities were constant: Jewish sovereignty and "the removal of a certain number of Arabs."[19]

Organized Arab guerrilla warfare spread to rural areas in 1938 and was accompanied by increased terrorism in the towns, which disrupted economic and social life. As the campaign gained momentum, the British exiled Palestinian Arab leaders. The neighboring nations of Syria, Lebanon, and Iraq lent a measure of support to the rebellion, especially Syria.[20] Prominent Palestinian Arabs accused by Arab rebels of being British collaborators were intimidated, abducted, and murdered. Some fled the country. Rebels particularly targeted village *mukhtars* (leaders) and police personnel for their connections with the government.[21]

British policy grew more repressive as the revolt spread. Determined to disarm the Arabs and destroy their leadership, the British outlawed the AHC and all national committees. They issued arrest and deportation orders for Arab politicians, including the mufti, who escaped to Lebanon disguised as a woman.[22] Anyone convicted of carrying weapons could receive the death penalty.

Meanwhile, the British government trained and armed 978 active and 3,881 reserve Jewish settlement police, indirectly boosting Zionist military potential.[23] Large-scale British military operations reduced the Arab rebel organization to comparative impotence. By the end of 1938, the rebellion was leaderless, torn by internecine violence, and defeated by superior British forces and systematic government repression. The British-trained Jewish settlement police would become the core element of organized Zionist forces in the coming years.[24]

Zionists Prepare for Decisive War against the Arabs

By the mid-1930s, a coterie of Zionist leaders recognized that the end of British rule would present a unique opportunity to rid Palestine of its indigenous Arabs. While publicly downplaying Arab hostility to Zionism during the 1936–39 Arab rebellion, the yishuv's leadership quietly prepared to implement the now widely accepted view that war was necessary to achieve its goals. New Jewish settlements increasingly were situated in strategic and defensible locations, and settlers were selected according to military usefulness. Settlers received military training both in Palestine and, prior to emigrating, in Europe. Zionist organizations also clandestinely transferred military personnel and materiel from Europe and the United States to Palestine. Buildings were constructed in cities with mixed Jewish and Arab populations to serve as defensible strong points.

After the British crushed the Arab rebellion, the government dispatched another commission to Palestine in 1938. The Woodhead Commission deemed partition "impracticable." Twenty thousand British troops in Palestine were fully engaged in suppressing a popular Arab peasant uprising while the outbreak of European war was imminent. In an attempt to reach a settlement between Arabs and Jews to pacify the strategic outpost, the government convened the 1939 London Conferences at St. James Palace. After the conferences failed, the British government issued a conciliatory white paper to placate the Arabs. It proposed the establishment of an independent binational state of Palestine within ten years while vowing to restrict Jews to no more than one-third of the country's total population.

Jewish reaction in Palestine to the white paper's rejection of Jewish statehood and liberal Jewish immigration was swift and violent. The Zionist Congress unanimously condemned the document. The yishuv held a general strike and angry Jews looted shops and stoned police. Newly formed Zionist dissident groups from the Revisionist political wing, the Irgun Zva'i Leumi (National Military Organization—IZL or Irgun) and its offshoot, the Lohamei Herut Yisrael (Freedom Fighters of Israel—LHI or Stern Gang), initiated a campaign of murder and sabotage directed against Arabs and the mandate government. Zionist terrorism and illegal immigration increased thereafter, though a relative lull followed the outbreak of World War II.

With the commencement of the global conflict, the official Zionist in-surgency ceased, although the one carried out by the LHI continued. The yishuv's leadership declared its support for the British war efforts against the Axis, and Jewish recruits volunteered for British infantry regiments. On the Arab side, the mufti fled to Baghdad and threw his support behind the Axis powers. Ordinary Palestinian Arabs did rally to Britain's side but with less enthusiasm than the Jews. Hazem Nuseibeh, who worked for Palestinian Broadcasting in Jerusalem, voiced Arab anger at repressive British policies in Palestine. He asked how the Arabs could "fight [along-side] the British when the British had already imprisoned thousands" of Arabs in "concentration camps."[25] Arabs had also criticized the British formation of a Palestine Jewish regiment "as a first step in the direction of a Jewish army."[26]

The disaster befalling European Jewry hardened Zionist resolve. As Hitler's armies advanced over Eastern Europe with its large Jewish popu-lations, the international Zionist movement called for the immediate establishment of a Jewish commonwealth in Palestine. It also demanded Jewish Agency control of unrestricted Jewish immigration and settlement, along with the formation and recognition of a Jewish military force fight-ing under its own flag. This agenda was known as the Biltmore program of May 1942.[27] These proposals reflected a fundamental shift in the Zionists' Arab policy. The Israeli scholar Simha Flapan has argued that the pro-gram "signified a basic change in relation to the Arab factor: it ignored it completely." Whereas prior to the 1939 white paper Zionists made some efforts "to reduce the degree of Arab opposition" to Zionist aspirations, after Biltmore "the Zionist movement . . . considered an agreement with the Arabs as unnecessary, if not harmful."[28]

Zionist organizations mounted a publicity campaign stressing the Nazi persecution of Jews and claiming Palestine as the only possible refuge. After the war, according to U.S. intelligence sources, Zionists forced some Jewish survivors in European refugee camps to emigrate to Palestine against their wishes.[29]

Prominent Palestinian Arabs turned their attention to their own post-war future. But individual jealousies and divergent opinions prevented Palestinian Arabs from forming a coherent political body. Local Arab politicians also began to rely on neighboring Arab rulers and states to champion the Palestinian Arab cause.[30] That dependency undercut Pales-

Legend:
- Proposed Arab State
- Proposed Jewish State
- International Zone

LEBANON

SYRIA

Safad

Acre

Tiberias

Haifa

Nazareth

Baysan

Jinin

Tulkarm

Nablus

River Jordan

Jaffa

Ramallah

Al-Ramla

Jerusalem

MEDITERRANEAN SEA

Dead Sea

Gaza

Hebron

Beersheba

EGYPT

0 10 20 30 40 50
Kilometers

TRANSJORDAN

JEWISH AGENCY PROPOSED PARTITION TO THE ANGLO-AMERICAN
COMMITTEE OF INQUIRY, 1946

tinian Arabs' preparedness for the Arab-Jewish civil war that erupted in November 1947.

As World War II progressed, the yishuv was also busily preparing men and materiel for an eventual war against the Arabs. In March 1943, the Palestine government uncovered a large-scale Zionist arms ring in Palestine. The Haganah, the underground Zionist military force, was illegally obtaining arms and ammunition from British soldiers.[31] Such acquisitions were in line with Ben-Gurion's prediction that "the end of [World War II] would not necessarily mean the end" of Jewish fighting "but might on the contrary be only the beginning of [our] own fight."[32] The reasons for his predictions were not difficult to discern given the irredentist demands among the Zionists. In December 1944, the yishuv's elected leadership reaffirmed its objective that the Jewish Agency control immigration and settlement in preparation for a Jewish state in an unpartitioned Palestine.[33]

Zionists at War with the Mandate Government

The end of World War II saw the beginning of a renewed Zionist insurgency against the British with the more sensational terrorist acts carried out by the "dissident" Revisionist factions. The IZL and LHI had declared their intention to fight the British with every means, legal or illegal, at their disposal.[34] The mandate government became convinced of a serious Zionist "determination to achieve their political aims, if necessary by violence."[35] The high commissioner of Palestine, Alan Cunningham, who assumed his position in November 1945, observed that Jews of all classes, as well as the Arabs, believed that "Great Britain always gives in to force." As for the Zionist insurgency, Cunningham believed that the Jewish Agency and the yishuv generally held a "large measure of sympathy if not of condonation of the terrorist acts" performed mostly by Revisionist Zionists.[36]

Most galling to the Palestine government was the Jewish Agency's indifference toward the dissidents' operations. The British military complained that "while the Jewish Agency professed horror at these attacks," it did nothing to curb them. "No Jew would give the slightest assistance to [the] Security Forces, or even own up to having seen a cold-blooded murder committed under their nose." Many British soldiers resented what they perceived as Jewish ingratitude for British sacrifices to save Jewish lives during World War II.[37] Because the yishuv refused to turn over the dissidents, British forces were perpetually on the defensive.[38]

Meanwhile, the United States emerged as a world power after 1945. Despite their British allies' entanglement in a bloody guerrilla war with underground Zionist military organizations, U.S. politicians were vocally denouncing Britain's Palestine policy. American politicians strongly favored the Zionists. To mollify the Americans, the British government invited U.S. participation in a commission to determine Palestine's future. Foreign Secretary Ernest Bevin also hoped to convince the Americans of "the inequity of creating a quasi-white settler community in Palestine."[39]

The Anglo-American Committee of Inquiry (AACI) was convened in 1946 to examine the question of surviving European Jewry in light of the Palestine situation. The Zionists' position was increasingly one of entitlement and rejection of compromise with Palestine's Arabs. Ben-Gurion testified before the AACI that Palestine "is and will remain our country," and "we are here as of right. We are not here on the strength of the Balfour Declaration or the Palestine Mandate."[40] Likewise, Moshe Shertok, director of the Jewish Agency's political department and a native of Russia, testified that "the right to return [to Palestine] was never, and is not today, considered by the Jews to depend on Arab consent."[41] The AACI recommended, despite Arab opposition, the immediate entry of 100,000 Jewish refugees into Palestine. Many Arabs felt this reflected the American government's susceptibility to Zionist pressures applied by the country's pro-Zionist Jewish community.

Meanwhile, the Zionist campaign of terror in Palestine grew as Britain delayed implementing the AACI's recommendations. Sabotage of the mandate government's installations was accompanied by the kidnapping and murder of British officers in 1946. The Haganah became more directly implicated in the terrorism.[42] British forces searched Jewish Agency headquarters and 26 settlements in June 1946 and declared war against "Jewish extremist elements." Terrorist suspects were arrested, including members of the Palmach, the Haganah's elite strike force, which the British had formed in 1941 to defend the Middle East against an expected German invasion.[43] Even though the British military declared its operations successful, dissident anti-British activities reached a devastating climax when IZL members, disguised as Arabs, planted a bomb in Jerusalem's King David Hotel on July 22, 1946.[44] Half of the British secretariat and military

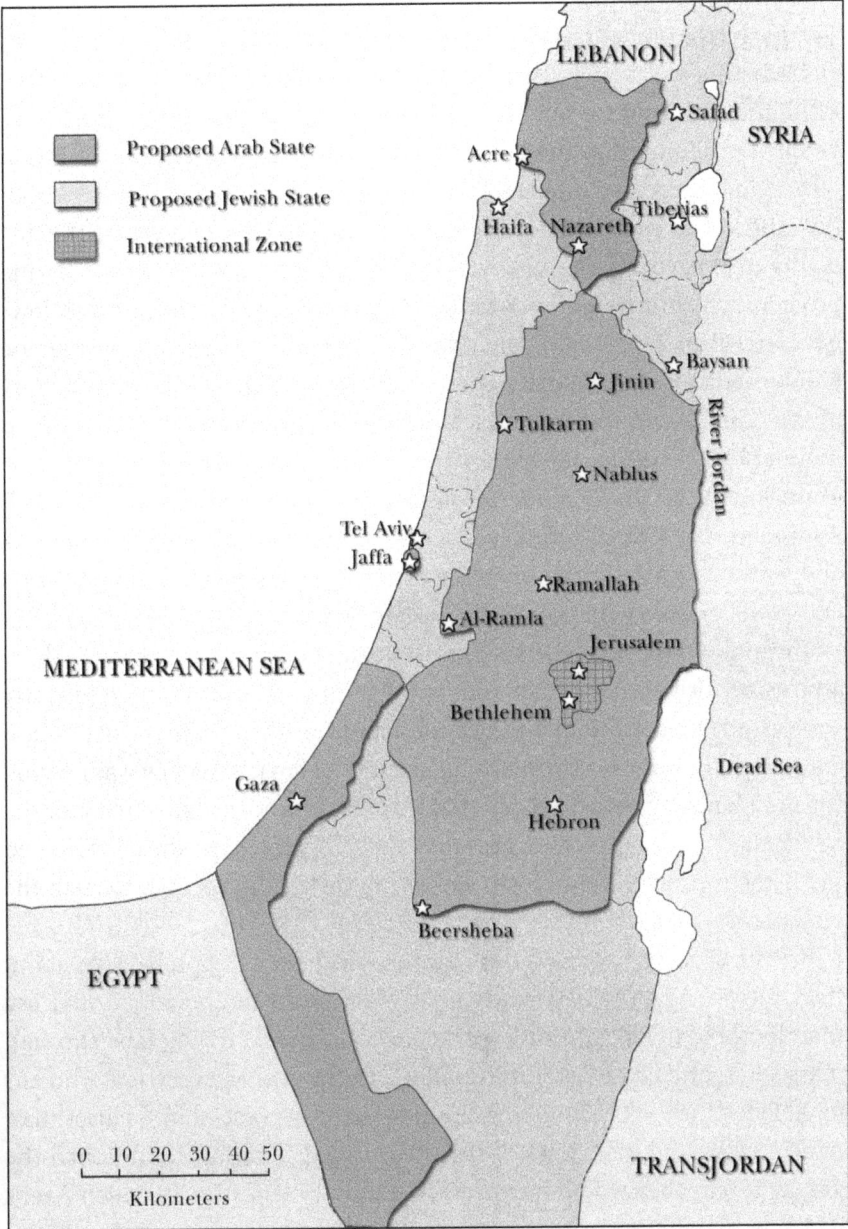

Proposed Arab State

Proposed Jewish State

International Zone

LEBANON

☆ Safad

SYRIA

Acre ☆

☆ Haifa Nazareth
☆

Tiberias ☆

☆ Baysan

☆ Jinin

River Jordan

☆ Tulkarm

☆ Nablus

Tel Aviv ☆
Jaffa ☆

☆ Ramallah

☆ Al-Ramla

Jerusalem
☆

MEDITERRANEAN SEA

Bethlehem

Dead Sea

Gaza ☆

☆ Hebron

☆ Beersheba

EGYPT

0 10 20 30 40 50

Kilometers

TRANSJORDAN

U.N. PLAN OF PARTITION, NOVEMBER 1947

offices, housed in the hotel, were destroyed when the bomb detonated. An unprecedented number of British military and civil servants were killed in a single terror operation.

Daily funerals were held to bury the 100 Britons, Arabs, Jews, and Palestinians with other ethnic backgrounds killed in the hotel. Another 47 people were injured in the bombing. Cunningham wrote: "This criminal outrage has increased inter-racial hatred and bitterness to an extent which it is difficult to over-emphasize and which will seriously increase the difficulty of persuading the Arabs to agree to any settlement of the Palestine problem which does not secure them against being delivered up to Jewish extremism."[45] The mandate government faced a dilemma: on the one hand, meting out immediate and severe punishment to the perpetrators of the King David terrorist attack seemed necessary to maintain British morale. On the other, the authorities wished to avoid punishing and aggravating the generally moderate yishuv, and thereby fanning anti-British sentiment. The British military was also anxious to avoid a two-front war and wanted to reduce the quantity of arms possessed by Zionists before expected "trouble with the Arabs" began again.[46]

Throughout the rest of 1946, Zionist insurgents perpetrated nearly daily attacks on British personnel and installations. Arab civilians frequently were also intended Zionist targets or caught in the crossfire.[47] Although Cunningham was uncertain to what extent the Jewish Agency was helping the dissidents, evidence existed that it had "pre-knowledge of most of the incidents."[48] But political expediency and a defensive posture forestalled the British security forces from exploiting their full potential to stem the violence.[49]

British observers viewed both Arabs and Jews as apprehensive about their future. Arabs feared Zionist settlers would rule them or would use their foothold in Palestine to expand and force them off their land through massive organized Jewish immigration. To the Arabs, every Jew who entered Palestine took them a step closer to their dispossession.[50] Palestinian Arab attacks and massacres of the preceding generation conditioned the yishuv to fear they would be unsafe in a unitary Palestine in which Arabs had a permanent majority.[51]

The British public grew weary of the continuing Zionist insurgency, the mounting British casualties, and the related economic drain. Winston Churchill criticized the Labor government's Palestine record in the House of Commons in January 1947. "How long are you going to stay there, and stay there for what?" he demanded. Churchill also expressed the widespread expectation that communal violence would erupt if the British withdrew, and the common indifference to this eventuality: "It is said that we must stay, because if we go there will be a civil war. I think it very likely, but is that a reason why we should stay? We do not propose to stay in India. The responsibility for stopping civil war in Palestine ought to be borne by the United Nations and not by this overburdened country."[52]

On February 12, 1947, British security forces in Palestine were assigned to a man who, it became clear, concurred with Churchill that inaction was the best policy. Lieutenant General Gordon H. MacMillan would remain in that position until the mandate ended. His decisions would have a great impact on events.

The mandate government meanwhile made a last effort at forceful control. To clear the field for concerted military action against dissident groups, nonessential British civilians and civil administration staff were evacuated in early February 1947. Remaining British subjects were concentrated in cantonment areas in Jerusalem, Tel Aviv, and Haifa to prevent their kidnapping by Zionist dissidents.[53] In spite of the British military crackdown, terrorist activity increased markedly from March through June 1947. One major difficulty for the British was that the security forces employed methods far less harsh than those used to crush the 1936–39 Arab insurgency, methods which had also significantly reduced the Arab community's fighting potential. Golda Meyerson [Meir], a native of Russia and acting director of the Jewish Agency's political department in Jerusalem, herself conceded the comparative leniency of the British vis-à-vis the rebellious Jews.[54]

Race-based perceptions contributed to policy decisions. Both the British and the Jews viewed the Palestinian Arabs as an inferior race that only understood force, whereas the British considered the Jews to be more Western and amenable to reason. The principle of collective responsibility and collective penalties used to combat the Arab mass insurgency "was one to which the Arab community had been accustomed from ancient times," Cunningham wrote. Applying it to the Jewish community, he believed, would have been out of place because of their Western social organization, and because Jewish terrorism was "the work of a dissident minority in which the Jewish community as a whole is not actively implicated," although many Jews were sympathetic to it.[55] The British military felt differently, however. They believed that the yishuv was in fact passively and actively supporting Zionist terrorism, which was "tacitly accepted by all and sundry." The military was increasingly frustrated by politically imposed restraints that limited the punishment of Zionist terrorists.[56]

The British Abandon the Palestine Question to the United Nations

With no settlement of the Arab-Jewish conflict in sight, Britain turned the problem over to the United Nations, in the first real test of the new international body. The United Nations accepted the British request but refused a petition by five Arab member states to consider terminating the mandate and declaring Palestine's independence. The U.N. Special Committee on Palestine (UNSCOP) was appointed to investigate the issue.[57] Abandoning Palestine to the United Nations did not necessarily entail a greater role for statesmanship. Ralph Bunche, special assistant to the representative of the U.N. secretary general, viewed UNSCOP as incompetent and characterized the members as "just about the worst group I have ever had to work with. If they do a good job" he said, "it will be a real miracle."[58] Palestinian Arab leaders distrusted the United Nations and feared that Zionist political pressure, especially in the United States, would lead the world body to decide against their interests.[59]

UNSCOP offered two alternative solutions to the Palestine problem in August 1947. According to Bunche, he essentially drafted both the majority and minority reports because UNSCOP members were incapable of doing the work themselves. The majority recommended partitioning Palestine into two states, one Arab and one Jewish, with an economic union between them and an international trusteeship for Jerusalem. The British Ministry of Defense considered the proposed Arab state, divided into two noncontiguous areas, unviable for geographic, economic, communication, and other reasons.[60] The proposed economic union was intended to resolve the issue of economic viability. The majority proposal ignored both Jewish Agency policy to employ only Jewish labor in Jewish enterprises and Arab rejection of partition.[61]

The UNSCOP plan was not regarded as unbiased. The British chief of staff observed that the majority plan frontiers were "more favorable to the Jews and more unfavorable to the Arabs than those drawn in" partition plans contemplated by the British government.[62] The U.K. colonial secretary, Arthur Creech Jones, commented later that "in all the confused and unreal discussion in Europe and America and among the Jews, the Arabs just did not exist and their views were hardly considered" in formulating future plans for Palestine.[63]

The British were not committed to accepting, much less to carrying out, the U.N. majority proposal, which the Foreign Office considered "manifestly unjust to the Arabs."[64] But they also did not wish to obstruct a U.N. recommendation by refusing to accept it. The Foreign Office believed the Palestinian Arabs' refusal to cooperate with the Jews would "inevitably mean the destruction of the viability of Palestine as a whole." It would portend the embitterment of Arab-Jewish relations and result in guerrilla warfare, except in those areas where British military authority was required to maintain order for the process of withdrawal. The Foreign Office feared that partition would lead to "considerable confusion in which neither the Jewish nor the Arab areas could be economically viable, even though they might fall into more naturally defensive boundaries."[65]

The establishment of these de facto boundaries would likely cause large-scale migration of Arabs and Jews from areas where they were a minority. Parallel events had been happening in India.[66] The Foreign Office also predicted that an attempt to enforce partition would precipitate an Arab uprising in Palestine, with the "more or less" active support of neighboring Arab states and the approval of the entire Muslim world. The Palestine government and military forces would be confronted with a situation in which the Zionists would establish as rapidly as possible a defensible and viable Jewish state. This area would "depend less on the boundaries defined by the partition plan than on the physical necessities of the situation."[67] The logical conclusion was that the outcome of partition would be influenced more by the nature of British withdrawal and its allowing a Jewish state to be established than by the U.N. partition plan.[68] Most of the Foreign Office's predictions proved correct.

At this point, the British made the crucial decision that would contribute to both the outbreak of the subsequent civil war and the concomitant mass dispossession of Palestine's Arabs. They refused to impose any solution by force on either community. If partition could not be peacefully implemented, they declared, Britain would surrender the mandate and withdraw unconditionally from Palestine.[69] The British government chose to disengage from Palestine by following the ill-planned India model, in which a military withdrawal without a political solution resulted in the deaths of hundreds of thousands of people and created a legacy of chaos, hatred, and unending war in South Asia.

Security in Palestine deteriorated markedly immediately after UNSCOP announced its recommendations in August 1947. Jews "became hysterically jubilant" while Arabs were stunned "that such a solution could be possible, involving as it did the gift to the Jews of such large areas of purely Arab population."[70] Not only was the Jewish state to be awarded the most fertile land under the majority plan, but 400,000 Arabs would be unwillingly incorporated into the Jewish state.[71] Because UNSCOP's report excluded the Bedouins in its calculations, the Palestinian Arabs would likely be the majority in both proposed states.[72] The Arab League political committee considered UNSCOP's recommendations "flagrantly devastating" to U.N. principles and to the Palestinian Arabs' natural right to independence, as well as "a breach of all promises made to the Arabs." Furthermore, the Arab League protested that the recommendations threatened "the peace of Palestine and of all Arab lands."[73]

High Commissioner Cunningham saw an unavoidable dilemma for Britain if it failed to secure an Arab-Jewish agreement. If partition could not be adopted, withdrawal was Britain's only alternative, but an unconditional withdrawal would end British prestige in the Middle East: "Although we may say we have fulfilled our promises to the Jews, the Arabs will feel that we have forced the Jews upon them and have then left them in the lurch to deal with the resulting problems, and I would suggest that this would inflict infinitely more damage on the possibility of retaining Arab goodwill than would result from a reasonable scheme of partition."[74]

Withdrawal without an Arab-Jewish agreement held "disadvantages which should not be underestimated," Cunningham noted. In the interval between the announcement of British intentions and the actual withdrawal the administration's task "might be more difficult than in any previous period." He also calculated that absent a government to which power could be transferred, the consequences of evacuation "would be unpredictable." Some or all of the Arab states could become involved in the resulting disorder, and "even quarrel among themselves over the country's future."[75] All of these fears, expressed in September 1947, would be borne out in the ensuing months.

Cunningham also saw the British situation as a dilemma. He conceded significant advantages to withdrawal even if effected "at the cost of a pe-riod of bloodshed and chaos" in Palestine. He recognized that "British lives would not be lost, nor British resources expended, in suppressing one Palestinian community for the advantage of the other." Passive with-drawal was preferable to enforcing the U.N. majority plan or a variant of it, since the latter would damage British Middle East interests.[76]

British military and police commanders agreed at their September 19, 1947, security conference that the U.N. majority plan was unlikely to be implemented effectively on the ground. They also saw a probability of the British facing trouble on two fronts concurrently. The military was never-theless confident that improved communications, modern weapons and equipment, and liaison with the Royal Air Force (RAF) had strengthened its position since the 1936 Arab rebellion. Meanwhile, seeing no future in Palestine, many police were submitting resignations to seek employment elsewhere, and military units were being continually released.[77]

Despite the drawdown of forces, MacMillan argued that the army would be able to cope with any threats against it resulting from Arab troubles. The military unanimously considered Arab leaders to be of poor qual-ity, except for the mufti. Although he would be proved wrong, MacMillan also believed that the army could control the situation in Palestine by preventive measures rather than through direct attacks against the Arabs. The military did foresee the danger of Arab attacks on outlying Jewish settlements and conceded that great pressure would need to be exerted to prevent Zionists from using "savage retaliatory methods."[78]

Cunningham attempted to impress on Jewish and Arab leaders that Britain had wearied of disturbances and intended to withdraw from Pales-tine with or without an agreement between the two communities. He told AHC Secretary Husayn al-Khalidi and Jewish Agency Chairman David Ben-Gurion on October 2, 1947, that Britain was "most desirous of leav-ing Palestine with a happy solution and in peace." But, he continued, it would "leave without that condition" if Arabs and Jews could not agree.[79] Cunningham believed that the Jewish leadership took more seriously than the Arabs the British intentions to withdraw their military forces and ad-ministration in the absence of a settlement. Like many Palestinian Arabs, Sami Hadawi, who worked for the mandate government, believed that the British would "never leave" Palestine.[80]

Cunningham's remarks had implied that the British would leave Palestine in chaos, if necessary. He felt the Jewish Agency viewed this contingency with equanimity because it believed the Haganah was "strong enough to hold" against Arab attack virtually all territory under Jewish occupation, and doubtless saw "in the resultant anarchy an opportunity for the yishuv to do for itself what Great Britain and the U.S. will not and Russia and others could not do."[81] In other words, Cunningham believed that the Zionist political leadership saw conflict as an opportunity to shape Palestine to suit its own aims. As this book will show, events would prove him correct.

The Arab governments were quite apprehensive about the planned British withdrawal. The president of Lebanon, Bishara Khouri, viewed the situation in Palestine as serious, particularly if British withdrawal created a power vacuum. He urgently stressed that a withdrawal without a replacement force would leave the Palestine Arabs at the mercy of an organized and experienced Zionist army. Arab League countries also feared that the Jews would "introduce into Palestine large numbers [of] potential reinforcements during [the] period of confusion following British withdrawal." The movement of small numbers of the Arab armies toward Palestine's frontiers, President Khouri said, was precautionary and these forces would not enter Palestine unless the British withdrew.[82]

The British Regional Command Predicts Civil War during Withdrawal

The British military regional command also assessed the risk of Arab-Jewish civil war early. In a note on the handover of Palestine, General Sir Harold Pyman, chief of staff to General John T. Crocker, commander of Middle East Land Forces (MELF), advised that "some authority must remain to govern the country and run the public services." He warned of "immediate civil chaos," which would "undoubtedly develop into civil war" unless the civil authority and the army transferred power to a new government before withdrawing. The Arab states would consider a withdrawal that created a power vacuum to be "a complete breach of trust and our swan song in the Middle East." Afterward, Pyman predicted, the British would never have any influence in the region. If the British wished "to remain a great power in the Middle East," he advised, "we cannot evacuate Palestine before we have handed over the country to some other authorities."[83]

Cunningham also feared Arab actions, warning that Palestinian Arabs were unlikely to wait for the British evacuation before attacking the Jews, thereby drawing the British "into the three-cornered conflict" they had "been trying so hard to avoid."[84] Cunningham advised London that however the mandate regime withdrew, it was essential that the Palestine government abrogate "its authority on one particular date for the whole of Palestine."[85] Otherwise, he believed, the Jews and Arabs would challenge the government's authority.

The Jewish Agency had already warned that it would ignore British authority since the latter was abandoning the mandate. Ben-Gurion maintained that as the British were relinquishing the mandate, "there is no law in Palestine and therefore anything the Jews wish to do is justified."[86] In October 1947, Ben-Gurion had already directed his "war cabinet"—"an ad-hoc group of Jewish officers who had served in the British army"—to prepare to occupy the whole country. He asked General Ephraim Ben-Artzi, the most senior officer, to create a military force capable of repelling a potential attack from neighboring Arab states and occupying "as much of the country as possible, and hopefully all of it."[87]

In the event that the U.N. General Assembly voted in favor of partition, Cunningham believed the Arabs would almost certainly oppose the implementation of a U.N. resolution favoring partition, even if they did not resist before practical steps were taken to implement it. MacMillan estimated he had sufficient forces to deal with "any trouble the Arabs may make," in the event of partition, but only "up to the 1st April 1948." His force estimate addressed the threat from only one side. It had always been MacMillan's view that he could "deal with either Arabs or Jews at one time, *but not both*." He believed that "he would only have to deal with the Arabs, with the possible exception of some Jewish terrorism."[88] Events would prove him wrong.

By November 28, 1947, the British had prepared a withdrawal plan that in theory continued civil administration and law and order until the mandate ended on May 15, 1948. Even though the British government and military were demonstrably aware that their unilateral withdrawal would create a power vacuum in Palestine resulting in civil war, the British based their planning on the mistaken assumption that the degree of violence would not escalate to uncontrollable levels until they had fully withdrawn their troops and police into the final enclave at the port of Haifa after May

15, 1948.[89]

To safeguard British withdrawal and in an attempt to preserve good relations with the Arab states, the British inhibited U.N. preparations designed to ensure a smooth transition of power to the envisioned Jewish and Arab states. Cunningham advised the British government that no steps should be taken toward implementing partition, even by a U.N. commission, as long as the civil administration and British troops remained in Palestine. His rationale for lack of cooperation with the United Nations was to avoid provoking the overwhelmingly anti-partition Arabs while the British needed to maintain lines of communication.[90] Although the United Nations had planned to send a commission to serve as an interim authority and oversee partition, the British government concluded it could not maintain the mandate and the civil administration for more than 15 days after the arrival of the U.N. Palestine Commission, because of expected Arab disorder. The British feared being forced to abandon their withdrawal plans and suffering "disastrous losses of stores," which they were not prepared to accept.[91] Consequently, the British barred the U.N. commission from arriving in Palestine until the beginning of May 1948.

The British also enacted policies that practically prohibited British subjects who staffed the mandate government from accepting employment in the proposed Arab or Jewish states' governments.[92] These policies further obstructed any governmental continuity, especially on the Arab side, where educated professionals were fewer in number. U.S. intelligence confirmed the U.N. Palestine Commission's difficulties in functioning effectively without the assistance of top-level British civil administrators in areas like public utilities and other essential services.[93] British unilateral withdrawal, along with the British failure to establish any other authority in Palestine (or to permit the United Nations to accept a handover of power when the British withdrew), ensured that the British evacuation would create a power vacuum.

On November 29, 1947, the U.N. General Assembly voted 33 to 13, with ten abstentions, in favor of UNSCOP's plan to partition Palestine into sovereign Jewish and Arab states, with an economic union administered by a joint board.[94] (Jerusalem was designated a demilitarized and neutralized *corpus separatum* under an international trusteeship.) Colonial Secretary Creech Jones had no illusions about the capacity of the United Nations to meet the postwar challenges. "The scandal of the partition vote," he wrote, "the behavior of the delegations and the treatment of the Palestine issue by the [UNSCOP] committee is on the records and is in truth a very sorry episode."[95]

The General Assembly resolution was the product of relentless politicking to overcome widespread skepticism about the plan's merits. U.S. Undersecretary of State Dean Rusk commented that the "pressure and arm-twisting applied by American and Jewish representatives in capital after capital to get that affirmative vote" would be "hard to describe."[96] The Palestinian Arabs and the Arab states were embittered by the U.S. support for partition. Saudi Arabia's foreign affairs minister, Amir Faisal, described the struggle in the U.N. General Assembly as between the Arab states and the U.S. delegation, with other nations as spectators rather than active participants.[97]

For the Arabs, the U.N. vote was the spark that ignited the 1948 war. The Arabs rejected a U.N. resolution they saw as unfairly partitioning their land, stripping them of their birthright, and forcing them to pay for European pogroms and the Holocaust. They also feared that the Jews would not be satisfied with their allotted area but would seek to acquire all of Palestine and also Transjordan, which many Jews openly proclaimed as their aim.[98] (The expansionist intentions of the State of Israel would be confirmed by future wars, ongoing illegal settlement on occupied Palestinian land, and discriminatory laws against the Palestinians.) Rather than maintaining international peace and security, as mandated by its charter, the United Nations, by voting in favor of partition, contributed to the outbreak of civil war in Palestine and the concomitant expulsion of the Palestinian Arabs.

֍

1. David Gilmour, "The Unregarded Prophet: Lord Curzon and the Palestine Question," *Journal of Palestine Studies* 25.3 (1996): 60–68. In deference to Lord Curzon's opposition to the Balfour Declaration, the final version contained the pledge that "nothing shall be done which may prejudice the civil and religious rights of the existing non-Jewish communities in Palestine."

2. NACP 319/270/15/31, Intelligence Estimate of the Enemy Situation, March 6, 1948, revised June 15, 1948.

3. John Norton Moore, ed., *The Arab-Israeli Conflict: Documents*, vol. 3 (Princeton, N.J.: Princeton University Press, 1974), 26.

4. The territories designated League of Nations mandates were previously controlled by states defeated in World War I, primarily imperial Germany and the Ottoman Empire. The mandate power undertook obligations to the inhabitants of the mandated territories and to the League of

Nations.

5. *Survey of Palestine: Prepared in December 1945 and January 1946 for the Information of the Anglo-American Committee of Inquiry* (Palestine: Government Printer, 1946 [reprinted by the Institute of Palestine Studies, Washington, D.C., 1991]), hereafter, *Survey of Palestine*. See chap. 1 of the Survey for the terms of the mandate.

6. Abu-Lughod, *Transformation of Palestine*, 144.

7. FRUS, *The Paris Peace Conference, 1919*, vol. 12 (Washington, D.C.: U.S. Government Printing Office, 1947), 758–62.

8. *The Political History of Palestine under British Administration*, Memorandum by His Britannic Majesty's Government presented in 1947 to the U.N. Special Committee on Palestine (UNSCOP) (Jerusalem: 1947), 2.

9. Ibid.

10. *Survey of Palestine*, 16.

11. *Haycraft Report, Commission of Inquiry*, Cmd. 1540, October 21, 1921.

12. *Survey of Palestine*, 20.

13. Aaron S. Klieman, *Foundations of British Policy in the Arab World: The Cairo Conference of 1921* (Baltimore: Johns Hopkins University Press, 1970), 204.

14. *Survey of Palestine*, 24; George Antonius, *The Arab Awakening: The Story of the Arab National Movement* (New York: Capricorn, 1965), 405–12.

15. *Survey of Palestine*, 27.

16. Ibid. The number of Jewish immigrants into Palestine jumped from 9,553 in 1932 to 30,327 in 1933.

17. *Survey of Palestine*, 37–38. For more information on the Arab Revolt see Ted Swedenberg, *Memories of Revolt: The 1936–1939 Rebellion and the Palestinian National Past* (Fayetteville: University of Arkansas Press, 2003).

18. David Ben-Gurion, Diary, July 12, 1937; emphasis in original; cited in Morris, *Birth Revisited*, 47–48n23.

19. CZA 28, protocols of the joint meeting of the Jewish Agency Executive and the Political Committee of the Zionist Actions Committee, June 12, 1938; cited in Morris, *Birth*, 27, and in Masalha, *Expulsion of the Palestinians*, 117.

20. Philip S. Khoury, *Syria and the French Mandate: The Politics of Arab Nationalism, 1920–1945* (Princeton, N.J.: Princeton University Press, 1987), 540–48.

21. *Survey of Palestine*, 45.

22. Ibid., 42.

23. *Report by His Majesty's Government in the United Kingdom of Great Britain and Northern Ireland to the Council of the League of Nations on the Administration of Palestine and Transjordan, 1937*.

24. NACP 218/190/19/4-5, AACI interviews, 10.

25. Hazem Nuseibeh, interviewed by author in Amman, Jordan, September 30, 2001.

26. *Survey of Palestine*, 65.

27. Ibid., 64.

28. Simha Flapan, *Zionism and the Palestinians* (London: Croom Helm, 1979), 283.

29. NACP 43/250/9/29/2-3, documentation of Zionist publicity campaign promoting Palestine as the sole solution to rescue the "remnant of European Jewry."

30. *Survey of Palestine*, 66.

31. Ibid, 67.

32. Ben-Gurion's speech at Tel Hai, March 20, 1943; cited in *Survey of Palestine*, 67.

33. Ibid., 74.

34. TNA AIR 23/8350, Report on RAF's Evacuation from Palestine, Air Vice Marshal W. L. Dawson,

air officer commanding, Levant [n.d.].

35. CP I/1/4, Cunningham to Creech Jones, no. 1710, December 1, 1945.

36. CP I/1/39, Cunningham to Creech Jones, no. 281, February 19, 1946.

37. TNA AIR 23/8350, Report on RAF Evacuation, Dawson.

38. TT, General Sir Horatius Murray interview.

39. Louis and Stookey, *End of the Palestine Mandate,* ix.

40. NACP 43/250/9/29/2-3, Jewish Agency Submission to AACI. Statement by David Ben-Gurion, Jerusalem, Monday, March 11, 1946.

41. Ibid., Statement by Moshe Shertok before the AACI, March 26, 1946.

42. CP I/1/105, Cunningham to Creech Jones, no. 993, June 19, 1946.

43. CP V/4/51, HQ Palestine and Transjordan Operation Instruction, no. 68, June 1946; David Tal, "Between Intuition and Professionalism: Israeli Military Leadership during the 1948 Palestine War," *Journal of Military History* 68 (July 2004): 888.

44. SP, Palestine: Narrative of Events from February 1947 until Withdrawal of All British Troops by Lt. General Gordon MacMillan, July 3, 1948, Fayid [Egypt], 1, hereafter the MacMillan Report.

45. CP I/2/7, Cunningham to Creech Jones, August 3, 1946.

46. CP I/1/175, Creech Jones to Cunningham, July 26, 1946; Cunningham to Creech Jones, no. 1226, July 27, 1946. Issa Nakhleh, *Encyclopedia of the Palestine Problem,* vol. 1 (New York: Intercontinental, 1991), 93–188.

47. Ibid., 93–118. Includes a chronology of terrorist incidents extracted from the British National Archives' War Office records.

48. CP I/1/39, Cunningham to Creech Jones, no. 281, February 19, 1946.

49. CP I/5/95, GOC Palestine to MELF, November 21, 1946; CP I/3/93, GOC Palestine to commander-in-chief MELF, November 21, 1946.

50. NACP 43/250/9/29/2-3, AACI hearing in Jerusalem, March 12, 1946, Jamal Husayni representing Palestinian Arabs.

51. CP 1/5/66, Creech Jones to Cunningham, no. 209, February 1, 1947.

52. *Keesing's Contemporary Archives* (London: Keesing's, 1987), February 1–8, 1947, 8408.

53. Christina Jones, *The Untempered Wind: Forty Years in Palestine* (London: Longman, 1975), 61–62.

54. Golda Meir, *My Life* (New York: G. P. Putnam's Sons, 1975), 206.

55. CP II/1/54, Cunningham to Creech Jones [April 1947].

56. TNA WO 261/708, Third Parachute Brigade, November 2, 1947.

57. Brian Urquhart, *Ralph Bunche: An American Life* (New York: W. W. Norton, 1993), 149.

58. Ibid., 140.

59. CP I/4/100, Cunningham to Creech Jones, no. 365, February 18, 1947.

60. TNA DEFE 5/10 COS (48) 45 (O) 26/2/48 annex.

61. Urquhart, *Ralph Bunche,* 146.

62. CP V/3/22, Chief of Staff to FO, September 5, 1947.

63. EMP, Arthur Creech Jones, October 23, 1961.

64. CP V/3/33, FO memo, September 18, 1947.

65. Ibid.

66. TNA CAB 134/527, Official Committee on Palestine: The Future of Arab Palestine, FO memo, January 10, 1948.

67. Ibid.

68. TNA CO 537/3899, CID HQ Jerusalem to Chief Secretary, December 12, 1947. Revisionists meeting in Tel Aviv, December 6, 1947.

69. CP V/3/37, FO Memo, September 19, 1947.

70. MacMillan Report, 10.
71. FRUS, Henderson to Marshall, September 22, 1947, *The Near East and Africa, 1947*, vol. 5 (Washington, D.C.: U.S. Government Printing Office, 1971), 1156.
72. TNA FO 371/61836, FO interview with 'Abd al-Rahman Azzam Pasha, October 6, 1947.
73. NACP 84/350/63/11/5-6, U.S. Beirut Legation and Embassy, Confidential Resolutions of Sofar Conference, September 16–19, 1947, enclosure no. 7 to dispatch no. 189, October 16, 1947.
74. CP IV/4/21, Cunningham's comments on the FO paper on Palestine 1947.
75. CP V/3/35, FO memo, September 18, 1947.
76. Ibid.
77. CP IV/1/85, Minutes of Security Conference, September 19, 1947.
78. TNA WO 261/708, Third Parachute Brigade Intelligence Summary no. 6, October 21, 1947.
79. CP V/1/77, Notes on Cunningham's interview with Khalidi and Ben-Gurion, October 2, 1947.
80. Quoted in Larry Collins and Dominique Lapierre, *O Jerusalem!* (London: Pan, 1972), 333.
81. TNA CO 537/2281, Situation Monthly Reports, Cunningham to Creech Jones, no. 249, October 11, 1947.
82. NACP 84/350/63/11/5-6, Beirut Legation to Creech Jones, no. 412, October 13, 1947.
83. PP, October 1947 file.
84. CP IV/4/22, Comments on the FO paper on Palestine [Cunningham, 1947].
85. CP II/3/1, Cunningham to Creech Jones, no. 2054, November 1, 1947.
86. Ibid.
87. Bar-Zohar, Ben-Gurion, vol. 2, 663; cited in Pappé, *Ethnic Cleansing of Palestine,* 42.
88. CP II/3/23-24, Cunningham to U.K. Delegate, New York, no. 1519, November 5, 1947.
89. CP III/3/31, Cunningham to U.K. Delegate, New York, no. 1529, November 8, 1947.
90. Ibid.
91. CP II/3/115, Creech Jones to Cunningham, November 11, 1947.
92. Ibid.
93. NACP 319/270/6/15/4, Memorandum for the Chief of Staff, Intelligence Division Special Briefing "Planned Partition of Palestine Encountering Serious Obstacles," January 27, 1948.
94. TNA CAB 134/527, Official Committee on Palestine: The Future of Arab Palestine, FO memo, January 10, 1948.
95. EMP, Arthur Creech Jones, October 23, 1961.
96. Richard Papp, ed., *As I Saw It, by Dean Rusk as Told to Richard Rusk* (New York: W. W. Norton, 1990), 146.
97. FRUS, Minister in Saudi Arabia (Childs) to the Secretary of State (Marshall), Jidda, January 13, 1948, *The Near East, South Asia and Africa 1948*, vol. 5, part 1 (Washington, D.C.: U.S. Government Printing Office, 1975), 210.
98. TT, General Sir John Glubb Pasha; *Times,* January 14, 1948.

PALESTINIAN HOUSE DYNAMITED BY THE HAGANAH, KILLING SEVEN
FAMILY MEMBERS, INCLUDING FOUR CHILDREN, 1947

III

Zionist Militarism and Arab Population "Transfer"

Not one village, not one tribe should be left.

Joseph Weitz, Jewish National Fund

Since the late 1800s, many leaders of the Zionist movement, beginning with its founder, had wanted the indigenous Arab population removed from Palestine. As Palestinian Arabs increasingly resisted Jewish settlement, Zionist leaders realized a Jewish state in Palestine could be established there only by force. They understood that the Palestinian Arabs would never voluntarily relinquish their homeland to the Jews—politically or physically. Thus, the yishuv undertook to prepare militarily to win any potential war for statehood and to reduce the Arab majority in Palestine. The Zionist leadership discreetly steered policy toward strategies that would prompt Arab dislocation, referring obliquely to these policies as "transfer."

Contemporary observers, including U.S. and U.N. military analysts, assessed the absolute and relative Zionist and Arab military capabilities in late 1947. These assessments show that Zionist policymakers were aware of their superior military strength and recognized the opportunity presented by the civil war to forcibly "transfer" Arabs. Their outlook had historical antecedents.

The Zionist Concept of Population "Transfer" or "Cleansing"

In the late nineteenth and early twentieth centuries, European attitudes of superiority toward indigenous peoples supported colonialists' removal of native populations to expand territorial holdings. Political, religious, territorial, and economic motives all drove compulsory "transfers." Population transfer, or "cleansing," is defined as "a planned deliberate removal from a certain territory of an undesirable population distinguished by one or more characteristics such as ethnicity, religion, race, class or sexual preference."[1]

During this period, compulsory transfer was an accepted policy to solve political problems and to resolve communal differences.[2] Population transfer was employed after World War I to solve problems of ethnic minorities. The exchange of minority populations between Greece and Turkey was one of the earliest of such organized undertakings. Sir John Hope Simpson, vice president of the League of Nations' Refugee Settlement Commission of 1926–30 (and later a special envoy to Palestine), oversaw the Greco-Turkish transfer. While he believed that compulsory population exchange could offer "an adequate solution for hopelessly complicated minority problems," he also emphasized that it is "inhumane, indeed a cruel remedy, entailing much suffering and hardship on the unfortunate to whom it is applied."[3]

Today, forced population transfer is commonly referred to as "ethnic cleansing." This term entered the international lexicon to describe crimes of aggression during the 1990s conflicts in the former Yugoslavia. "Ethnic cleansing" describes the intent to drive victims, and often all traces of their existence, from territories that perpetrators desire and claim for themselves. Forced deportation "seldom takes place without violence, often murderous violence." In his study of twentieth-century ethnic cleansing, Norman Naimark observed how people cling to their homes: "People do not leave their homes on their own. They hold on to their land and their culture, which are interconnected. They resist deportation orders; they cling to their domiciles and their possessions; they find every possible way to avoid abandoning the place where their families have roots and their ancestors are buried."[4]

From its inception, Zionist ideology intended to establish a Jewish state in Palestine, which necessitated the reduction of the non-Jewish population to relative insignificance. Contemporary sentiments are exemplified by Moshe Menuhin, who was schooled in Palestine at the elite Zionist-oriented Herzlia Gymnasia in the early twentieth century. He wrote that "it was drummed into our young hearts that the fatherland must become ours *'goyim rein'*" (clear of Gentiles).[5]

The Zionist concept of "transfer" entailed the organized removal of the indigenous Palestinian Arab population and its resettlement elsewhere. Theodor Herzl, the founder of political Zionism and the World Zionist Organization, wrote in his diary in June 1895 that it would be necessary to remove the non-Jews from the Jewish state, recording his plans to displace the indigenous population and expropriate private property. Herzl, a native of Hungary, based his transfer ideas on white, minority-ruled Rhodesia, established by Cecil Rhodes in southern Africa. He believed it prudent not to publicize the idea of transfer because the extreme measures he advocated to colonize Palestine would "temporarily alienate civilized opinion."[6] Secrecy and discretion were necessary to implement such plans, he advised.[7]

The historic links between the Zionist political goal of establishing a Jewish state in Palestine and the leadership's ideological advocacy of transfer have been well-established by various researchers using declassified Israeli state archives. Nur Masalha concluded in his comprehensive study that transfer was not merely a strategic expedient but inherent in Zionist aims and policy. Transfer, he wrote, "can be said to be the logical outgrowth of the ultimate goal of the Zionist movement, which was the establishment of a Jewish state through colonization and land acquisition—in other words, through a radical ethno-religious-demographic transformation of a country, the population of which had been almost entirely Arab at the start of the Zionist venture."[8]

Many leading Zionists, across the political spectrum, endorsed or advanced the idea of population transfer, both voluntary and compulsory, as a solution to the "Arab question." They include David Ben-Gurion, Berl Katznelson, Leo Motzkin, Arthur Ruppin, Chaim Weizmann, Nachman Syrkin, Joseph Weitz, and Israel Zangwill.[9] Contemporary evidence is somewhat elusive because many official Zionist documents referring to transfer planning remain classified, particularly those concerning the 1948 Arab exodus.[10] Nonetheless, Zionist support for population transfer is well documented in letters, speeches, diaries, and meeting minutes. Indeed, Zionist tactics went beyond mere military actions to drive out much of the Arab population in the early period of the 1948 war.

Forced Depopulation: A Strategy for the "Arab Problem"

Since Zionists had begun to settle in Palestine, many of them had viewed the indigenous population with hostile indifference or patronizing superiority. They believed the *fellahin* (peasants) were base and that the only language the Arabs understood was force. The European Jewish author Ahad Ha'am observed the settlers' behavior, writing, "They treat the Arabs with hostility and cruelty, deprive them of their rights, offend them without cause, and even boast of these deeds."[11]

Many Zionist settlers were convinced that the Palestinian Arabs could be harassed into leaving. By 1907, settlers had organized a boycott against the use of Arab labor on Jewish agricultural settlements, which became increasingly institutionalized. The boycott was later extended to Arab produce. Settlers forcibly evicted Arab tenant farmers from the Sejera settlement in the lower Galilee[12]—the same settlement where David Gruen (Ben-Gurion) lived for a time as a young Jewish immigrant from Plonsk, Poland. Deadly conflict between the Sejera settlers and the local Arabs made an impression on Ben-Gurion. He said later, "I realized that sooner or later there would be a trial of strength between us and the Arabs. . . . We had to be prepared to meet them."[13]

At this time, European Zionist settlers organized the Hashomer (the Guard), an armed security force to protect and defend Jewish villages and colonies. This militant organization, which adopted Arab Bedouin garb, was modeled on the secret Jewish self-defense groups in Russia and derived its basic values from Russian revolutionary ideology and practice. Members believed that "every revolutionary ideology harbors within it the legitimation of the use of violence, since the end justifies the means."[14] The Hashomer was the first Zionist militia and the forerunner of the official underground Zionist army, the Haganah (defense). It adopted the slogan: "In blood and fire Judea fell, in blood and fire shall Judea rise again."[15]

During the Palestinian Arab rebellion of 1936–39—sparked by accelerated Jewish immigration, from 5,249 in 1929 to 61,854 in 1935[16]—the idea that force was the only option to deal with the Arabs became more institutionalized and overt. The Jewish leaders' declared policy of *havlaga* (self-restraint)—based on moral principles and political-pragmatic considerations—soon ceded to popular pressure, spurred by the Revisionists, to use force to counter Arab attacks. For the Revisionists, the "war for the conquest of the homeland was already being waged," and the object of force was "the conquest of the homeland Israel by the sword of Israel."[17]

The Israeli historian Anita Shapira identifies a crucial factor in the Jewish military forces' development: their training by Captain Orde Charles Wingate, a British officer dedicated to the Zionist cause. Wingate, a zealot and a controversial World War II commander, introduced commando techniques to Zionist militias. Without authorization, he set up small, mobile Jewish units, training and familiarizing them with Palestine's terrain. They were the forerunner to the officially sanctioned Anglo-Jewish Special Night Squads, which exploited darkness and surprise in operations against Arab paramilitary groups. Wingate was unimpressed by the Arabs' fighting abilities. "They are feeble and their whole theory of war is cut and run. Like all ignorant and primitive people they are especially liable to panic," he wrote in an official assessment.[18]

With Wingate, the Jews went beyond simply defending their settlements to initiating "offensive actions in areas inhabited by Arabs," which "increased the [Jews'] sense of ownership of Palestine, raising it from a theoretical to a practical level."[19] Jewish volunteers were trained to follow tossing a hand grenade with an attack on a village. Wingate used "methods of intimidation and considerable brutality against Arab villagers." He reportedly lined up rows of villagers suspected of murder and executed every tenth one. Wingate mounted merciless raids on Bedouin encampments, humiliating the inhabitants and destroying their property.[20] He also had no compunction about employing collective punishment, such as home demolitions (still practiced by the Israeli government against families of suspected terrorists). The most important psychological as well as tactical lesson that Wingate taught the Jewish settlers was "to go beyond the wire," said Polish-born, American-raised Zvi Brenner, "not just to defend our settlements but to go out and confront the enemy in his lair."[21] The Jewish fighters absorbed these norms and techniques and used them against the Arabs in the 1948 war.

The Zionist leadership took the opportunity of the Arab Revolt to strengthen and expand the Haganah in the belief that the "Arab problem" could only be solved from a position of military strength and by creating economic, military, and settlement predominance.[22] Ben-Gurion concluded: "What will drive the Arabs to a mutual understanding with us?

. . . Facts . . . only after we manage to establish a great Jewish fact in this country . . . will the precondition for discussion with the Arabs be met."[23]

Jewish youth in particular responded to the use of force as a means to realize Zionist goals. The violence awakened their awareness that the Arabs would not accept the colonization of Palestine by Jews. The Polish-born Yisrael Galili founded Ha-Noar ha-Oved (Working Youths), and inspired young Jews "to take on the burden of defense."[24] Galili, who served as Haganah chief of staff from 1946 to 1948, was among those stressing to the youth movement the seriousness of the conflict between the Arabs and the Jews and the necessity of creating an independent Jewish military force. Many Zionists had reached the conclusion during the Arab Revolt that "there is no possibility of building Palestine without waging a war for every inch of its soil."[25]

The yishuv's increasing militarism was coupled with the Zionist leadership's continued transfer planning. In 1937, the Jewish Agency set up the Committee for the Transfer of Arabs. The committee met regularly and assembled information and statistical data to prepare plans for the compulsory transfer of Arabs from Palestine.[26] Zionist experts meticulously mapped each Arab village in great detail on reconnaissance missions, including topographic location, access roads, land quality, water springs, income sources, sociopolitical makeup, religion, mukhtars' names, relationships to other villages, the age of men between 16 and 50, and how best to attack it. In addition to this information, Zionists used Arab informants to gather data on a village's hostility to the Zionist project and its level of participation in the Arab Revolt. Arabs who had participated were listed, as were families that had lost a member in the fighting against the British or had allegedly killed Jews. Ilan Pappé asserts the last bit of information influenced the villages that Zionist forces targeted for mass executions, massacres, and torture during the 1948 war.[27]

Zionist transfer plans were soon formally endorsed by the British government. Yet another British commission was dispatched to Palestine to ascertain Arab grievances that led to the 1936 Arab Revolt. The 1937 Royal (Peel) Commission proposed to terminate the mandate and to partition the country between the Arabs and the Jews. The partition plan explicitly included the forced depopulation of large numbers of Arabs from the proposed Jewish area to the Arab area (but not vice versa). The Zionist leadership publicly accepted and advanced the concept of forced transfer in the context of the Peel plan. Ben-Gurion wrote: "In many parts of the country new settlement will not be possible without transferring the Arab peasantry. . . . Transfer is what will make possible a comprehensive settlement program. . . . Jewish power which grows steadily, will also increase our possibilities to carry out the transfer on a large scale."[28]

At that time, even at the accelerated rate of Jewish immigration, the yishuv never would have exceeded the Arab birth rate if the indigenous Arabs were left in place. The Zionist leadership deemed depopulation essential to the stable Jewish character of the envisioned Jewish state. Ben-Gurion stated that he would accept the Peel partition plan only if Jews were given complete sovereignty in matters of immigration and transfer of the Arabs.[29] A mass Arab depopulation, he reasoned, would solve the problem of land requirements for Jewish settlers, eliminate cheaper Arab labor competing against Jewish labor, and solve the problem of Arab agricultural products and markets competing with those of the yishuv.[30]

Zionist leaders accepted force as a necessity for statehood and to establish Jewish demographic preponderance because they understood that Palestinian Arabs were not likely to depart on their own. This policy preference, along with a certain consciousness of its immorality, continued even after the British abandoned the Peel Commission proposals. Outlining future Zionist policy in 1941, Ben-Gurion wrote about the practicalities of transfer, arguing that the mass of the Arab population could only be transferred by "ruthless" compulsion. With a keen political eye, he also warned against openly advocating compulsory transfer as it would be unacceptable in the West.[31] Adding to this realization was the idea that a state of war was needed to facilitate depopulation.

Ethnic cleansing is closely related to war and upheaval. Both Weizmann and Ben-Gurion had studied the large-scale forcible transfer of Greeks and Turks after World War I. They became convinced that the Greco-Turkish experience illustrated that forcible transfer was a practical and secure way to evict national minorities, and that the optimal condition for transfer was a state of war.[32] Ben-Gurion openly reflected on war as an opportunity, or preferred means, to deal with the Arabs' opposition to removal. He observed that war "turned the world upside down: regimes fell, new regimes arose from the ruins, empires collapsed, borders were erased, and new states were born." What was unthinkable in settled times was to "be taken for granted during great upheavals."[33]

War provides governments and leaders with strategic justification for ethnic cleansing. It also provides cover to carry out ethnic cleansing, which would be condemned by the public and the international community during peacetime. Chaotic conditions provide an opportunity to suspend civil law for military exigency, while reporting is restricted and military censorship precludes the investigation of atrocities. "The Young Turks decided to deal with the Armenian 'problem' during the war, just as the Nazis dealt with the Jewish 'question' after the attack on Russia." Both tried to conceal their actions, Naimark observed.[34] Ben-Gurion also saw war as an opportunity to deal with the Arab problem. "The Arabs will have to go," he wrote his son Amos in 1937.[35]

Many Zionist leaders continued to press for forced transfer. In 1942, after Nazi Germany advanced into Eastern Europe and commenced its persecution, removal, and genocide of European Jews, Chaim Weizmann called on Western powers to support the creation of a Jewish commonwealth in all of Palestine and to pressure the Arabs to accept a population transfer.[36] Such depopulation plans had the general support of "mainstream official and Labor Zionists, particularly those leaders who were to play decisive roles in 1948—Ben-Gurion, Weizmann, Shertok, Kaplan, Golda Meyerson, Weitz." The support of the Zionist leadership highlights "the ideological intent that made the Palestinian refugee exodus in 1948 possible."[37]

Ben-Gurion appears, from his writings, to have a high level of confidence in Zionist military superiority as early as the 1930s, or at least in its potential. In a 1937 letter to his son, Ben-Gurion predicted a decisive war in which the Arab states would come to the aid of the Palestinian Arabs. He counted on Zionist military superiority to achieve victory: "It is very possible that the Arabs of the neighboring countries will come to their [Palestinian Arabs] aid against us. But our strength will exceed theirs. Not only because we will be better organized and equipped, but because behind us there stands a still larger force, superior in quantity and quality.... the whole younger generation [of Jews from Europe and America]."[38]

Ben-Gurion spoke again of the likelihood of a decisive war at the Jewish Agency executive meeting on June 20, 1944, and at the 22nd Zionist Congress in Basle, Switzerland, in December 1946.[39] The reiteration of his acceptance of war in late 1946 indicates Ben-Gurion's belief that Zionist forces retained superior strength, actual and potential, despite the loss of most of the young generation of Europe's Jews in the Holocaust.

A turning point in the Haganah's strategic thinking occurred in December 1946, when Ben-Gurion assumed responsibility for the Jewish Agency's defense planning. He believed that the struggle with the British ended when Britain turned the Palestine problem over to the United Nations. He identified the Arabs as the enemy posing the greatest threat to Jewish national aspirations and he warned the Haganah command in June 1947 that "we should expect" an invasion by the neighboring Arab states.[40] The Palestinian Arabs he dismissed as a non-threat; he held that "an attack by the Palestinian Arabs will not jeopardize the yishuv," a view shared by Haganah high command.[41] Ben-Gurion ordered the Haganah's reorganization as a regular military force to resist the expected invasion by regular Arab armies.[42]

The Zionist leadership demonstrated its confidence that the Palestinian Arab population in the Jewish state would be reduced in some way (physically, politically, or both) by completely excluding the Arabs from the provisional Jewish state's government planning. The constitution and the list of planned ministries published in October 1947—even before the U.N. partition vote—made "no provision at all for the rights of the minority of nearly 1/2 million Arabs," the mandate government observed. Furthermore, the U.N.-envisioned Jewish and Arab state militias "were national [i.e., territorial] and not racial." Therefore, the approximately 500,000 Palestinian Arab residents in the assigned Jewish state had "a claim to 2/5ths membership of the Jewish [state] militia."[43]

By the end of January 1948, the Jewish Agency and the Vaad Leumi (Jewish National Council) had completed their arrangements for the establishment "at the appropriate moment" of the Jewish state's provisional government. The Revisionists were excluded from the provisional government and "no thought seems to have been given to the large Arab minority's right to a share in the [Jewish state's] Government," High Commissioner Cunningham noted.[44] It was evident to him, if not to the Arabs themselves, that the Zionists had no intention of accommodating the Arab minority in the proposed Jewish state. Cunningham believed that the Arabs would have been better served by asserting their rights rather than by boycotting the United Nations to demonstrate "the dangers" of the U.N. policy, which "as interpreted by the Jews" was neither "more nor less than the most flagrant racial discrimination."[45]

Zionist "Transfer" Planning Debated

The role played by Zionist "transfer" thinking in creating the Palestinian Arab refugees continues to incite debate. Pro-Palestinian writers have criticized the conclusions of some of the "new historians" for ignoring or marginalizing the role that "transfer" played in Zionist thinking during the 1948 war. In contrast, pro-Zionist critics deny that Zionist leaders ever seriously considered the idea of transfer, accusing Benny Morris of exaggerating its importance.[46]

Morris argues that the declassified documentary evidence on transfer is only partial. Because "transfer" was a very sensitive issue, any references were usually excised from texts or proceedings, even though transfer was repeatedly discussed at the meetings of the Jewish Agency Executive, the "government" of the yishuv. Nevertheless, Morris had no doubt as to the extent of Zionist acceptance of transfer before the 1948 Palestine war. He concludes that "the consensus or near-consensus in support of transfer—voluntary if possible, compulsory if necessary—was clear."[47]

Morris's argument also lends support to pro-Palestinian writers who contend that transfer arose "inherently" out of Zionism. He noted that a homogeneous Jewish state could be created or at least one with an overwhelming Jewish majority "by moving or transferring all or most of the Arabs out of its prospective territory. And this, in fact, is what happened in 1948."[48]

Yet Morris retreats from the logical inference that the ideology of transfer lay behind what actually happened. Rather, he contends that the way the concept of transfer affected the unfolding of Zionist policy and actions during the 1948 war "remained more complicated than some Arab researchers have suggested." Morris holds that early Zionist thinking about transfer and the subsequent actions in 1948 were not a direct, causal, one-to-one correspondence. Rather, he views the connection as "more subtle and indirect." He suggests that "the haphazard thinking about transfer before 1937 and the virtual consensus in support of the notion from 1937 on contributed to what happened in 1948" by conditioning the Zionist leadership, and the officials and officers managing the civilian and military agencies, "for the transfer that took place." The mindset of all these men, influenced by "anti-Zionist Arab violence" and the growing persecution of Jews in Central and Eastern Europe, "was open to the idea and implementation of transfer and expulsion" in 1948. The "transfer" that occurred "encountered almost no serious opposition from any part of the Yishuv."[49]

Morris seems to highlight the very points he is attempting to dispute. He concedes that the yishuv's political and military leadership was essentially unanimous in supporting transfer prior to the outbreak of fighting in 1948. Morris merely describes the emotional and moral perception that might have led the Zionist leaders to more readily and fervently accept compulsory and violent population transfer. Instead of supporting his argument, Morris's observations of the Zionists' frame of mind bolster the evidence that the Zionist leadership and the yishuv felt justified in implementing forcible population transfer. His broad view of Zionist transfer thinking undermines the tentative conclusion of his *The Birth of the Palestinian Refugee Problem* that the refugees "were born of war not by design."

Ilan Pappé, in his book *The Ethnic Cleansing of Palestine*, leaves no question as to Ben-Gurion's attitude toward the Arabs. In the clearest possible terms, Ben-Gurion stated on November 2, 1947 (before the U.N. partition resolution passed), that ethnic cleansing was the means to ensure that the new state would be exclusively Jewish. He warned that Palestinians in the Jewish state could form a fifth column, and if so, "they can either be mass arrested or expelled; it is better to expel them," he said.[50] When war erupted in 1947–48, senior Haganah field commanders, handpicked by Ben-Gurion,[51] led their troops in expelling the Palestinian Arab population as systematically as circumstances allowed, as shown by the results on the ground.

Assessing Arab and Jewish Forces

Without Zionist military superiority and the Jewish Agency leadership's awareness of it, the Arabs could have been driven out only by another force, such as the British military. A review of Arab and Jewish military capabilities at the time shows that the balance strongly favored Zionist forces in the civil war period, creating opportunities to evict Arabs. (Zionist military capabilities would be superior for the second period of the war as well.) It also shows that the Zionist leadership was aware of this superiority and had taken steps to make certain that it endured.

A wide variety of sources support these conclusions. British and Zionist sources include testimony by British and Haganah military commanders and Jewish Agency leaders before the 1946 Anglo-American Committee of Inquiry (AACI) and the 1947 U.N. Special Committee on Palestine (UNSCOP). Other British assessments include a 1945 British general staff intelligence (GSI) report, the March 1948 Palestine Police intelligence report, and a July 1947 report by Lieutenant Colonel C. R. W. Norman, head of British military intelligence. American observations are reflected by U.S. army intelligence reports of December 1947 and March 1948, and by the director of the Joint Chiefs of Staff's report of March 31, 1948. Reports by the Arab League military committee, General Ismail Safwat commanding the Arab Liberation Army (ALA), and the Egyptian minister of war, Colonel Muhammad Nouh, provide Arab assessments. U.N. observations are provided by U.N. military advisor Colonel Roscher Lund and the Guatemalan representative to the UNSCOP, Jorge García Granados. As we will see, international observers, as well as the Arab and Jewish military experts themselves, also arrived via separate paths at a consensus that the Zionists enjoyed decisive military superiority over the Arabs both during the civil war and the subsequent regional war.

Palestinian Arabs: Unprepared for War

World War II saw a moratorium on hostilities between the yishuv and the British, and the Zionists and the Arabs, with the exception of LHI, which continued its terrorist activities.[52] The end of the war left the Arabs of Palestine in a state of apprehension due to their disunity and lack of preparedness. British general staff intelligence reported that the war's end had aroused a "sense of urgency" and "sometimes almost of desperation" in the Palestine Arabs. This 1945 report concluded that "unless a radical change takes place in the near future the Palestine Arabs will find themselves unprepared to meet coming events."[53]

In contrast, the yishuv's attitude continued to be a mixed sense of nervous fear and committed determination, while a cautious confidence prevailed among the Jewish community's leadership. Morris reported the sense of trepidation among the yishuv during early 1948 when he wrote that they fought and prepared for the end of the mandate on May 15 "believing and feeling that the Arab armies, if not the Palestinian irregulars, were stronger than they, were more numerous and professionally trained and led, and were better armed."[54]

This conclusion describes yishuv popular sentiment at most. The Zionist leadership and contemporary British, U.S., and even U.N. military observers all assessed the military capabilities of the Palestinian Arabs and the Arab states as poor to mediocre, with the exception of the British-financed and led Transjordan Arab Legion. However, King Abdullah of Transjordan, the Legion's commander in chief, had been negotiating privately with Jewish Agency leaders to avoid direct conflict with the Jews and to divide Palestine between the Zionists and Transjordan. Furthermore, all observers and parties to the conflict, including Zionist leaders, were cognizant of long-standing political, economic, and interstate Arab rivalries that prevented a united Arab front.

Zionist Military Superiority Recognized by 1946

The confidence of the Zionist leadership was rooted in a realistic appraisal of their side's overall military capabilities. Even before the United Nations recommended partition, British military commanders recognized the Zionists' active preparations and their potential to conquer Palestine. The AACI of 1945–46 pointedly asked British military officials whether Jewish military preparations had advanced to the point of becoming an effort at "conquest" regardless of U.N. recommendations. Air Chief Marshal Sir Charles Medhurst testified that the Jews could hold Palestine against the Arabs at that time, and he also believed that "their [Jewish] army is there to enforce by illegal means the policy they want to pursue there, gradually to extend their territory by displacing the Arabs and to make it as difficult as possible for the Mandatory Power—us at the moment—to carry out its obligations."[55]

The General Officer Commanding (GOC) Palestine, Lieutenant General John D'Arcy, estimated the Haganah force in 1946 at 40,000, which included settlers and townsfolk, in addition to a field army of 16,000. The Haganah's base of recruits was the Jewish settlement police, which the British had trained and paid to protect Jewish settlements against the Arabs. The Haganah had "completely abused the settlement police by incorporating them in, and indeed making them the backbone of an illegally armed organization," D'Arcy stated.

During World War II, the Haganah had trained 7,000 of its members by making them join the Jewish settlement police, serve the six-month term, and then retire from the organization, which normally had between 1,000 and 2,500 members at any given time. The Palmach, an elite commando force, numbered approximately 2,000, which could be increased to 6,000 for war. D'Arcy estimated membership of the Irgun Zva'i Leumi (National Military Organization—IZL) at between 3,000 and 5,000 fighters. The Lohamei Herut Yisrael (Freedom Fighters of Israel—LHI, or Stern Gang) he disdainfully dismissed as a "gang, a terrorist organization pure and simple, using assassination for the furtherance of political aims."[56] D'Arcy testified to the AACI "that a very large section of the Jewish community in this country is determined to get and to hold this country by force. It is a fact that large illegal Jewish armed organizations exist and it is my opinion that they exist for the purpose I have mentioned and none other."[57]

D'Arcy described the situation in 1946 as a state within a state, with the Jewish Agency acting as an "opposition government . . . assuming all the functions of government and holding in the background a large well-armed reasonably well-trained army as a threat."[58] He predicted that if the British withdrew from Palestine in 1946, the Jews would be "able to look after themselves extremely well and probably conquer the country." Strategically, he believed the Jews would first "consolidate themselves in their own areas," including the coastal plain, "and then extend their domination. . . . where they wanted to go; where, in fact, the good land is," that is, Arab-owned land.[59] A Jewish conquest of Palestine, D'Arcy warned, would mean a considerable slaughter of the Arabs. He saw no chance of a successful political settlement in Palestine "bristling with arms on both sides," and with "both sides completely intransigent."[60]

The Zionist Command's Confidence in Military Superiority

The Zionist military knew it was superior to the Arabs' and that it could carry out Zionist political goals. The Haganah's commander testified before the AACI in 1946 that "there is no doubt that the Jewish force is superior in organization, training, planning and equipment, and that we ourselves will be able to handle any attack or rebellion from the Arab side without calling for any assistance from the British or Americans. If you accept the Zionist solution but are unable or unwilling to enforce it, please do not interfere, and we ourselves will secure its implementation."[61]

The Zionists fully expected Arab acquiescence if they were faced with a fait accompli. In all past crises, the commander assured the committee, Arabs "have always acquiesced" to Zionist-created facts in Palestine. "If they were to be faced now with the fait accompli of the Jewish State, they will at length acquiesce in that too," he said.

The Haganah commander felt confident that the Arab states would not interfere in the conflict because of their own national interests. He testified that any Arab state dispatching troops to Palestine during the transition period would propel "that Arab country into a state of war with the Great Powers, and into a serious dispute" with the United Nations. No Arab state would be willing to run this risk, he stated. "They all take good care of their own interests above all things."[62] Although events would disprove the prediction of a U.N. confrontation, Zionist military strength nevertheless was sufficient to convince Zionist leaders that intervention by the Arab states could be overcome.

During the UNSCOP's 1947 investigations, the Haganah high command informed the committee that its actual trained and armed strength was approximately 55,000 without reserves and about 90,000 with reserves. UNSCOP members acknowledged that any solution admitting the Jewish claim to Palestine would provoke Arab resistance and questioned whether the Haganah could cope independently with possible Arab armed attacks. The officers responded that Zionist forces could "repulse any attack from the Arab population in Palestine." Further,

> if Palestine Arabs receive help from the Arab states, as they did during the previous riots, we can meet that situation, too. Haganah is training the Jewish forces underground. . . . our army has a very high morale. It is a voluntary army. . . . Our forces are more able than the Arabs; and Jewish Palestine now has a munitions industry which can put us far ahead of all Arab countries in the next few years. . . . we can stand up against the Arabs alone.[63]

In addition, Haganah commanders believed they could depend on the Jewish community abroad for help, particularly American Jews. They predicted that they would be able to defend themselves if the struggle continued. "We realize that the Arab countries cannot send all their forces to aid the local Arabs; we can resist what they can send." Not just unofficial foreign Arab aid was considered stoppable but even direct regular military intervention, subject to the security and freedom of maneuver provided by Jewish autonomy. Autonomy of action would indeed become a reality in the civil war period due to the vacuum created by British withdrawal. The Haganah commander continued: "If the Arab countries intervene, we can strike back at their main air and naval bases. All this assumes that your [UNSCOP's] decision will be in favor of the Jews and will give the Jews a legal basis for arming and defending themselves."[64]

The Zionist leadership soon realized that even though it could count on American Jewish support, it could not count on the U.S. military to enforce partition, and furthermore, that Great Britain and the United States would block any Russian offer to implement partition itself, to prevent Communist infiltration into the Middle East.[65] With no other promising suggestion, and confident of its own military capabilities, the Jewish Agency considered placing the Haganah under U.N. authority if necessary to establish the Jewish state.[66] The British policy of preventing a handover to the United Nations would stop this from happening. Yet it would allow Zionist forces to operate with the impunity desired to meet local and regional Arab forces and to engage virtually unhindered in Arab depopulation operations.

The Yishuv's Preparations for War

The Zionists' superiority lay in their extensive preparations over many years for a decisive war, in contrast to Arab passivity. A Jewish brigade, recruited in Palestine, fought alongside the British Eighth Army in Italy during World War II. This nucleus of a battle-hardened Jewish field army was trained, equipped, and even clothed like the British.[67] The British had an infantry battle school to train noncommissioned officers and junior officers in Nathania, Palestine. Within one mile of it was a Jewish battle school. Throughout 1947 and 1948, the Jews had "machinery for ensuring whatever field army they had was kept up to standard,"[68] observed the British military commander of the Lydda district, General Horatius Murray. He believed that in a war with the Arabs, the Jews would have "a flying start" because the Jews were organized, equipped, and formed a closely knit community with a very strong military background.[69] The yishuv also had a relatively advanced arms industry.[70]

The Arabs had no such advantages. Murray said that even though the Palestinian Arabs had arms "of some sort," they were not organized, and they relied on the promise of military assistance from the Arab League countries. Palestinian Arabs had been rendered ill-prepared for self-defense by very effective British measures "to crush organized" resistance during the 1936–39 Arab rebellion, including exiling the leadership, suppressing the activities of the Arab Higher Committee (AHC), and disarming the Arabs. In addition, the Palestinian Arab population consisted of predominately militarily and technologically inexperienced illiterate farmers grouped around localized and clan loyalties. Intense factional feuding contributed to the disarray.[71] Murray also suggested that the Arabs were paradoxically overconfident, believing that ultimately because of their superior numbers they were bound to win, and that they were therefore unwisely passive: "They didn't really do anything about getting themselves lined up for war in the way that the Jews did."[72]

In actuality, the ratio of potential combatants drawn from men of fighting age in Palestine favored the yishuv, owing to selective immigration policies by the Zionists. In December 1947, U.S. army intelligence reported that Jewish males aged 15 to 44 outnumbered Arab males in this age group.[73] Jewish females, who also received military training and participated in combat, tipped the balance of potential combatants overwhelmingly in favor of Zionist forces. These figures do not account for the 60,000 to 70,000 illegal Jewish immigrants the British estimated to be in Palestine in November 1947. The Arab perspective that Zionist forces were invaders was aggravated by the fact that by 1946 two-thirds of the Jewish population was composed of immigrant settlers, according to Ben-Gurion.[74]

The Probability of Forced Partition

Lieutenant Colonel C. R. W. Norman, head of British military intelligence in Palestine from 1946 to 1948, assessed the potential of a Jewish state to defend itself against Arab aggression as highly capable, even after British security forces completely withdrew from Palestine.[75] Norman assumed in his July 1947 report that the Jewish state would be sovereign; that the Haganah would be the Jewish army; that its total strength would number

60,000, with a field army of 16,000, and 5,000 Palmach; that the mufti would lead the Palestinian Arabs; and that the Jewish state would include the Galilee and the Negev.

Norman considered, in turn, the likelihood and extent to which each Arab state would support the Palestinian Arabs in resisting partition. Lebanon was not considered much of a threat; it was poor, with a "very small and inefficient army." Lebanon was the only Arab country with a Christian majority, and it was considered possible that the Lebanese would hold a "certain fellow feeling with the Jewish state in their attitude towards the Moslems." Syria was considered the greatest threat as "the traditional rallying point for dissidents of all types." The mufti was believed to be building up a base in Syria for operations in Palestine, with the conniv-ance of the Syrian government. Like Lebanon, he wrote, "Syria is rotten internally. . . . Her army is in a bad state and is still suffering from the departure of the French." Potentially, Norman believed, Syria, although preoccupied by "troublesome minorities" and suspicious of Transjordan, could make war on the Jewish state if confident of the full support of at least one other Arab League member.

Transjordan was considered the most important factor in the equation. King Abdullah was Great Britain's ally, and Transjordan possessed the British-commanded Arab Legion, "the most efficient army in the Arab League." King Abdullah's participation in any action offensive to the Brit-ish government or the United Nations was considered doubtful. Norman asserted that if King Abdullah were to invade Palestine, he would do so "with the object of annexing the Arab portion of the country and that he would leave the Jews severely alone." Events subsequent to May 15 would prove this prediction correct.[76]

Iraq, "a vociferous agitator on the Palestine problem," had a moderately efficient army and a small air force. Its ruler, a member of the Hashemite dynasty, was influenced in some measure by King Abdullah. Furthermore, Iraq required its forces domestically to contend with continual trouble with its Kurdish population. It could not afford to risk sending many armed forces abroad but could "continue moral and financial support." If Saudi Arabia had sent its forces, these would almost certainly have had to pass through Transjordan, which King Abdullah would not have permitted in view of the animosity between the two countries, dating from the 1920s, when the Saudis displaced the Hashemites from the Hijaz. Any support

Saudi Arabia was prepared to give to the Palestine Arabs was estimated "to be limited to talk and money."

Yemen was not considered to constitute a menace to a Jewish state apart from the possible persecution of Yemen's own Jews. The British expected little from Egypt either. The Egyptian army was considered unlikely to "put up a very brilliant performance in the face of a determined foe." Egypt also was fully occupied with the evacuation of British forces from the Suez Canal and with its relations with the Sudan. Any act of aggression would severely prejudice the Egyptian case at the United Nations for the full and immediate withdrawal of British troops from Egypt and Sudan. Egyptian support was therefore expected to be limited to finance and propaganda.[77] (This estimation proved false, as Egyptian forces did intervene directly after May 15, largely in response to the ongoing expulsion of Palestinian Arabs.)

The Palestinian Arabs believed that they successfully had used violence to force the British to issue the 1939 white paper, and they therefore concluded that "by threatening violence again they will be similarly successful," Norman stated. Nevertheless, in view of the existing political unrest and economic uncertainty in many Arab states, British military intelligence concluded (incorrectly) that support from the Arab states was unlikely. Assistance to the Palestinian Arabs, with the sole exception of Syria, was expected to be nothing more than "moral and financial support, the clandestine supply of arms," small numbers of volunteers, and "the usual Arab provision of refuge for those fleeing from Palestine." The Zionists' prospects of implementing partition were considered therefore to be highly probable.[78] Despite some errors in its estimates, British military intelligence reflects the prevailing high level of confidence in future Zionist success enabled by Jewish forces' relative strengths vis-à-vis the Arabs.

Haganah Ability to Repel Arab Attacks

The Jewish leadership had been preparing political institutions and offensive military plans since the 1937 Peel Commission first recommended partition. According to the head of British military intelligence, the Haganah had prepared "complete plans for [its] own police and army to establish the Jewish state" in 1938, when a decision in favor of partition had seemed likely. Since then, the Haganah had gained experience and was "very much better equipped and trained." British intelligence assumed the Haganah was "fully prepared for the implementation of partition."[79] Furthermore, the yishuv was confident of receiving the full support of its American friends. It envisaged an enormous pool of Haganah reinforcements from those Jews who had served in the U.S. armed forces, as well as the provision of arms, money, and even a small air force. Confidence in American support was not misplaced. Zionist recruiters were aggressively canvassing for experienced U.S. servicemen to fight in Palestine, U.S. army intelligence reported.[80] As a result of the Nazi genocide in Europe, the Zionists were considered a formidable foe psychologically, as they were "more than ever determined to see their nation established." British intelligence doubted the Arabs were equally determined to oppose them.[81]

British military intelligence foresaw three possible Arab military reactions to partition, presented here in the order of assessed probability. First, mufti-organized raids from Syria on northern Jewish settlements, without the active assistance of Palestinian Arabs, were considered extremely likely to occur. Zionist forces, however, were not expected to have any great difficulty repelling these isolated raids. The Jewish leadership had anticipated Arab raids after August 1947, regardless of the Jewish state's establishment.

Second, an invasion of the Jewish state area by Palestinian Arabs, similar to the 1936–39 Arab rebellion, with the clandestine assistance of one or more Arab states, was also considered probable. Although the mufti would direct such a rebellion, its success would largely depend on the measure of ordinary Palestinian Arab support, and many Arabs realized that they had more to gain "by co-operating with the Jews than opposing them." Because Zionist forces would be better armed and organized than Arabs in Palestine or Syria, the Zionists would be able to repel any attacks and further organize commando raids on Arab villages in Palestine, and if necessary in Syria. Therefore an invasion of the Jewish state area by Palestinian Arabs was not considered a serious threat. The third scenario, an invasion of the Jewish state area by the Palestine Arabs with the full and open support of one or more Arab states, was considered "improbable" by the British.[82]

International observers also generally believed that intervention by the Arab states' regular armies was improbable. Subsequent events would prove them incorrect. Arab states did eventually engage reluctantly and half-heartedly in overt warfare because of the British withdrawal, to preserve the Arab League, and especially due to intense public pressure and popular support from their populations, which grew insistent due to Zionist forces' aggressive actions against Palestinian Arab civilians in the latter stage of the civil war.[83] The Arab states' intervention in Palestine on May 15 requires further research to illuminate Arab decision making, motivations, and ultimate purpose. Unfortunately, Arab state archives relevant to 1948 remain closed.

Arab Inability to Stop Partition

Palestinian Arab military organization was virtually nonexistent in 1946. By November 1947, only the most rudimentary organization existed. The *shabab,* or youth organization, composed of rural forces and town garrisons, existed only in theory. The shabab's rural forces had units in the Galilee and areas of Gaza, Haifa, Jaffa, Jerusalem, and Tulkarm. Their total rifle strength was about 1,000 by the mandate's end. Palestinian Arabs had to purchase their own guns and ammunition, which were prohibitively expensive for peasants, so the majority of Arab villagers remained unarmed. Rural units were not fully mobilized and the AHC had minimal control over them. Unit organization, in practice, was along tribal or clan rather than military lines, and coordination problems were never resolved due to the distance between units and unit commanders' reliance on the mufti's directives.[84]

The larger town garrisons "were even more tenuously under the command of the AHC than the rural forces," as Walid Khalidi has noted. Local municipal councils could find themselves at odds with the local national or defense committees or town commanders appointed by the Arab League military committee. Town garrisons were "static defense forces, loosely organized on a locality basis with no reserves and no effective overall command." The garrisons varied in numbers and ranged from "unpaid part-time amateur citizen volunteers to full-time professional Palestinian ex-servicemen." In some cases, there were small Arab Liberation Army (ALA) contingents in the major cities of Haifa, Jaffa, and Jerusalem. By April 1948, the total maximum Arab rifle strength in the town garrisons was only 1,563. The rifles were distributed among the nine cities of Acre, Baysan, Gaza, Haifa, Jaffa, Jerusalem, Nazareth, Safad, and Tiberias.[85]

The AHC began recruiting groups of two to three dozen young men for training in Damascus after the November partition vote, but the effort was amateurish. Ayoub Talhami, from the village of Shafr 'Amr, was a student at the Arab College in Jerusalem when he and his friend were selected for AHC training in Damascus. He said no one knew what to do with them: "We went from office to office. After a week or two, we both were running out of money. Nothing was happening; nothing was prospect, so we both gave up."[86]

The relative weakness of the Arabs in Palestine was known at the higher levels of the Arab League, while at the popular level, overconfidence in the Arab armies and Arab numerical strength endured. In a March 23, 1948, report to the Arab League military committee (established to coordinate Arab state forces), General Ismail Safwat, assistant chief of staff for the Iraqi army and the ALA commander, estimated Jewish forces in Palestine, with some accuracy, at fewer than 50,000 armed and equipped fighters.[87] This estimate combined the force strength of the Haganah, LHI, and IZL. He estimated the highly trained mobile Palmach at 5,000 to 6,000 combatants. Organized local Jewish defense forces drawn from settlers were approximately 20,000 strong, a third of them young women.

The total Arab combat force before the mandate ended was approximately 7,700, according to Safwat. Armed groups of full-time, enlisted Palestinian Arab guerrillas, receiving regular pay, numbered 2,500. The total non-Palestinian Arab force was about 5,200. Of these, only 4,000 had entered Palestine by mid-March 1948.[88]

A Palestine Police report of March 1948 gave a higher assessment of the number of Arab forces because it included Arab members of the Palestine Police. This report listed Arab forces as including a number of components: the Arab Liberation Army (ALA) fielded by the Arab League was estimated at 5,000 to 6,000 men, composed of Syrians, Iraqis, Egyptians, Circassians, Druze, Turks, Yugoslavs, Transjordanians, Germans, and a few British. Palestinian Arab organizations included the National Guard, youth organizations, and permanent members of armed guerrillas.

Armed villagers and townsmen were available for sporadic engagements, and among them were trained and partially trained men, such as former members of the temporary additional police, supernumerary police, and the Transjordanian Frontier Force. Arab personnel of the regular cadres of the Palestine Police, municipal police, and the village and tribal police forces together totaled 6,159. Regular police were armed with either a rifle or a pistol. Eighty-one percent of the municipal police and 82 percent of the village and tribal police were armed with rifles.[89]

The ALA regular and semi-regular units had completed training at the Qatana camp near Damascus. The Palestine Police considered the ALA and Palestinian Arab organizations to be partially trained in guerrilla tactics in rural areas. A number of these Arabs reportedly had served with the armies of Syria or Lebanon, the Transjordan Frontier Force, or the French Colonial Forces. A few, particularly officers, had served with the British army or with Axis forces during World War II. The ALA reportedly had a number of demolition and bomb experts, mostly Germans and Yugoslavs, but also Syrian and Palestinian Arabs who were trained by the British and French armies.

Armed villagers and townsmen were assessed quite differently. They had "only an aptitude for limited guerrilla tactics." Considered "ill-disciplined, excitable and reckless," they were "of little use except for minor engagements, ambushes and harassing road communications." The Arabs had a variety of small arms and light automatic weapons. Nevertheless, their ammunition supplies were estimated to be "limited and precarious."[90]

Haganah intelligence assessments corroborate Palestine Police estimates, at least in approximate numbers. Zionist analysts reported in mid-February that 3,000 Arab fighters had entered the country, another 9,000 planned to do so, and 5,000 troops were to be recruited among local Arabs. The Zionists expected to face Arab forces numbering no more than 17,000 men, with out-of-date arms and insufficient ammunition for their French rifles.[91]

The Arab League commander also thought that the Zionist forces were far better equipped than the Arabs. General Safwat believed that Zionist forces possessed large numbers of light weapons such as rifles and machine guns. The Arabs possessed a few thousand rifles of various makes which were "antiquated and unfit [as] modern weapons." Ammunition was extremely limited, and for some rifles no ammunition existed at all. Logistic and operational problems were compounded because available ammunition was often not interchangeable among the various firearms. "Some of the weapons issued to the men killed more of them than the enemy was able to kill," according to Jordanian Major Wasfi al-Tal.[92]

Machine guns were few in number and unsuitable to "modern military organization." While Zionist forces were using mortars in almost every battle, the Arabs had no more than fourteen Syrian-supplied mortars. Zionist units possessed British armored cars, and others that they had assembled themselves. Arab irregular forces had neither armored cars nor tanks "and not a single anti-tank or anti-armor weapon." Zionist forces also used machine-gun-fitted aircraft to attack Arab guerrillas. They had limited their use in combat, Safwat believed, out of fear of British intervention.

Safwat warned the Arab League against underestimating the training and capabilities of the Jewish forces, many of whom had served in European and U.S. armed forces. As for the Arab forces, he assessed the training among the volunteer units as "less than middling, and with poor fighting capabilities, and a lack of military discipline." The Arab guerrillas "whether full-time salaried fighters or those participating on an occasional basis . . . have no military capability." Whereas the Zionist forces could draw on reserves and reinforcements from a general mobilization of the Jewish population in Palestine, illegal Jewish immigrants detained in Cyprus, and a continual flow of illegal immigrants into Palestine itself, Safwat had "no hope of recruiting large numbers of Palestinian volunteers." Even though the Palestinian Arabs as a whole far outnumbered the Jews, the general population lacked any established military tradition or training.

As for volunteers from other Arab countries, Safwat suggested that though it was possible to recruit with some difficulty, they would number only a few thousand more, and only if the necessary arms and means to train and equip them were obtained. He cautioned that volunteers and guerrillas needed "a large number of officers to lead them," and they had but a small number, mainly from the Syrian army. The situation of arms and equipment was far worse, and therefore "more cause to expect failure and disappointment." The Arab countries did not deliver the promised arms and equipment, even when the quantities requested "were for emergency aid only," and not "sufficient for sustaining long-term combat." Egypt, Iraq, Syria, and Saudi Arabia were to deliver to Palestine 2,000 rifles each, and Transjordan and Lebanon, 1,000 each. By February 8, "neither Saudi Arabia nor Transjordan had delivered a single rifle." Egypt, Iraq, and Lebanon delivered a fraction of the promised rifles. Only Syria fulfilled its quota.

Safwat reported that all Jewish colonies were well-fortified and strongly defended. Many had bunkers for mortars and machine guns, and experience had shown it was impossible to overcome them with light arms. The Arabs had established static garrisons in the cities where the danger was greatest. These garrisons, however, were conspicuously weak, "possessing only antiquated rifles and hand grenades and a few machine guns each." Arab forces and scattered groups also were hindered by lack of contact with a general command. The rise in factionalism and local alliances among Palestinian Arabs had pitted them against each other when the need for unity was most pressing. Safwat concluded his assessment on a sober and pessimistic note: "Our forces in Palestine—whether trained volunteers or armed Palestinian guerrillas—cannot achieve a decisive military victory. All they can do is prolong the fighting for a certain period in accordance with the reinforcements they receive and the arms available to them."[93]

The Egyptian war minister, Colonel Nouh, visited Palestine before the mandate ended to assess the military situation. He echoed Safwat's pessimism, concluding that "it would be impossible to destroy the Jewish state and the rest of Palestine would be taken by King Abdullah." He saw no practical advantage for Egypt, Iraq, or Syria to go to war. In fact, Nouh stated that Egypt eventually did go to war "in order not to break up the Arab League."[94]

U.S. Military Expectation of the Zionist Scenario

In March 1948, U.S. Chief of Staff Admiral William Leahy asked the director of the Joint Chiefs of Staff to evaluate requirements for a U.S. peacekeeping force in Palestine in case the United States was asked to furnish troops under a U.N. trusteeship. The director concluded that the United States should not under any circumstances send forces to Palestine alone or as a part of an international force, neither to preserve order nor to enforce partition.[95] As for creating a peacekeeping force, the director believed that a number of political factors were of particular significance in determining the force's required size.

His report turned to the question of Zionist aspirations in the Middle East. He foresaw a number of stages defined by a progressive expansionism:

(1) the initial recognition of Jewish sovereignty even in a portion of Palestine, (2) acceptance by the great powers of the right to unlimited immigration, (3) the extension of Jewish sovereignty over all of Palestine as presently constituted, (4) the extension of the Jewish Palestinian borders to include Transjordan and parts of Lebanon and Syria, (5) the establishment of sufficient Jewish power over the whole Near East so as to assure preferential treatment for Jewish capital and manufactures in the Near Eastern states adjoining Palestine.

All stages, he concluded, were "equally sacred to the fanatical concepts of Jewish leaders." Furthermore, the Zionist program's ultimate goals were "openly admitted by some leaders," and "privately admitted to United States officials by responsible leaders of the presently dominant Jewish group [in Palestine]—the Jewish Agency."[96]

The Joint Chiefs of Staff report also warned that "the more extensive the fighting in Palestine" became, the greater the opportunity would be for "virile extremist Jewish leaders to gain control." The "struggle for political power" would be expressed "through military power."[97] The British Foreign Office held a similar opinion about Zionist expansionist aspirations. The Jewish state's formation "would necessarily establish a bridgehead from which the Jews would be bound to break out sooner or later."[98]

U.S. military planners evaluated basic economic and logistical factors in their assessment of force requirements. Among the most important were that the Palestinian Arab population was 70 percent rural and able to subsist on local produce, and upper-class Arabs could and would travel across the border to neighboring Arab countries where they had friends or relatives. The Arab majority rural population relied on camels and donkeys for transport requirements, which "would greatly assist the maintenance of Arab urban communities."

The U.S. planners also reported, however, that the majority of the Jewish population was urban and dependent in part on food shipments from abroad, even when Arab-grown produce was available. The Jews would therefore suffer serious disruption from military operations. Their agricultural colonies could, however, "subsist on local produce for an indefinite period except insofar as constant sniping by Arab guerrillas would prevent cultivation of food and fodder."[99] All classes of the rural and urban Jewish population relied on motor and railway transport, except for those coastal communities serviced by boat. The report pinpointed the weakness of the yishuv as the vulnerability of the roads and roadway transportation. Jewish transportation requirements were easy to disrupt, as they were subject to the availability of motor vehicles and fuel, and the railways and highways were susceptible to sabotage.[100]

The Joint Chiefs of Staff's report offered several likely scenarios in the event that U.S. military were assigned to Palestine. Planners theorized that if the military assignment was enforcing a political decision unacceptable to a majority of the Arabs, and if the military problem was "one limited to restoration of order inside Palestine," then "given a policy of ruthless suppression the local Arab population could be forced into outward submission in a few months." The mission would then be reduced to continuous maintenance of a heavy border force if the frontiers were effectively sealed against infiltration by Arab volunteers: "If the frontiers could not be sealed effectively it would become necessary to expel a substantial portion of the Arab population from Palestine—one of the objectives of the Zionists."[101]

Contemporary and informed U.S. analysts understood this objective unambiguously. Additionally, and perhaps more importantly, the report also illustrated that armed conflict would present a favorable context in which to force out Palestine's Arabs. The report was incorrect, however, in assuming that suppression of Arab resistance would require expelling the Arab population. During the 1930s Palestine rebellion, the British proved quite capable of forcing the Arab population into quiescence despite being unable to seal the borders and despite the fact that the Palestine Arabs were then better armed, organized, and more popularly engaged than they were in 1947–48. Thus, expulsion was not vital to suppression of Arab resistance to partition. Nevertheless, the American assessment illustrates how conflict could create a situation in which transfer's implementation became more justifiable, as the Zionist leaders Ben-Gurion and Weizmann had anticipated.

U.S. military planners believed no legal basis allowed the United Nations to enforce partition. Furthermore, they saw that, politically, "forcible imposition of the present partition plan would be tantamount to a declaration of war on the Arab States." They estimated that enforcement of the U.N. decision would require sufficient strength to defeat both the Palestinian Arabs and the Arab League forces. The United States was not prepared or inclined to take on duties that would commit its forces to that extent. Also, the U.S. military believed that pursuing a course of forced imposition of partition "would be inimical to the peace and security of the world."[102]

U.S. analysts estimated Haganah forces in early March 1948 at 85,000, with recruitment for more under way. They considered the Haganah to be well organized and possessing a preponderance of automatic weapons among its small arms. They estimated that the IZL forces had 7,000 members and believed that they cooperated closely with the LHI, estimated at "400 extreme fanatics." Both groups were supplied with small arms and cooperated with the Haganah when "the Jewish military situation demanded it." The IZL's importance was growing to the point that it played an "increasingly influential part" in Haganah policies and actions.[103]

As for Arab forces, U.S. army intelligence considered the Arab irregulars semi-trained, poorly led and equipped, but capable of being effective in "purely guerrilla-type warfare." The U.S. military predicted that Zionist forces would initially "score some successes" against Arab irregular forces, but that they would be incapable of withstanding a long war of attrition unless they had a continuous supply of men, munitions, and other needs. If, however, Zionist forces received substantial assistance, U.S. intelligence concluded, the Arab states could not maintain their regular troops in prolonged fighting.[104] After May 1948, with the new State of Israel possessing stores seized in the civil war and procured soon after, the requisite supplies were indeed sustained to exhaust and defeat the Arab state armies.

U.N. Expectation of Partition

The U.N. military advisor Colonel Roscher Lund, who had served in the Norwegian army, also assessed the military situation. He arrived in Palestine on March 2, 1948. Lund was a member of the U.N. advance group preparing for the arrival of the U.N. Palestine Commission charged with implementing partition.[105] Lund's preliminary April 6, 1948, report on the security situation was based primarily on Jewish sources, since U.N. personnel could not travel securely in Arab areas where they were unwelcome. Lund believed the Palestine Arabs would "fight only within their own districts under their local chiefs." He estimated the ALA's total mobile force at between 6,000 and 11,000. Of these, 80 percent were foreign volunteers, and a number of them he viewed as "adventurers" more interested in "looting and destroying" than in the Arab cause. "One cannot expect militia built on the human material of Palestine Arabs and volunteers to reach any high quality," he wrote.[106]

The main difficulties facing the Zionist forces, Lund observed, were difficult lines of communications between population centers and the lack of a suitable harbor to receive outside aid. Haganah leadership told him they intended to create a force of about 35,000 soldiers. Lund assessed Jewish troop quality as generally good and viewed Zionist propaganda as effective. The Haganah radio station stressed that neutral Arab villages had "nothing to be frightened of [a claim that proved false], but those who harbor [hostile] bands will be destroyed."[107]

Lund determined that partition could be imposed only by a "substantial military force." Would neighboring Arab countries' armed forces intervene in Palestine "either to promote [their own] national purposes or to assist the Palestinian Arabs"? Lund believed "that none of these [Arab] countries eventually will be able to use their whole forces in Palestine. The political feelings between the Arab States are not too amicable and they have, to a certain degree, to watch each other."[108] He concluded that "the two parties in Palestine will fight the situation out to a practical partition" at the mandate's end, as neither party wanted to engage British forces. He assumed the Haganah had offensive plans prepared, as the Zionists knew "no war so far in history has been won by defensive action."[109]

British Expectation of a Zionist Coup d'Etat

Neither the Palestinian Arabs nor the Arab League believed sufficient votes could be garnered to pass the U.N. partition plan, which would place so high a proportion of Arabs under Jewish rule. Many Arabs also believed that the U.N. recommendation would never be implemented, because Great Britain would not relinquish Palestine as a strategic base. As the U.N. General Assembly deliberated in 1947, Palestinian Arab leaders remained "stubborn, uncompromising and clinging to the idea of a unitary Arab state," according to the British Third Parachute Brigade's intelligence report. Faced with violent Palestinian Arab rejection, backed by the Arab states' military assistance, the brigade believed that "no power would face the responsibility of bloodshed on the scale necessary to implement partition."[110]

The Arab League's leadership was fully aware of the Zionist forces' superior strength and the Arabs' inability to win a decisive military victory. In contrast, average Palestinian Arabs, typically isolated, illiterate villagers, had no comprehension of the odds against them. They were compelled to rely on the Arab states' repeated promises of military assistance to save them from forced partition.

For its part, the British government avoided fully committing to any policy until after the General Assembly's vote. The mandate government predicted that if the United Nations accepted the proposition of a Jewish state—without any country being prepared to implement the partition—the Jews would "likely ask to be allowed to do so themselves." By resisting the Jewish state's establishment, the mandate government feared antagonizing the yishuv and acting contrary to a U.N. decision. By tacitly agreeing to partition, even if the Arabs were to see some subtle conspiracy between the British and the Zionists, the high commissioner believed Britain would have already made its position clear in the General Assembly.

> It is obvious that UNO will not be able in fact to carry out any plan which the Arabs oppose and in which we [the British] do not participate. Nobody knows this better than [the] UNO and the Jews. If the position is reached in which the Jews, confident in non-interference by UNO, establish by a coup d'état a Jewish government of a Jewish State as approved by the Assembly we should be ready with a plan to withdraw from the State all our services and forces.[111]

The Zionist leadership was believed to be considering this eventuality. Cunningham viewed as politically preferable the Zionists' seizure of power to form a Jewish state and thereby present the Arabs with an established fact. Under these circumstances, Great Britain believed it could still maintain the appearance of neutrality and thus its good relations with the Arab states.[112]

The Mandate Ends with Overwhelming Zionist Military Superiority

On the eve of the Arab armies' entry into Palestine, the British commander in chief of Middle East Land Forces sent an intelligence report to the War Office assessing the relative strength of the Jewish fighting troops at 74,000, including 70,000 fully mobilized and trained Haganah and Palmach and 4,000 IZL. The Arabs' assessed fighting force totaled 19,200, composed of 5,000 ALA; 5,000 Arab Legion; 2,000 Iraqis; 5,000 Egyptians; 1,500 Syrians; and 700 Lebanese. In spite of the Arab states' preponderance of artillery, armored fighting vehicles and aircraft, the British believed that the Arab forces were "numerically too small to sustain major offensive operations in [the] Jewish occupied area." The Arabs were handicapped by divided command; lack of operational experience; communication and supply problems; and lack of reserves. The Zionists meanwhile had superior intelligence, good communications, mobile interior lines, battle experience, and strong offensive spirit.

The British command predicted that if the United States supported the Jewish forces, it would likely make up equipment deficiencies and create an efficient air force at an early date.[113] British military intelligence concluded, and the GOC Palestine concurred, that in the event of partition, the Jewish state would by the time of the mandate's end "be sufficiently well organized to defend itself against aggression from the Arabs of Palestine and Syria."[114] These conclusions by British military officers corroborate that in the civil war period, Zionist forces held numerical and operational military superiority over Palestinian Arab and foreign Arab forces in Palestine.

The following table compiles the comparative numerical strength of Zionist and Arab military forces prior to May 15, according to estimates of contemporary sources.

Estimates	British	Arab	Zionist	U.S.	U.N.
Zionists					
Haganah	40,000–70,000	50,000	55,000	85,000	35,000
Field Army	16,000	20,000	35,000		
Palmach	2,000–6,000	5,000–6,000			
IZL	3,000–5,000				
LHI	400				
Palestinian Arabs					
ALA	5,000–6,000	5,200	13,000–17,000		6,000–11,000
Police	6,159				
Guerrillas		2,500			

All sources support the assessment of Zionist superiority over combined Palestinian Arab and ALA forces during the civil war period, whether in raw numbers or in training, organization, and armament. When one also considers the powerful consensus on Zionist qualitative superiority, it is clear that Zionist forces were decisively superior during the civil war period and beyond it as well.

On the eve of the U.N. partition vote, the military balance favored the Zionists. The Palestinian Arabs had no organized army; the rural and urban Arab militias they did have were, from the outset, outnumbered by a trained and battle-hardened Zionist fighting force. The Zionists were highly organized, equipped, and motivated, and had been preparing and planning for a decisive war since the 1930s. The Zionists shared the British, U.S., and U.N. military view that the Arab states were highly unlikely to enter Palestine before the mandate ended, to avoid conflict with British forces or international condemnation.

Zionist leaders were aware of their own superior military potential and reiterated to the international community their ability to establish and defend a Jewish state by their own means if necessary. Zionist dissident groups had, after all, cowed the British Empire with an eighteen-month campaign of terror, even without the full strength of the Haganah in place. The Zionist forces not only could defend themselves, predicted British and U.S. commanders; they had the manpower and ability to take and hold by force all of mandate Palestine.

As U.S. and British military analysts predicted, and Palestinian testimony will show, the Zionist leadership found it expedient militarily, acceptable ideologically, and justifiable politically to implement an Arab population transfer through terror and armed violence. This depopulation or "transfer" of a substantial portion of Palestinian Arabs from what would become Israel was facilitated by Britain's tacit acceptance of partition. Mass expulsion also was facilitated by Britain's enabling the ensuing civil war through the unilateral abandonment of the mandate, despite its awareness that the result would be a vacuum of power, law, and order.

�֍

1.   Andrew Bell-Fialkoff, *Ethnic Cleansing* (New York: St. Martin's, 1996), 3.
2.   See Norman M. Naimark, *Fires of Hatred: Ethnic Cleansing in Twentieth-Century Europe* (Cambridge: Harvard University Press, 2001); and Bell-Fialkoff, *Ethnic Cleansing*.

3. *Spectator*, December 5, 1941, 530; cited in Joseph B. Schectman, *European Population Transfers, 1939–1945* (New York: Oxford University Press, 1947), 460. Sir John Hope Simpson was the author of the 1930 Hope-Simpson Report on Palestine. It concluded that without developing the current lands, "there was no room for a single additional settler if the standard of life of the Arab villager was to remain at its existing level. Palestine could absorb no additional Jewish settlers."

4. Naimark, *Fires of Hatred*, 4.

5. Moshe Menuhin, *The Decadence of Judaism* (New York: Exposition, 1965), 52; cited in Erskine B. Childers, "The Wordless Wish: From Citizens to Refugees," in Abu-Lughod, *Transformation of Palestine*, 169.

6. Desmond Steward, *Theodor Herzl: Artist and Politician* (London: Hamish Hamilton, 1974), 192.

7. Chaim Simons, *International Proposals to Transfer Arabs from Palestine, 1895–1947: A Historical Survey* (Hoboken, N.J.: Ktav, 1988), 6.

8. Masalha, *Expulsion of the Palestinians*, 1.

9. Simons, *International Proposals to Transfer Arabs*, 31, www.geocities.com/CapitolHill/Senate/7854/transfer.html.

10. Masalha, *Expulsion of the Palestinians*, 2–3.

11. Ahad Ha'am, "The Truth from Palestine," in *Nationalism and the Jewish Ethic*, ed. Hans Kohn (New York: Schocken, 1962).

12. Robert St. John, *Ben-Gurion* (New York: Doubleday, 1959), 31–32; cited in Childers, "Wordless Wish," 168, 174.

13. Quoted in Michael Bar-Zohar, *Ben-Gurion: The Armed Prophet* (Englewood Cliffs, N.J.: Prentice-Hall, 1966), 22.

14. Anita Shapira, *Land and Power: The Zionist Resort to Force, 1881–1948* (Oxford: Oxford University Press, 1992), 70.

15. Ibid., 75.

16. TNA FO 371/20025/E5967, Vansittart to Eden, September 19, 1936; *Survey of Palestine*, 141, 185.

17. Zeev Jabotinsky, "Havlagat ha-Yishuv—ad Matai?" ("Self-Restraint of the Yishuv—How Much Longer?"), in *Havlaga o teguva (Self-Restraint or Response?)*, ed. Yaakov Shavit (Tel Aviv, 1983), 73; cited in Shapira, *Land and Power*, 246n71.

18. John Bierman and Colin Smith, *Fire in the Night: Wingate of Burma, Ethiopia, and Zion* (New York: Random House, 1999), 85.

19. Shapira, *Land and Power*, 250–51.

20. Ibid., 251–52.

21. Bierman and Smith, *Fire in the Night*, 91–93.

22. Masalha, *Expulsion of the Palestinians*, 26.

23. Shabtai Teveth, *Ben-Gurion and the Palestinian Arabs from Peace to War* (New York: Oxford University Press, 1985), 155.

24. Shapira, *Land and Power*, 268–69.

25. Nineteenth Conference of the Permanent Council of Ha-Noar ha-Oved, Tel Aviv, August 19, 1938, LA, sec. 213 IV, file 14; cited in Shapira, *Land and Power*, 267n141.

26. Simons, *International Proposals to Transfer Arabs*, www.geocities.com/CapitolHill/Senate/7854/transfer.html.

27. Pappé, *Ethnic Cleansing of Palestine*, 19.

28. CZA S5-1543, Speech by Ben-Gurion and others at the Twentieth Zionist Congress in Zurich, August 1937; cited in Morris, *Birth Revisited*, 48–49n24. The Zionist Organization issued an edited version of the speeches with most references to transfer deleted.

29. *Ben-Gurion Memoirs*, vol. 2 (Tel Aviv: Am Oved, 1974), 365; cited in Flapan, *Zionism and the Palestinians*, 261.

30. Masalha, *Expulsion of the Palestinians*, 67.

31. CZA Z4-14632, Ben-Gurion, "Outlines of Zionist Policy," October 15, 1941; cited in Morris, "Revisiting the Palestinian Exodus of 1948," in *The War for Palestine: Rewriting the History of 1948*, ed. Eugene L. Rogan and Avi Shlaim (Cambridge: Cambridge University Press, 2001), 45.

32. Masalha, *Expulsion of the Palestinians*, 136.

33. "The fulfillment of Zionism," *Yiddisher Kemfer*, no. 41, November 14, 1917; cited in Teveth, *Ben-Gurion and the Palestinian Arabs*, 35–36. See also Morris, *Birth Revisited*, 370–71. In discussing his settlement policy, Ben-Gurion admits that "in peacetime we would not have been able to do this."

34. Naimark, *Fires of Hatred*, 188–89.

35. David Ben-Gurion, Diary, July 12, 1937, and in *New Judea*, August–September 1937, 220; cited in Pappé, *Ethnic Cleansing of Palestine*, 23n40.

36. Chaim Weizmann, "Palestine's Role in the Solution of the Jewish Problem," *Foreign Affairs* 20.2 (1942): 337–38.

37. Masalha, *Expulsion of the Palestinians*, 165.

38. Ben-Gurion's letter to his son Amos, October 5, 1937; cited in Teveth, *Ben-Gurion and the Palestinian Arabs*, 189.

39. Masalha, *Expulsion of the Palestinians*, 88n52.

40. Instructions to the Haganah Command, June 18, 1947, David Ben-Gurion, *Be-hilahem Yisrael* (Tel Aviv: Mapai, 1975); cited in David Tal, "The Forgotten War: Jewish-Palestinian Strife in Mandatory Palestine, December 1947–May 1948," *Israeli Affairs* 6.3 (2000): 5n7.

41. David Ben-Gurion's speech at the Jewish Congress's political committee, December 18, 1946, David Ben-Gurion, *Ba-ma'arakha*, vol. 5 (Tel Aviv, 1969), 135–36; cited in Tal, "Forgotten War," 6n12.

42. Instructions to the Haganah Command, Ben-Gurion, *Be-hilahem Yisrael*, 16–17, Ben-Gurion's speech at the Security Committee, June 8, 1947, Meir Avizohar, *Paamei Medina* (Tel Aviv, 1994), 295, 297–98, 291–301; cited in Tal, "Forgotten War," 6n12.

43. TNA CO 537/2281, Cunningham to Creech Jones, Monthly Reports, no. 249, October 11, 1947; CP III/1/40, Cunningham to U.K. Delegate in New York, no. 180, January 23, 1948.

44. CP III/1/52, Cunningham to Creech Jones, Intelligence Appreciation, no. 113, January 24, 1948.

45. TNA CO 537/2281, Cunningham to Creech Jones, Monthly Reports, no. 249, October 11, 1947; CP III/1/40, Cunningham to U.K. Delegate in New York, no. 180, January 23, 1948.

46. Morris, "Revisiting the Palestinian Exodus," 39.

47. Ibid., 44.

48. Morris, *Birth*, 40.

49. Morris, "Revisiting the Palestinian Exodus," 48.

50. Pappé, *Ethnic Cleansing of Palestine*, 49n20, Central Zionist Archives, 45/1 Protocol, November 2, 1947.

51. Eliot A. Cohen, *Supreme Command* (New York: Anchor, 2002), 145.

52. NACP 218/190/19/4–5, Anglo-American Committee of Inquiry, 10.

53. NP, The Palestine Problem GSI (14), GHQ Middle East Land Forces, October 1945.

54. Morris, *1948 and After*, 13.

55. NACP 43/250/9/29/2–3, AACI interviews with Generals Tennant, Oliver, and Air Chief Marshal Medhurst, HQ Cairo, March 5, 1946.

56. NACP 218/190/19/4–5, AACI interviews, 10.

57. Ibid., 3–4.

58. Ibid., 128.

59. Ibid., (ii). Regarding Zionists' strategic acquisition of Palestine territory, see also Yossi Katz,

Partner to Partition: The Jewish Agency's Partition Plan in the Mandate Era (London: Frank Cass, 1998).

60. NACP 218/190/19/4–5, AACI interviews, iv.

61. NACP 43/250/9/29/2–3, Testimony by head of command, Jewish resistance movement [Haganah] to AACI, March 25, 1946.

62. Ibid.

63. Jorge García Granados, *The Birth of Israel: The Drama as I Saw It* (New York: Alfred A. Knopf, 1948), 185. García Granados was Guatemala's representative to the UNSCOP and supported partition.

64. Ibid.

65. CP II/2/131, Creech Jones to Cunningham, October 9, 1947; CP II/2/134, Cunningham to Creech Jones, Monthly Report, October 11, 1947.

66. CP II/2/133, Cunningham to Creech Jones, saving 249, October 11, 1947.

67. NP, Lieutenant Colonel Norman Personal Lectures, "The Situation of Palestine Today," June 7, 1947. Jewish units in Europe initiated the organization of large-scale illegal immigration.

68. TT, General Sir Horatius Murray interview.

69. Ibid.

70. Morris, *Birth Revisited*, 16.

71. Walid Khalidi, *From Haven to Conquest: Readings in Zionism and the Palestine Problem until 1948* (Beirut: Institute for Palestine Studies, 1971), appendix 8, Note on Arab Strength in Palestine, January–May 15, 1948, 858. TT, Farid Assad and Youssuf Khamis interviews.

72. TT, General Sir Horatius Murray interview.

73. NACP 319/270/6/15/4, Army Intelligence, Memorandum for the Executive Assistant, Office of the Assistant Secretary of State for Occupied Areas, Armed Forces Data, Palestine, December 10, 1947.

74. NACP 43/250/9/29/2–3, AACI hearing in Jerusalem, Palestine, March 11, 1946, David Ben-Gurion.

75. NP, Appreciation prepared by HQ Palestine, July 10, 1947, for Cunningham from Lieutenant-General, GOC, British Troops in Palestine and Transjordan, July 15, 1947, hereafter, the Norman Report. Lieutenant Colonel C. R. W. Norman was head of military intelligence in Palestine from October 1946 through July 1948.

76. See Avi Shlaim, *Collusion across the Jordan: King Abdullah, the Zionist Movement and the Partition of Palestine* (New York: Columbia University Press, 1988); and Mary C. Wilson, *King Abdullah, Britain, and the Making of Jordan* (New York: Cambridge University Press, 1987).

77. Norman Report.

78. Ibid.

79. Ibid.

80. NACP 319/270/6/15/4, Army Intelligence, Memo for the Executive Assistant, Palestine, December 10, 1947.

81. Norman Report.

82. Ibid.

83. UN DAG 13 3.2:2, U.N. Truce Commission Palestine, Mediator, November–December 1948. Record of conversation with Bunche and Colonel Nouh, November 18, 1948. Simha Flapan, *The Birth of Israel: Myths and Realities* (New York: Pantheon, 1987), 121–52.

84. Khalidi, *From Haven to Conquest*, 859.

85. Ibid., 860.

86. *Collecting Stories from Exile: Chicago Palestinians Remember 1948* (film) (Chicago: American Friends Service Committee, 1999), Ayoub Talhami interview.

87. "A Brief Report on the Situation in Palestine and Comparison between the Forces and Potential of Both Sides," by General Ismail Safwat, GOC, Arab League Military Committee, Damascus, to Syrian Prime Minister Jamil Mardam Bey and Chairman of the Palestine Committee of the Arab League, March 23, 1948, in Walid Khalidi, "Selected Documents on the 1948 Palestine War," *Journal of Palestine Studies* 27.3 (1998): 60–72, hereafter Safwat Report. The Arab League political committee appointed a technical committee of military experts which became the military committee after the U.N. partition vote of November 29, 1947.

88. Safwat Report. For a detailed description of the ALA battalion organization based on AHC and ALA files see Khalidi, *From Haven to Conquest*, 860.

89. NP, Appreciation from HQ Palestine by Palestine Police for U.N. Commission, March 27, 1948. CP IV/4/35, Appreciation with MacMillan's handwritten comments, July 10, 1947.

90. Ibid.

91. IDF Archives, War of Independence Collected Files 1/65, Haganah intelligence reports of February 13, 1948; cited in Uri Milstein, *History of Israel's War of Independence*, vol. 3, *The First Invasion*, trans. and ed. Alan Sacks (Lanham, Md: University Press of America, 1998), 58.

92. Maan Abu Nowar, *The Jordanian-Israeli War, 1948–1951: A History of the Hashemite Kingdom of Jordan* (Reading, U.K.: Ithaca, 2002), 14n9.

93. Safwat Report, 69–71.

94. UN DAG 13 3.2:2, U.N. Truce Commission Palestine, Mediator, Bunche and Colonel Nouh conversation, November 28, 1948.

95. NACP 218/190/1/19/4–5, Report by the director of the Joint Chiefs of Staff on Force Requirements for Palestine, March 31, 1948.

96. Ibid., appendix C.

97. Ibid., 65.

98. CP IV/4/21, Comments on the Foreign Office Paper on Palestine presumably written by Cunningham, 1947.

99. NACP 218/190/1/19/4–5, Report by the director of the Joint Chiefs of Staff on Force Requirements for Palestine, March 31, 1948, 67–68.

100. Ibid., 68.

101. Ibid., 69.

102. Ibid., 71.

103. NACP 319/270/15/31/7, Intelligence Estimate of the Enemy Situation, case 9, March 6, 1948, revised June 15, 1948.

104. Ibid.

105. See Pablo de Azcárate, *Mission in Palestine, 1948–1952* (Washington, D.C.: Middle East Institute, 1966). Azcárate was deputy principal secretary of the Palestine Commission and head of the 1948 advance mission.

106. UN 0453-0003 (UNPC), Advance Party Communication AP/1–AP/39, March–April 1948, 6.

107. Ibid., 8.

108. Ibid., 10.

109. Ibid.

110. TNA WO 261/708, Third Parachute Brigade intelligence summary, no. 5, October 8, 1947.

111. CP IV/4/28, Note on the Establishment of a Jewish State in Palestine by the Jews Themselves.

112. Ibid.

113. TNA CO 537/3926, Arab-Jewish Military Situation in Palestine, Weekly Intelligence Appreciation, no. 5, May 17, 1948; DEFE 4/13, COS (48) First Meeting, May 25, 1948, annex 1.

114. CP IV/4/35, Cunningham, July 10, 1947. Appreciation of the potential capability of a Jewish State in Palestine defending itself against Arab aggression.

Destroyed Jerusalem neighborhood, 1948

IV

Creating a Vacuum
The British Withdrawal

It must be agreed that law and order is not being maintained at present.

Sir Alan Cunningham, January 1948

Less than six months after the U.N. partition vote, the British withdrew from Palestine without a handover to another competent authority. The accelerated withdrawal left a chaotic power vacuum that the Zionists were far better prepared and equipped to exploit than were the Arabs. Although aware that their actions could result in civil war, the British withdrew their military forces, materiel, and civil administration as quickly as possible while avoiding conflict with either Jews or Arabs. This "scuttled" British withdrawal from Palestine led directly to Arab-Jewish civil war. Decisions made by the central and local British authorities contributed to the catastrophic outcome of the 1948 war. The expected vacuum created was filled by ethnic conflict resulting in the mass Arab exodus, which continues to foment regional conflict to this day.

The end of the British mandate was overseen by the Labour government of Prime Minister Clement Attlee, Foreign Secretary Ernest Bevin, and Colonial Secretary Arthur Creech Jones, which had taken office in 1945. The Foreign Office and the Colonial Office were the two offices of state concerned with Palestine. Since 1922, Palestine had been a Colonial Office responsibility. During the late 1930s, it also became a major political and strategic concern of the Foreign Office and the chiefs of staff. In fact, the Foreign Office and the Colonial Office often clashed over Palestine policy. But when Attlee, Bevin, and Creech Jones were in accord on ministerial

LEBANON

SYRIA

☆ Safad

☆ Acre GALILEE

☆ Haifa Tiberias ☆

HAIFA Nazareth ☆

Baysan ☆

Jinin ☆

—— Military Boundary

SAMARIA

Tulkarm ☆

Nablus ☆

☆ Jaffa

Al-Ramla ☆ ☆ Ramallah

LYDDA

☆ Jerusalem

MEDITERRANEAN SEA

JERUSALEM

Dead Sea

☆ Gaza

☆ Hebron

GAZA ☆ Beersheba

EGYPT

0 10 20 30 40 50

Kilometers

TRANSJORDAN

BRITISH CIVIL AND MILITARY ADMINISTRATIVE BOUNDARIES, 1947–48

policy, their joint decisions were "virtually invulnerable to challenge by other members of the Cabinet or the Chiefs of Staff."[1]

In London, the Palestine crisis reached a climax in February 1947. The London Conference, convened in September 1946, was Britain's final attempt to find a negotiated solution to the Palestine problem. Discussions occurred against a backdrop of other postwar international and domestic issues, including the emotional debate on withdrawal from India, the collapse of defense arrangements with Egypt, Near East strategic planning to prevent Soviet infiltration, and a "sense of impending economic disaster."[2]

The cost of maintaining the Palestine mandate had become prohibitive. In 1946 approximately 100,000 British troops—one-tenth of the armed forces of the entire British Empire, about one soldier for every 18 inhabitants—were occupying a territory the size of Wales.[3] British security costs in Palestine had risen "far beyond the means of the British taxpayer." Military costs alone were close to £40 million per annum. And increasing Zionist terrorism against British security forces resulted in public pressure to "bring the boys home."[4] The London Conference came to an abrupt end when the Labour government decided on February 14, 1947, to refer the Palestine issue to the United Nations.

The British government decided to terminate the Palestine mandate and to withdraw unilaterally once it became obvious that no political solution satisfactory to both Palestinian Arabs and Jews was likely to be found through the United Nations. The British executed the unilateral withdrawal without any formal de facto or de jure turnover of authority, and without regard to consequences for the people living in Palestine.

The mandate government decided that May 15, 1948, was the earliest that it could withdraw the civil administration. All remaining British security forces were to be completely withdrawn from Palestine by August 1, 1948. Parliament approved that decision on December 11, 1947.[5] General Sir Horatius Murray, commander of the First Infantry Division, summed up the military's attitude about the decision to abandon the mandate, saying that the British had "done as good a job as we reckoned we could do but it's [also] true to say we had no qualms about leaving Palestine at high speed."[6]

Britain's decision to abdicate authority without a prior handover to another government was not without precedent. The Attlee government's

hasty withdrawal of military and civilian administration from British India in mid-August 1947, without achieving a political solution, abandoned
one-fifth of humankind to partition and bloody civil war. During the partition of India, an estimated one million civilians perished, and about ten
million inhabitants fled their ancestral homes in one of the largest mass
migrations in history.[7] Like British India, mandate Palestine would suffer
the ravages of hatred, fear, depopulation, and continued conflict wrought
by Britain's decolonization.

Military Decision Making in Palestine

A complex command structure fostered competing interests in British
military decision making, which, at times, pitted the military command
in Palestine against both London and the mandate civil government itself.
Palestine forces served under the joint military command of the British
Army and Royal Air Force (RAF). The Imperial General Staff issued instructions through the War Office in London to British forces in Palestine via the Egypt-based commander in chief of Middle East Land Forces
(MELF). The commander of MELF in turn issued orders to the general
officer commanding (GOC) Palestine, Lieutenant General Gordon Mac-
Millan.

MacMillan exercised some latitude in interpreting his orders, based on
the "facts on the ground." When MacMillan received orders, he would
confer with High Commissioner General Sir Alan Cunningham on how to
implement them most effectively "in step with [local] civil policy." As the
Dayr Yasin massacre and the Haifa battle of April 1948 would respectively
demonstrate, the military's interpretation of orders during the evacuation
could conflict with both the high commissioner's and London's policy.[8]
In these cases, local British concerns in Palestine usually took precedence
over London's dictates.

Despite public statements to the contrary, the military was overstretched
and unable to implement the British government's expectations to maintain law and order in Palestine while troops evacuated. The military in
the field attempted to compensate for deteriorating security by making
decisions based narrowly on whatever it faced. These ad hoc choices, made
in many cases by local commanders, contributed to, rather than inhibited,
the increasing lawlessness in Palestine during the civil war's dénouement.

Withdrawal: A Major Setback for the British

The British chiefs of staff viewed the long-term political and strategic consequences of enforcing the U.N. majority plan as even more serious than its military aspects.[9] The chiefs believed, much as the high commissioner had, that by enforcing the majority plan they would have been "suppressing Arab resistance in Palestine, and thus antagonizing the independent Arab States" when Great Britain's entire political and strategic system in the Middle East was founded on cooperation with the Arab states. A firm strategic hold on the Middle East was indispensable to Commonwealth defense policy. Strategic British military considerations thus were contrary to enforcing the U.N. plan. Also, logistical factors posed problems: the chiefs estimated that no less than an additional division would have been required to enforce partition—a quantity of troops that could not be spared.[10]

British strategists based in the Middle East viewed the general idea of withdrawing from Palestine "as a disaster harmful in the extreme" and as "a major strategic reverse."[11] Events affecting Palestine had an impact on the Middle East as a whole. The area was strategically important as a gateway to Africa and as a land bridge between Europe, Asia, and Africa, which they could not permit an enemy to possess. From the region, "allied forces could strike at Russian production in the heart of Russia." Land, sea, and air communications were centered there and Middle East oil was a vital factor in war and peace. To defend the Middle East during war, cooperation with the Arabs during peacetime was essential.[12]

The British considered access to military facilities in Palestine and Egypt vital to the postwar defense of the whole Middle East in the event of future conflicts. Consequently, after World War II, the British built up Palestine to serve as a strategic military base in its own right, and as a fallback from Egypt for future wars. To accommodate anticipated force requirements, military camps in Palestine had been expanded for a reserve of five divisions, and equipped with enormous requisite stores of explosives, weapons, and vehicles.[13] Great Britain's withdrawal from Palestine presented three additional immediate strategic implications: the need to further redeploy Middle East forces, the effect on British oil interests, and the issue of control of Palestine after withdrawal.[14] The decision to withdraw was an unexpected policy reversal, and it necessitated a complete revision of British defense plans.[15]

British Efforts to Save Military Stores

Preserving military stores, and the troops removing the stores from Palestine, became the chief policy consideration of the British at the end of the Palestine mandate. Evacuation was a daunting task, requiring the withdrawal and redeployment of approximately 70,000 army and RAF personnel along with their equipment and vehicles. An estimated 250,000 tons of navy, army, and RAF stores and machinery also had to be evacuated. The military was further charged with disposing of approximately 100,000 tons of surplus stores, 8,000 vehicles, fixed assets, 208 military camps, and releasing 1,133 employees.[16]

The chiefs-of-staff committee determined the timetable. The main consideration for evacuation was how fast Britain's military could reduce its fighting strength and reassign released units. The timing was determined by how fast stores could be transferred to other Middle East locations from Haifa and Egypt.[17] The security of these stores was paramount; the civilian population's safety in Palestine was considered a secondary goal at very best. Jerusalem was to remain the site of British headquarters until the mandate ended on May 15; after that, evacuating forces were to be moved into the Haifa enclave until the end of July 1948, when the remaining British forces were to be withdrawn.

In January 1948, the organizational command in Palestine was as follows:

Sector	Operation Command	Civil District Area
North Sector	Sixth Airborne Division	Haifa and the Galilee
Central Sector	First Infantry Division	Lydda and Samaria
East Sector	Second Infantry Brigade	Jerusalem
South Sector	Lorried Infantry Brigade	Gaza[18]

The British evacuation was planned as a four-phase operation. Mandate Palestine was divided administratively into six districts: the Galilee, Haifa, Samaria, Jerusalem, Lydda, and Gaza. Each district was subdivided into subdistricts, which together totaled 16. After the civil administrative boundaries were reorganized into military districts, the geographically phased evacuation program through Haifa and Egypt proceeded as follows: In the first phase, the Gaza civil district, excluding Rafah, was evacuated by February 29. In phase two, troops in Jerusalem, Lydda, and part of Samaria were withdrawn by May 31. By June 30, in the third phase, the remaining troops withdrew from Samaria and the Galilee. In the fourth and final phase, the military enclave at Haifa was evacuated by July 31.[19]

Throughout the country, civil administration was to be maintained officially only until the mandate ended on May 15, during the second phase of withdrawal. Thereafter, certain administrative staff were to be retained in occupied enclaves to assist military authorities in the efficient conduct of withdrawal, and in the case of the Gaza district to safeguard the evacuation route through Egypt for as long as possible.[20]

The evacuation of men and stores through Haifa port and overland to Egypt was scheduled to begin on December 1, 1947. Stores were not to be left in Palestine for fear that Jews and Arabs would employ them against each other. If materiel could not be evacuated before troops withdrew, it was to be destroyed. Military planners estimated that roughly 150,000 tons of useful stores would be completely lost, even under the most favorable conditions.[21] As predicted, the security forces were unable to destroy or remove all materiel before their departure. In most cases, Zionist forces were able to seize control of stores and use them against the Arabs.[22]

Withdrawal went faster than expected. Even under the most favorable conditions, military planners had calculated that the withdrawal would take eight months, due to uncertainties on the ground during evacuation. The chiefs of staff estimated as much as an 18-month time frame.[23] In the end, British withdrawal from Palestine took less than six months.[24] This accelerated and haphazard evacuation would foster the state of lawlessness that allowed the civil war, and Arab expulsions, to occur. The British focus on military concerns and desire to avoid confrontation did not bode well for maintaining local law and order, as nationalist clashes grew between Palestine's two communities.

British Withdrawal: An Open Secret

Cunningham, MacMillan, and the commanders in chief of the Middle East met in Jerusalem on November 14, 1947, to outline the evacuation plan. The civil administration felt it could control the country only from Jerusalem, where the entire government apparatus was located. The military was dissatisfied with this arrangement. Holding Jerusalem—located in the central highlands—while the military withdrew from the rest of the country presented significant tactical difficulties. At the same time, the military feared that terminating the civil administration before military evacuation was completed would result in confusion that would prolong the withdrawal.

In the end, they agreed that the civil administration should continue to function during the withdrawal because it was "vital for the maintenance of law and order." They also agreed to hold on to Jerusalem as the political center until the mandate ended.[25] Additionally, without the U.N. commission's presence in Palestine to assume the civil government's responsibility "with sufficient force at its disposal," the British administration would withdraw before the military. Without military protection, the government acknowledged that it could not function. Cunningham stressed the importance of remaining in Jerusalem and maintaining the civil government until the last possible moment to give the United Nations as much time as possible to find a solution "acceptable to the inhabitants of Palestine." He also hoped "some special arrangement could be made for the safety of the Holy Places in Jerusalem."

The commanders in chief met again with Cunningham on November 24, 1947, to discuss the specific administrative details of the evacuation. They accepted that some part of the administration needed to remain in Haifa after disbanding the government "in order to wind up the legal aspect of land holdings." Failure to do so, they feared, would result in the Arabs' losing a great deal of their land.[26] In fact, by the time the British left Palestine, over 50 percent of the Palestinian Arabs who would be displaced had already been driven from their lands by Zionist forces.

After the partition plan was adopted, the military's concern over removing British equipment and stores within the allotted time continued to dominate planning. The removal was complicated by the limited capacity of the exit routes and the economic importance of giving precedence to local rail transportation of citrus fruit, a major export crop.

The planners also foresaw trouble. There would be a "certainty of civil disturbances, and the probability of fighting, at least between Arabs and Jews."[27] Yet none of the planning included a military effort to suppress the violent disturbances foreseen, and this contributed to the lack of willing-ness to quell the burgeoning civil war and check the decades of geopoliti-cal conflict that would result.

British evacuation plans were meant to be top secret, but they were not. The details were soon widely known.[28] Jews and Arabs both had "excel-lent intelligence" from the British service installations, which employed considerable numbers of civilians in clerical positions and as laborers.[29] The Jewish Agency learned from the Colonial Office in December 1947 that the "British withdrawal would proceed from south to north."[30] By mid-January 1948, at the latest, Ben-Gurion had detailed knowledge of the British evacuation schedule—advance notice of the decisive reduction of British forces in April 1948.[31]

In early March 1948, a 17th Airborne Division field security report acknowledged that future British troop movement and the division's disbandment and evacuation was common knowledge among Jews and Arabs due "to loose talk among the troops, and snippets of information intelligently collated."[32] Knowledge of the evacuation calendar allowed the Jewish Agency to plan its military strategy to take advantage of the weakening British presence in Palestine. This contradicts Benny Morris's conclusion, based on his assumption that Haganah commanders lacked intelligence on the British withdrawal, that the Zionists were mostly im-provising.[33]

Among the most far-reaching political decisions affecting the war's out-come was the joint decision of the civil administration and the military to delay the United Nations' implementation of partition. The commanders emphasized that the U.N. commission's arrival in Palestine should be de-layed as long as possible to preserve British-Arab relations.[34] They wanted at all costs to minimize any violence in Palestine that could disrupt their evacuation plan. The Palestinian Arabs had threatened violence if the U.N. commission arrived to enforce partition. However, the U.N. commission's delayed arrival in Palestine, a mere fortnight before the mandate ended, precluded any handover of administrative authority. The resulting atmo-sphere of uncertainty and violence contributed to the rapidly disintegrat-ing delivery of civil services and to the increasingly violent chaos, during which the Palestinian refugee crisis would be created.

Fallout from the U.N. Vote

Prior to the partition announcement on November 29, British forces were occupied in battling dissident Zionist violence. After the U.N. vote in favor of partition, the British military noted that the "Arabs realized that they would have to fight for their independence." To obtain weapons, vehicles, and ammunition, the Arabs also began attacking British servicemen.[35] Although conflict between Arabs and Jews had been expected, the British withdrawal plan was based on the assumption that their own evacuation would not be "actively opposed by either Jews or Arabs." They believed it possible for the "civil administration to continue for the greater part of the period of withdrawal." Indeed, British evacuation was not opposed by either side, but the extensive British military supplies were coveted by both sides, putting the security forces at risk of becoming targets.[36]

Some military worries about Palestine's facilities overlapped with civilian concerns. Of particular importance to the military was maintaining communications and essential public utilities throughout Palestine.[37] British evacuation planning counted on a measure of restraint on all sides, yet neither side would act as expected. The British grossly underestimated the Arabs' violent response to a U.N. vote for partition, as well as the willingness, if not eagerness, of Zionist military and terror groups to join in and expand the conflict.

Immediately after the partition decision was announced, sporadic hostilities between Jews and Arabs broke out throughout Palestine. As security deteriorated rapidly, a mere month after the U.N. announcement, Colonial Secretary Creech Jones wrote Cunningham on January 5, 1948, to inquire whether he had rethought maintaining the civil administration's presence until May 15. Circumstances in Palestine had already endangered the planned evacuation program, as it had been based on the assumption that the Arabs "would produce no strong reaction" until after the U.N. commission had arrived. But by January 1948, wrote Creech Jones, the British military realized that whatever preparations the U.N. commission would make, there was "very little prospect of an orderly handover of the administrative machine."[38]

The British nevertheless continued their evacuation. Once fighting over partition erupted, the argument that the civil administration should be maintained until May 15 to effect an orderly handover was invalidated.[39] Even though effective government was more necessary than ever to deal with the breakdown of order, Great Britain continued its rush out of Palestine. Security forces in Palestine advised advancing Jerusalem's evacuation to as early as February 1948, but civil authorities rejected this proposal, saying they would be unable to function after leaving Jerusalem. Military withdrawal plans were thus forced to adapt somewhat to the civil situation, but it is clear that law and order had ceased to be a significant policy concern for the military, unless the British evacuation was affected. The policy became to abdicate any practical responsibility for the state of affairs in Palestine.[40]

On a visit to Palestine, the British minister in Transjordan, Sir Alec Kirkbride, described the mandate's impotence. Civil administration, except in circumscribed localities, was "operating from within the relatively safe refuge of the army security zones," with its control over events beyond the barbed-wire enclosures diminishing as time passed. The vacuum outside had created a corresponding vacuum inside. Kirkbride observed that in their closely guarded safety zones, Cunningham and Chief Secretary Sir Henry Gurney "were, in a sense, functioning in a vacuum. . . . They . . . issued orders which were intended for observance by Jews and Arabs who had, by this time, taken charge of their own affairs and no longer regarded themselves as being bound, either legally or morally, to take any notice of the British authorities. [The civil administrators] were on the way out and did not care if the edifice of government was on the point of collapse."[41]

British Policy: Do Not Intervene

Intervention in Palestine's turmoil, where it did occur, was determined by several principles. None reflected a fundamental concern with responsible governance. Instead, military action was taken to ensure that local violence caused no interruption in the military's lines of communication to Haifa or Egypt. Security was to be maintained in the main port of Haifa, but only as necessary to evacuate British troops.[42] Security forces also intended to protect Haifa's oil installations until May 1948. Military instructions emphasized the importance of doing everything possible "to be on good terms with the Arabs and Jews," though keeping the communities at peace with each other was not a priority. Instead, security forces avoided

forceful pacifying intervention against Arabs or Jews unless locally necessary to protect British evacuation. The military was especially anxious to
avoid inflicting heavy punishment on either community, fearing retaliation against the British during evacuation, when the military was least
prepared to meet opposition.

The British even speculated that intercommunal conflict could deflect
hostilities from themselves. Members of the cabinet's Palestine committee posited that "there was much advantage in abandoning certain areas
[in Palestine] as soon as possible." Without British control, those areas
"would act, as it were, as lightning conductors for any trouble that might
develop, and we ourselves should thereby avoid the trouble."[43]

The British defined their goal as the continued maintenance of "law and
order," but by using the "absolute minimum of force in doing so," and
avoiding "at all costs unnecessarily inflaming either side in the process."[44]
This contradictory policy to use minimum force while aspiring to maintain law and order meant relative inaction. The Palestine government's
existence was mostly formal in the final six months of the mandate. Both
Jews and Arabs exploited British passiveness to attack each other with escalating fury and to seize strategic ground. Despite their policy and their
attempted impartiality, the British were nevertheless viewed as partisan
by both communities, which were conditioned to suspect British policy
vacillations over the mandate years and cynical about Britain's regional
interests.

It was MacMillan who finally articulated and enforced with the rank
and file the decision not to intervene in Jewish and Arab disputes. Troops
had orders not "to carry out futile operations" unless an incident threatened British lines of communications. MacMillan surmised that with the
available forces, he could not take on commitments that would entail dis-
persing or engaging his forces, and thus risk delaying evacuation.

MacMillan did not have sole responsibility for the abdication of law
and order inherent in the policy—or so he maintained. The chiefs of staff
in London also endorsed the decision, he stressed. Instructions from
Whitehall also supported MacMillan's nonintervention policy. He summarized Secretary of State for War Emanuel Shinwell's orders as stating:
"You have overriding military jurisdiction in certain areas specified by
ourselves, but you should exercise only in so far as it is essential for the
protection of our forces and for the orderly progress of the evacuation.

. . . you have no responsibility for the preservation of law and order in any part of Palestine except as required by you for the protection of our forces and for the purpose of evacuation."[45] Whatever the ultimate origin of the policy, the noninterference in communal conflicts and the spiraling social breakdown would make possible the civil war, the resulting Arab population displacement, and subsequent generations of regional war.

The Breakdown of Law and Order

The evacuation contributed to the growing strife, as the contending communities raced to fill the vacuum. The British military withdrawal, "based upon a series of clear cut backward moves,"[46] proceeded from the Egyptian frontier in the south to Haifa in the north. To prepare for evacuation, and before each "backward move" of the departing security forces, the troops were relieved of their responsibilities to assist the civil government in maintaining law and order and guarding stores even before they physically evacuated an area.[47] When the area was evacuated, it was not to be reoccupied. This policy was intended to preserve British-Arab relations by preventing clashes with Arabs in the Arab areas through which British troops withdrew. Yet as evacuation proceeded, Arab-Jewish fighting intensified as each side rushed to seize strategic, newly evacuated positions before the enemy did. Concurrently, as British forces progressively withdrew, the ability of the remaining British fighting forces to control the security situation was diminished due to reduced numbers, less strategic positioning, and increased Arab or Jewish military activity in the abandoned area.

On January 2—four and a half months before the mandate ended—Cunningham issued a directive confirming MacMillan's orders and stating that the civil government was more formal than functioning: "The role of the Security Forces was no longer the preservation of law and order, in the normal sense, but to preserve a state of affairs in which it remains possible for the Civil Government to function on a restricted basis. The run-down of the Army and police rendered the RAF ability to hit quickly without becoming involved on the ground, even more important."[48] The RAF, however, was not to be used offensively against Arabs or Jews, except in emergency cases. An "emergency" was narrowly defined as any occasion when the failure to employ the RAF would result in casualties or increased casualties to British forces only.[49] The directive held dire implications for general order and security in the country.

The guerrilla nature of the civil war before April 1948 provided an additional rationalization for British inaction. The RAF commander reported that the security forces were driven into a defensive role throughout the evacuation period because they "never had an enemy in the open," and every soldier and British vehicle was a potential target. Every civilian "was a potential thief or murderer, and both Arabs and Jews could therefore choose the time and place of their attacks." As time passed, Arab attacks became bolder, particularly armed holdups on the open road and in towns.

The absence of a British security presence revealed the superiority of Zionist military potential and permitted its employment. "The more ambitious attacks, aimed at destruction and murder" in the majority of cases, "were carried out by Jews,"[50] the British military reported. The Zionists' anti-British attacks were directed against army or police installations.

Many British soldiers resented Palestine's Jews because of these attacks. Their resentment was aggravated by pent-up rancor due to prior terrorism during the Zionist insurrection immediately after World War II. Many Jews in turn suspected British partisanship and claimed that British soldiers gave preferential treatment to Arabs.

Arabs simultaneously denounced the British for delivering Palestine, their country, to the Jews. The British complained that neither side believed in "the perfectly fair and impartial position of the average British soldier," who looked "forward to being able to leave" Palestine "quietly and without disturbances."[51] Throughout the withdrawal, British troops received instructions and frequent reminders that in the interest of law and order, it was important to show Arabs and Jews complete impartiality and "thus inspire confidence."[52]

How could confidence be inspired when British withdrawal was abandoning the territory with obvious indifference to the escalating violence between Arabs and Jews? Both communities accused the British of evacuating so as to favor the other side. Though evacuating security forces resented accusations of partiality, they feared more the anti-British attitudes emanating from the Palestinian Arabs. British lines of communication ran largely through Arab areas, so widespread anti-British sentiment could pose a serious threat to safe evacuation.

Leaders of Arab states were also concerned about British withdrawal through their areas for tactical military reasons. Syria's president, Shukri al-Quwatly, feared that the mechanics of British evacuation would be advantageous to the Zionists and "enable them to consolidate their position or perhaps even take over Arab parts [of] Palestine" because the Palestinian Arabs would be more constrained in their military actions by the continued presence of the British in the much larger areas of Palestine in which the Arabs lived.[53]

In the process of evacuation, the British-trained Arab security forces in Palestine, which had shared security responsibilities with the British security forces, were also disbanded or relocated. The Arab Legion was phased out of Palestine and the Transjordan Frontier Force (TJFF) was withdrawn from the northern Palestine frontier and disbanded in Transjordan by February 27.[54] This not only diminished frontier security, it also provided additional demobilized personnel for Arab guerrilla fighting units in the civil war.

A combined British force designated CRAFORCE was formed in the northeast sector to assume the majority of the TJFF commitments patrolling the northern Palestine border.[55] The southern sector was left comparatively devoid of troops. A detachment of the 12th Anti-tank Regiment was concentrated at al-Burij in the south and tasked with keeping open the coast road to Sarafand, and also with restraining local violence. The east and center of Palestine, running from Nazareth to Beersheba and thence to Gaza, was predominately populated by Arabs.[56]

Logistical Difficulties of Evacuation

Throughout the British evacuation, the army was charged with keeping abreast of the changing situation and adjusting its methods accordingly. Progress hinged on three factors: labor, transport, and shipping. The failure to manage these factors accelerated the extent and speed with which disorder took over.

The growing antagonism between Jews and Arabs made the procurement of labor very "uncertain and timid." Employees' attendance at work varied daily and widely, threatening a breakdown of the railways and the docks. As early as the end of January 1948, "labor troubles," while not yet endangering operation of the railway and docks, had nevertheless so "seriously interfered" with the fuel oil supply that the functioning of the railway and public utilities were direly threatened.

Road transportation fared little better. The movement of tons of stores from the country along the roads was at constant risk of armed holdups and hampered by a railway system that "ceased to work a full month before the date of final evacuation." Furthermore, there was a considerable shortage of military transport drivers because Jewish and Arab drivers had "little freedom of action outside depot and cantonment precincts."[57]

Shipping through the port city of Haifa was the focus of evacuation. The turnaround of ships was extremely slow and the harbor was congested. Before withdrawing troops could be redeployed to the British-administered province of Cyrenaica in Libya, construction materials to build accommodations for those troops had to be shipped there.[58] The difficulties of shipping, labor, and transport made law enforcement an even lower priority for the mandate.

The evacuation of both military and civilian authorities was to be governed by several principles. All personnel and equipment were to be removed by August 1, 1948. The withdrawal was supposed to be done "in step," in a "clean and tidy" manner. No actions were to be taken that could be interpreted as favorable to either Arabs or Jews. There was an overriding awareness that antagonizing either community could prevent the full working of the port facilities and railways, for which both Jews and Arabs provided the workforce.[59] Hostility from either could delay the evacuation and prevent the removal of a considerable portion of essential stores.

The evacuation from Jerusalem was in itself a major task, complicated by the uncertainty of the city's final evacuation date. To meet every contingency, the British prepared four separate detailed evacuation plans, and the final plan was not selected until some ten days before it was implemented. The Second Infantry Brigade's task of maintaining law and order in Jerusalem and the surrounding countryside, known as east sector, was rendered increasingly difficult by such practical uncertainties, as well as by the nonintervention policy. As the mandate's end approached, Zionist and Arab forces "tended more to open warfare against each other" and both "resented all British intervention which was not entirely favorable to their own side." While trying to carry out heavy security tasks to protect itself, the brigade was also planning for complete evacuation. British troops in Jerusalem were, "in fact as well as in name, on active service," though active service was not designed to include sustained actions to suppress Arab-Jewish fighting.[60]

The British had considered, but dismissed, the idea of retaining a small force in Jerusalem to protect the holy places and maintain order. The main argument for maintaining such a force had not been the population's security but fear that disorder in the Holy City would harm British prestige internationally. The counterargument was that retaining forces to protect Jerusalem's holy sites could ensnare British forces in riots and negate the political benefit of Britain's withdrawal policy, particularly vis-à-vis the Arabs.[61]

The nonintervention policy persisted despite British knowledge of Zionist plans to seize additional territory. The Sixth Airborne Division's internal security instructions of January 30, 1948, drew attention to plans "for the illegal appropriation of land in Palestine by the Jews in order to est[ablish] new settlements." Each company or equivalent unit had been issued maps delimiting Arab, Jewish, and state-owned land. The codeword *autonomous* appeared on communications and orders concerning illegal land appropriation. Because the problem was considered "largely political," the military was to take no action, pending Palestine government decisions.[62] As a result, the mandate's exit policy knowingly acquiesced in Zionist territorial expansion.

British security forces, occupied with evacuation-oriented shipping concerns, also realized that they could not prevent some illegal Jewish immigration after February. Zionist-sponsored immigrants intercepted by the navy had been transshipped to Cyprus, where they were held in detention camps.[63] The military ruled that illegal Jewish immigration could not be prevented once the Cyprus camps were filled to a capacity of 34,000, or after February 1, 1948. After that date, to avoid interference with British withdrawal, ships conveying illegal Jewish immigrants were to be accepted in Haifa port only in case of bad weather and unseaworthiness. Otherwise ships were to be directed to Tel Aviv and illegal Jewish immigrants disembarked and directed to where they would not interfere with British evacuation.[64]

The British military thereby abdicated its responsibility to interdict Jewish illegal immigration three and a half months before the mandate ended. As the Arabs had feared, the Palestine coast had become permeable to illegal Jewish immigrants, including potential combatants. The policy of noninterference further enabled the Zionists to pursue unilateral military measures and made possible the civil war's escalation.

Troop Deployment and Command Restructuring

The mandate government's reduction of its military and civilian payroll helped to determine the course of the civil war. Not until the number of British troops had been cut in half at the beginning of April 1948 did the Haganah unleash its Plan D offensive. By May 1, 1948, another 17,000 British troops withdrew, an additional 61 percent drop, while full-scale civil war waged in Palestine. Remaining British troops were redeployed to maintain open communications for the evacuation of troop and service stores until final administrative tasks were completed. The following table shows the reduction of British personnel during the evacuation.[65]

Personnel Statistics

Date	British Military	Civilian Drivers	Other Civil Employees
1 Jan. 1947	53,100	1,328	33,186
1 April 1947	64,800	1,309	32,312
1 July 1947	70,200	1,277	28,185
1 Oct. 1947	57,500	1,213	25,546
1 Jan. 1948	38,000	1,299	22,045
1 April 1948	27,600	272	11,992
1 May 1948	10,730	20	7,832
1 June 1948	8,500	10	2,079

As the British withdrew into their evacuation routes, security zones, and out of the country, armed Arabs and Jewish fighters entered illegally and with considerable impunity, fanning out across the land and joining with locals. An estimated 7,000 trained and armed Arabs from neighboring states infiltrated Palestine between January and March 1948, establishing their headquarters in the Nablus-Jinin area. With fewer British forces left to intervene, both sides began "pushing ahead with their arrangements for the battle they both propose[d] to wage."[66] General MacMillan's April

18 message to commanders, even as Palestine was being torn by civil war, conveyed the main concern of the commander in chief: not to inhibit the conflict but to "avoid prejudicing future relations with both contestants and to take all steps possible to avoid [an] embarrassing withdrawal."[67] Violence increased from December 1947 to May 1948, but the British evacuation was not significantly affected. MacMillan would recall that the withdrawal plan set in place on November 28, 1947, was carried out "with very little alteration."[68]

Great Britain's goal of withdrawing British troops from Palestine with minimal British casualties, succeeded to a great extent. From October 1, 1947, to June 30, 1948, British military casualties totaled 129 killed and 271 wounded out of a starting force of over 50,000. However, law and order would disintegrate completely during the mandate's last six months. Both nationalist Arabs and Zionist Jews utilized the atmosphere of chaos allowed by British evacuation policy to pursue their political and strategic goals. Because of the Zionists' superior organization and planning, they benefited tremendously, and disproportionately, from British preoccupation with safe evacuation. Under the cover of war, Zionist forces would seize Arab territory and rid the conquered lands of their Arab inhabitants, reducing the non-Jewish population consistent with their leaders' ideological aims.

⚙

1. Louis and Stookey, *End of the Palestine Mandate*, 4–5.
2. Ibid., 15; J. C. Hurewitz, *The Struggle for Palestine* (New York: W. W. Norton, 1950), 276.
3. TNA CAB 21/1686, Use of armed forces in Palestine; WO 46/145, Cabinet Defense Committee, Palestine, December 19, 1946; Louis and Stookey, *End of the Palestine Mandate*, 19–20.
4. Hurewitz, *Struggle for Palestine*, 282; Louis and Stookey, *End of the Palestine Mandate*, 20. Security forces included British military (army and RAF), Palestine Police, and Arab Legion detachments.
5. TNA AIR 23/8350, Report on the RAF Evacuation from Palestine, Air Vice Marshal W. L. Dawson, Air Office Commanding, Levant [n.d.].
6. TT, General Sir Horatius Murray interview.
7. Stanley Wolpert, *Shameful Flight: The Last Years of the British Empire in India* (Oxford: Oxford University Press, 2006), 1–2.
8. See chap. 6 for an account of the Dayr Yasin massacre and chap. 7 for the Haifa battle.
9. TNA DEFE 5/6, COS 47/223(0), Palestine–Implications of Withdrawal, October 27, 1947.
10. Ibid., CP V/3/33, FO Memo, September 18, 1947.
11. TNA WO 216/686, General Crocker to Field Marshal Montgomery, June 24, 1948; WO 216/686, Lt. General Templer to Montgomery, July 13, 1948.

12. TNA DEFE 4/13, COS 48/71st meeting May 25, 1948, annex 2.

13. TNA WO 32/15037, Crocker to WO, October 20, 1948.

14. TNA DEFE 5/6, COS 47/223 (0), October 27, 1947, 176, 169.

15. TNA WO 32/15037, Crocker to WO, October 20, 1948.

16. MacMillan Report, Third Appreciation for the Evacuation of Palestine, November 14, 1947, appendix E. TNA AIR 23/8350, RAF Evacuation from Palestine, Air Vice Marshal W. L. Dawson.

17. TNA DEFE 5/6, COS 47/223 (0), October 27, 1947, 176, 169.

18. SP 1/6/11, Sixth Airborne Division Internal Security Instruction No. 1 (revised), January 30, 1948.

19. PP 6/1/11, Middle East Land Forces to Ministry of Defense, November 17, 1947.

20. CP II/3/117, Creech Jones to Cunningham, no. 3034, November 28, 1947.

21. PP 6/1/11, Middle East Land Forces to Ministry of Defense, November 17, 1947.

22. Hanna Braun, "Memoirs of an Anti-Zionist Jew," *Olive Stone*, Autumn 1994, 3–4. Braun was a Haganah and later an IDF member. She immigrated to Palestine from northern Germany in 1937.

23. MacMillan Report, Diary of Events, 1948, 48.

24. Ibid.

25. Ibid., 12.

26. PP 6/1/11, Minutes of Chiefs of Staff's Committee Meeting, November 24, 1947.

27. TNA AIR 23/8350, RAF Evacuation from Palestine, Air Vice Marshal W. L. Dawson.

28. TNA WO 275/79, 17th Airborne Field Security Section, no. 69, March 4, 1948.

29. Ibid.

30. Israel State Archives (ISA), *Te'udot mediniyot ve-diplomatiyot, Detsember 1947–Mai 1948* (*Political and Diplomatic Documents, December 1947–May 1948*), ed. Gedalia Yogev (Jerusalem, 1979), no. 86, Ben-Gurion: Report of D. Horowitz, December 31, 1947, 121.

31. ISA, F72/P105; 93.01/2180/23, Shertok to Ben-Gurion, January 17, 1948.

32. TNA WO 275/79, 17th Airborne Field Security Section, no. 69, March 3, 1948.

33. Morris, *Birth*, 62.

34. PP 6/1/11, Minutes of Chiefs of Staff's Committee Meeting, November 24, 1947.

35. TNA AIR 23/8350, RAF Evacuation from Palestine, Dawson; TT, General Sir Horatius Murray interview.

36. Ibid.

37. CP II/2/163, Creech Jones to Cunningham, no. 2650, October 31, 1947.

38. TNA DEFE 7/388, Creech Jones to Cunningham, Withdrawal from Palestine Administrative Implications, January 5, 1948.

39. Ibid.

40. MacMillan Report, Third Appreciation for the Evacuation of Palestine, November 14, 1947, appendix E.

41. Sir Alec Kirkbride, *From the Wings: Amman Memoirs, 1947–51* (London: Frank Cass, 1976), 10–11.

42. TT, General Gordon MacMillan interview.

43. TNA CAB 134/526, Official Committee on Palestine 1947, second meeting, November 3, 1947.

44. TNA WO 261/654, QHR, First Infantry Division, March 1948. Major General H. Murray assumed command of First Infantry Division, December 10, 1947.

45. TT, General Gordon MacMillan interview.

46. PP 6/1/11, Signal from MELF, Col. Light Infantry. G. O. Jenkins to Ministry of Defense, from Commanders in Chief for Chiefs of Staff, November 17, 1947.

47. Ibid.

48. TNA AIR 23/8350, RAF Evacuation from Palestine, Dawson.

49. Ibid.

50. Ibid.

51. TNA WO 275/79, 17th Airborne Field Security Section, no. 58, December 17, 1947.

52. TNA WO 275/78, Sixth Airborne Division, Internal Security, Road Restriction Orders, January–April 1948.

53. NACP 84/350/63/11/5–6, Damascus to American Legation Beirut, October 10, 1947.

54. MacMillan Report, Third Appreciation for the Evacuation of Palestine, November 14, 1947, appendix E.

55. CRAFORCE consisted of 17th/21st Lancers, First Irish Guard, First Parachute Battalion, and supporting units under the command of CRAFORCE Sixth Airborne Division.

56. TNA WO 261/573, HQ Palestine G Branch, Historical Record, January–March 1948.

57. TNA WO 261/193, Second Infantry Brigade, April–June 1948.

58. TNA WO 216/249, Palestine, Evacuation of Progress Report and Appreciations, January 26, 1948; TNA WO 216/686, Crocker to Montgomery, June 24, 1948.

59. MacMillan Report, Third Appreciation for the Evacuation of Palestine, November 14, 1947, appendix E.

60. TNA WO 261/193, Second Infantry Brigade, April–June 1948.

61. CP II/2/151, Creech Jones to Cunningham, no. 2551, October 22, 1947.

62. SP 1/6/11, Sixth Airborne Division Internal Security Instruction no. 1 (revised), January 30, 1948, appendix E to Sixth Airborne Division, Illegal Appropriation of Land.

63. CP II/3/117, Creech Jones to Cunningham, no. 3034, November 28, 1947.

64. PP 6/1/11, Signal from MELF, Col. Light Infantry G. O. Jenkins to Ministry of Defense, from Commanders in Chief for Chiefs of Staff, November 17, 1947.

65. MacMillan Report, appendix.

66. CP V/4/99, Statement on the Military Situation in Palestine, March 28, 1948.

67. SP 1/6/1–14.

68. MacMillan Report, 12.

ZIONIST TERRORIST ATTACK ON THE KING DAVID HOTEL, JERUSALEM, 1946

V

From Provocation and Reprisal
to Open Warfare

*Present and future events in Palestine are leading
to a catastrophe in that country.*

British Chiefs of Staff, February 1948

The U.N. adoption of the partition resolution on November 29, 1947, precipitated the civil war period of the 1948 Palestine conflict. On that date, the Jewish and Arab struggle shifted from a drive for liberation from the British by both communities to a fight between the two populations for sovereignty over Palestine or its parts. The U.N. endorsement of partition was viewed by Palestinian Arabs and the Arab League as a declaration of war against the sovereign national rights of Palestine's Arabs. In waging war against the proposed partition, the Arabs felt it was not only their right but "their sacred duty" to defend their country and patrimony.[1]

Palestinian Arabs staged emotional protests against the U.N. partition vote, Zionist forces responded with indiscriminate provocation and reprisal, and the pattern was established to expand the conflict. The spontaneous joyful Jewish and angry Arab reactions rapidly gave way to intercommunal attacks and retaliations that spiraled into "undisguised civil war."[2]

Response to the U.N. Vote: Violence, Apprehension, and Planning

Initial public reactions to the partition resolution came largely from the Jewish community. An early British military report described the mood on the day of the announcement: "When it became known that partition

LEBANON

SYRIA

Safad

Acre

Haifa

Tiberias

Nazareth

Baysan

Jinin

Tulkarm

Nablus

Jaffa

Ramallah

Al-Ramla

River Jordan

Jerusalem

MEDITERRANEAN SEA

Gaza

Dead Sea

Hebron

Beersheba

EGYPT

——— Highway

——+—— Railway

0 10 20 30 40 50
Kilometers

TRANSJORDAN

MAIN ROADS AND RAILWAYS IN 1948

had achieved the necessary two-thirds majority the news spread rapidly from Jew to Jew and hysterical demonstrations began to take place. . . . There were no Arab reactions."[3]

The majority of Jews welcomed the U.N. decision as "official recognition to the right of the Jews to independence."[4] Ben-Gurion considered the United Nations' recognition of the Jewish right to establish their state in Palestine a tremendous political success. Although the 54 percent of mandate Palestine designated as the Jewish state did not satisfy maximalist ideological aspirations of the Zionists, the fact that a "majority of mankind" sanctioned its establishment, including the United States and the Soviet Union, was deemed a very significant step forward.

Ben-Gurion also believed the U.N. General Assembly resolution gave the Zionists an internationally recognized legal mandate to establish a Jewish state, although the Jewish Agency and other Zionists did not consider U.N. endorsement essential. With or without U.N. approval, British support, or indigenous Arab acquiescence, the Jewish Agency had every intention of moving toward statehood.[5] Ben-Gurion viewed the acceptance of partition as a first step toward extending the Jewish state throughout the entire territory of mandate Palestine.[6]

The dissident Revisionists' goals were even more far-reaching. Polish-born Menachem Begin, the leader of the IZL and later prime minister of Israel, also believed the Jews were entitled to statehood, and not only within the boundaries established by the United Nations. Begin's greatest worry had been that the Arabs might accept the U.N. partition plan. This, he said, would have resulted in "the ultimate tragedy, a Jewish state so small that it could not absorb all the Jews of the world."[7]

Others in the right-wing Revisionist party stressed their strong opposition to partition, vowing to "continue to struggle for the establishment of a Jewish state on both sides of the Jordan." At a meeting in Tel Aviv on December 6, 1947, the Revisionist party leader Herzl (Rosenblum) Vardi, from Lithuania, expressed misgivings about a truncated Jewish state's ability "to survive in a hostile Arab world." The Jews would have to fight for themselves, he said. Vardi doubted that they would receive any effective assistance from the United Nations or the United States. "Since a struggle was therefore inevitable," he concluded, "they might as well fight for a Jewish State in the whole of Palestine."[8] The Ukrainian native Arieh Altman, the principal speaker at that Revisionist meeting, also supported the immediate conquest of the whole of Palestine. He warned that those who optimistically believed partition was "but the first step and that the Jewish state would continue to expand" held a fatal illusion. He wrote—ironically in light of future events—that "if the Jews were unable to secure the whole of Palestine at the present time, with the Arabs weak and unorganized, they would certainly never be in a position to do so later when the Arabs had become stronger."[9]

More mainstream Zionist expansionist ambitions were analyzed by the U.S. Central Intelligence Agency (CIA) in a November 28, 1947, report titled "The Consequences of the Partition of Palestine":

> In the long run no Zionists in Palestine will be satisfied with the territorial arrangements of the partition settlement. Even the more conservative Zionists will hope to obtain the whole of the Nejeb [Negev], Western Galilee, the city of Jerusalem, and eventually all of Palestine. The extremists demand not only all of Palestine but Transjordan as well. They have stated that they will refuse to recognize the validity of any Jewish government which will settle for anything less, and will probably undertake aggressive action to achieve their ends.[10]

Meanwhile, the U.N. vote stunned the Arab states. The Arab League secretary general, 'Abd al-Rahman Azzam Pasha, told the U.S. first secretary at Cairo, Philip W. Ireland, that "the Arab states had never expected that partition would be voted and that they would be obliged to take up arms." The outcome of the vote was unexpected, and the Arabs had not made any "real preparation" to oppose it, he said. In contrast, Azzam Pasha further noted that the Jewish Agency "had begun to prepare for an all-out campaign of armed destruction of the Arabs' interest in Palestine" since the 1936–39 Palestinian Arab rebellion against the mandate.[11] This assertion is supported by British military intelligence reports that acknowledge the existence in 1938 of Zionist offensive plans to conquer all of Palestine.[12]

The U.N. vote caught the Arab Higher Executive (AHE), a four-member committee dominated by Husayni family supporters, completely by surprise.[13] The AHE had been confident that the partition plan would fail to obtain the necessary two-thirds majority, or that the decision would be postponed until the following summer, at which time Arab plans would have been completed. In order to gain time, the mufti called a three-day strike on Monday, December 1, 1947, as a safety valve for popular pressure.[14] It was not, however, unanimously supported by Palestinian Arabs. The local Arab national committees were opposed to the mufti's strike because they were unprepared for it.[15]

A cycle of violence quickly began nonetheless. Sporadic and spontaneous Arab violent reaction to Jewish celebratory outbursts commenced along with opportunistic violence by dissident Zionists. The general officer commanding (GOC) Palestine, Lieutenant General Gordon MacMillan reported that disorders started with Arab attacks on the consulates of countries that had voted for partition. The British military attributed the Arab attacks to "hooligan elements" rather than to coordinated efforts by Arab leaders.[16] There was sporadic shooting in Haifa, Tel Aviv, and Jaffa and isolated Arab attacks on Jewish transport.[17] The IZL and LHI used the disorder to renew their attacks against British police and soldiers.[18]

Arab attacks were not just politically motivated. The Arabs were provoked "by loss of face," the Sixth Airborne Division observed. They "were furious at the Jews [for] rejoicing as though they had won a war." British soldiers reported scenes in Jerusalem "reminiscent of VE Day," and celebrations "continued with staggering endurance for almost two whole days." They commented that if Jewish celebrations had been restrained, "instead of arrogant and ostentatious, the Arabs would not have been so angry."[19]

Tensions were increased by spontaneous British actions as well. The *Palestine Post* reported that the "British in town caught the spirit" and joined in Jewish celebrations. The Polish-born Haganah member Shulamith Hareven recalls riding around Jerusalem in British jeeps all night.[20] The Sixth Airborne intelligence reasoned that the soldiers' behavior "was understandable since the characteristic good nature of the Briton impels him to assist in any form of happy celebration." The Arabs were incensed. They "naturally misinterpreted" the soldiers' "contagious enthusiasm" as genuine and biased,[21] the Sixth Airborne reported.

The recollection of Abu Yusuf, of Dayr Yasin village, confirms that Jewish celebrations were associated with provocative triumphalism. Yusuf was taking a taxi home from work in Wadi Joz and saw "Jews dancing on top of a British tank, celebrating happily" in Jerusalem's Jewish Mea Shearim neighborhood. He feared for his life as the taxi passed through the Jewish throng, which he said cursed him, calling him "dirty Arab" and shouting, "We took Palestine!"[22]

Arab rioting erupted on Tuesday, December 2, when the "Jews were facing the results of their party," in the words of the Sixth Airborne: "The crowds of Arab hooligans got out of hand, and set fire to and looted shops all over Jerusalem. Throughout Palestine, Jewish vehicles and buses were stoned, and in some cases fired at. Throughout the day, reports were received of minor brushes, with casualties on both sides."[23] The Zionists had anticipated the Arab riots on December 2, but they had not expected them to last long, according to British military intelligence. Arab rioters burned the Jewish Commercial Center, and the IZL set fire to the Arab-owned Rex Cinema in Jerusalem.[24] The Jewish Agency severely criticized the British police's "unwillingness to prevent the rioting" in Jerusalem and for arresting 16 Haganah members but not a single Arab during the riot.[25]

The cycle of violence that would devolve into civil war continued. An officer with the Sixth Airborne observed that the Jewish community would not simply dismiss the rioting "as the acts of irresponsible elements." Instead, the intelligence officer observed: "Reprisals had to follow, and, furthermore, retribution had to be exacted several fold. Much blood was spilt therefore as a direct result of both sides taking hasty action in the early stages, and thereafter the situation was never wholly restored."[26] Although the yishuv was confident it could successfully defend itself, "vigorous counter measures" by the Haganah were not anticipated by the Palestine Police until the mandate government's attitude toward the rioters became clear. Ben-Gurion discussed the security problem with the high commissioner, who assured him (despite the actual civil military posture of initial passivity) of the "government's intentions to fulfill its obligations in the field of security and to remain responsible for law and order." Ben-Gurion interpreted these assurances as a warning that the government would "not tolerate open action" by the Haganah. The veiled threat, albeit negated by the ultimately passive British policy, momentarily restrained the Haganah.[27]

Nevertheless, Zionists eventually retaliated for the early December Arab rioting in Jerusalem. The Haganah launched an offensive of sabotage and terror, blowing up buildings they alleged were centers for armed Arabs. These included a flour mill in the village of Bayt Safafa, a soda-water factory near the entrance to Jerusalem's Romema quarter, and the Supreme Muslim Council headquarters.[28] During the first week of December 1947, Palestine Police sources believed that the Haganah would adopt a "more vigorous policy" because of the riots, even though they maintained that the Haganah was "still anxious to avoid an open conflict with the Arabs."[29]

Ben-Gurion struck a moderate propartition position in public. He advised that "everything should be done, by way of persuasion, to prevent irredentist propaganda and talk of conquering [the] rest of [the] country and Jerusalem." At the same time, Ben-Gurion was calling for immediate expansion of Jewish settlements in three areas assigned to the Arab state—the southwest area of the Negev; the Etzion settlements in the southeast; and the western Galilee—because such action might not be possible after the mandate's termination.[30] This combining of rhetorical restraint with aggressive creation of facts to achieve political objectives characterizes Ben-Gurion's actions throughout the civil war period (and beyond).

During this early phase of spontaneous exchange of violence, officials on both sides seemed to counsel restraint. Neither seemed sure how the British or the other side would react. The Jewish leadership was very concerned about armed Arab attacks on road traffic. They feared the disruption of economic activities, particularly in Jerusalem, which relied on the roadways for supplies. As British and U.S. military analysts had predicted, Jewish lines of communication were the Achilles' heel of the yishuv. Even untrained Arab peasants could easily disrupt them.

On December 6, 1947, a British military report observed that "so far, the Jews have kept themselves fairly well in hand," but it predicted that if the Arabs continued reactive attacks to the partition resolution, "retaliation [against the Arabs] by the dissidents [IZL and LHI]," and probably by the Haganah too, "would be inevitable."[31] Arab leaders may have sensed the risk of inciting the Zionists. The U.S. consulate general in Jerusalem reported that the Palestine Police had information that the mufti had instructed the AHE to "do all possible [to] curb present disorders."[32] Contrary to Zionist historical accounts, the mufti realized the Arabs were weaker than the yishuv, and he was not trying to incite Arab reaction in early December.[33]

The Palestinian Arab community generally desired to continue life as normal and not become embroiled in civil war. Palti Sela, a Haganah intelligence officer observing the daily trends and moods of the rural Arab population, reported in December 1947 that "normalcy is the rule and [Arab] agitation the exception." Zionist leaders thus could not use the guise of "retaliation" to expel rural communities.[34] Increased attacks on Jewish convoys and settlements by Arab volunteers from neighboring states gave the Zionist leadership the rationale and opportunity to justify its occupation and expulsion policy. The Jewish leadership saw less and less need for a pretext for offensive operations. The new aggressive strategy against Palestinian Arabs on lands coveted for the Jewish state required "initiative" (*yotzma*), or taking action without waiting for a pretext for "retaliation" (*tagmul*).[35]

Meanwhile, according to British sources, the Revisionists were mounting a vigorous pressure campaign against the Haganah's policy of *havlaga* (restraint) "to secure popular support" for the IZL's adoption of "strong-arm retaliatory measures against the Arabs." Those included large-scale reprisals in the form of arson, murder, and bus attacks. Such actions were becoming increasingly popular among the yishuv as a result of the continuing disturbances.[36] The Revisionists warned that continued restraint "would entail catastrophic results for the yishuv since its only effect would be to encourage further Arab riots."[37]

Internal Zionist political rivalry also contributed to the Revisionists' adoption of aggressive retaliatory measures. The Revisionists believed that Ben-Gurion's refusal to admit them into the Haganah indicated his intention to exclude them from the future Jewish state government. The British expected the Revisionists "to make considerable political capital out of the Arab disturbances" and the Haganah's passive attitude to them. Many sections of the yishuv were increasing their criticism of the Haganah's response.[38] British military headquarters had predicted IZL activism as far back as November 1947: "There can be no doubt that should the Arabs attack the Jews, the IZL will take an active part in expelling them, but at the same time, if this threat should not materialize, the Irgun will continue to prove a thorn in the side of the Jewish Provisional Government, unless the Revisionists form a strong part of it."[39] Richard Crossman, a pro-Zionist member of Parliament, also warned that if Arab guerrilla attacks started, the IZL would "have to be restrained from massacring local Arabs."[40]

During its December 12, 1947, security conference, the Palestine government discussed the Zionists' changing offensive strategy, at least among the dissident groups. The government informed the Jewish Agency it was aware that "the IZL had often started attacks on Arabs" and that "the Jews were now attacking Arabs to gain reprisals for Arab attacks on Jews." High Commissioner General Sir Alan Cunningham insisted that the Jewish Agency "must cooperate with the Security Forces in eradicating the dissidents and that reprisal raids would not be tolerated."[41] Whether the Haganah was incapable of reining in the dissidents or simply chose not to do so, no restraint proved effective. Additionally, the British were increasingly unwilling or unable to maintain security because of the military's progressing evacuation and policy of nonintervention.

Intercommunal hit-and-run fighting escalated rapidly as December continued. On December 11, IZL members attacked Arabs at Shufat on Mount Scopus, and Arabs ambushed an armed Jewish supply convoy on the Jerusalem to Bethlehem road, killing ten Jews and injuring two. On December 12, the IZL carried out an attack on al-Tira village near Haifa, indiscriminately killing 12 villagers, including children and elderly, and injuring six. In another IZL attack on al-'Abbasiyya village near Jaffa on December 13, six villagers were killed and 36 were wounded. The same day, an IZL bombing near the Damascus Gate in Jerusalem killed four Arabs and one Jew, and wounded 15 Arabs and two Britons. The IZL freely admitted that it was "responsible for attacks on Arabs all over the country."[42]

Despite the escalating violence, the mandate government began turning over partial administrative control to local authorities to reduce its internal security commitments, confirming Britain's declining interest in governing. On December 15, British police evacuated Tel Aviv and handed over administration to Jewish forces. The Arab press criticized the British for implementing partition and also for not withdrawing from Arab areas and handing over self-administration to them as well. The early British pullout from Tel Aviv left the Arabs of Jaffa feeling vulnerable.[43] AHE Secretary Husayn al-Khalidi strongly protested the government's decision to withdraw British police forces from the Tel Aviv area. The pullout contradicted Cunningham's reassurances during their last meeting that the British would "maintain civil administration and police and security forces until the last moment," al-Khalidi argued. The Jews were "longing to disembark immigrants in the area dominated by them," he protested, warning that the British pullout would place 5,000 Arabs in this area "at the mercy of Jews."[44]

December 1947: The Beginning of Haganah Offensive Action

Zionist violence grew mainstream and systematic over the course of December 1947, escalating the civil conflict from spontaneous acts of violence to premeditated, sustained fighting. According to MacMillan, "the Haganah began the first of a series of Jewish attacks on Arab villages" when two lorry loads of armed Jews attacked Khisas village north of Lake Hula on December 18, 1947.[45] Haganah forces destroyed two houses, killed ten Arab villagers, including children, and wounded five. Scattered pamphlets claimed the raid was in reprisal for incidents in Hula and Safad.

The yishuv's two leading Arabists, Ezra Danin (from Jaffa) and Elias (Eliahu) Sasson (a Syrian native), "criticized various Haganah and Palmach operations, such as the one at Khisas[,] . . . which had unnecessarily 'spread the fire' to hitherto quiet areas of Palestine." Ben-Gurion had agreed to appoint Arab specialists like Danin and Sasson to advise the Haganah regional brigade headquarters, but Danin complained that the brigades rarely observed the Arabists' guidelines.[46] While Ben-Gurion attempted to placate the Arabists and the moderate elements of the yishuv, his military officers understood Ben-Gurion's thinking to be, as Ilan Pappé summarizes it, that "any military action, authorized or not, helped contribute to the expulsion of the 'strangers.'"[47]

Ben-Gurion summarized his view in a January 1 diary entry: "There is a need now for strong and brutal reaction. We need to be accurate about timing, place and those we hit. If we accuse a family—we need to harm them without mercy, women and children included. Otherwise, this is not an effective reaction. During the operation there is no need to distinguish between guilty and not guilty."[48]

By mid-December, as the security situation worsened, Cunningham observed that the situation had deteriorated into a "series of reprisals and counter-reprisals between Jews and Arabs in which many innocent lives are being lost." The tempo of violence, he feared, would accelerate: "I must state that the provocative action of the Jews and their admission that the Haganah is authorized to take what they call counter-action but what is in effect indiscriminate action against any Arabs, is hardly calculated to have a calming effect."[49]

By December 29, it was clear that the weight of attacks now emanated from Zionist forces. On that day, Chief Secretary Sir Henry Gurney told Golda Myerson (Meir), the acting director of the political department in Jerusalem, that the government "would not be able to enforce law and order as long as Jewish attacks on Arabs continued." Meyerson's response illustrates how the British unilateral abandonment policy enabled and rationalized the ensuing civil war, now in its formative phase. She said that the IZL and LHI, and now the Haganah, had given up on a policy of restraint "in view of continued Arab attacks and government inaction." She further complained that British measures to protect Jewish transportation were inadequate and ineffective. Myerson also protested that Jewish settlement police were not permitted to use armored cars on the roads, and arms were confiscated from the Jews, "on pretext that they were the attackers."[50] The yishuv widely believed that Britain allowed the hostilities to continue in order to "demonstrate that partition could not be implemented."

Gurney was annoyed—in light of past Zionist insurrections—that a Jewish Agency official complained of British failure to maintain law and order. At the same time, he conceded that British actions were inadequate for the country's needs. He wrote to his colleague John Martin in the Colonial Office: "It is in a sense fantastic for the Jews to be criticizing anybody for failing to maintain law and order (seeing that the one thing they have been doing successfully for years is breaking the law), but nevertheless I hope that the Army will soon feel able to do much more than they have been doing."[51]

To mitigate the increasingly dangerous situation, High Commissioner Cunningham suggested that the British government approach the Arab League to pressure the mufti to dissuade the local Arabs from further violence while the British still held the mandate. He believed the approach to the Arab League had to be matched by parallel pressure on the Jewish Agency. By mid-December 1947, it was becoming clear that the Haganah was now aggressively participating in the violence.

The Haganah maintained that "all the acts committed against the Arabs were carried out by the dissident groups." But both British and U.S. intelligence reports contradicted this assertion. Cunningham reported to London that the Haganah and dissident groups were working so closely together that "the [Jewish] Agency's claims that they cannot control the dissidents are inadmissible."[52] Ben-Gurion and his advisors had in fact approved a new policy of systematic intimidation on December 10, 1947.[53]

The Haganah now operated in the open and termed its military actions "aggressive self-defense." However, Cunningham stated, the number of killed and injured demonstrates that Zionist forces inflicted "many more casualties on the Arabs than the reverse." Furthermore—heralding a pattern of intimidation that would lead to Arab displacement—most of the casualties were innocent civilians purposely targeted. "Practically all the attacks have been against buses or in civilian centers," Cunningham reported to Colonial Secretary Arthur Creech Jones. Casualties on either side through December 14, a mere fortnight after the partition announcement, were 84 Jews killed, 155 injured, and 93 Arabs killed, 335 injured.

The Jewish leadership implemented a policy of indiscriminate violence against the Arabs to terrify them and render "help from the Arab world useless." Ezra Danin suggested "destroying the traffic (buses, lorries that carry agricultural products and private cars) . . . sinking their fishing boats in Jaffa, closing their shops and preventing raw materials from reaching their factories" to show the Arabs that their fate was sealed. Ben-Gurion summarized in a letter to Sharett that the new policy would put the Arabs "at our mercy," and the Jews could do whatever they wanted, including "starving them to death."[54]

For Ben-Gurion and his small group of advisors, the opportunity had come to implement an aggressive policy to achieve a Jewish majority state, which would be impossible without the forced transfer of the Arabs. Ben-Gurion approved a series of attacks on Arab villages to cause maximum damage and kill as many villagers as possible. "Every attack has to end with occupation, destruction, and expulsion," he stressed.[55] Palmach commander Yigal Allon concurred that "collective punishment" was required "even if there are children living in the [attacked] house."[56]

Cunningham was appalled by the Zionist reprisal attacks and the horror they engendered:

> It will be remembered that even though our own policy over the past two years has been based on the avoidance of reprisals against innocent Jews, we have never at any time on the slightest excuse escaped the vociferous and hysterical accusations of the Jews that we were a people who were prone to brutal reprisals. Now they themselves have come out with reprisals of a nature which would not even have crossed the mind of any soldier here, and which are an offence to civilization.[57]

The British military assessment of December 28, 1947, reflected concern over the deteriorating security countrywide. But the British government, instead of reconsidering its rapid hands-off withdrawal, chose to accelerate it. Cunningham wrote that his support for the military timetable of withdrawal and the May 15 deadline, apart from military necessity, was based mainly on his belief in the repeated assurances by representatives of the Arab Higher Committee (AHC) that "they would hold their hands against the Jews" until the British left Palestine. He had no doubt "the Arabs recognized that it was very much in their own interest to have a period of quiet during which they could organize themselves." Nevertheless, a much different situation presented itself from what the British had envisaged when they studied the problem of withdrawal. In the "face of Jewish provocation and reprisals," it was now evident to Cunningham that neither the Palestinian Arab leadership nor the Arab League could restrain the Palestinian Arabs.[58]

Cunningham believed that the disturbances would almost certainly continue until the British left and "of course beyond," and security forces could not "avoid becoming involved with both Jews and Arabs." Moreover, as Arabs were now attacking British ammunitions stocks in order to obtain weapons, it was "inevitable" that more "drastic action" would have to be taken against them. Still, British forces were hampered from "using the full rigor/vigor of the law" because of their focus on a low-casualty evacuation. Consequently, their authority continued to weaken. These factors supported the civil administration's termination as early as possible. While Cunningham would not yet say definitely in late December that the British could not "hold the situation," he recognized that it would "become increasingly difficult."[59]

The Reign of Terror in Palestine

Merely a month after the U.N. vote, the U.S. consulate general in Jerusalem wrote that "normal life" was disappearing. "Terror is prevalent," he said, and the situation one of "extreme uncertainty. . . . It is tragic that many of the present casualties comprise innocent and harmless people, going about their daily business. They are picked off while riding in buses, walking along the streets, and stray shots even find them while asleep in their beds."[60] From Jerusalem, Thomas Wasson, the U.S. consul general, observed that ever since the British announced their intention to give up the mandate, "their chief desire seems to be to prevent any organized warfare before their departure." As a result, strong-arm measures formerly characteristic of British occupation were no longer observed. Increasingly frequent outbreaks of violence were not stemmed by the police or army: "When the British interfere in local troubles, they seem to do so only if the violence is of such a nature as would seem to be capable of spreading. The British attitude seems to be one that is governed by a desire not to precipitate general trouble by interfering too much in local situations."[61]

In fact, the U.S. consul's observations were overly deferential to the British administration, whose policy was one of nonintervention except to protect the British evacuation. As British documents from the time overwhelmingly attest, their actions' effect on local conflict was not a decisive consideration.

Arab decision making proved hard for the British to read. Despite repeated assurances by the Arabs that "they were most anxious not to make trouble," Arab leaders appeared unable or unwilling to take firm steps to control disorder. Although the AHC did make efforts to stem the violence, the British suspected that these efforts were sabotaged by "certain individuals in Palestine acting independently."[62] Still, the British remained confident that the Arab states' armies would not march on Palestine as long as Britain held the mandate, "with the possible exception of the Hashemite bloc." Cunningham had always held the opinion, for military reasons alone, that the Arab armies did not have the training, the equipment, or the ammunition reserves "to maintain an army in the field far from their bases for any length of time, if at all."[63]

Although the British had predicted civil strife, they were caught off guard by how quickly the violence grew and were unprepared to commit the reinforcements to stop it.[64] In an attempt to stabilize the situation, the Palestine government tried to prevent arms-running across the frontier, but the British had never achieved an impenetrable frontier.

British representatives did try diplomacy to dissuade the Arab states from encouraging violence, at least before the British departure. "The provocative action of the Jews" made this task difficult. At the same time, Arab attacks on the railways and roads, primarily to steal weapons and ammunition, tended to delay the movement of stores, as well as the British troops' departure. The Arab League had "no clear idea of the outcome of its present action," which it undertook "merely to save face in view of past utterances," Cunningham surmised. He believed the Arab League accepted partition as unpreventable.[65]

Organized Internecine Strife

As 1948 began, GOC MacMillan reported that military "operations on both sides assumed a more organized shape."[66] The Arab Liberation Army (ALA) set up by Syria, ostensibly to defend Palestine and to thwart King Abdullah's plans to take over parts of Palestine, grew restive.[67] Under the command of Fawzi al-Qawuqji, a Lebanese veteran of the 1936–39 Arab rebellion, the ALA undertook "one or two abortive attacks on Jewish settlements."[68] The mixed cities of Jerusalem, Haifa, and Jaffa/Tel Aviv remained the chief centers of growing communal disorder, and conditions in Safad were also deteriorating. The rural districts were relatively quiet except for intermittent reprisal attacks. Bitterness between Arabs and Jews was increasing, as was blaming the British for a situation that was "becoming intolerable to both sides and most difficult for the police." Cunningham observed a paradox in the reaction created by the escalating strife:

> The outrages perpetrated by the Haganah and IZL in Jerusalem, Jaffa and Haifa, and the activities of Arab snipers and raiding bands, though they have deeply embittered feeling, have also revived in both communities a desire for peace. Dr. Khalidi's thoughts are for the moment only of defense against Jewish attack; the Arab[s] are not ready, and they know it. The Haganah on their side promise that they will stop shooting the moment the Arabs do so; they feel that such a truce would be only temporary, but are confident that they could use it to re-arm at an even greater rate than could the Arabs. The burning question is, who is to stop first?[69]

A climate of terror was evident even among government employees. About half of the British headquarters offices had not functioned since the end of December 1947 because the Palestinian staffs feared to venture near them. Although the employees were anxious to return to work, "every new outrage sends their heart into their boots."[70] The terrorist reprisal policy was being encouraged in internal yishuv publicity, with themes that would make internal restraint and criticism of the terrorizing violence difficult. The high commissioner observed that

Haganah actions are lauded in the press as operations of war, and the yi-shuv generally is being encouraged in an attitude of smug self-righteousness in a situation for which in fact Jews as well as Arabs are responsible. This atmosphere naturally favors the Jewish dissidents, whose publicity condemns Government apathy while pointing to its own deeds of daring as evidence that it is the dissidents alone who have the will and determination to defend the yishuv against Imperialism and the Arabs alike.[71]

On January 5, the terrorizing of civilian Arabs escalated dramatically. The Haganah, disguised in British uniforms, blew up the Semiramis Hotel in the wealthy, densely populated Arab quarter of Qatamon in Jerusalem, killing 12 Arabs and injuring two. The majority of the dead were civilian Christian Arabs, including women and children. The Spanish vice consul was also killed. According to Amina Rifai, a schoolteacher from Qatamon, "this incident alone caused half the residents, where we lived, to flee."[72] The bombing caused some embarrassment for the Haganah, which blew up the hotel on the grounds that it was the Iraqi volunteers' headquarters.[73] The British believed the Semiramis bombing was an "unauthorized venture," a view corroborated by the U.S. consulate in Jerusalem.

By this point, it was clear to outside observers that Zionists of all political leanings had taken the military initiative and moved into a more regular fighting posture. The U.S. consul characterized Zionist military operations, which the Jewish Agency termed "preventative defense," as offensive actions: "The blowing-up of the Old Serail in Jaffa (by the Stern Gang), the same type of action against the Semiramis Hotel in Jerusalem (by the Haganah), and the shooting of Arabs in Tireh Village (by the Irgun) are all examples of Jewish offensives. Such activities are designed, according to the Jews, to force the Arabs into a passive state."[74] In January 1948, the director of U.S. military intelligence also observed that "Jewish fighting was more or less defensive in character" for only about a month after the partition announcement—with the exception of the IZL's "punitive attacks on Arabs" and the LHI's attacks against the British: "Since the first of this year, however, Jewish forces have taken the offensive. Arab villages have been attacked; known Arab headquarters bombed; and Jewish forces are reported to be in a position to blockade the Arab city of Jaffa."[75]

The Zionist offensives had the intended effect on the Palestinian Arab civilian population. Terrorized by deliberate Zionist attacks, Palestinian

Arabs generally did not respond actively but migrated passively in search of safety, a behavior that increased with the fighting and intimidation. "If we had to deal only with the Palestine Arabs," Ben-Gurion confidently asserted in January 1948, "I think we could have already won the war." Haganah experts agreed with his assessment and reiterated this opinion in March.[76]

Open Organized Warfare

During the first large-scale skirmish of the civil war, approximately 1,000 Arabs gathered to attack the Kefar Etzion settlement on January 14. The fighting was provoked by Zionist forces sniping at an Iraqi consulate car driving along the road to Hebron.[77] The Arab forces retreated, not because of Zionist defense or the British military's arrival, but due to an order received by the AHC from the mufti to stop the attack. Still, the assault's failure showed the weakness of Arab military efforts. The British military observed that the Arabs' massive frontal attack on the Jewish colonies in the Hebron subdistrict demonstrated "the almost entire absence of existing co-ordination and organization" of the Arab war effort. Although the Arab press made "fantastic claims of a resounding success," it soon became known among the Arabs that the operation was "a most ignominious failure."[78]

British forces moved in to restore order on January 15 to prevent an escalation of hostilities along British lines of communication. Cunningham was relieved that the Kefar Etzion battle was "far less serious than it might have been." The Arab press sarcastically alluded to British intervention in the battle and "to the damage done to the Arabs by 'neutral' British forces protecting the Jews." The high commissioner was sensitive to Arab criticism, and he remained concerned about long-term Arab-British relations. He remarked on the constant danger "lest the necessity actively to protect Jewish colonies against Arab attack should attract Arab attentions." Still Cunningham framed his concerns in terms of mandate withdrawal policy, noting that anti-British sentiment would complicate the British evacuation through predominately Arab areas and damage future Anglo-Arab relations.[79]

As January 1948 progressed, organized fighting between the Jewish and Arab communities grew. Intercommunal strife had become "endemic" in the Shaykh Jarrah quarter of Jerusalem, the Wadi Rushmiyya area in Haifa, and the Manshiyya quarter of Jaffa, according to Cunningham. Husayn al-Khalidi and Emile al-Ghoury, of the AHE, feared the situation was "passing out of the control of the Arab Higher Executive" and regarded "the restoration of order in the large towns as being of the first importance and urgency." By the end of January, Arab losses in Haifa were already estimated at £2 million.[80] Cunningham observed that "nothing but drastic military intervention" could have restored the situation in those areas. "Even if it were politically desirable" to intervene in intercommunal fighting, Cunningham was dependent on the military to determine whether there were "enough troops in Palestine to undertake such severe action."[81]

Elsewhere, sniping and minor incidents were common, and attributed "to panic as much as to deliberate aggression."[82] Hints of the actual or potential power of psychological warfare prevailed. One of the most difficult obstacles to restoring normalcy was "the apparently ineradicable fear which permeates both communities," which Cunningham attributed to the provocation of rumors and "ill-considered action."[83]

The high commissioner was acutely aware of the effects of the collapse of civil government and military security, as seen in his correspondence with his superiors. On January 19, he informed Colonial Secretary Creech Jones that "law and order is not being maintained" and "British prestige is diminishing daily," which was negatively affecting the British community's morale in Palestine. Was the British government "prepared to accept this position until May 15th?" Cunningham asked.[84] Existing and subsequent decision making, documented by the contemporary record, shows that the answer was yes.

British Decisions Contribute to Further Chaos

In addition to the British military's nonintervention policy, the British government chose not to cooperate with the U.N. commission charged with implementing partition. Thus chaos burgeoned in the absence of clear authority in Palestine. The British U.N. representative, Sir Alexander Cadogan, announced on January 14 that the British government would agree to the U.N. commission's arrival in Palestine to provide some overlap, but only shortly before the mandate's termination. Fearing a violent

Arab reaction, the British agreed to its arrival only a fortnight before the British departure on May 15, during which time the commission would be permitted to assume its responsibilities.[85] The Palestinian Arabs had made it clear that the commission's arrival "would be the signal for their full armed revolt."[86] The mandate's response further evaded responsibility for government and security continuity: Britain would not provide security, accommodations, or transportation to the U.N. commission once it arrived in Palestine. That decision, in effect, guaranteed the commission's inability to operate.

Chief Secretary Gurney predicted that the U.N. commissioners would no doubt "seek to hide their failure behind our unwillingness to have them in Palestine before the 1st May." Mandate officials realized that without a military force to implement partition, the U.N. commission "could have done nothing" in the midst of a civil war.[87] By choosing a course of military and political abandonment, British authorities consciously accepted chaos and conflict. The Zionists and Arabs no doubt also realized that the U.N. commission was unlikely to implement partition in a two-week period, and that the fate of the country would depend on their own resources. Each community, therefore, continued its campaign to establish the Jewish state or to prevent partition.

The British also set a date to terminate remaining operative authority. This was based on several considerations. The deteriorating situation in Haifa caused grave concern, because it could seriously affect the operation of the railway network and therefore the withdrawal of British troops. Furthermore, work interruptions at the Haifa oil refinery resulted in severe economic disruptions. Cunningham himself admitted at January's end that the civil administration had "no object, not much function and very little authority." Still, he would not be the one to say it could not go on.[88]

Military considerations finally decided the matter. GOC MacMillan sent an amended withdrawal plan to London, as he felt "it would be wrong for the soldiers to press for the maintenance of the civil government beyond March 31st."[89] After this date, he believed the military would be unable to maintain the situation at any level. Zionist forces launched countrywide military offensive operations under the framework of Haganah Plan D after March 31, indicating that the Jewish leadership knew the British military no longer felt it could maintain control after April began.

To avoid "divided control," the mandate government did not contemplate a "progressive transfer" of its general authority to any party, including local Jews and Arabs,[90] thus effectively preventing the formation of replacement security forces. Armed Jewish or Arab militias were not permitted to be openly established before the mandate ended. Accordingly, the communities' military and security apparatuses were not subject to public accountability either locally or internationally.[91] For example, potential sources for professional Arab militia, including the Arab Legion, the Transjordan Frontier Force, and the Palestine Police force, which combined Arab and Jewish members, were moved away or disbanded before May 15. Ahmad Tell, an Arab Legion officer, wrote that it could be suggested that, despite its technical legal correctness, the British insistence on the Arab Legion's withdrawal, when it could have served to maintain order, "led to the ruin of a large part of Jerusalem."[92]

Because organized Arab security forces depended more on external organization—British or Transjordanian—the lack of transitional bodies meant effectively abandoning protection of Palestine's Arabs. Further, the Arab Legion tended to act in a more restrained fashion than either Arab militia or Jewish Agency forces. Arab Legion units in Palestine had been employed only on static guard and escort duties and not sent to quell communal disorders. Jewish Agency allegations that Arab Legion forces fired on Jewish convoys passing Arab Legion camps were investigated "and in no instance," the British told the United Nations, was it established the Arab Legion fired first.[93] But this did not lead the British to disband or disarm the Jewish Agency's military force, the Haganah, or any Zionist dissident organization.

Cunningham's public warnings that armed aggression prior to the mandate's termination would be resisted by force were undermined by his own addendum: "provided of course that the administration has not withdrawn from the area attacked."[94] Thus, as evacuation proceeded, warnings were less of a deterrent to both communities. British policy discussions make clear that as British troops prepared to withdraw into their final Haifa enclave, they were not so much transferring areas of Palestine to new local or international control as abandoning them to whichever side established its presence by sheer firepower. Given their superior organization, Zionist forces were more likely to exploit the British noninterventionist evacuation and the British forces' dissipating strength. Further, the Arabs' efforts to escalate their threats and military strength in the face of the growing British absence would ultimately backfire, provoking Zionist advances and intimidation.

Infiltration of Arab Volunteers

To serve as a counterforce to the Zionist militia, volunteer units composed of Palestinian Arabs and Arabs from neighboring states, which were sponsored by the AHC and the Arab League, began infiltrating the borders in January 1948. Cunningham observed the overall effect of this development: "It seems likely that a new phase of the Arab-Jewish struggle is about to begin, with foreign trained guerrilla forces doing the bulk of the attacking and the local Arabs (apart from more or less permanent bands under such leaders as Abdul Qadur Husseini and Hassan Salameh which will continue to act on the offensive against the easier objectives) being relegated to the defensive role for which they are better fitted."[95]

The first large-scale entry of Arab volunteers occurred as early as January 9, 1948, when 250 to 300 Syrians crossed the frontier and attacked the Jewish settlements of Kefar Dan and Kefar Szold.[96] Cunningham believed this force also carried out an intense attack on the Yechiam settlement on January 20 using mortars, heavy automatic weapons, and rifles, with settler casualties of eight killed and eight wounded. A second band of some 700 Syrian soldiers, believed to be part of Fawzi al-Qawuqji's command, entered Palestine during the night of January 20–21 via Transjordan. Although King Abdullah exacted assurances that this band would remain passive in central Palestine until the mandate ended, Cunningham doubted public opinion would allow a well-equipped portion of the ALA to do nothing "while local Arabs get the worst of it in Jaffa, Haifa, and Jerusalem and while villages bear the brunt of Jewish reprisals."[97]

Arab volunteers continued to infiltrate Palestine as January progressed. During the last week of January, a force of 200 to 300 men, believed to be led by a German officer, established itself in Acre and Safad.[98] In early February, British forces encountered a group of Syrian volunteers from Idlib, a village southwest of Aleppo. Some of them had enlisted only 14 days before entering Palestine. Their orders were "to attack Jewish convoys and to disrupt Jewish communications," but they had also received strict instructions not to engage British military or police vehicles and personnel. "They seemed to have little or no idea of the geography of the country, and obviously intended [on] relying on local guides" for their operations, the Sixth Airborne reported.[99]

The Arab volunteers would ultimately prove a liability to the Palestinian Arab cause, as well as a political and military complication for the mandate government. They generated three difficulties: destabilization of "the already difficult problem of maintaining law and order"; embarrassment for Great Britain before the United Nations; and complications in British-Arab relations. Cunningham warned London that it was ill-advised to be concerned "with the precarious maintenance of day-to-day good relations with the Arab governments" rather than with the prevention of events that could have potentially disastrous results for British relations with the entire Arab world. Preventing Arab incursions into Palestine early, he argued, would be preferable to large-scale military engagements at the frontier with Arabs from several Arab states and the resultant political repercussions with those states and in Palestine. Cunningham requested that London apply the strongest possible pressure on the Arab League to secure the withdrawal of the Arab bands that had entered Palestine.[100]

The British government did not take up the cause. While the mandate government's ostensible goal of maintaining security in Palestine was officially pronounced by the British government, London was anxious at the same time to maintain good relations with all Arab states for strategic, economic, and defense purposes, and would not go so far as to directly confront or censure the Arab states over Palestine. In fact, the Colonial Office took a favorable view of Arab infiltration, which might benefit its protégé King Abdullah of Transjordan, or at least enable a peaceful transfer of power to a friendly or stable Arab authority. The Colonial Office viewed the buildup of Arab militia dispersed in Samaria as a precursor to a "fairly peaceful transfer to Abdullah's authority," or possibly Syrian control, as soon as the British pulled out.[101] London's policy was at odds with the day-to-day realities in Palestine, and this dissonance contributed to further destabilization.

The United Nations was also concerned with Arab volunteer forces and the escalating violence in Palestine. Embarrassed British representatives responded to U.N. queries about the "infiltration of non-Palestinians" by characterizing and downplaying these forces as "irregular formations and not organized units of any national armed force." Among themselves, the British acknowledged that the Arab infiltrators were "armed and organized bands," but they minimized their destabilizing effect and defended British efforts to control the entry of both Arab infiltrators through the land frontiers and Jewish illegal immigrants by sea.[102] Security forces were increasingly unsuccessful in interdicting either Arab or Jewish infiltration, especially as Britain abandoned aggressive control of illegal immigration. On February 11, as 50 Arab volunteers crossed the Damiyyah Bridge into Palestine, the ship *Jerusalem the Besieged* arrived in Haifa with 678 illegal Jewish immigrants.[103]

The competing territorial aspirations of Syria, Transjordan, and the mufti exacerbated the already obvious lack of coordination among the infiltrating Arab bands.[104] At its February 4 meeting in Damascus, the Arab League military committee had divided Palestine into three operational zones. The northern front comprised the Galilee and was under the command of Adib Shishakli (who later became president of Syria). The Negev made up the southern front and was under Egyptian command. 'Abd al-Qadir al-Husayni commanded the Jerusalem area, and the Husayni influence also dominated Jerusalem and Jaffa.[105] Jordanian Major Wasfi al-Tal observed that Palestine was divided into military areas for "party political, local, and familial considerations," and not for military purposes.[106]

The Sixth Airborne considered the Arab irregulars in northern Palestine "comparatively well-disciplined" and viewed their intervention as a stabilizing influence, at least in the Nablus-Jinin-Tulkarm triangle.[107] In contrast, King Abdullah remarked, "every Arab criminal in the Mid-East was pouring" into Palestine. He believed that some of the infiltrators were creating chaos and some were mercenaries merely seeking loot.[108]

The infiltrating Arab forces caused considerable consternation for the Zionist leadership. The British army's First Guards Brigade, based in Bayt Lid, observed in its February 10 intelligence report that the main concern of the yishuv in the Samaria district was to know what was "going on in the hills. . . . The Jewish Agency spoke in easy terms of the mythical Arab rabble and its complete lack of organization and strength. Since then, they learn daily of a well equipped force infiltrating into the country. 'We must fight or die' is the new attitude and no more 'We shall push Tulkarm into Nablus and Nablus over the Jordan river.'"[109]

The civil war escalated a new order of magnitude as February progressed. The First Guards Brigade saw major preparations under way and growing violence, particularly against Arab villages. Militarily, both Jews and Arabs were "feverishly preparing themselves" in early February, the brigade observed. While the ALA was "still entering the country at various points," the Haganah had been "intensifying attacks on Arab strongholds and transport," and the IZL and LHI "perpetrated rather vicious attacks on Arab villages and transport." Arab affairs experts reported to the Jewish leadership that rural Palestine "showed no desire to fight or attack, and was defenseless." Ben-Gurion counseled "to continue to terrorize the rural areas . . . through a series of offensives . . . so that the same mood of passivity reported . . . would prevail."[110] Psychological warfare was observed to be deliberately employed by the Zionist side to widen the conflict. The First Guards believed that "by attacking Arab villages, disguised as British soldiers," Zionist forces hoped "to start an all-out anti-British offensive by the Arabs so as to draw the British Army on their [Jewish] side."[111]

The increasingly organized violence hastened the collapse of British military control. In late February 1948, the First Guards admitted that it was "now practically impossible to control the number of Arab "fighters entering the country." A proportion of these Arabs permanently reinforced existing garrisons, while other parties came in "to execute a raid and leave the country" when that particular fight was over.[112] For Cunningham, the Arab infiltration was a "grave embarrassment" and a political as well as a military problem. "They are just as much illegal immigrants as the Jews whom the Arabs have constantly clamored for us to stop," he said.[113] Gurney made the same observation from the opposite perspective and one which better reflected the almost fatalistic indifference of prevailing British policy: "These Arab incursions are no more illegal than the Jewish immigration and importation of arms which have been the policy of the Jewish Agency for years."[114]

Azzam Pasha justified the infiltration of Arab forces by arguing that this "was intended to counter-balance organized Jewish forces."[115] The Arab forces were composed of a higher proportion of Palestine-born than was the Haganah, he added.[116] According to Cunningham, Arab morale rose sharply as a result of the Arab reinforcements, the "spectacular success of the Hebronites in liquidating a Haganah column near Surif," and the Arab National Guard's capture and dismantling of a Jewish van filled with explosives intended for detonation in an Arab locality: "Even the severe losses of life and damage to property caused by Jewish reprisals have failed to check a revival of confidence on the part of the fellahin [peasants] and the urban proletariat."[117] Nevertheless, the uptick in morale was far from universal, and the fear generated by reprisals continued. "The panic of the middle classes persists," Cunningham observed, "and there is a steady exodus of those who can afford to leave the country."[118] As fighting escalated, that increased confidence would ebb, and fear and panic would return in greater measure.

Beginning of the Arab Exodus

The Palestinian Arab exodus began mainly from the cities, especially Jerusalem, Haifa, and Jaffa, which had suffered most severely from heavy night fighting, mortar actions, and daily explosions. According to the Sixth Airborne Division, the evacuation was "by no means confined only to the lower classes" or the panicky middle class. Members of leading families were leaving Jerusalem.[119] The Haganah's indiscriminate attacks on Palestinian Arab civilians, including women and children, intimidated them into moving to safer areas of the city, to their native villages, or to neighboring countries.

Palestinian Arab leaders did not encourage the displacement. British military observers recorded that the AHE was "becoming very perturbed by the large number of Arab families leaving the Arab areas." The mufti ordered them to return, and if they refused, he warned that their houses would be occupied "by other Arabs sent to reinforce the areas."[120] The mufti also wrote the prime minister of Egypt on March 8 that the exodus would "adversely affect the national movement, reflect badly on the Palestine Arabs, and create conditions which will weaken Arab morale in adjacent Arab territories in their defense of Palestine."[121] Arab League committee members told Palestinian Arab refugees arriving in Egypt by rowboat that they would be trained in the Egyptian army and sent back to Palestine to fight. The mufti stated that the AHC had resolved that "no Palestinian should be permitted to leave the country except under special circumstances." The AHC, in consultation with local committees, would determine valid reasons for departure, which had to be presented to Arab governments' consular officers before exit visas would be issued.

Not only did the mufti attempt to stem the exodus, he also wrote to Arab leaders asking them to return those who had already sought refuge abroad.

There are at present time resident in the adjacent Arab countries a number of Palestinians who left Palestine as soon as Arab defense operations commenced. The national interest demands that these persons should return to Palestine to carry out their obligations according to their abilities and each in his own sphere. . . . The Arab Higher Committee requests that their residence permits should not be renewed and that they should be returned to Palestine, except in cases where it is found that there are health or other extenuating circumstances for them to stay.[122]

The AHC's actions and proposals were not effectively enforced.

In Jerusalem, many Jews under siege wished to leave the Old City. The Haganah, "considering no doubt that any large-scale exodus would have a demoralizing effect both locally and on world Jewry," forcibly prevented Jewish families from leaving the city.[123] Jewish authorities also decided that "no settlement, however isolated or vulnerable," would be evacuated, although women and children were removed from some areas. If the Jewish Agency had evacuated the settlements, the British observed, the right wing and the IZL would have made "great capital out of it."[124]

The pace and brutality of Arab and Jewish attacks increased in February 1948. Frequent Arab attacks on British troops and police were geared to obtaining arms, but also due to hypervigilance to psychological warfare. To preserve the element of surprise, Zionist forces often wore British uniforms to conduct offensive actions, particularly in rural areas. The explosion at the *Palestine Post* newspaper office in Jerusalem on February 1, which killed one and injured 20 Jews, greatly alarmed the Zionist leaders, who blamed the British. Thereafter, the Haganah intensified its policy of reprisal, "scarcely troubl[ing] to conceal its indifference to casualties thereby caused to noncombatants," Cunningham observed.[125] On February 15, the main Arab attack on the Jewish settlement of Tirat Zvi by ALA members based in the Jinin subdistrict was aborted because of a rare intervention by British forces. The curtailed attack nevertheless resulted in 44 Arabs known dead and about the same number wounded. Jewish casualties, on the other hand, were one dead and one injured. The Arab press "claimed a great victory" with Arab occupation of Tirat Zvi and claimed that 200 Jews had been killed. The high commissioner observed: "Such distortion of the truth by both Jewish and Arab press is now the rule, though the former is rather more artistic in its manipulation of the facts."[126]

The Sixth Airborne reported that the Arab attack failed when the Arabs lost the element of surprise and employed poor tactical troop deployment—all frontal attacks by "badly trained men" and without adequate covering fire. The report concluded that "this attack has proved conclusively that Jewish settlement defense[s] are adequate enough to withstand large scale attacks" when artillery was not employed.[127]

In an effort to "disrupt the flow of Arab reinforcements," the Haganah attempted to blow up the Shaykh Husayn bridge, destroyed road culverts at Metulla, and blew up a number of houses and their occupants in Khirbat Sa'sa' village. Yigael Yadin ordered the midnight attack on Sa'sa'. Palmach's Third Battalion, led by Moshe Kalman, dynamited one house after another, each with its sleeping inhabitants. Thirty-five homes were demolished and 60 to 80 villagers killed in the attack. Ben-Gurion had been unhappy with the limited scope of operations; he envisioned terror on a grander scale: "A small reaction [to Arab hostility] does not impress anyone. A destroyed house—nothing. Destroy a neighborhood, and you begin to make an impression!" Ben-Gurion approved of the Sa'sa' attack because it caused "the Arabs to flee."[128]

Zionist expectations of an international force materializing to enforce partition were dissipating. Nevertheless, yishuv confidence was buoyed by Jewish Agency statements that the Haganah could "hold its own unaided." Jewish mobilization was proceeding, and registration was extended to Jews abroad aged 17 to 25. The Jewish Agency was exerting "strenuous efforts to prevent [Jewish] departures from Palestine."[129]

Escalation: Bombing and Offensives

The U.S. consul general in Jerusalem, Robert Macatee, wrote on February 9 that in "two brief months" since the U.N. vote, "more than one thousand persons are reported to have lost their lives, and more than two thousand have been wounded. . . . One should remember that these casualties have occurred with the British still doing a considerable amount of interfering in Arab-Jewish melées."[130] At the same time, Macatee conceded the long-term trend: the Palestine government was in "a state of disintegration." Vital services were interrupted for long periods because of disturbances in the neighborhoods of government offices and "due to the unwillingness of local Jews and Arabs to work together." In Jerusalem no day passed without shooting or incidents; rifle and machine gunfire and heavy explosions in central Jerusalem were commonplace, even in daytime.[131]

The situation in Jerusalem became far worse after the Ben Yehuda Street bombing on February 20, which was planned by Arab forces and executed by British deserters who sided with the Arabs. Fifty-two Jews were killed and 123 injured. Everything else in Palestine was "overshadowed," the high commissioner noted. After surveying the destruction, Ben-Gurion noted in his diary that he could not forget that "'our' thugs and murderers had blazed this trail in Haifa [blowing up a police station], at the King David [government secretariat bombing], the Goldshmidt House [explosion at the British officers' club] and elsewhere." He could not help remembering, he said, that "the Jews were the first to do this [bombings]."[132]

The Jewish Agency attributed the explosion to British security forces, and a wave of dissident reprisals ensued against British servicemen, including the murder of a British soldier in a Jewish hospital.[133] Jewish leaders feared the demoralizing effect on the yishuv if it became known that Arabs were capable of such devastating operations.[134] Arabs claimed responsibility for the attack in retaliation for a Jewish bomb in al-Ramla. Tensions induced by the bombing increased the number and severity of attacks throughout the country. The British noted a marked tendency on both sides to resort to heavier weapons such as mortars.[135]

Politically, the Haganah's "increasingly virile role in defending the yishuv" contributed to its increased popularity in relation to the IZL, in Palestine and in the United States.[136] The Haganah let it be known that it was going on the offensive, according to Cunningham's February 23 report.[137] The British believed this was due to the steadily growing Arab strength and the Haganah's hope that the ALA would be provoked into large-scale actions involving clashes with the British army.

The high commissioner was becoming firmer in his views on the outcome of the war. He had been one of the few to consider, initially, the possibility of Arab success on the battlefield. But as events unfolded, he saw little sign of any Arab state's "intending at any time to exert [its] full military strength" in the fighting. "Apart from the blowings-up," the Arab operations were "lamentable from a military point of view," he wrote. The Arabs should have been "able to paralyze the Jews[,] who depend entirely on open communication," he wrote. The Arabs were lacking in military sense and could not prevent partition of some sort, even if no international military force implemented it, he predicted—correctly—in late February 1948.[138] What had begun as localized riots, unsuppressed by the mandate, escalated into what the Austro-Jewish philosopher Martin Buber described as "the strangest war in history. . . . There are three participants, all occupying the same territory, and one of them is fighting both for and against the other two. There are no battle lines, and when two of the participants are fighting they do not know, when the third comes along, whether he will stop them, join one side or the other, or amuse himself by shooting at both."[139]

❧

1. Izzat Tannous, *The Palestinians: Eyewitness History of Palestine under British Mandate* (New York: IGT, 1988), 470.
2. "Peril in Palestine," *Times* (London), April 10, 1948.
3. TNA WO 275/79, 17th Airborne Field Security Section, no. 56, December 3, 1947.
4. Ibid.
5. ISA, David Ben-Gurion: Speech at meeting of Executive Committee of General Federation of Jewish Labor in Palestine, December 3, 1947, no. 8, 21. NACP 38/370/15/5/2, Macatee, American Consulate General Jerusalem, no. 518, November 11, 1947.
6. Zeev Tzur, *From the Partition Dispute to the Allon Plan* (Tel Aviv, 1982); quoted in Flapan, *Birth of Israel*, 22.
7. Nicholas Bethell, *The Palestine Triangle* (New York: G. P. Putnam's Sons, 1979), 354.
8. TNA CO 537/3899, CID HQ, Jerusalem, to Chief Secretary, December 12, 1947. Account of Revisionists' meeting in Tel Aviv, December 6, 1947.
9. Ibid.
10. NACP ORE 55, CIA: The Consequences of the Partition of Palestine, November 28, 1947.
11. NACP 84/35061/23/4–5, Memorandum of Conversation between Secretary General of the Arab League Azzam Pasha and First Secretary of U.S. Embassy, Cairo Philip W. Ireland, enclosure 1, no. 83, January 30, 1948.
12. See chap. 3 regarding Zionist offensive plans formulated in 1938 after the Peel Commission recommended partition and population transfer.
13. The AHE was created at the Arab League's June 1946 conference in Bludan, Syria. It consisted of Vice-Chairman Jamal al-Husayni (the chairmanship was left vacant for the mufti), Secretary Husayn al-Khalidi, Hilmi Pasha, and Emile al-Ghoury.
14. TNA WO 275/79, 17th Airborne Field Security Section, no. 56, December 3, 1947. LCP, Emile al-Ghoury interview.
15. TT, Palestinian Arab research notes by Nigel Maslin, Jerusalem, April 1977. Interview with Farid Assad of Jinin.
16. Major R. D. Wilson, *Cordon and Search: With Sixth Airborne Division in Palestine* (Aldershot, U.K.: Gale and Polden, 1949), 155.
17. TNA WO 275/64, Sixth Airborne Division, no. 56, November 22–December 5, 1947. See also Wilson, *Cordon and Search*, 155.
18. MacMillan Report, 10.
19. TNA WO 275/64, Sixth Airborne Division, no. 56, November 22–December 5, 1947.

20. Lynne Reid Banks, *Torn Country: An Oral History of the Israeli War of Independence* (New York: Franklin Watts, 1982), 15.

21. TNA WO 275/64, Sixth Airborne Division, no. 56, November 22–December 5, 1947.

22. Interviews with Abu Yusuf and Umm Yusuf of Dayr Yasin, www.badil.org.

23. TNA WO 275/64, Sixth Airborne Division, no. 56, November 22–December 5, 1947.

24. TNA CO 537/3899, CID HQ, Palestine Police, Jerusalem to Chief Secretary, December 4, 1947. The Haganah was rumored to be not altogether displeased with the Jewish merchants' losses in Jerusalem. Many were Sephardic Jews who refused to contribute to the yishuv's emergency security fund; MacMillan Report, Diary of Events 1947, 17.

25. Ibid.

26. Wilson, *Cordon and Search*, 155.

27. TNA CO 537/3899, CID HQ, Palestine Police, Jerusalem, to Chief Secretary, December 4, 1947.

28. Dov Joseph, *The Faithful City: The Siege of Jerusalem* (New York: Simon and Schuster, 1960), 34.

29. TNA CO 537/3899, CID HQ, Palestine Police, Jerusalem, to Chief Secretary, December 4, 1947.

30. ISA, Yogev, D. Ben-Gurion: Speech at meeting of Executive Committee of General Federation of Jewish Labor in Palestine, December 3, 1947, no. 8, 21, and D. Ben-Gurion (Tel Aviv) to members of the Agricultural Center, December 4, 1947, no. 12, 26.

31. TNA WO 275/64, Sixth Airborne Division, HQ Palestine, no. 56, December 6, 1947.

32. NACP 84/350/63/11/5–6, Secretary of State to American Legation Beirut, Lebanon, December 5, 1947.

33. Morris, *Birth*, 31.

34. HA 205/9; cited in Pappé, *Ethnic Cleansing of Palestine*, 52n26.

35. Pappé, *Ethnic Cleansing of Palestine*, 50–52.

36. TNA CO 537/3899, CID HQ, Jerusalem, to Chief Secretary, December 12, 1947.

37. Ibid.

38. Ibid.

39. TNA WO 261/57, HQ British Troops in Palestine, no. 54, November 8, 1947.

40. NACP 38/370/15/5/2, London Embassy to Secretary of State, "Implementation of U.N. Decision on Palestine as Source of Bloodshed and Social Upheaval in Arab World," December 11, 1947.

41. CP IV/1/102, Minutes of Security Conference, December 12, 1947.

42. TNA WO 275/64, Sixth Airborne Division, no. 56, December 20, 1947.

43. Ibid.

44. FBIS, "British Troop Withdrawal Protested," Cairo, Egyptian Home Service in Arabic, December 10, 1947.

45. MacMillan Report, 10.

46. KMA–Yisrael Galili Papers, Protocol of the Meeting on "Shem" [Arab] Affairs, January 1–2, 1948, Yisrael Galili to brigades, January 18, 1948, and CZA S25/426, Protocol of a Meeting of the Political Department, March 25, 1948; cited in Ian Black and Benny Morris, *Israel's Secret Wars* (New York: Grove Weidenfeld, 1991), 51–52.

47. Pappé, *Ethnic Cleansing of Palestine*, 69.

48. Ibid., n. 62, Ben-Gurion, Diary, January 1, 1948.

49. CP II/3/149, Cunningham to Creech Jones, no. 2437, December 15, 1947.

50. ISA, G. Meyerson meeting with Sir Henry Gurney, Jerusalem, December 29, 1947, no. 85, December 31, 1947, 116.

51. TNA CO 967/102, Gurney to Martin, December 24, 1947.

52. CP II/3/149, Cunningham to Creech Jones, no. 2437, December 15, 1947. See also Stockwell papers file 26. NACP 319/270/6/15/4, Memo for the Chief of Staff; Intelligence Division Special Briefing. Planned Partition of Palestine Encountering Serious Obstacles, January 27, 1948. S. J.

Chamberlin, Lieutenant General, GSC, Director of Intelligence.

53. Pappé, *Ethnic Cleansing of Palestine*, 55.

54. Ben-Gurion, Diary, December 11, 1947, and letter to Moshe Sharett, G. Yogev, Documents, December 1947–May 1948, 60; cited in Pappé, *Ethnic Cleansing of Palestine*, 54n30.

55. Danin testimony for Bar-Zohar, 680n60; cited in Pappé, *Ethnic Cleansing of Palestine*, 64.

56. Pappé, *Ethnic Cleansing of Palestine*, 64–65.

57. CP II/3/149, Cunningham to Creech Jones, no. 2437, December 15, 1947. See also Stockwell papers file 26.

58. CP IV/5/68, Cunningham's appreciation of Palestine situation, December 28, 1947.

59. Ibid.

60. NACP 84/350/61/34/4–5, Wasson, American Consulate General, Jerusalem, December 31, 1947.

61. Ibid.

62. CP II/3/149, Cunningham to Creech Jones, no. 2437, December 15, 1947.

63. CP IV/5/68, Cunningham's appreciation of Palestine situation, December 28, 1947.

64. CP II/3/161, Cunningham to Creech Jones, no. 2517, December 18, 1947.

65. Ibid.

66. MacMillan Report, 10.

67. TNA FO 371/61583/E12129, Amman to FO, September 24, 1947; cited in Tal, "Forgotten War," 8n23.

68. Ibid.

69. CP III/1/15, Cunningham to Creech Jones, no. 15, January 10, 1948.

70. Ibid.

71. Ibid.

72. "Memories of Palestine," interview with Amina Rifai from Jerusalem, *Guardian*, May 15, 1976.

73. NACP 84/350/61/34/4–5, Wasson to Marshall, no. 43, January 12, 1948, and no. 67, January 19, 1948, and Macatee to Marshall, no. 26, January 7, 1948. Milstein, *History of Israel's War of Independence*, 3:89.

74. NACP 84/350/61/34/4–5, Macatee to Marshall, February 9, 1948.

75. NACP 319/270/6/15/4, Chief of Staff, Intelligence Division Special Briefing. Planned Partition of Palestine Encountering Serious Obstacles, January 27, 1948, S. J. Chamberlin, Lt. General, GSC, Director of Intelligence.

76. IDFA, 922/75/595, Guidelines for Plans in Case of [British] Evacuation, unsigned document from late December 1974; LPA 25/48, Ben-Gurion's speech in Mapai Center, January 8, 1948; HA 80/50/21, Ezra Danin's assessment, protocol of a meeting on Arab affairs, January 1–2, 1948; BGA, Memoranda Files, Ben-Gurion to Shertok and Meyerson, March 14, 1948; cited in Tal, "Forgotten War," 12n40.

77. MacMillan Report, Diary of Events 1948, 21.

78. CP III/1/23, Cunningham to Creech Jones, no. 113, January 16, 1948.

79. Ibid.

80. CP III/1/60, Cunningham to Creech Jones, no. 252, February 2, 1948.

81. CP III/1/33, Cunningham to Creech Jones, no. 128, January 19, 1948.

82. CP III/1/23, Cunningham to Creech Jones, no. 113, January 16, 1948.

83. Ibid.

84. CP III/1/33, Cunningham to Creech Jones, no. 128, January 19, 1948.

85. CP III/1/45, Creech Jones to Cunningham, no. 235, January 21, 1948.

86. GP folio 1/1, April 9, 1948.

87. Ibid.

88. CP IV/1/85, Cunningham to J. M. Martin, CO, January 24, 1948.

89. Ibid.

90. CP III/1/41, High Commissioner to U.K. Delegate, New York, no. 180, January 23, 1948.

91. Ibid.

92. Ahmad Tell, "The Battle of Old Jerusalem in 1948," part 1, www.jerusalemites.org/ahmad.html. Ahmad Tell served as an officer in the Arab Legion from 1946 to 1950 and fought in the Arab-Israeli war. His brother, Major Abdullah Tell, commanded the Arab Legion forces in Jerusalem.

93. UN 0453/0003, Communications from U.K. Delegation, U.K./1-U.K./79, January–March 1948, Note: Incursions of Armed Arab Bands into Palestine, U.K./64, March 12, 1948.

94. CP III/1/41, High Commissioner to U.K. Delegate, New York, no. 180, January 23, 1948.

95. CP III/1/51, Cunningham to Creech Jones, no. 113, January 24, 1948.

96. TNA WO 275/64, Sixth Airborne Division, no. 37–67, March 1947–May 1948.

97. CP III/1/51, Cunningham to Creech Jones, no. 113, January 24, 1948; TNA WO 275 64, Sixth Airborne, HQ Palestine, no. 37–67, March 1947–May 1948.

98. CP III/1/51, Cunningham to Creech Jones, no. 113, January 24, 1948.

99. TNA WO 275/60, Sixth Airborne Division Intelligence Summaries, nos. 37–68, April 1947–March 1948

100. CP III/1/76–77, Cunningham to Creech Jones, no. 288, February 4, 1948.

101. CP VI/1/82, J. M. Martin to Cunningham, February 12, 1948.

102. UN DAG 13/3.1.0.3 (S-0453 0003), U.N. Palestine Commission 3, Communication from the U.K. Delegation U.K./1-U.K./79, January–March 1948. Memorandum to President Dr. Ting Fu Tsiang, President, Security Council, UN from V. G. Lawford for Sir Alexander Cadogan.

103. Ibid.

104. CP III/1/60, Cunningham to Creech Jones, no. 252, February 1, 1948.

105. Safwat Report, 65. MacMillan Report, Diary of Events 1948, 25. CP IV/1/94, Cunningham to Creech Jones, no. 372, February 14, 1948.

106. Abu Nowar, *Jordanian-Israeli War, 1948-1951,* 14. Major Gen. Maan Abu Nowar served in the Arab Legion from 1943 to 1972.

107. TNA WO 275/64, Sixth Airborne Division, HQ Palestine, no. 58, January 11–28, 1948.

108. CP VI/1/84, Alan Cunningham to J. M. Martin, CO, record of conversation with Rabbi Silver and King Abdullah, February 2, 1948.

109. TNA WO 261/189, First Guards Brigade QHR, March 31, 1948.

110. Ben-Gurion, Diary, February 19, 1948; cited in Pappé, *Ethnic Cleansing of Palestine,* 79n76.

111. TNA WO 261/189, First Guards Brigade QHR, March 31, 1948.

112. Ibid.

113. CP III/2/35 Cunningham to Creech Jones, no. 654, March 15, 1948.

114. GP, folio 1/1, Sir Henry Gurney diary.

115. CP III/2/91, Beirut to Cunningham, no. 37, March 22, 1948.

116. NACP 84/350/63/11/5–6, Beirut Legation and Embassy, Pinkerton to Marshall, no. 101, March 18, 1948.

117. CP III/1/51, Cunningham to Creech Jones, no. 113, January 24, 1948.

118. Ibid.

119. TNA WO 275/64, Sixth Airborne Division, HQ Palestine, no. 58, January 14–28, 1948; NACP 84/350/61/34/405, Jerusalem Consulate to Secretary of State, no 67, January 19, 1948.

120. TNA WO 275/64, Sixth Airborne Division, HQ Palestine, no. 58, January 14–28, 1948.

121. Mufti to Prime Minister of Egypt, March 8, 1948; cited in Robert John and Sami Hadawi, *The Palestine Diary,* vol. 2, 1945–1948 (New York: New World, 1970), 383–84. See also NACP 84/350/61/34/5–5, Consulate's Report no. 111, April 29, 1948.

122. John and Hadawi, *Palestine Diary,* 383–84.

123. CP III/1/52, Cunningham to Creech Jones, no. 113, January 24, 1948.

124. TNA WO 275/64, Sixth Airborne Division, HQ Palestine, no. 58, January 14–28, 1948.

125. CP IIV/1/94, Cunningham to Creech Jones, no. 372, February 14, 1948.

126. CP III/1/112, Cunningham to Creech Jones, no. 432, February 23, 1948.

127. TNA WO 275/49, Sixth Airborne Division Operations and Incidents, February 1948.

128. Ben-Gurion, Diary, February 19, 1948; quoted in Pappé, *Ethnic Cleansing of Palestine*, 77–78.

129. CP III/1/113, Cunningham to Creech Jones, no. 432, February 23, 1948.

130. NACP 84/350/61/34/4–5, Jerusalem Consulate General, Macatee to Marshall, February 9, 1948.

131. Ibid.

132. Milstein, *History of Israel's War of Independence*, 3:112nn30, 31.

133. CP III/1/120, Cunningham to Creech Jones, no. 491, February 28, 1948.

134. Ibid.

135. Ibid.

136. CP III/1/95, Cunningham to Creech Jones, no. 372, February 14, 1948.

137. Ibid.

138. CP VI/1/81, Cunningham to J. M. Martin, CO, February 24, 1948.

139. Thomas Sugrue, *Watch for the Morning: The Story of Palestine's Jewish Pioneers and Their Battle for the Birth of Israel* (New York: Harper and Brothers, 1950), 157.

*AL-QASTAL AFTER VILLAGE WAS TAKEN AND ITS
INHABITANTS EXPELLED BY THE HAGANAH, APRIL 1948*

VI

The Collapse of the Palestinian Arab Community

They made us leave the village. As I looked back, it was all destroyed and dusty. Dead bodies were lying in the streets.

Muhammad Ismail, Dayr Yasin survivor

March 1948 proved decisive for Palestine's destiny. Major developments converged to heighten tensions between the warring communities. The rapid evacuation of the British and their security forces was removing what little check remained to deter violence. The retreat of the United States from its support of partition had infuriated the Zionists, already provoked by the yishuv's declining economic situation and vulnerable geographic position vis-à-vis the predominately rural Palestinian Arabs. Meanwhile, Arab volunteer fighters continued to infiltrate, while Zionist forces increased in raw military strength and qualitative superiority. These factors led the Haganah to prepare and launch coordinated offensive operations, designated Plan D, at the beginning of April.

In fact, since mid-December 1947, when the Zionists had implemented a policy of "offensive defense," their forces had already been on a de facto offensive. They had also announced to the British their intent to take the fight to the enemy. Both British and U.S. military observers viewed Zionist actions as unambiguously offensive ground operations against the Arabs, and they regarded these operations as partly responsible for the infiltration of Arabs into Palestine to defend their Palestinian brethren.[1] Not until British forces were too few to repulse Zionist forces did the Jewish Agency leadership launch major offensive operations with the goal of establishing the Jewish state. The British withdrawal reached that critically low stage at the end of March 1948.

In early March, both sides in Palestine were primarily jockeying for position. According to the First Guards Brigade, Zionist efforts were aimed at reinforcing outlying settlements while removing noncombatants to safer areas. The Zionist military was strengthening its hold on vital communication points, while laying mines and conducting raids against Arab communications. For both training purposes and retaliation, Zionists also destroyed Jordan valley bridges. The Arabs attacked Jewish lines of communication and blocked the reinforcement of settlements, while strengthening their own lines of communication. They also established bases from which to attack after May 15 and carried out bombing attacks, raids, and sniping on outlying Jewish settlements.[2] Each side harassed the other and prepared for battle during this transition from reprisal to open warfare.

Meanwhile, the British civil and military administration grew ever more focused on its own exit, which despite (and because of) the increasing Arab-Jewish hostilities proceeded on an accelerated timetable. On March 6, more than two months before the mandate ended, High Commissioner Sir Alan Cunningham informed London that the British military's effectiveness was rapidly diminishing: "The GOC [general officer commanding] has no longer sufficient troops to introduce controlled areas. . . . In fact in view of countrywide commitments & rapidly reducing manpower, the extent of military operations the troops can carry out is already limited and will become increasingly so from now on."[3]

Already, any decision to undertake military operations was "an extremely delicate matter" due to insufficient troops. For this reason, the frontiers were "increasingly less guarded" and Arab infiltrators were not interdicted. Yet, Cunningham continued to hope that his administration would be able to maintain a "modicum of civil control" until the mandate ended, despite an "extremely delicate" balance.[4] In fact, the balance was already disrupted; as Arab-Jewish hostilities escalated and British security forces withdrew, the mandate government was forced increasingly to resort to political methods to lower tensions—methods that would prove unsuccessful.

Despite Palestine's escalating violence and the Arabs' own bellicose rhetoric, the Arab League states still evidenced no serious practical intentions of intervening in Palestine overtly. Arab League Secretary General Azzam Pasha told Lowell Pinkerton, the U.S. consul in Beirut, that the Arab governments believed the civil war in Palestine could be contained within the country and "must be settled by Arabs and Jews there." He also stated that the Arab regular armies would not enter Palestine unless "those of other countries did" or if action was necessary to "prevent massacre [of] Arab residents."[5] Meanwhile, international developments threw the entire partition scheme into limbo.

The U.S. Retreat from Partition

The violence ignited by the partition resolution was causing the United Nations grave concern. Pablo de Azcárate, head of the U.N. advance mission to Palestine, observed in mid-March that partition as a whole, and particularly in Jerusalem, was being implemented by "the common action of the British administration, the Jewish administration and . . . the Arab local authorities." But, he added, Palestine was being destroyed rather than partitioned: "To speak in this situation of 'enforcement of partition' sounds rather unreal. In some respects partition is going too far in the sense that the two populations are not only 'partitioned,' but killing and destroying each other."[6]

Despite intense pro-Zionist lobbying, the United States proposed a new plan for Palestine to the U.N. Security Council on March 19: a trusteeship. It had become obvious to the U.S. administration that partition could not be implemented peacefully. The U.S. reversal on partition was also influenced by the conclusion that the General Assembly's recommendations were not legally binding on the Security Council. Even though the latter had the authority to use its powers to maintain international peace and security, it was not authorized to enforce the political recommendation of partition on Palestine.[7]

The trauma to Jewish state planning was profound. U.S. Assistant Secretary of State Dean Rusk said the trusteeship idea "exploded like a bomb and raised hell with the Zionists."[8] The LHI spoke of "American treachery."[9] The trusteeship proposal gave the Zionists additional incentive to force a favorable on-the-ground reality. Chaim Weizmann stated that the Zionists "had no choice but to 'create facts.'"[10] Robert Macatee, the U.S. consul general in Jerusalem, reported that local Jews believed the United

States had betrayed them in the interest of Middle East oil and in fear of Russian designs on the Near East. He observed that foreign journalists reported that the Jewish Agency was determined to set up a state "in any event" and that the only decision remaining was whether the state was to be in the "area given under [the] partition scheme or in all Palestine with Jerusalem as [the] capital and Tel Aviv as [the] seat of government."[11]

Palestine's Arabs regarded the U.S. retreat from partition as a natural return to American "principles of democracy and justice."[12] Azcárate himself, after surveying the situation, wrote to Ralph Bunche, the principal secretary to the U.N. Palestine Commission, observing that "Palestine is an Arab land," and that the Arabs, in trying to prevent the establishment of a Jewish state in Palestine, "far from having behaved like 'aggressors' or troublemakers, [had] only been doing what any other people would have done under similar circumstances."[13] From his perspective, "what is being asked of the Arab States in requesting their 'acquiescence' to the existence of a Jewish state in Palestine is nothing less than to set aside their rights in order to meet the convenience—or need—of the Jews."[14] The Palestinian Arabs were willing to accept trusteeship provided that Jewish immigration was limited and that trusteeship would not ultimately end in partition.[15]

The British cabinet convened on March 22 to discuss the new situation. Cabinet members foresaw only more trouble, as they clearly believed the trusteeship proposal would be unacceptable to either the Jews or the Arabs. The British strongly objected to a U.S. suggestion that a joint U.S., British, and French force maintain order in Palestine. Moreover, the cabinet calculated that the Jewish Agency would seek to establish a Jewish state in those areas allotted to it in the partition plan, which Zionist forces might reasonably be expected to defend. Meanwhile, King Abdullah of Transjordan might seek to assume control of the Arab areas allotted in the partition plan, a move that would incite trouble among the other Arab states, in addition to the disturbance it would create in Palestine itself. Furthermore, the cabinet was concerned that the U.N. commission was unlikely to be in Palestine when the British surrendered the mandate.[16]

With the new U.S. trusteeship proposal, a decisive moment had come for Britain to end or alter its policy of recklessly abandoning a functioning government in Palestine. The British chose to alter their course only modestly. They would still pull out by May 15, but they would not interfere with a Jewish state being set up in Palestine, or with a Transjordanian entry into the Arab areas. The chiefs of staff were then tasked with examining the possibility of accelerating the pace of British military evacuation. The cabinet wanted particular care taken to avoid leaving isolated units of the civil administration or military forces at points where their retreat might be cut off. That situation was to be avoided "even at the cost of allowing the efficiency" of the "civil administration to run down over wide areas of Palestine, before the surrender of the Mandate."[17] This course fostered a further, accelerated breakdown in security, creating an immense power vacuum—one that, given the Arabs' relative political and military weakness, explicitly favored Zionist goals of "creating facts" driven by ideological aims. Largely unarmed Palestinian Arabs in towns and villages were left virtually defenseless against Zionist forces that were showing fewer and fewer scruples about terrorizing and killing civilians.

The Jewish Agency and the Vaad Leumi (Jewish National Council) declared on March 24, 1948, that "the Jewish people and the yishuv in Palestine will oppose any proposal designed to prevent or postpone the establishment of the Jewish state," and they "categorically reject any plan to set up a trusteeship regime for Palestine." The Jewish Agency further declared that "upon the termination of the Mandatory administration and not later than May 16, next, a provisional Jewish government will commence to function in cooperation with the representatives of the United Nations in Palestine."[18]

Cunningham and MacMillan began exploring the possibility of securing a truce until the political situation clarified itself. By now, they considered Britain all but impotent to create order on its own. In a foreboding March 28 telegram, Cunningham warned London that "unless something is done almost at once the situation may deteriorate."[19]

The high commissioner was also considering terminating the mandate earlier, sometime between April 29 and May 5, because of the highly volatile situation.[20] Remaining British forces were struggling, in the face of increased Arab-Jewish clashes, to maintain some semblance of order in those limited areas required to carry out their evacuation. At the same time, the maintenance of British communications, particularly to Jerusalem, absorbed so many military units that insufficient forces remained to intervene effectively in large-scale clashes, even if they had been ordered to do so.[21] In case after case, British military pullbacks left poorly defended Arab population areas at the mercy of well-organized and better-equipped

Zionist forces, as Palestinian Arab testimony will reveal.

British commanders shared the high commissioner's fears about the security situation for Palestine's inhabitants. On March 28 they characterized the situation as bleak. A general deterioration was in progress "all over the country," and particularly in the Jerusalem area. Each side was increasing attacks on the other's isolated settlements and villages, and destroying its opponent's key buildings with bombs, mines, and explosives. There were more frequent Arab attacks on Jewish communications: "ambushes of convoys, mining and blocking of roads, and sniping and mortaring of key positions." The British attributed the deterioration to increasing antagonism between Arabs and Jews as a result of U.N. discussions, continuing preparations "for the battle they both propose to wage," Zionist employment of "the weapons that they have for long been accumulating," increasing Arab absolute strength due to "infiltration of armed Arabs in considerable numbers" across all the land frontiers, and "the propaganda on either side for the creation of a Jewish state and the rejection of partition respectively."[22]

Cunningham asked the British government on several occasions to protest formally to the Arab states whose nationals were crossing into Palestine, and to emphasize that the British remained responsible for maintaining law and order until the mandate ended. British diplomats did warn the Arab state governments that infiltrating bands might encounter British forces whose duty it was "to repel the invasion." The British also intimated that the U.N. Security Council and the General Assembly were "bound to be affected by the extent to which Arab states" demonstrated their sense of responsibility as U.N. members to avoid resorting to force and war.[23] How much effect these warnings had is uncertain, but it is clear that sufficient Arab forces remained in the country to sustain hostilities, unchallenged by the British military.

By the end of March 1948, all British troops stationed in the civil district of Lydda and Samaria had withdrawn and were concentrated in Sarafand and Bir Ya'acov, with small defensive detachments at Bayt Nabala and the Lydda railway station. The rest of the country was left to fend for itself.[24] The impotent approach of the British and the uncompromising stances of the Zionist and the Arab leaderships culminated in Zionist leaders' seizing territory militarily.

The Implementation of Haganah Plan Dalet

The Haganah high command assigned the name Plan Dalet or Plan D to a set of military measures and goals that took shape in a series of 13 offensive operations from April 1 to May 15.[25] Plan D called for the conquest and permanent occupation of contiguous areas of territory and, in cases of resistance, it explicitly authorized the forced removal of Arab civilians from these areas. When it was implemented, the Haganah had 50,000 troops, half of which the British army had trained during World War II.[26] Operational orders on March 10, 1948, included "destruction of villages (setting fire to, blowing up, and planting mines in the debris), especially [in] those population centers which are difficult to control continuously. Mounting search and control operations according to the following guidelines: encirclement of the village and conducting a search inside it. In the event of resistance, the armed force must be destroyed and the population must be expelled outside the borders of the state."[27] Yigael Yadin, the chief of Haganah planning and a native of Jerusalem, explained that Plan D's main objective was to seize and maintain at all costs key positions and roads, including the strategically located British police stations. In spite of some British officers' plans to evacuate the police stations "in such a way that the Arabs will take over," the Haganah was determined to seize these targets first, on or before May 16, to control the roads.[28]

Lieutenant Colonel Netanel Lorch, an Israeli military historian, wrote that "zero hour" for the implementation of Plan D would arrive "when British evacuation had reached a point where the Haganah would be reasonably safe from British intervention and when mobilization had progressed to a point where the implementation of a large-scale plan would be feasible."[29]

British evacuation reached that point on March 31. Although Benny Morris argues that the Haganah did not know whether the British would withdraw piecemeal or pull out abruptly en masse, the British in fact had informed both Jews and Arabs of their general plans.[30] Both communities could also witness British demobilization and gauge the strength of British forces in their areas through each stage of withdrawal.

The nature of Plan D is a matter of debate between Zionists and pro-Palestinians. Morris writes that Plan D was not a "political blueprint for the expulsion of Palestine's Arabs: it was governed by military considerations and was geared to achieving military ends." Given the nature of the war, Morris explains, "in practice [it] meant the depopulation and destruction of villages that hosted hostile local militia and irregular forces."[31] Simha Flapan, Walid Khalidi, and Ilan Pappé, however, hold that Plan D was the Zionist plan to expel Palestine's Arabs from their homes.[32]

Flapan, Khalidi, and Pappé are correct in their assessment. Brigade commanders received a list of villages or neighborhoods to be occupied, destroyed, and the inhabitants expelled by certain dates.[33] No village would be exempt from expulsion because Arab resistance to occupation was expected. In every operational order from Haganah high command to the units in the field, the word *tihur*, or "cleansing," appeared, directing "the expulsion of entire populations from their villages and towns."[34] Even before the troops had their orders, they clearly knew what was expected of them. Shulamit Aloni, an Israeli civil rights activist and former Haganah officer, recalls that "special political officers" incited the troops "by demonizing the Palestinians and invoking the Holocaust," frequently the day before a scheduled operation was carried out.[35]

After a meeting of the Jewish Agency's main policymakers on May 11, 1948, David Ben-Gurion sent a letter reminding Haganah brigade commanders that their troops should not be distracted from their principal task of ethnically cleansing Palestine. He wrote, "The cleansing of Palestine remained the prime objective of Plan Dalet (D)." Ben-Gurion used the Hebrew word *bi'ur*, meaning either "cleansing the leaven" during Passover, "root out," or "eliminate," according to Pappé.[36]

Contemporary British civil and military observers also support the pro-Palestinian view that, whatever the precise nature of Plan D, Zionist forces did purposefully expel Arabs during the final six months of the mandate. General Horatius Murray, commander of the First Infantry Division, described the Zionist forces' strategy as the seizure of maximum territory and the removal of the Arabs through forcible intimidation, replacing them with Jewish immigrants. The tactical method employed by Zionist forces, Murray stated, "was to frighten the Arabs out of isolated villages by dropping two or three mortar bombs at night" and then occupying "the vacated territory with their own people."[37]

Under Plan D, Palestinian Arab testimony and British military documents reveal, Zionist forces frequently made no distinction between

hostile or neutral villages. Haganah commanders might arbitrarily determine that any village was hostile and attack it, including villages that
had already entered nonaggression treaties with the Haganah and local
officials. Such was the case with the Arab villages of 'Aqir, Biyar 'Adas,
al-Maliha, Kafr Saba, and Dayr Yasin, as well as with the cities of Acre
and Haifa.[38] Haganah commanders argued in late March that "war was
war and that there was no possibility of distinguishing between good and
bad Arabs."[39]

Although subject to a formal hierarchy, "Haganah commanders were
encouraged and trained to shoulder extensive responsibility in the field
and to be capable of improvising," the Israeli military historian David
Tal has explained. In fact, "improvisation was considered as important
as planning." This doctrine had been inculcated into Haganah members
during the Arab Revolt of 1936–39, when they engaged in skirmishes with
poorly armed and trained, and loosely organized Arab guerrilla group-
ings. Haganah commanders were expected to act "independently, and
decisively, while demonstrating a high level of flexibility."[40] The fighting
in 1947–48 was similar to that of the 1930s, except that the Palestinians
were more poorly armed, organized, and led in 1948. As a result, Zionist
attacks rarely encountered armed Arab resistance, "allowing Jewish forces
to invade the Arab villages quite easily."[41]

The vulnerability of the Palestinian Arab population at this time is
shown by the tactical picture unfolding in Palestine on April 4. On the
Arab side, about 6,000 Arab Liberation Army (ALA) soldiers, led by Fawzi
al-Qawuqji, had taken over operations in northeastern Palestine. 'Abd
al-Qadir al-Husayni, with some 3,000 Palestinian and other Arabs, was
based in Bir Zeit, north of Ramallah, and operating in and around Jerusalem. Hassan Salamah was near Jaffa, with an estimated 1,000 to 2,000
Palestinians and Iraqis. The Arabs' positions at Haifa and in the northwest
were confused. In Gaza and the southwest were a few hundred Egyptians
and a "retired Egyptian major-general." Chief Secretary Gurney, who
made the above assessment, estimated that the Arab forces in Palestine
"with any sort of training and discipline thus do not exceed 10,000, armed
mostly with all sorts of antiquated small-arms, some automatics and a few
mortars."[42]

On the Zionist side, Gurney estimated the Haganah could field about
40,000 better-armed and better-equipped members, including 200 to 300

members of the IZL and a few hundred LHI. A large delivery of modern arms and ammunition from Czechoslovakia arrived in April just as Plan D was being implemented. Gurney viewed the Arab tactics as fundamentally incompetent.[43] He noted that the Arabs showed scant appreciation that direct attacks on strongly defended Jewish settlements "cost them dearly and can scarcely succeed," while they could have "easily throttle[d] communications such as the Jerusalem-Jaffa lifeline."[44] Arab operations were ineffective in stymieing Zionist communication lines because of a lack of coordination and follow-through.

The Battle for the Roads

From the outbreak of civil war, in one of the few Arab operations with tactical significance and a measure of success, Arab irregulars and militiamen from villages dominating the Tel Aviv to Jerusalem road attacked Jewish traffic to prevent weapons and supplies from reaching the Jews in Jerusalem. By the end of March, the 100,000 Jewish inhabitants of Jerusalem were suffering acutely from the siege. Ben-Gurion and the Haganah general staff met the night of March 31 (which coincided with the time that evacuating British forces had reached a critical level of weakness). They decided that the yishuv's first priority was to dislodge the Arab siege of Jerusalem. Three battalions of Palmach and Haganah troops were mobilized for Operation Nachshon (April 5–20), the first operation in the framework of Plan D and the largest Zionist offensive to date.

The Haganah's Givati Brigade commander, the German immigrant Shimon Avidan, directed Operation Nachshon. His operational orders were that "all the Arab villages along the [Khulda to Jerusalem] axis were to be treated as enemy assembly or jump-off bases." Plan D stipulated to destroy such villages and to expel their inhabitants. The Arab villages of Dayr Muhaysin, Khulda, and Saydun were the first targets under Operation Nachshon.[45]

According to the Royal Irish Fusiliers, Zionist forces attacked Dayr Muhaysin (pop. 534) on April 6 and "succeeded in driving the population to the surrounding hills." A British army statement reported that the fighting continued into the night. The Fusiliers warned the Zionist forces that if they continued occupying the village, which lay on a British communication line, the Fusiliers would use force against them. The Zionists evacuated Dayr Muhaysin on the night of April 6.[46]

Years later, Palestinian Arabs targeted by Operation Nachshon described in vivid detail their traumatic memories of the Haganah's attacks on their villages and towns. Ahmad Rashid Mizhir, from the village of Khulda (pop. 325), said "there had been daily skirmishes with the Jews," who would occupy areas and "purposely antagonize" the villagers. Well-armed Jewish convoys would collect near the settlement of Hulda to travel together to Jerusalem. The villagers' movements were restricted; they could not access other villages for food or other needs, putting them effectively under siege. Eventually, a confrontation ensued. 'Abd al-Jabbar al-Shammari, who fought in Haifa and Salama village, came with a group of Palestinian Arab fighters to the nearby military camp, Abu Sarab. The attacks on Jewish convoys started from there. "The Arabs initiated it and then the Jews reacted," Mizhir said.

The battles were intense and the Jews suffered numerous casualties, he reported. The villagers realized that Jewish forces were preparing to ambush the village, and "huge numbers" attacked it, although the ambush was not very disciplined, Mizhir recalled. The Jews occupied what they could, and most villagers fled. Mizhir commented that "the Jews from abroad were more brutal" than the native Palestinian Jews. Perhaps 50 to 60 village fighters remained, but they "did not have the ability to stand up to a huge army. . . . The British tried to intervene with their tanks to stop the fighting. The British stayed until the end, and toward dusk they retreated. Fighting continued until nightfall. . . . After three days, the village fell. . . . After that battle people started leaving for Hebron, Bethlehem, and Ramallah. . . . No one returned to Khulda. The Jews put barbed wire around the village because it had a strategic location and they wanted to control it at any cost."[47]

Qaluniya (pop. 1,056) was another Arab town targeted during Operation Nachshon. Hostilities between Qaluniya and nearby Jewish settlements began when two Jews parked their trucks by the village and started shooting at the villagers, according to townsman Hamdi Muhammad Matar. Even then, the villagers decided "no one should leave the village." But after the news reached them of the Dayr Yasin massacre of April 9, in which Zionist militias killed more than 100 villagers (reported as over 250 killed at the time), the inhabitants of Qaluniya decided to evacuate the women and children to village-owned land near Bayt Surik. On April

12, "Qaluniya was occupied and most of its homes bombed." Haganah forces destroyed much of the village, even removing stones, Matar said, to obliterate its existence.[48]

> Our only option was to go to Bayt Surik. Unfortunately when we reached Bayt Surik we found that its people had left. There was a state of chaos. Then we went to Biddu, a village further along the way. We found it empty. After that there was a Christian village called al-Qubayba where people were hiding in the convent. Then we went to Jerusalem. . . . When the Jews came and found nobody, [the Jews] went to Bayt Surik, where there was a group of elderly people who had stayed behind because they could not keep up with the others who had run away. The Jews killed them at the mosque.[49]

Matar's testimony is corroborated by Israeli sources, which indicate that Biddu and Bayt Surik were raided and demolished in part on April 19–20, but Zionist sources apparently fail to mention any massacre of elderly villagers in Bayt Surik. Explicit expulsion orders were unnecessary for Dayr Muhaysin, Khulda, and Qaluniya, since Arab villagers were driven out violently by Zionist forces.[50]

The Battle of al-Qastal

The Arab village of al-Qastal (pop. 102) was the site of one of the most important battles in the civil war. The charismatic Palestinian commander 'Abd al-Qadir al-Husayni was killed attempting to retake the village. Also, al-Qastal was strategically located on a summit overlooking the main Jerusalem to Jaffa road, and Arab forces had used it in their effort to prevent convoys from transporting supplies to Jerusalem's Jews.

On Saturday, April 3, as part of Operation Nachshon, Palmach's fourth battalion attacked and occupied al-Qastal after a short engagement with the villagers. Bahjat Abu Gharbiyya, a Jerusalem schoolteacher involved in the fighting, recalls that "the Palmach expelled all the inhabitants and proceed[ed] to fortify [the village] with barbed wire and bunkers of reinforced concrete."[51]

The fall of al-Qastal "aroused great concern in Jerusalem and the surrounding villages, as well as in Damascus and the other Arab capitals." 'Abd al-Qadir sent a brief order from Damascus, where he was meeting with the Arab League military committee: "Reoccupy Qastal. Qastal is Jerusalem." Arab forces began an offensive from the south of al-Qastal on April 4. Meanwhile, 'Abd al-Qadir was appealing unsuccessfully to the military committee for arms. He was said to have stormed from the meeting shouting: "You're all traitors, and history will record that you lost Palestine!"[52]

U.S. naval intelligence had been monitoring the situation and reported that the mufti's influence in the Arab League was steadily diminishing. His repeated complaints that the Palestinian Arabs were not receiving a just proportion of the arms and ammunition imported for irregular Arab forces became so acute that the Arab League formed a subcommittee to mediate. According to British Major Stephen Meade, this appeared to be simply "a measure to stall off sending" aid to the Palestinian Arabs.[53]

When 'Abd al-Qadir attempted to procure reinforcements, arms, and ammunition for his counterattack on al-Qastal, the Arab League responded that resources were not available, and that if he attacked al-Qastal, "it would be on his own responsibility." The military committee's response angered the Husaynis, who nonetheless forged ahead with the attack. U.S. intelligence reported that this incident increased the friction between the Palestinians and other Arab factions.[54]

Anwar Nusseibeh, secretary of the Jerusalem National Committee, wrote that a number of Jerusalemites participated in the battle to retake al-Qastal on April 8, during which 'Abd al-Qadir was killed. In the aftermath of their victory, militiamen returned to their villages or went to 'Abd al-Qadir's funeral in Jerusalem. An estimated 30,000 Arabs attended the funeral, leaving only 15 men to guard al-Qastal. As a result, Zionist forces reoccupied the village virtually unopposed on April 9. Considering the high price, Nusseibeh viewed the battle as "in vain; absolutely, completely and wastefully in vain."[55] The Jewish Agency was reportedly pleased that Hassan Salamah, whom they considered "completely incompetent," was to assume command of 'Abd al-Qadir's forces.[56]

The Dayr Yasin Massacre

The massacre at nearby Dayr Yasin proved to be a pivotal event in the civil war, a turning point in the battle for Jerusalem, and a heavy psychological blow to the Arab population during the civil war and beyond. The feroc-

ity and horror of this joint IZL-LHI attack on a neutral village terrified
the Palestinian Arabs like no other action. Many Palestinian refugees cite
Dayr Yasin as contributing to the terror that emptied their towns and villages.[57] Typically, such evacuations did not occur, however, until precipitated by an attack on their villages or towns by Zionist forces. Reports of
the killings and mutilations of villagers, as well as the degrading treatment
and rape of Dayr Yasin's girls and women, spread panic among the Palestinian Arabs. The following account draws on eyewitness Arab, Jewish,
and British testimony.

The village of Dayr Yasin (pop. 750) was located about two kilometers south of the Jaffa to Jerusalem road, on a hill overlooking six Jewish
settlements. A ridge blocked its access to the road; its only direct route
to Jerusalem was an eastbound truck path passing directly through the
Jewish settlement of Givat Shaul. Relations between the village and the
settlements were usually good. Because of the village's vulnerability, the
inhabitants had signed in mid-January 1947 a Haganah-approved, mutual
nonaggression agreement with the Jews of the Givat Shaul and Montefiore
settlements located to the east. Under the agreement, the villagers agreed

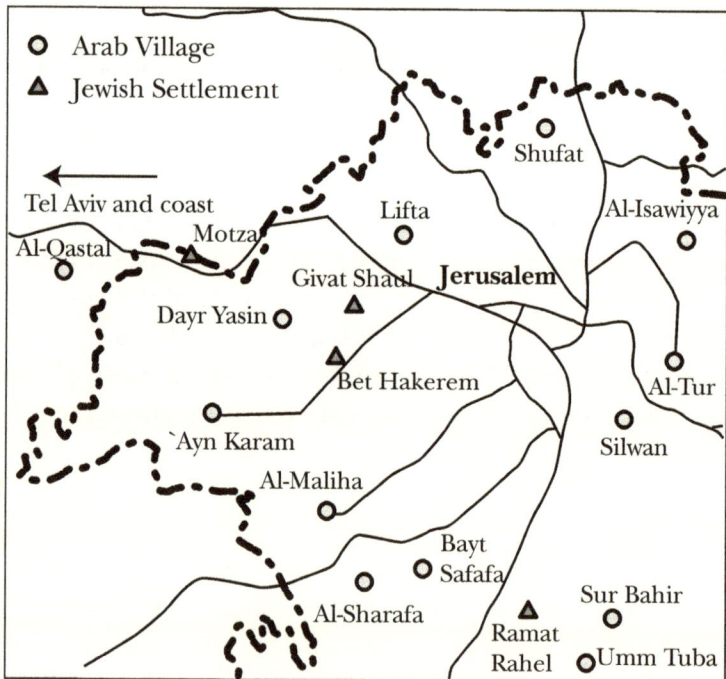

O Arab Village
△ Jewish Settlement

Tel Aviv and coast

Al-Qastal

Motza

Lifta

Shufat

Al-Isawiyya

Givat Shaul Jerusalem

Dayr Yasin O

Bet Hakerem

Al-Tur

`Ayn Karam

Silwan

Al-Maliha

Bayt
Safafa

Al-Sharafa

Sur Bahir

Ramat
Rahel

Umm Tuba

to prevent foreign fighters from using Dayr Yasin as a base or to inform the Haganah if they could not bar their entry. In January 1948, four months before the attack, the agreement was renewed.[58]

According to one villager's account, the nonaggression agreement was violated the first time by Jews "shooting [at] people [in Dayr Yasin] with Bren guns" from great ranges. The Arab villagers did not want to return fire and break their agreement with the Haganah. Instead, they dispatched the village commission, which had negotiated the agreement, to reiterate that they "did not have any intentions of aggression." The Haganah representatives apologized and said "the people who had opened fire were irresponsible."[59] Nonetheless, the villagers took precautionary measures by forming a village guard.[60] According to Abu Mahmud, after news reached the village of 'Abd al-Qadir al-Husayni's death in the April 8 battle at al-Qastal, the men guarded the village until 2:30 the next morning.[61]

IZL and LHI members informed the Haganah that they planned to attack Dayr Yasin, in violation of the nonaggression agreement. The Jerusalem Haganah commander, David Shaltiel, did not approve and instead proposed an attack on the strategically important villages of Qaluniya or 'Ayn Karam. But IZL and LHI members argued that the other targets were too difficult. Shaltiel replied that he would not stand in the way, and that IZL-LHI should take and hold the whole village to prevent its reoccupation by Arab irregulars.

When IZL and LHI members discussed their plan of attack, one LHI member "put on the table the idea of killing the Arabs." The IZL rejected the idea, according to Meir Pa'il, a Palmach intelligence officer.[62]

Before the attack, the villagers "felt very secure and did not expect any attack." Two nights prior, however, they detected movements and preparations in two nearby Jewish settlements, whose Jewish neighbors reassured the villagers that they would not attack. "But they broke their word and the agreement," said Abu Mahmud. "They used this agreement to surprise us and to attack us."[63]

About dawn on April 9, approximately 130 IZL and LHI members attacked Dayr Yasin from the northeast and southeast.[64] The attack was chaotic, as the IZL and LHI units converged from the east, south, and north. The villagers, armed with "only some old guns and pistols," put up effective resistance and inflicted casualties. After a brief Haganah intervention, the town ceased resisting about late morning. It appears that atrocities, which began during the attack, spread and were sustained over the ensuing hours and even days. One villager recounts that

> there were twenty-five people living in the first house they entered. Of them, twenty-four were killed and only one could escape through the window. They used the Mills hand grenades and after that stormed the house with machine guns. In another house they captured a boy who was holding the knee of his mother, and slaughtered him in front of her. A whole family raised their hands high as a gesture of capitulation; nevertheless, the Jews threw Mills grenades at them and shot them with machine guns. In this family alone, eleven people were killed, among them old people over eighty years old and children [aged] three to four years. There was no way out: to run away meant getting killed, and to capitulate also meant getting killed.[65]

Twelve-year-old Fahimah Ali Mustafa Zaidan, who suffered a grenade wound in the attack, lost her mother, grandmother, grandfather, two brothers, and a baby sister three months old. "The whole village was asleep. . . . About 500 Jews with heavy guns and tanks started attacking. Our 30 or 40 guards tried to stop them, but it was useless," she said. The family hid, but the baby's cries revealed their hiding place. At about 9:00 a.m., "[the Jews] put us all in line, my old grandmother included, and shouted insults at us. They started firing with Bren guns. Some of us ran away and got back into the house and hid. The Jews came in and took our olives and lemons and turned all the jars over." The family was then taken to the edge of the village where the Jews forced them to stand until 5:00 p.m. The Jews "just laughed when the older women asked for food for the children," Zaidan recounted.[66]

Ahmad Ayish Khalil reported that the Jewish attackers tied dogs in the four corners of the village, which barked incessantly and frightened the villagers as they tried to flee.[67] Those who were able to escape "ran in the shadow of walls and headed west," downhill toward 'Ayn Karam village.

The mukhtar and a number of villagers fled Dayr Yasin soon after the Revisionist units attacked. They reached Jerusalem between 8:00 and 9:00 a.m., reported the incident to the Jerusalem police rural division headquarters, and requested that a military party be dispatched to assist in rescuing villagers buried under the debris of wrecked buildings.[68] Families were so fearful of leaving their homes that they were killed when IZL-LHI forces blew up the houses on top of them.[69]

District police headquarters received the request and passed it to the Second Brigade duty officer. The reply stated, "The military authorities were not prepared to send troops to Dayr Yasin because they might become involved in Arab/Jewish fighting."[70] The mukhtar's appeal for British assistance and the rejection of this request were widely publicized and resented. Arabs generally believe that "the slaughter and atrocities could have been prevented" if the British had intervened in Dayr Yasin. Arabs saw the refusal of assistance as anti-Arab, in contrast to the British use of heavy guns to disperse Arab forces after an attack on a Jewish convoy at Shaykh Jarrah a few days later on April 13.

The massacre's intensity ebbed about 2:00 or 3:00 p.m. on Friday, April 9. The Zionist attackers looted great quantities of food, money, and home furnishings, with officers and soldiers fighting over the booty.[71] Pa'il reported that "the dissidents were going about the village robbing and stealing everything: Chickens, radio sets, sugar, money, gold and more."[72] Umm Yusuf said that the attackers rounded up the villagers and loaded them on trucks and took them to the nearby settlement: "They took us off the trucks, the youth they shot, the old people they left. . . . They said, finished now, go to the Bedouin king, he should take you. . . . Go, go, to King Abdullah. They took us off the trucks in Jerusalem, in a place called Salahiya."[73] Umm Yusuf's account of abuse is corroborated by Fahimah Zaidan, who told her story to a *Chicago Daily Tribune* reporter while recovering from her injuries in a government hospital: "They searched the village for men and shot them dead when they found them. Two trucks came for us about 7 o'clock and we were hauled thru Givat Shaul where the Jews laughed at us and mocked us."[74]

Most shocking and horrifying to the conservative and traditional Palestinian Arab population, whose honor was embodied in their women's purity, was the degrading treatment of the village girls and women. Zaidan, 12 years old at the time, told how she was publicly humiliated, stripped, and robbed: "[The Jews] drove us into the main road of town and made us get out. They told us: 'Give us everything you've got, or we'll shoot you.' Then the men formed a circle and the Jewish girls stripped us naked and took our rings and earrings. While we were naked they took pictures of us and then told us to get dressed and walk to Jaffa Gate [Jerusalem]."

Shaykh Mahmud, who lived in the neighboring village of 'Ayn Karam, saw dazed women from Dayr Yasin sitting under fig trees, and "some of them were without shoes and clothes." Many of the villagers were injured. "They told us that Jews entered the houses, raped women, and machine-gunned young people. It was a horrible massacre."[75] The AHC delegation to the United Nations angrily charged that in addition to rapes, the perpetrators of the massacre removed women and young girls from Dayr Yasin, "stripped off all their clothes, and put them into trucks[,] and after parading them in the Jewish quarters, photographed them in that condition."[76] Some spectators in the Jewish quarter "jeered and even spat [at] and stoned" the surviving women and children as they were paraded through the streets.[77] Others were apparently repulsed by the display. S. Shereshevsky wrote that the "scene reminded him of how the Nazis had transported 'us' through the streets of Berlin."[78]

The Palestine government undersecretary, Sir John Fletcher-Cooke, confirmed to the United Nations that Arab men, women, and children were killed with great savagery. "Women and children were stripped, lined up, photographed, and then slaughtered by automatic firing," and survivors told of "even more incredible bestialities." Those taken prisoner "were treated with degrading brutality." Furthermore, Fletcher-Cooke confirmed that the joint IZL-LHI operation was undertaken with the foreknowledge and covering fire of the Haganah.[79] Two squads of Palmach also helped to take some of the houses and evacuate wounded Jewish soldiers.[80]

Colonel Yitzhak Levy (Levitza), head of the Haganah Intelligence Service in 1948, confirmed years later that after the conquest of the village, "men, women and children were loaded onto trucks and driven through the streets of Jerusalem. Afterwards, most of them were returned to the village and shot with rifles and machine guns. This is the truth."[81] Meir Pa'il observed and photographed the dissidents' operation at Dayr Yasin for the Jewish Agency. He reported on April 10 that "in the quarry near Givat Shaul I saw the five Arabs they had paraded in the streets of the city. They had been murdered and were lying one on top of the other. . . . I saw with my own eyes several families [that had been] murdered with their women, children and old people, their corpses were lying on top of each other. . . . Each dissident walked about the village dirty with blood and proud of the number of persons he had killed."[82]

The Haganah sent an official letter of apology to King Abdullah and issued a statement accusing the IZL and LHI of "massacre, robbery, looting and barbarism" in the murder of 254 Arab men, women and children.[83] The Jewish Agency called on the IZL and LHI to "realize the depth[s] of the shame you have inflicted on Jewry, to whom such acts are utter abomination."[84]

The number of Arab villagers massacred at Dayr Yasin is debated. The Palestinian anthropologist Sharif Kanaan and the historian Walid Khalidi both have investigated the massacre, based on interviews with survivors and genealogies. Their findings indicate that approximately 110 villagers were murdered.[85]

My interviews with Dayr Yasin survivors indicate that immediately after the attack, the village elders counted more than 100 dead.[86] Although this figure appears to be correct, the larger number became embedded in the record—apparently the result of an attempt by the Revisionists to intimidate Palestinian Arabs. The IZL leader Mordechai Raanan later explained, "I told reporters that 254 were killed so that a big figure would be published, and so that Arabs would panic . . . across this country."[87]

The news of Dayr Yasin was "carried by the wind; people heard about it the same day it happened," recalled Masud Ali Masud of Haifa.[88] The Palestinian Issam Shawwa was with a British police patrol in Jerusalem when he saw a newspaper's graphic description of the massacre. Everybody was "talking about the terror," he said, and there was a "sense of sorrow among people and a sickening feeling." Shawwa and a police officer friend went to Dayr Yasin following the International Red Cross's visit there and found "dead bodies . . . of people ranging from young kids up to old people men and women . . . . [There was] someone uncovering something which turned out to be the body of the woman whose abdomen was opened with a bayonet and next to her was a little embryo dead and bloody. . . . I really felt really sick."[89]

Shawwa believed the publicity given to Dayr Yasin by the AHC was counterproductive for the Palestinian Arabs. The local and regional Arab press printed "glaring headlines and front page publicity" for days.[90] Photographs of Dayr Yasin reportedly were sold in the markets in Jerusalem, Amman, and Beirut. Husayn al-Khalidi, secretary general of the AHC, emphasized in a Damascus press conference that a "great number of Arabs are threatened with [the] fate of Deir Yassin," and it was "therefore the duty of Arab governments to take [a] decisive stand for their protection."[91] The AHC intended to mobilize international public opinion, but the publicity backfired. The Palestinian Arabs "were scared to death," and in some villages, any expectation or experience of Zionist attack spurred people to flee to relatives in other towns.[92] Nevertheless, for many others, the massacre strengthened their resolve for revenge and continued resistance.[93]

Dayr Yasin: The British Factor

The British military did not intervene to mitigate the Dayr Yasin massacre, underscoring the contribution of British decision making to the civil war's chaos and terror. When MacMillan learned of the attack, he told General Murray, who had divisional responsibility for the area, "I'm giving you a definite order that you will not intervene there in any event, at any cost, you will leave it alone."[94] Although MacMillan said that he could have easily sent in ground troops to Dayr Yasin from Jerusalem, he "would have probably had to use them all." MacMillan did not want to embroil British troops in what he considered to be a "quite almost irrelevant operation." He feared that if the British were occupied at Dayr Yasin, Arab or Jewish forces might take advantage of this to seize other areas, such as the Shaykh Jarrah quarter of Jerusalem, and that this would interfere with British communications. Although MacMillan viewed the massacre as "a really horrible affair," it had no relevance to the British military, "in view of the policy which was laid down that we would only take action if our communications were threatened."[95]

Nonetheless, Cunningham and MacMillan debated possible punitive action for Dayr Yasin, including bombing the IZL and LHI forces that had occupied the village. When these groups learned of British retaliatory plans, they asked the Haganah to take control of the village "on the premise that the British would not bomb *them*."[96] By the time the RAF was ready to strike, the Haganah had formally announced it was in possession of Dayr Yasin. The British then decided against the air operation to avoid "attacking the moderate element of the Jewish population, the Haganah."[97] Also, Cunningham had doubted that the Arabs would return to the village, and he felt the British military did not have enough ground troops to hold it. On April 14, Palestine government officials were still not able to enter Dayr Yasin, and a Jewish police officer sent to investigate was barred by the Haganah from proceeding beyond Givat Shaul.[98] In the end, the British took no punitive action. Regarding the canceled air strike, Chief Secretary Gurney wrote to the Colonial Office:

The situation in Jerusalem has now degenerated into such a bloody, continuous day and night battle that it is difficult to write with moderation of suggestions that there should have been military intervention at Deir Yassin [Dayr Yasin]. As you know, there is one brigade in Jerusalem. The force available to deal with any but the routine duties is one platoon. I've missed the bus with an air strike, but shall not do so again, in spite of its repercussions. The RAF orders are not to use the air except in case of danger to British lives.[99]

In the aftermath of Dayr Yasin, Cunningham told MacMillan that he intended to publish the details of the atrocities. MacMillan worried that any explanation of the British military's lack of assistance to the Arabs might reveal British military weakness.[100] He realized that "certain elements" were taking full advantage of the reduction in British army and police forces. Because the RAF was the only force available that could "still hit hard and effectively," pressure grew on it to remain available for future air strikes in Palestine.[101]

A contingent of ALA fighters had been stationed not far from Dayr Yasin, and like the British, could have intervened. Because of inter-Arab rivalries and the April 9 funeral of 'Abd al-Qadir al-Husayni, however, it did not. Hilwi Muhammad 'Atallah, who escaped the fighting at Dayr Yasin, affirmed that 500 Syrian and Iraqi fighters were stationed in the plains of 'Ayn Karam, but "not a single one of them fired a single shot."[102] Anwar Nusseibeh criticized the ALA for not intervening at Dayr Yasin or in the al-Qastal battle, despite the fact that a small detachment led by the Iraqi officer Fadl al-'Abdullah was in the vicinity of Jerusalem. Al-'Abdullah took orders from the Damascus-based Arab League military committee, and he followed a policy of "non-cooperation and rivalry with the mufti's supporters."[103]

Dayr Yasin's Impact

The terror induced by the IZL-LHI massacre at Dayr Yasin ultimately benefited the Jewish Agency's political objective of creating a Jewish state with a small non-Jewish minority. On April 14, Ben-Gurion wrote to Sharett: "From day to day we expand our occupation. We occupy new villages and we have just begun."[104] The Sixth Airborne Division reported that the violence at Dayr Yasin "so impressed the Arabs all over the country" that a Haganah attack on the village of Saris "met with no opposition whatsoever." It derisively reported that "after killing three old women who could not run away and demolishing most of the houses the attackers withdrew content in the knowledge that yet another key position on the Jerusalem–Tel Aviv road had been rendered untenable."[105]

Dayr Yasin elevated terror to a new level for the Palestinian Arabs. Amina Rifai of Jerusalem said, "It was a situation where I had become used to terror. The incident of Dayr Yasin was something infinitely more terrifying." Rifai and her family decided to leave Palestine "when it became quite obvious to me that to stay would mean certain death." They left their Qatamon neighborhood for Damascus on April 15 by taxi. Rifai said that "cars were reported going along the roads saying, 'See Deir Yassin? You are next!'"[106] Hala Sakakini wrote in her diary entry of Wednesday, April 14, that following Dayr Yasin her family began thinking about leaving Jerusalem.

> The most terrible stories have reached us from eyewitnesses who have escaped from this unbelievable massacre. I never thought the Jews could be so cruel, so barbarous, so brutal. Pregnant women and children were tortured to death; young women were stripped naked, humiliated and driven through the Jewish quarters to be spit upon by the crowds. The "civilized" Jews are not ashamed of their crime at all and we know that they are capable of repeating it whenever and wherever possible. One day, perhaps soon, we may be forced to leave our house.[107]

In New York, 28 prominent Jews, including Hannah Arendt, Albert Einstein, and Sidney Hook, denounced the IZL as a "terrorist, right-wing, chauvinist organization" and condemned the Dayr Yasin massacre in a letter to the *New York Times*.[108]

Haganah intelligence worried about the effects on friendly Arab communities; Dayr Yasin might cost Jews the "trust of all those Arabs who hoped to be saved from destruction by agreements with us."[109] It reported that inciters were using the incident to frighten "the Arab community arguing that there is no sense in maintaining peace and good relations with the Jews, because they do not understand this and will slaughter their friends even before they slaughter their enemies. The only choice was to fight as strongly as possible against the Jews."[110] As events show, even those villages and cities that concluded nonaggression pacts with Jewish officials and the Haganah, including al-Maliha, al-Shaykh Muwannis, Abu Kishk, Miska, Jaffa, and dozens of others, were attacked and their people expelled.[111]

Palestinian Arabs learned several lessons from the massacre that affected their reactions in the months to follow: (1) The Zionists could not be trusted; (2) Even nonbelligerent Arabs could be massacred; (3) The ALA forces were unable or unwilling to protect them; and (4) British guarantees to maintain security until the mandate ended were hollow. In fact, British inaction was emboldening Zionist forces to fight in the open.

The attitudes of the Arab League states also hardened considerably after Dayr Yasin. More moderate leaders, such as King Abdullah, who had been negotiating with the Jewish Agency, decided to intervene militarily in Palestine with the entire Arab Legion after May 15.[112]

The Battle of Mishmar Ha'emek

The April 4–15 battle of Mishmar Ha'emek—a settlement astride the Jinin to Haifa road, which was considered by Haganah commanders to be one likely route for a major Arab attack—was initiated by al-Qawuqji's forces, according to Morris.[113] My research, however, suggests a different genesis. The Third King's Own Hussars' field report indicates that al-Qawuqji's attack on Mishmar Ha'emek was in retaliation for Zionist attacks and sniping on neighboring Arab villages and vehicles. ALA forces began to fire near Mishmar Ha'emek, not into the settlement, after Haganah forces attacked and demolished the Arab village of al-Ghubayya al-Tahta.[114] Three British armored-car troops investigated the shooting on April 7 and told ALA Iraqi Colonel Mahdi Bey Salah that the fighting must stop. Salah responded that he and his troops, composed mostly of about 1,000 Iraqis and Syrians, were protecting the Arabs in the area. There were also "a large number of local Palestinian Arabs, inadequately armed, totally undisciplined, and thoroughly despised" by the ALA irregulars, wrote Major R. D. Wilson of the Royal Northumberland Fusiliers.[115] The Arabs wished to use the Jinin to Haifa road, Salah said, which was important for military lines of communication and for commerce. The British concurred that Haganah forces, which had taken over the settlement, had started firing on road traffic. Salah agreed to withdraw his troops if Mishmar Ha'emek's Jews would guarantee not to carry out reprisals against the two neighbor-

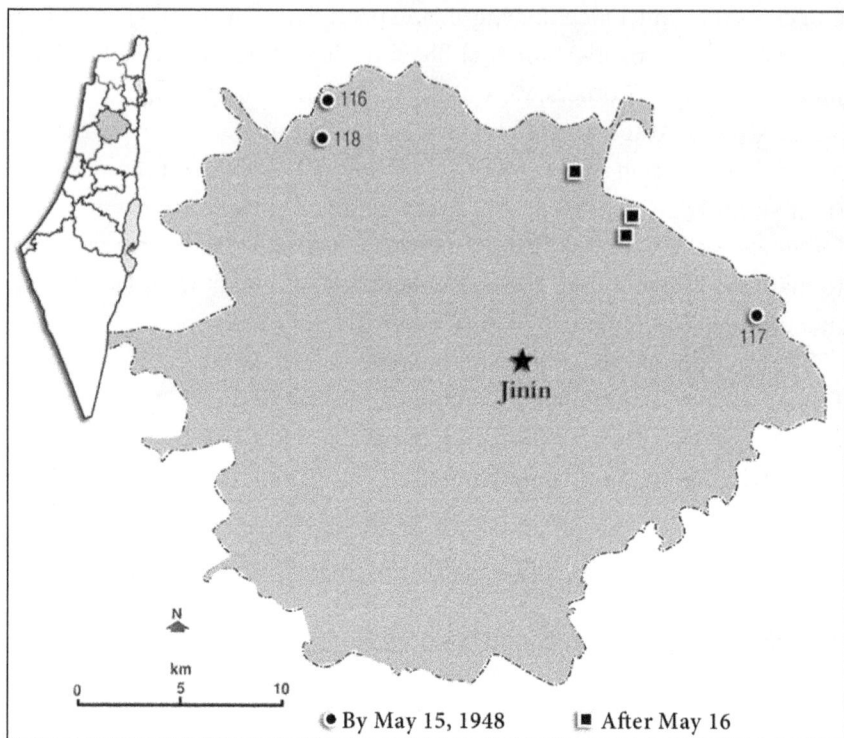

JININ SUBDISTRICT DEPOPULATED TOWNS AND VILLAGES

116. ʿAyn al-Mansi
117. Khirbat al-Jawfa (Mazraʿat al-Jawfa)
118. Al-Lajjun

ing Arab villages, and would also agree to stop sniping at Arab vehicles.

The British attempted to secure a truce with the settlement leadership. A Jew posing as the settlement's leader said he "could not give that undertaking as it would have to be referred to Tel Aviv," but he could obtain authority for a 24-hour truce from Haifa.[116] During the lull in fighting, and with the agreement of Colonel Salah, the British assisted the settlement in evacuating women and children to another colony.[117] The Haganah seized the opportunity to bring in "a great number of reinforcements from Afula and the neighboring settlements," and then attacked and partially destroyed the Arab village of Abu Shusha.[118]

Ben-Gurion and Haganah commanders rejected the proposed ALA cease-fire. They decided instead to launch a vast offensive, expel the local

Arab inhabitants, and demolish their villages.[119] For the first time, Benny Morris writes, "Ben-Gurion explicitly sanctioned the expulsion of Arabs from a whole area of Palestine." Morris argues, however, basing his conclusion on Zionist archival records, that "expulsion was largely preempted by a mass Arab flight from the area because of, and during, the fighting."[120] Palestinian testimony suggests otherwise—that the attacks were deliberately designed to terrorize the Arab villagers into leaving, amounting to expulsion orders.

With the truce broken, the British commander decided there was nothing further he could do, given the force strength at his disposal, "without risking many British lives and incurring the antagonism of certainly one and possibly both sides." The British troops were therefore withdrawn, allowing the battle to rage.[121]

Without the threat of British military interference, Haganah forces drove out villagers from al-Ghubayya al-Fauqa and al-Ghubayya al-Tahta (pop. 1,311) through direct attacks on civilians, whose fear was amplified by reports of Dayr Yasin. Afterward, they were intimidated from returning to their homes. The villages were "blown up piecemeal during the following days."[122] Jamil 'Abd al-Rahman Musa Muhsin explained that both villages were collectively called "Ghubayya." (This area is known as "Turkman" or "Arab Turkman," due to the seven Arab tribes inhabiting it.) Inhabitants of Jewish settlements interspersed among the Arab villages clashed several times with the villagers. The battle began, Muhsin recounts, when Jews attacked al-Ghubayya a day after the Dayr Yasin massacre. The villages had six rifles among them, and some members of the ALA were stationed there. Zionist forces entered al-Ghubayya from the mountains in the west. "When they entered the villages, they fired very heavily, like rain," Muhsin recalled.

The villagers fled under fire. When they reached the village of al-Mansi (pop. 1,392), Zionist forces cut off their return route by bombing a bridge in Tall al-Musalam in 'Ayn al-Ras. Then, Zionists attacked al-Mansi on April 12, killing two brothers and wounding another. The villagers from al-Ghubayya and al-Mansi fled and took refuge in al-Lajjun (pop. 1,279), which the Haganah attacked on April 13. The attack was sufficiently destructive to terrorize the villagers and included the taking of young female prisoners, a particularly intimidating tactic due to cultural issues of family status and honor associated with female inviolability. Muhsin described the attack: "After Zionist forces attacked al-Ghubayya al-Fauqa, some of the villagers fled to Abu Shusha, others ran to Marj Ibn Amir [Jezreel Valley], but most of the villagers ran to Abu Zurayq. When Abu Zurayq was attacked, Zionist forces destroyed and burned the houses, killed twelve villagers and took some women hostages."[123]

Other ill-protected villages were also attacked. On the evening of April 8, the Haganah had attacked Abu Shusha (pop. 835) from the direction of Kefar Barukh settlement.[124] On April 12, Palmach units attacked the village of al-Kafrayn (pop. 1,067), which had participated in the battle of Mishmar Ha'emek. Morris relies solely on Zionist records in claiming that al-Kafrayn was found empty.[125] Yusif Muhammad Husayn al-Jammal, from al-Kafrayn, recounts, however, that some villagers stayed and fought, armed with 15 guns and a small amount of ammunition.

> Young men stayed in the village to defend it, and women, children and elderly were evacuated. At night the Jews burst into the village, and there was a fierce battle because there were some men of the ALA there. Many Jews were killed. The battle was fought in the hills around the village. . . . The second day the Jews relaunched a huge attack on the village and controlled it fully. We had few guns to fight back while Jews owned machine guns, tanks [armored vehicles] and even war [Piper] planes. There was no way to win a battle there. . . . People started to run. Jews were shooting all the way.[126]

The remaining Arab villages to the west of Mishmar Ha'emek were cleared by IZL forces on May 12. The villages of Sabbarin (pop. 1,972), al-Sindiyana (pop. 1,450), Burayka (pop. 336), Khubbayza (pop. 336), and Umm al-Shawf (pop. 557) were all attacked and their populations driven out.

Morris claims, based on Zionist sources, that most of these villagers fled as Jewish forces approached and laid down mortar fire.[127] In contrast, Jamila Hatib, a mother of three from Sabbarin, related that Zionist forces entered the village and committed atrocities.

> The Jews entered our village from nearby hills. They had tanks [armored vehicles] and machine guns with them and killed everyone they found in the streets of the village. They even followed young men from house to house to snipe and shoot them. Nobody defended the village because we

did not have guns and whoever had a gun could do nothing in the face of tanks. Even while we were leaving the village we were followed by shots. We met people from other villages who were also running away.

It appears that reports of Dayr Yasin were a major factor in decisions to flee especially when similar behavior continued: "Everybody was frightened of rape. They were trying to hide their women away. . . . In our village, [the Jews] tried to rape a girl, but she managed to run away. We left the village on foot. The injured were left to die." The villagers took nothing with them. Hatib said, "Jews later entered the village and killed elderly people and shot young men and even burned some of them."[128] Palestinians interviewed commonly reported that elderly and infirm villagers who were unable to leave were killed by Zionist forces. Some villages where such atrocities were reported to have been committed include Bayt Mahsir, Bayt Surik, Hadatha, Sabbarin, and Saris.[129] The Sixth Airborne Division corroborated the Haganah's killing of elderly women in Saris "who could not run away."[130]

The villagers of al-Sindiyana did not flee; they were ordered to leave. Ahmad 'Abdullah al-Swalma, a farmer, recalls that the villagers of Kafr Qariya ran to al-Sindiyana after their village was bombed for two days. Al-Swalma said, "Jews told the influential people [of the village] that we must leave." The villagers had only "48 hours to leave" or be attacked. Terrified because of Dayr Yasin, the villagers left for Qafin. According to al-Swalma, approximately 50 to 60 elderly villagers remained behind, but Zionist soldiers ordered them to leave. Those villagers who tried to return to retrieve food or belongings were killed or taken prisoner. The village was then destroyed.[131]

Some local kibbutzniks complained to senior defense officials about unnecessary cruelty by Zionist forces. Eliezer Bauer (Be'eri) from Kibbutz Hazore'a wrote that "there are still rules in war which a civilized people tries to follow." He accused Haganah forces at Abu Zurayk village of murdering unarmed captured Arabs, those that surrendered or had hidden in the village after the battle. "And these were not gang members as was later written in [the Mapam daily] Al Hamishmar but defenseless, beaten peasants." He was also concerned about charges of rape and said the unrestrained looting by soldiers and neighboring kibbutzniks was "nothing but theft." Bauer asked Mapam leaders to ensure that Jewish soldiers had orders to abide by the Geneva Conventions.[132]

The battle of Mishmar Ha'emek, the largest-scale operation to date in the civil war period, demonstrates in microcosm the Jewish leadership's use of the cover of war to drive out the Arabs. The ALA had attempted to forge a truce with the Haganah, but Ben-Gurion seized on the battle as an opportunity to expel inhabitants of the Palestinian villages in the area of the settlement.

U.S. intelligence officers observing the Palestine conflict reported that Arab and Jewish military operations "increased on a scale in proportion to the decrease in British intervention." The officers also criticized British forces for exerting "practically no effort . . . to carry out their responsibility of maintaining law and order as the mandatory power" and for focusing on their sole objective "of leaving Palestine by the 15th of May with a minimum loss of [British] life."[133]

An Earlier End to the Mandate?

By mid-April, full-blown civil war was raging throughout Palestine. British forces still in Palestine appear to have independently pressured the chiefs of staff in London to end the mandate even earlier than planned. Field Marshal Bernard Montgomery, chief of the Imperial General Staff, who harbored hostility toward Cunningham, blamed him for mismanaging the Palestine situation. Cunningham indignantly wrote to Colonial Secretary Arthur Creech Jones on April 12 insisting it was the military that had pressured him to evacuate Jerusalem earlier than May 15. He protested that the civil administration was not "trying to run out," as Montgomery claimed. Although he had always believed "the sooner we went the better," Cunningham realized that external politics affecting British prestige and the military's withdrawal were important reasons to continue the mandate until May 15.

Citing Dayr Yasin, Cunningham observed that British authority had "progressively weakened to a greater extent than what even I had foreseen." While he personally wanted the military to drive out Haganah forces that had occupied Dayr Yasin after the IZL-LHI's departure, MacMillan informed him that British troops were "not in a position to do so" or indeed to do anything else that could provoke "a general conflict with either side." This was only one example of many where the civil government had "to stand idle while its authority [was] flouted in all directions." In fact, Cunningham stated that "it would be true to say that we remain in our present positions in Palestine entirely by courtesy of the Arabs."[134]

No military reason justified the British remaining in Palestine after April 20, because the evacuation program was well advanced. MacMillan had suggested withdrawing the Palestine civil administration to the Haifa enclave, but because of past misunderstandings with military commanders in London, Cunningham hesitated to suggest the idea himself, fearing their ridicule. Since abandoning Jerusalem to become a battlefield while the British remained in Haifa unable to function would be "even more damaging to British prestige" than all that had happened thus far, the high commissioner advised reconsidering an early termination of the mandate if the United Nations was unable to do anything before May 15.[135]

The civil and military administrations were frustrated with London's lack of responsiveness to the escalating conflict. MacMillan and the troops complained that no government official had bothered to visit Palestine for more than two years. The government's inattention had negatively affected morale. MacMillan felt that His Majesty's government had "let the whole thing fall apart badly from lack of knowledge" and by being out of touch with the local situation.[136]

The Battle for Jerusalem

Life in Jerusalem, where fighting commenced in the immediate aftermath of the partition vote, had rapidly declined into chaos and misery. The U.S. consul general there reported that Arabs living in the Jerusalem area feared that the Haganah planned to force them out of certain residential areas in order to connect and defend dispersed outlying Jewish areas.[137] Subsequent events would prove their fears well founded. "Jewish plans for the domination of the Holy City" were "becoming clear," Chief Secretary Gurney lamented, "and not a single Christian nation is prepared to do anything to help."[138]

On December 29, 1947, IZL operatives detonated a bomb at Damascus Gate, killing 11 Arabs, three of them children. "The Arabs retaliated by preventing supply convoys from entering the Jewish Quarter" of the Old City. After the bombing, Jews could enter and leave their "quarter only under British protection and only by British arrangement with the Arabs.[139]

During a January 26 meeting with Ashkenazy Chief Rabbi Isaac Halevy Herzog, in response to the rabbi's complaints about the siege and the lack of British security, Gurney retorted: "That's your fault. It is because the Jews threw bombs at Damascus Gate that the Arabs became afraid and imposed a siege."[140]

Pablo de Azcárate, with the U.N. advance committee, wrote a pessimistic letter on April 1 to Ralph Bunche about the "unpleasant events of daily life" in Palestine. Among these, he listed constant firing and explosions, fighting all over the country, shortages, and the virtual impossibility of moving around in Jerusalem or the rest of the country. Azcárate could not imagine how the U.N. commission would be able to live, let alone work, in Jerusalem. "As for being able to carry out the very complex and delicate operation of taking over the present administration, it is simply unthinkable," he said.[141] Azcárate reported that the "minor war" was caused chiefly "if not exclusively by the Arab offensive against the Jews and partition." He felt, however, that the partition plan was defective and that the Arabs were reacting "as any other threatened people."[142]

MacMillan reported that the Arabs' success in attacking Jewish convoys traveling from Tel Aviv to Bab al-Wad had caused Jerusalem to be cut off for about a fortnight. Attack and counterattack rendered the Jerusalem to Jaffa road unsafe even for military convoys, which were therefore diverted to the road linking Jerusalem, Ramallah, and Latrun.[143]

Because of serious food shortages in the Jewish quarter, Cunningham approached the AHC in April to obtain its consent to allow food convoys to pass.[144] Brigadier Sir Iltyd N. Clayton, head of the British Middle East Office in Cairo, approached the Arab League with the same proposal. Azzam Pasha strongly objected to British requests that the blockade on Jerusalem be lifted. He vehemently protested that the Jewish Agency's ability to feed the Jews in Jerusalem was the one weak link in the Zionist position, and "it was out of the question to expect Arabs to forego their main advantage." Further, Azzam Pasha could see no reason why the Arabs should allow food to go through the blockade to maintain the considerable number of Haganah, IZL, and LHI members stationed in Jerusalem.

The Arab League secretary general did, however, propose an opening if the British removed Jewish fighting forces from Jerusalem. Azzam Pasha protested that it was unfair for the British to threaten to use force to feed the Zionist fighting force in Jerusalem, while the British "were entirely unable to protect the Arab villages against outrages which are occurring daily and of which [the] most dramatic was that of Deir Yassin."[145]

The high commissioner felt that he made considerable progress toward an agreement with the Arabs for the passage of food convoys along the road from Jerusalem to Tel Aviv and Jaffa. But British proposals were overtaken by events. The Jewish Agency decided to launch Operation Nachshon to take Arab villages dominating the road. In the process, Zionist forces committed "such atrocities" like Dayr Yasin that "the Arabs became more violently hostile than before," MacMillan observed.[146]

An important local zone of conflict was the mixed Shaykh Jarrah area north of Jerusalem, the main Arab outlet to Ramallah and the north. Hebrew University and Hadassah Hospital were located to the east. Ben-Gurion's January 31 instructions to David Shaltiel, commander in Jerusalem, included expanding Jewish territory to create territorial continuity and liquidating Shaykh Jarrah while avoiding clashes with the British.[147]

From the outset, Arabs controlled the main road to the north, along which Jewish traffic to the hospital and the university was required to pass, according to the Second Infantry Brigade. Arab attacks on this road increased during the civil war period until Jewish traffic, with the exception of armored convoys, came to a standstill.

On April 13—almost certainly in response to Dayr Yasin—Arab forces ambushed a ten-vehicle Jewish convoy traveling the two and a half miles from Jerusalem to the Hadassah Hospital and murdered more than 70 Jews, mostly medical personnel, researchers, and scholars. Two IZL members, wounded at Dayr Yasin, were also in the convoy.[148] At 9:35 a.m., the convoy's lead armored car fell into a mine crater, trapping four vehicles. Hundreds of Arab irregulars from the neighboring villages poured toward the convoy, raining gunfire and shouting, "Vengeance for Dayr Yasin!" The Jews in the armored car held off the Arabs, firing their Sten submachine guns through the car's slits.

The British commander of a Highland Light Infantry platoon called for a cease-fire, unsuccessfully. At 11:15 a.m., Major Jack Churchill attempted to rescue the Jews himself by backing an armored car against the trapped vehicles, but the Jews refused to leave due to heavy Arab gunfire, saying they preferred to wait for the Haganah to rescue them. At least three British soldiers were wounded or killed in these initial rescue efforts. A half troop of Life Guards arrived about 11:30 a.m. to provide supporting firepower with two-pounder guns and three-inch mortars, followed by Jewish reinforcements from Mea Shearim, who raked the houses along the road with Spandau fire. Another half troop of Life Guards arrived at 1:30 p.m.

At 3:00 p.m., after a six-hour standoff, British command authorized a platoon of Highland Light Infantry Reserve Company B with armored carriers to evacuate Jewish casualties under covering fire. Two of the trapped buses were ablaze. The few survivors of the Mount Scopus massacre were extricated with the company's assistance. British forces sustained additional casualties in the rescue effort.[149] The British were harshly criticized by both sides for their intervention. Jews blamed the massacre on the slow and ineffective British actions. MacMillan conceded that he could have moved faster.[150] The Arabs were angry that the British intervened at all.

The Arab National Committee (ANC) stated that Arab forces attacked the convoy because it carried Jewish military forces. The ANC received information that Zionist forces had been concentrating near Hadassah Hospital and Hebrew University, from where "they launched attacks on neighboring Arab quarters, particularly the area of Wadi al-Goz [al-Joz] and Bab al-Sadera." The Jewish convoy apparently did have armed escorts. The International Red Cross's chief delegate confirmed that the "Jews had committed a breach of the Geneva Conventions by providing armed escorts for vehicles which claimed the protection of the Red Shield." He had discovered another instance of Jews transporting arms in a Red Shield ambulance.[151] An American war correspondent witnessed the removal of "large quantities [of] arms and ammunition" from trucks in the convoy.[152]

The ANC in Jerusalem issued a communiqué "strongly repudiating the [British] Army's interference" in the battle. The Palestinian Arabs accused the British of blatant bias in hastening to assist the "Jewish gang" that had committed "aggression against the Arabs." The Arabs also were furious that the British had not taken any action at Dayr Yasin, "a crime where the Jews did not hesitate to kill children, women, pregnant women, and old men and women."[153] British forces in the Jerusalem area intervened in select battles, but only to protect their evacuation routes and lines of communication.[154]

The Haganah reprisal for the Mount Scopus massacre precipitated one of the few heavy firepower British interventions in Jewish-Arab fighting during the civil war period. On April 24 a major Haganah attack commenced on the Shaykh Jarrah quarter of Jerusalem—the first Palestinian neighborhood outside the Old City walls and home to the leading Arab families—driving out many Arab inhabitants and destroying about 20 homes. The bombing caused panic. The hospital was filled with wounded, and shrouds to cover the dead were in short supply.[155] The Haganah's orders were to "occupy the neighborhood and destroy all its houses."[156] The Second Infantry Brigade predicted that Arab forces would stage a counterattack which would plunge Shaykh Jarrah into a battle. The brigade commander concluded that he could not "under any circumstances" accept this possibility; the area was a key route in the British evacuation plan. The commander therefore gave an ultimatum to the Jewish Agency that the Haganah must withdraw to their original positions or be forcibly driven out. The Haganah refused the order, so Second Infantry troops mobilized, went on the offensive and proceeded to overrun Haganah positions.[157] The area required for British evacuation was thereafter demilitarized to facilitate withdrawal.[158]

Another Arab neighborhood of extensive conflict was Qatamon, southeast of Jerusalem. British troops could not stop the fighting, even with six-pounder antitank guns. Emboldened by their success against the Arabs in Shaykh Jarrah, the Haganah mounted a full-scale attack against Qatamon on the night of April 29. They were determined "to try their hand at liquidating Qatamon once and for all," reported the Second Infantry Brigade.

By the morning of April 30, "it was clear that their attack was succeeding." The Arab commander departed in the middle of the Qatamon battle, the high commissioner learned. Arab forces, Cunningham noted, "had been shooting at the Jews from this quarter for weeks and really brought the attack on themselves."[159] However, the Second Infantry Brigade record suggests that Arab forces had been trying to prevent a complete takeover of this quarter by Zionist forces and were attempting to reach a ceasefire. After the Zionist bombing of the Semiramis Hotel in January 1948, which caused many of the prosperous Arab inhabitants to flee Qatamon, Palestinian Arab forces and Iraqi volunteers had moved in to protect the neighborhood.[160] Arab forces then tried to mediate a truce through the commander of the Second Infantry Brigade, but the Haganah "were resolved not to give up any of their gains."[161] The whole of Qatamon fell into Jewish hands by the evening of May 1. "As the Jews captured one house after another, the well-to-do Arab residents began to abandon their homes."[162] Cunningham observed that in house-to-house fighting, "the

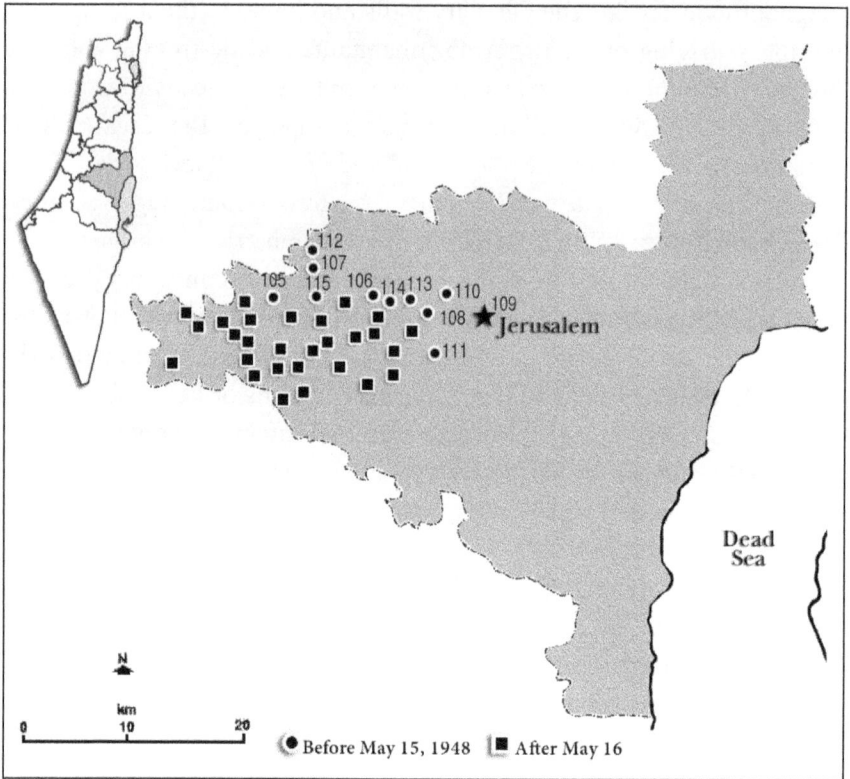

JERUSALEM SUBDISTRICT DEPOPULATED TOWNS AND VILLAGES

105. Bayt Mahsir
106. Bayt Naqquba
107. Bayt Thul
108. Dayr Yassin
109. Jerusalem-Qatamon quarter
110. Lifta

111. Al-Maliha
112. Nitaf
113. Qalunya
114. Al-Qastal
115. Saris

Jews win every time."[163]

Ghada Karmi recalled the city's civilians as being "terrorized and in flight." Karmi writes that hers was one of the last Palestinian Arab families to flee Qatamon. Her father intended to evacuate the war zone temporarily and return in two or three weeks. It was inconceivable that the Jews would win "or that we would lose our country and our home," she wrote.[164] Once the family was safe at her grandfather's house in Damascus, her father attempted to return to Jerusalem, but the news that Qatamon had fallen to the Zionists and was impassable stopped him in Amman.[165]

U.S. consular officers toured the Qatamon and German Colony sectors of Jerusalem and found that "heavy fighting had caused [an] appalling amount [of] destruction." Houses in certain sections of Qatamon had been completely destroyed, principally by explosions. Organized groups of Haganah, IZL, and LHI broke into and looted all the houses and shops, the German hospice sisters reported.[166] Jewish families rushed to occupy some of Jerusalem's most beautiful Arab-owned homes after the inhabitants were evicted.[167]

The mandate government's main interest in the fighting in Jerusalem remained to maintain open lines of communications to evacuate security forces. MacMillan feared "troops being cut off in Jerusalem and perhaps elsewhere," and that units would sustain casualties "in fighting their way out, possibly against troops from Arab states." British authorities seriously considered leaving Jerusalem prior to May 15 to avoid the "grave risk of losing Haifa." But the immediate response was the opposite: additional British troops arrived to reinforce Jerusalem's Second Infantry Brigade. One squadron, plus a troop of tanks, a parachute battalion, and the 42 Commando Royal Marines fresh from Malta would remain in Jerusalem for the final month. Haifa's British garrison was also reinforced.[168]

Cunningham did exert great personal effort to obtain a truce, if not in all of Palestine, at least in all of Jerusalem. British interests were paramount; he believed a truce would ease British military as well as political problems, although a truce would be to the Arabs' advantage as well, given their weak position. If the British finally left Jerusalem without a truce, he feared the Jews would "undoubtedly dominate" and the British would again be blamed by the Arabs.[169]

The Jerusalem Subdistrict: Driving Out the Arabs

Most of the subdistrict of Jerusalem lies in the occupied West Bank and did not fall into Zionist hands in 1948. The area of Jerusalem that Zionist forces eventually occupied in the 1948 war had either been designated part of the Arab state in the partition plan or lay in the proposed internationalized city of Jerusalem. The latter included the villages of 'Ayn Karam, Dayr Yasin, Lifta, and al-Maliha. The Jerusalem subdistrict was 88.4 percent Arab-owned and 2.1 percent Jewish-owned in 1945. The population was 59.6 percent Arab and 40.4 percent Jewish. Of the 41 Arab villages on the eventual Israeli side of the 1949 armistice line, Zionist forces occupied, depopulated, and demolished 37, or 90 percent of the subdistricts' villages. Ten of these villages, or 24 percent, were depopulated before the mandate ended in May 1948.[170] The following accounts of expulsion are based on Palestinian testimony.

Along the Jerusalem road, armed men from the farming town of Bayt Mahsir (pop. 2,784) had sniped at British-guarded Jewish convoys. After the Dayr Yasin massacre, village families with girls older than age 12 left to protect their daughters. On May 9, the Palmach's Har'el Brigade surrounded and attacked Bayt Mahsir at dawn during Operation Maccabi, the goal of which, like that of the earlier Operation Nachshon, was to control the area around Jerusalem. A small plane bombed the school, killing a number of fighters. The villagers fled west under fire, through the only route open. Fifty fighters remained to defend the village until they ran out of ammunition. Villagers from Saris fled and died with the Bayt Mahsir villagers during the Palmach attack. They were fleeing direct attack and a realistic fear of death if they remained. 'Aysha 'Ali Mahmud Tayim said villagers who remained in Bayt Mahsir were killed, including a handicapped girl. "[The Jews] entered and mined the village and killed the old people who could not escape. Those who were hiding were killed."[171] Numerous villagers also were killed trying to return to recover food and belongings.[172]

Zionists carried out several hit-and-run attacks on Lifta (pop. 2,958). 'Ali Mahmud Abu Ta'ih said one of the first incidents, on December 18, 1947, occurred when Haganah members drove a car into the village, then went on foot to the coffeehouse, spraying the men sitting inside with machine-gun fire. Nearby, LHI members stopped a bus and fired into it randomly. The LHI had issued pamphlets to its members reading: "Destroy Arab neighborhoods and punish Arab villages."[173] Despite several intimidation attacks, the villagers remained until they "heard about what happened in Dayr Yasin," although some women and children had been evacuated already. This contradicts other historical accounts which suggest that the villagers had evacuated completely after the attack on the coffeehouse.[174]

In Lifta, located in a deep valley surrounded by Jewish settlements, villagers became fearful of attacks. Lifta's inhabitants left on January 1, 1948, because of a direct Haganah assault: "The Jews attacked the village from the south and shot at the village. . . . After Dayr Yasin, people were afraid of Jewish attacks; for this reason they ran away. They thought they could return after two weeks."[175] Some villagers left to Bayt Hanina, others to al-Ramla and Shufat. Zionist forces attempted to kill villagers trying to sneak back into the village for provisions.[176]

According to Wadha Yusif 'Ammar, then a mother with an infant and a 13-day-old daughter, Zionist forces sniped at al-Maliha (pop. 2,250) from Dar Sofar settlement. Some of the women from Dayr Yasin, she said, fled to al-Maliha "undressed and uncovered." She heard from Dayr Yasin villagers that "the Jews had massacred the people in a way you cannot imagine. Some were burned in ovens; some were killed and thrown in wells." (The burning of bodies is confirmed by declassified Israeli archive documents.)[177] After Dayr Yasin, the elders of al-Maliha held a meeting and told the villagers to leave. The woman and children left for Bayt Jala, while the men stayed to defend the village. The villagers fled on April 21, under Zionist attack and fearing a massacre. 'Ammar said many young men and women from al-Maliha were killed.[178] Fighting also occurred in al-Maliha in July 1948 after most of the inhabitants had already left in April.[179]

According to Mahmud Ahmad Ziyad, from the farming village of Saris (pop. 659), "We recognized the Dayr Yasin massacre and the horrible things we heard about were aimed to make us fearful and leave our lands." The villagers gave food and other provisions to fighters attacking Jewish convoys on the Jerusalem road. Haganah forces attacked the village on April 13.

> [Zionists] attacked our village and left an exit for people to leave. . . . They aimed to expel people from the village. . . . They surrounded the village in the early morning and started shooting at the village to terrorize people. The people ran away. In the beginning [the Jews] did not enter the village. They waited until the people ran out of the village. We went to Bayt Mahsir. [The Jews] advanced to the village and put mines in it. Then they blew up the entire village. We stayed one month in Bayt Mahsir. Then Jews attacked Bayt Mahsir in the early morning. . . . Two old women could not be carried; the houses were destroyed on top of them. One of them was my wife's grandmother. . . . All the people in the village left together—no one before and no one after. To what could we return? All the houses were destroyed.[180]

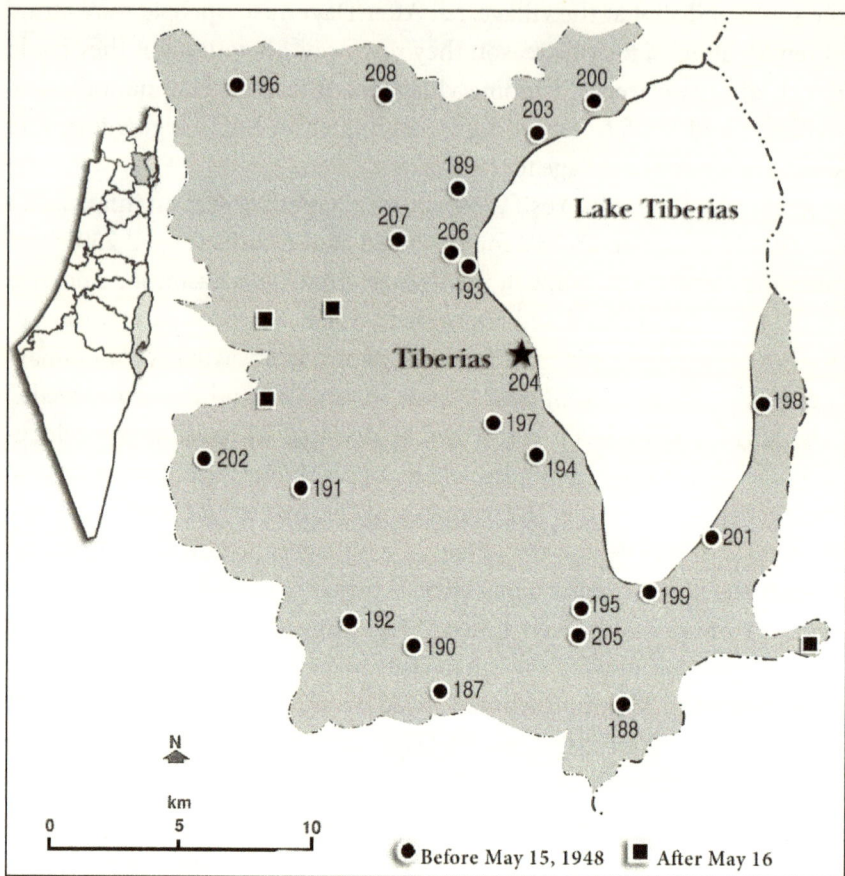

TIBERIAS SUBDISTRICT DEPOPULATED TOWNS AND VILLAGES

187. 'Awlam ('Ulam)
188. Al-Dalhamiyya
189. Ghuwayr Abu Shusha
190. Hadatha
191. Kafr Sabt
192. Ma'dhar
193. Al-Majdal
194. Al-Manara ('Arab al-Manara)
195. Al-Manshiyya
   (Manshiyyat Samakh)
196. Al-Mansura
197. Nasir al-Din

198. Al-Nuqayb (al-Naqib)
199. Samakh
200. Al-Samakiyya
201. Al-Samra
202. Al-Shajara
203. Al-Tabigha (Tall al-Hunud)
204. Tiberias (Arab)
205. Al-'Ubaydiyya
206. Wadi al-Hamam
207. Al-Wa'ra al-Sawda'
   ('Arab al-Mawas)
208. Yaquq

Morris attributes the abandonment of Bayt Mahsir, Lifta, Maliha, and Saris to military attack, but Palestinian recollections suggest that direct lethal force, accompanied by atrocities in a post–Dayr Yasin atmosphere of terror, was employed to force out the villagers.

The Capture and Depopulation of Tiberias and Subdistrict

The Zionist siege of Tiberias resulted in the first large-scale eviction of Palestinian Arabs, even while British forces were still stationed in the town. In 1944, Tiberias was home to approximately 5,310 Arabs and 6,000 Jews, who traditionally had lived together in general harmony.[181] The Arabs lived in the old city near Lake Tiberias, while the Jewish population lived around the periphery of the old city overlooking it, a prime strategic location.

Khalil al-Tabari, an Arab Tiberias landowner, stated that soon after the partition vote, several incidents gave rise to intercommunal tensions. Although the civilian Jews of Tiberias were urging Arab-Jewish cooperation, Zionist paramilitary organizations set out to intimidate the Arab population. Zionist fighting units distributed leaflets threatening the Arabs, warning them not to cooperate with Arab irregular forces stationed in Tiberias and not to hinder the implementation of the partition plan.[182] The Reverend 'Abdullah Sayigh said that Jews and Arabs began to block all roads leading to Tiberias, making movement dangerous, "particularly when the British were lax in the protection that they had guaranteed us."[183]

Haganah forces began attacks in the area in early March. The neighboring village of al-Manara (pop. 568) was raided on March 2. Inhabitants were expelled, according to al-Tabari. The Haganah chased out the villagers, destroyed some houses, and "left leaflets behind warning the inhabitants not to return because the village had been mined."[184] The villages of al-'Ubaydiyya (pop. 1,009) and al-Manshiyya, south of Tiberias, fell next. Morris reports that the inhabitants of al-'Ubaydiyya left for the Nazareth area on March 3 "out of a feeling of isolation and a sense of vulnerability to Jewish attack."[185] Although some villagers may have moved women and children to safer areas, the primary cause for the villagers' departure, according to Arab recollections, was the Haganah's March 3 attack and the expulsion of inhabitants from both villages. The fleeing residents of al-'Ubaydiyya and al-Manshiyya sought shelter in Samakh, and told the villagers there what had happened. Samakh's inhabitants were particularly horrified by reports that Zionist forces had entered the home of Ibrahim al-Bitar in al-Manshiyya and knifed him and his daughter-in-law to death.[186] The villagers understood that they were not safe in their own homes.

The British minister in Amman, Sir Alec Kirkbride, characterized unprovoked Zionist attacks on Arab locales as expulsions. He warned Foreign Secretary Ernest Bevin that the failure of British forces to deter Zionist aggression, which amounted "to the expulsion of the Arab population from Jewish areas," would "make it impossible" for the British government to maintain the pretense in any Arab country that "the British Mandate continued to exist in" Palestine.[187] Haganah forces laid siege to Tiberias from April 3 to 6, attacking any Palestinian Arabs entering or leaving the city except during a British-supervised truce. The Haganah had surrounded the city from all directions except from the sea, cutting Tiberias off from neighboring villages, which supplied its produce.

About April 10–12, only days after Dayr Yasin, two platoons of the Haganah's Golani Brigade attacked the village of Nasir al-Din (pop. 104), killed a number of inhabitants (including women and children), destroyed houses, and "expelled all of its villagers," according to Palestinian eyewitness accounts.[188] The Palestinian Arabic daily *Filastin* reported that eight men, one woman, and an unspecified number of children were killed.[189] Relying solely on Israeli documents, Morris attributes the Arabs' exodus from Nasir al-Din to military assault, fear, and the fall of a neighboring village and refers to the "alleged or actual killing of non-combatants."[190]

The AHC accused "Zionist gangs" responsible for the Dayr Yasin atrocities of committing a massacre during the attack on Nasir al-Din. In a memorandum submitted to the United Nations in July 1948, the AHC claimed that "in the early hours of the morning, while the villagers were peacefully asleep in their homes, the Zionist gangs dashed into the village, attacking with hand grenades and machine-gun fire defenseless women and children."[191] The attack—which the AHC attributed to the IZL and LHI—was actually perpetrated by Haganah members, who appear to have employed homicidal tactics comparable to those used by the IZL-LHI at Dayr Yasin, which the Jewish Agency had publicly denounced. The Zionist troops used massacres to terrorize and precipitate flight from nearby villages and cities. This was the case for Dayr Yasin near Jerusalem, 'Ayn al-Zaytun close to Safad, Balad al-Shaykh and al-Tira bordering Haifa, and Nasir al-Din near Tiberias.

When news reached Tiberias that neighboring villages had fallen, Khalil al-Tabari, a native of Tiberias, said, "I began to feel our turn was next." Despite the fact that the First Parachute Battalion was stationed in Tiberias, the battalion claimed it could not control the city, and its members "themselves were afraid of being killed."[192] The battalion nonetheless broke the Zionist siege of Tiberias on different occasions, according to Mustafa Sahtut, a teacher in Tiberias. This "tense and unbearable" situation of attack and counterattack lasted until the British military announced on April 16 that it would remain responsible for the Arabs' protection only for "an additional three days," or until April 18. In an effort to demilitarize Tiberias, Arab leaders met with the head of the Arab military garrison, Muhammad Kamal al-Tabari, at the Latin Convent on April 17 and asked the ALA to depart the city to forestall further fighting. Truce negotiations were in progress, directed by Brigadier W. G. Colquhoun.[193] But British efforts had no effect, as "the Haganah had decided to pacify [sic] Arab Tiberias."[194] Once again, the timing of the Haganah attack corresponded to British demobilization.

On the night of April 17, Haganah forces attacked and bisected the Arab quarter of Tiberias, killing many Arab civilians. Zionist psychological warfare included "barrel-bombs"—explosives loaded into barrels and rolled downhill into communities—"loudspeakers and 'horror sounds' . . . to frighten the civilians."[195] During the battle, and after, the town was looted by Jewish residents and soldiers. Zionist troops "sacked and desecrated Christian religious establishments in the town including the 'Holy Place' convent." The destruction was verified by the U.N. investigator, Captain F. Marchal of Belgium. He reported that despite repeated guarantees by "Jewish authorities to respect churches, convents, schools and other buildings belonging to the religious community, those places have been submitted to depredations."[196] The desecration of Christian and Muslim religious places served to further "terrorize the population and convince them of the necessity to flee."[197]

The British military gave the Arabs of Tiberias two choices: accept "safe passage to either Nazareth or Samakh" or "stay and fend" for themselves without British protection.[198] The Arabs accepted the British offer to evacuate their besieged city. The city was inadequately protected by about 100 poorly armed men, including approximately 30 ALA irregulars.[199]

The Arabs of Tiberias were confident that they could return soon after May 15, once Arab armies entered Palestine. They relied on repeated Syrian and Transjordanian promises to defeat "the attempted Jewish occupation of Palestine."[200] Responding to pleas for assistance, King Abdullah—fearing another Dayr Yasin—sent 30 trucks to assist in evacuating the women and children from Tiberias.[201] The British encouraged the men to leave as well. By 7:00 p.m. on April 18, British commanders reported that all of the Arabs were gone, "leaving the town completely in Jewish hands."[202]

Terror and demoralization induced by the Dayr Yasin and Nasir al-Din massacres, along with the expulsion of al-Manara's villagers, influenced the Arabs' decision to evacuate Tiberias.[203] They had already suffered numerous casualties, and they believed it was too dangerous to remain in the city, particularly since they could not withstand Haganah attacks. Such attacks on neighboring Arab villages had isolated Tiberias from the rest of Palestine, leaving its population incapable of defending itself. The British nonintervention policy also influenced the Arabs' decision to evacuate. Almost all of them left together on April 18, 1948. The British did not permit them to take any belongings except for the clothes on their backs.[204] The Jewish Community Council of Tiberias publicly declared: "We did not dispossess them. . . . They themselves chose this course but the day will come when they will return to this town. Let no citizen in the meantime touch their property."[205]

The Reverend Sayigh recalled, "[The Jews] forced their will on us because they were in a better position." He believed "it was God's mercy" that the Arabs "were able to leave the city unharmed."[206] Jamal al-Husayni informed the United Nations that the Jews had "compelled the Arab population to leave Tiberias," and the Haganah officer commanding the Golani Brigade affirmed the charge that the brigade had "forced the Arab inhabitants to evacuate."[207] Kirkbride, the British minister in Amman, wrote that the "expulsion of [the] Arab population from Tiberias following the Deir Yassin incident" and the Palestinian Arabs' growing realization that British forces and Arab partisans could not protect them from Jewish forces resulted in increased "pressure from both inside and outside Palestine for immediate intervention of the Arab Legion to contain the Jews."[208]

Other Depopulated Villages and Towns of Tiberias Subdistrict

Villagers and townspeople from Arab localities in northeast Palestine near Tiberias would soon be forced out. In 1945, the Tiberias subdistrict's land was 52.6 Arab-owned, 40 percent Jewish-owned, and 7.4 percent public property. The population was 66.6 percent Arab and 33.4 percent Jewish. Twenty-nine Arab villages, including two Bedouin communities, existed in 1948. Zionist forces subsequently demolished 24 of these, mostly in 1948.[209] Twenty-two of these locales, or 92 percent, were depopulated before the mandate ended, including the city of Tiberias.

Most inhabitants from Arab villages and towns expelled before May 15, 1948, were forced into Syria or Lebanon. In the majority of cases, the Arabs left following a Zionist attack on their home village. In other cases, such as that of the village of Ma'dhar—the only village in the Tiberias subdistrict that evacuated in fear *before* a Zionist attack—the villagers were subsequently expelled from the locality where they had sought shelter. Thus, the great majority of civilians from this subdistrict were driven out either by a realistic fear of attack or by a lethal assault directed at all the inhabitants.

Husayn 'Ali Yusuf, from Ghuwayr Abu Shusha (pop. 1,438), said a delegation from the Jewish settlements of Migdal and Genossar met with the village mukhtar and advised the Arab villagers to seek refuge in al-Rama, which was located in the "Arab state" of the partition plan. Otherwise, the delegation threatened, the villagers would "confront the Jewish army which would inflict heavy suffering on the villagers."[210] The villagers refused to abandon their village, although they were convinced that the Jews would attack Ghuwayr Abu Shusha. They did evacuate the elderly and children to al-Rama, a few hours' walk away, and left armed men behind to guard the village. Haganah forces attacked on April 24. The village militia did not engage the Zionists but retreated to join their families in al-Rama. The villagers of Ghuwayr Abu Shusha then sheltered in al-Rama but were expelled by Zionist forces.[211] Palmach forces took 40 men hostage, according to the parish priest.[212] Only Druze Arabs were permitted to remain.[213] Salih Ramadan Shatawi Hamudi recounts that his family "stayed on the borders of Syria, but Zionist forces did not allow us to stay there. They shot at us until we crossed the Syrian border."[214]

Morris attributes Ghuwayr Abu Shusha's fall to the exodus or to the fall of a neighboring town. In fact, the villagers were threatened with violence, and when they refused to leave, they were attacked.[215]

After the fall of Tiberias, the mukhtar of al-Tabigha (pop. 383), Ahmad Yusif 'Ali, stated that Zionist forces often shelled his village on their way from Tiberias to Rosh Pinna. Those villagers near the road moved from their homes, but continued Zionist shelling caused casualties. The villagers left al-Tabigha on April 5 to avoid a Zionist attack. According to the mukhtar, "Jewish shelling made us leave." They sought safety in al-Samakiyya (pop. 441), from where they watched Zionist forces burn their village.

The villagers of al-Samakiyya, with only four or five rifles, began to worry after Zionist forces attacked Tiberias and expelled its inhabitants. Mustafa Qrayam said the Jewish mukhtar at Genossar settlement also warned al-Samakiyya's mukhtar to surrender or depart to Syria, but the villagers refused to leave their homes and did not surrender. Haganah forces in armored cars attacked al-Samakiyya on April 28. The villagers of al-Samakiyya and al-Tabigha fled together as Haganah forces "fired over our heads, making us run to Syria, with nothing but the clothes we were wearing."[216] "No one was permitted to stay. The Jewish soldiers ordered us to leave," Qrayam said.[217] At least two civilian villagers of al-Tabigha were killed as they ran under fire toward the Syrian border.

The townspeople of Samakh (pop. 4,014) had heard about Zionist attacks and atrocities at al-Manara, Nasir al-Din, and Dayr Yasin in early April. They feared an attack after the neighboring villagers of al-Manshiyya and al-'Ubaydiyya "were forced to leave their homes." The Golani Brigade finally attacked Samakh on the evening of April 24. Although the local village committee forbade anyone to leave, women and children were moved to safer areas. Zionist attackers cut the village water supply and electricity. British forces stationed at Samakh police fortress then announced their own departure on April 27. Zionist forces attacked again on April 28. The few defenders were unable to repel the attack and retreated to join their families. The only exit was to Transjordan, because Haganah and Palmach forces had closed off all other retreats. The villagers felt "it was wise to leave and come back when the Arab armies had liberated Palestine."[218]

For Arab population centers in the Tiberias subdistrict, Morris assigns "fear, military attack, and the influence of fall of, or exodus from, neighboring town" as the decisive causes of the Arabs' departure.[219] However, Palestinian testimony indicates that psychological intimidation was utilized against the villagers of Ghuwayr Abu Shusha and al-Samakiyya. When this tactic was not completely effective, a Haganah military attack followed. The Haganah intended to push the Arabs from their homes and out of the country, as evidenced by the pattern of surrounding villages and driving villagers, with bullets flying, to the border of Transjordan, in the case of Samakh, and to the Syrian border, in the case of al-Tabigha.

Zionist forces employed similar tactics to drive out the villagers of 'Awlam, Hadatha, and Ma'dhar on May 12. All three were subjected to psychological or physical Zionist intimidation, according to villagers' accounts. None of these villages were abandoned on Arab orders, as Morris asserts based on Zionist intelligence sources.[220]

Isma'il Salih al-Ta'ib, a farmer in 'Awlam (pop. 835), said that his village had skirmished with the Jews. Then on May 12, Golani Brigade units besieged 'Awlam. "When they started to shoot at the village, the people became afraid, and they preferred to leave rather than be killed," al-Ta'ib said. In fact, Zionist forces killed several villagers during the attack, and others were killed while attempting to return to retrieve the wheat harvest.[221]

Ahmad 'Abd al-Salam Abu al-Hayja, a farmer from Hadatha (pop. 603), said his village was surrounded by Jewish settlements. Golani Brigade units besieged Hadatha on May 12. Al-Hayja said the villagers left after making "an agreement with the Jews to surrender and to leave to Syria and Lebanon." Elderly villagers who remained behind "were killed later by the Jews," al-Hayja said.[222]

Salah Ahmad Gharib, a farmer in Ma'dhar (pop. 557), recalled that a Jew gave the villagers an ultimatum: war or surrender. The unarmed villagers, who had heard about the massacres in Haifa and Dayr Yasin, chose to leave. Some went to Syria, others to Irbid in northern Transjordan and the Jordan valley.[223]

A Pattern of Forced Transfer

The Palestinian exodus varied in different parts of the country over time, but the causes of flight were not as "markedly different" as Morris suggests. Only local tactics differed, from rural areas to town, or according to circumstances. In all cases, the Zionists exploited Palestinian Arab fears, disorganization, and unpreparedness for war.

At the same time, Palestinian Arab testimony and British military observations corroborate that rural Arabs very often did attempt some defense of their villages. The villagers wanted to stay, and only after reports of atrocities, particularly the Dayr Yasin massacre, did they move women, children, and elderly to safer areas. Zionist forces did little to dispel and much to recreate the fear of another Dayr Yasin.

In most cases, villagers were finally driven out through direct intimidation and force. Immediately after an attack, Zionist forces would often prevent villagers from returning by using snipers, demolishing homes and villages, placing land mines and barbed wire enclosures, and destroying crops and livestock. Villagers unable to evacuate, such as the elderly, sick, wounded, and handicapped, were reportedly killed by Zionist forces in a number of locales, including Bayt Mahsir, Bayt Surik, Hadatha, Sabbarin, and Saris.

Villagers' testimony also indicates that when Arab villagers remained in or near their homes, Zionist forces employed any tactic necessary to compel their flight, prevent return, and speed frontier crossing when possible. In case after case, Zionist forces drove Arab villagers from areas in which they had sought sanctuary after an initial expulsion from home locales. Zionist forces began, in this way, to intimidate the Arabs into leaving their homes—through military attacks and physical and psychological terror, exploiting villagers' fears of what might happen if they fell into Jewish hands.

1. CP III/2/91, Beirut Consul to Cunningham, no. 37, March 22, 1948; CP III/1/20 Cunningham to Creech Jones, no. 15, January 12, 1948.
2. TNA WO 261/189, First Guards Brigade, QHR, March 31, 1948.
3. CP III/2/5, Cunningham to Creech Jones, no. 558, March 6, 1948.
4. Ibid.
5. NACP 84/350/63/11/5–6, Pinkerton to Marshall, no. 101, March 18, 1948.
6. UN DAG 13/3.1.0:1, Palestine Commission advance party, Azcárate to Bunche, March 19, 1948.
7. FRUS, Marshall to U.N. representative Warren Austin, 501.BB Palestine/3-1648, 728; UN, SC, OR, 253, 254, 255 and 258 meetings, February–March 1948; cited in Gabbay, A Political Study, 69; Harry Truman, Years of Trial and Hope, vol. 2 (Garden City, N.Y.: Doubleday, 1956), 163.
8. Papp, As I Saw It by Dean Rusk, 147.

9. *Times* (London), March 23, 1948.

10. Urquhart, *Ralph Bunche*, 156.

11. NACP 84/350/61/34/4–5, Macatee to Marshall, March 22, 1948.

12. Ibid.

13. UN 0455-0013, Reports-Cairo, part 2, August–September 1948, Azcárate to Bunche, Rhodes, September 3, 1948.

14. Ibid.

15. NACP 319/270/6/15/4, G2 Intelligence Report, for Chief of Staff, Situation in Palestine, April 27, 1948.

16. TNA CAB 128/12, CM (48) 24th Cabinet Meeting, March 22, 1948.

17. Ibid.

18. NACP 218/190/2/15/4, Admiral Leahy's files, Palestine 1948–49, U.S. Mission to the United Nations.

19. CP III/2/110, Cunningham to Creech Jones, no. 791, March 28, 1948.

20. Ibid.

21. CP V/4/99, Statement on the Military Situation in Palestine, March 28, 1948.

22. Ibid.

23. CP III/3/3, Creech Jones to Cunningham, no. 1220, April 1, 1948.

24. TNA WO 261/173, HQ South Palestine District, QHR, March 31, 1948.

25. See Khalidi, *Haven to Conquest*, appendix 7 for a list of Plan D operations, 856–57.

26. Pappé, *Ethnic Cleansing of Palestine*, 87.

27. Text translated from Shaul Avigur et al., eds., *Sefer Toldet Hahaganah* [History of the Haganah], vol. 3, ed. Yehuda Slutsky (Tel Aviv: Am Oved, 1973), appendix 48, 1955–60, www.electronicintifada.net.

28. TT, Yigael Yadin interview. See Khalidi, *Haven to Conquest*, for the evolution of Haganah Plans A, B, and C, 755.

29. Netanel Lorch, *The Edge of the Sword: Israel's War of Independence, 1947–1949* (New York: G. P. Putnam's Sons, 1961), 87–89.

30. TNA WO 275/79, 17th Airborne Field Security Section, no. 69, March 3, 1948.

31. Morris, *Birth*, 62.

32. Flapan, *Birth of Israel*; Khalidi, "Plan Dalet: Master Plan for the Conquest of Palestine," 4–20; Pappé, *Making of the Arab-Israeli Conflict*, 94.

33. Pappé, *Ethnic Cleansing of Palestine*, 82.

34. Ibid., 72.

35. IDFA 1950/2315, file 47, May 11, 1948; the plan distributed to the soldiers and the first direct commands are in IDF Archives; cited in Pappé, *Ethnic Cleansing of Palestine*, 83n84.

36. BGA, Ben-Gurion, Diary; cited in Pappé, *Ethnic Cleansing of Palestine*, 128n2.

37. TT, General Sir Horatius Murray interview.

38. Morris, *Birth*, 41.

39. CZA S25-426, protocol of the Jewish Agency political department meeting, March 25, 1948; cited in Morris, *Birth*, 41; Tal, "Forgotten War," 10, 19n34.

40. Tal, "Between Intuition and Professionalism," 888–89.

41. Ibid., 897.

42. GP, diary entry April 4, 1948, 34.

43. Amitzur Ilan, *The Origin of the Arab-Israeli Arms Race: Arms, Embargo, Military Power and Decision in the 1948 Palestine War* (New York: New York University Press, 1996), 63.

44. GP, diary entry April 4, 1948, 34.

45. KMA-PA 130-I, Nachshon Forces HQ to battalions, etc., April 1948; cited in Morris, *Birth*, 111.

46. TNA WO 261/381, Second Battalion Royal Irish Fusiliers, QHR, January–June 1948. Khalidi, *All That Remains*, 378. Population figures for 1948 are derived from Salman Abu-Sitta's estimates, calculated using a 3.8% natural Palestinian Arab population growth above the mandate government's 1944 census statistics; *Palestine 1948,* in Abu-Sitta, *Palestinian Nakba,* 12.

47. Ahmad Rashid Mizhir, interviewed by author in Amman, Jordan, July 26, 2001.

48. Hamdi Muhammad Matar, interviewed by author in Amman, Jordan, August 1, 2001.

49. Ibid.

50. KMA-PA 130-10, Report on the Capture of Qaluniya; cited in Morris, *Birth,* 112.

51. Walid Khalidi, "Selected Documents on the 1948 War: The Fall of Qastel and the Death of 'Abd al-Qadir," *Journal of Palestine Studies* 27.3 (1998): 72. Bahjat Abu Gharbiyya fought with 'Abd al-Qadir as a member of the Jihad Muqaddas, a Palestinian irregular force.

52. Ibid., 75.

53. NACP 38/370/15/5/2, Current Development in the Palestine Situation, Major Stephen J. Meade, April 20, 1948.

54. Ibid.

55. Musa Budeiri, "A Chronicle of a Defeat Foretold: The Battle for Jerusalem in the Memoirs of Anwar Nusseibeh," *Jerusalem Quarterly File,* nos. 11–12 (2001), www.jqf-jerusalem.org/journal/2001/jqf11-12/anwar.html.

56. NACP 84/350/61/34/4–5, Jerusalem consulate, no. RPJ-325, Jewish battle order, April 20, 1948, meeting with Jewish Agency representatives; *Times* (London), April 10, 1948.

57. Palestinians interviewed by the author repeatedly invoked the Dayr Yasin massacre as a major terrorizing event of the 1948 war.

58. IDF Archives 2644/49/359 427; Ma'as number ayin heh; *Lehi, Collected Writings,* 2:972, 989, 990. The Haganah had a similar arrangement with Abu Gosh village, which was not depopulated during the war; Yitzhak Levy (Levitza), *Nine Measures* (Hebrew) (Tel Aviv: Ma'arachot [Israel Defense Army Press], 1986), 340; cited in Ami Isseroff, "Deir Yassin: The Evidence," Peace Middle East Dialog Group, www.ariga.com/peacewatch/dy/dycg.htm. Levy was Haganah's chief of intelligence in Jerusalem during 1948; HA 20/253, Levy to Begin; cited in Benny Morris, "The Historiography of Deir Yassin," *Journal of Israeli History* 24.1 (2005): 85.

59. TT, Deir Yassin, uncatalogued interviewee not named.

60. Testimony of Abu Mahmud, www.alnakba.org/testimony/abu.htm.

61. Ibid.

62. Daniel A. McGowan and Marc H. Ellis, eds., *Remembering Deir Yassin: The Future of Israel and Palestine* (New York: Olive Branch, 1998), 37.

63. TT, Deir Yassin, uncatalogued unnamed interviewee; Survivors' Testimonies, www.alnakba. org, testimony by Abu Mahmud.

64. McGowan and Ellis, *Remembering Deir Yassin,* 35.

65. TT, Deir Yassin uncatalogued unnamed interviewee. For details of the attack see "A Jewish Eye-Witness: An Interview with Meir Pa'il," in McGowan and Ellis, *Remembering Deir Yassin;* and Daniel A. McGowan and Matthew C. Hogan, eds., *The Saga of Deir Yassin: Massacre, Revisionism and Reality* (Geneva, N.Y.: Deir Yassin Remembered, 1999). See also Matthew C. Hogan, "The 1948 Massacre at Deir Yassin Revisited," *Historian* 63.2 (2001), 309-33.

66. *Chicago Daily Tribune,* "Key Fortress of Arabs Again in Jewish Hands," April 13, 1948. Zaidan overestimated the number of Zionist fighters, and there were no tanks, only armored cars.

67. Staughton Lynd, Sam Bahour, and Alice Lynd, eds., *Homeland: Oral Histories of Palestine and Palestinians* (New York: Olive Branch, 1994), 22–23.

68. TNA WO 275/117, V. Fox Strangeways for Chief Secretary, Jerusalem to HQ British Troops in Palestine, April 16, 1948. Ahmad Ayish Khalil, who worked as a house servant for the British

army at Allenby Barracks about two kilometers from Dayr Yasin, heard the news of the attack on the radio in the barracks and immediately left to find his family. See Lynd, Bahour, and Lynd, *Homeland*, 22–23.

69. Morris, "Historiography of Deir Yassin," 91.

70. TNA WO 275/117, V. Fox Strangeways for Chief Secretary, Jerusalem to HQ British Troops in Palestine, April 16, 1948; Lynd, Bahour, and Lynd, *Homeland*, 22–23.

71. IDF Archives 500/48/3512; op.cit. 5440/49/1/317; cited in Isseroff, "Deir Yassin."

72. HA/20/253, "Avaraham" (Pa'il) to Jerusalem District OC, April 10, 1948, HGS/Operations/ Intelligence to Haganah corps, Lessons from the Dissidents' Operations in Deir Yassin 12.2.48 [*sic*, probably should be 12.5.48 or 12.6.48, according to Morris]; cited in Morris, *Birth Revisited*, 238n564. The IDFA has not released Pa'il's full report on the massacre or accompanying photographs. Morris includes what appears to be part of the original report.

73. Interview with Abu Yusuf and Umm Yusuf of Dayr Yasin, www.badil.org.

74. *Chicago Daily Tribune*, "Key Fortress of Arabs Again in Jewish Hands," April 13, 1948, 6.

75. Shaykh Mahmud, interviewed by author in Amman, Jordan, September 2, 2001.

76. NACP, Microfilm 1390, Records of the Department of State Relating to the Internal Affairs of Palestine, 1945–1949, "Jewish Atrocities in the Holy Land, Memorandum to the U.N. Delegation, submitted by the Arab Higher Committee delegation for Palestine, July 20, 1948. See also Musa Khuri, ed., *Tension, Terror and Blood in the Holy Land* (Damascus: Palestine Arab Refugees Institution, 1955), 118.

77. Morris, "Historiography of Deir Yassin," 86–87nn32, 33.

78. Quoted in ibid.

79. UN 0453-0004, U.N. Palestine Commission, IV, Communications from the U.K. Delegation, March–July 1948, Fletcher-Cooke to Bunche, April 20, 1948.

80. Morris, "Historiography of Deir Yassin," 86.

81. Quoted in ibid., 84.

82. HA/20/253, "Avaraham" (Pa'il) to Jerusalem District OC, April 10, 1948, HGS/Operations/ Intelligence to Haganah corps, Lessons from the Dissidents' Operations in Deir Yassin 12.2.48; cited in Morris, *Birth Revisited*, 238n564.

83. UN DAG 13/310: 4 [S04530004], U.N. Palestine Commission 6, January–May 1948, daily news summary, April 13, 1948. According to Meir Pa'il, the Gadna youths who were sent in to bury the bodies counted "about 250," Banks, *Torn Country*, 58.

84. *Chicago Daily Tribune*, "Key Fortress of Arabs Again in Jewish Hands," April 13, 1948, 6.

85. Sharif Kanaan and Nihad Zitawi, *Deir Yassin*, monograph no. 4, Destroyed Palestinian Villages Documentation Project (Bir Zeit University, 1987); and Walid Khalidi, *Deir Yassin: 9 April 1948* (Beirut: Institute for Palestine Studies, 1999).

86. Umm Bassam, interviewed by author at Amman, Jordan, September 2001.

87. IZL commander Mordechai Ranaan; cited in Uri Milstein, *History of Israel's War of Independence*, vol. 4, *Out of Decision Came Crisis*, trans. and ed. Alan Sacks (Lanham, Md.: University Press of America, 1998), 269.

88. Masud 'Ali Masud telephone interview by author, September 11, 1998.

89. TT, Issam Shawwa interview.

90. NACP 84/350/61/34/4–5, U.S. Embassy Cairo to Marshall, no. 329, April 22, 1948, Egypt press reactions to recent acts of violence in Palestine.

91. NACP 84/350/61/34/4–5, Jerusalem Consulate Damascus to Marshall, April 20, 1948.

92. TT, Issam Shawwa interview.

93. Masud 'Ali Masud telephone interview by author, September 11, 1998.

94. TT, General Sir Horatius Murray interview.

95. TT, General Gordon MacMillan interview.

96. Banks, *Torn Country*, 63, account of Dayr Yasin battle by Ezra Yachin, LHI member.

97. TT, General Gordon MacMillan interview.

98. UN 0453-0004, U.N. Palestine Commission, IV, Communications from the U.K. Delegation, March–July 1948, Fletcher-Cooke to Bunche, April 20, 1948; CP III/3/63 Cunningham to Creech Jones, no. 956, April 13, 1948.

99. TNA CO 967/102, Gurney to Martin, CO, 1946–48; CP III/3/64, Cunningham to Creech Jones, no. 966, April 13, 1948.

100. CP IV/1/136, Minutes of security conference, April 16, 1948.

101. CP V/4/95, Advance Air HQ Levant to HQ RAF Mediterranean and Middle East, April 14, 1948.

102. Hilwi Muhammad 'Atallah, interviewed by author at Mahatta Camp, Jordan, August 21, 2001.

103. Budeiri, "Chronicle of a Defeat Foretold."

104. Ben-Gurion Archives, correspondence section 23.02-03.1 doc. 113; cited in Pappé, *Ethnic Cleansing of Palestine*, 100n56.

105. TNA WO 275/64, Sixth Airborne Division Historical Section HQ Palestine, no. 58, April 7–19, 1948.

106. "Memories of Palestine," interview with Amina Rifai from Jerusalem, *Guardian*, May 15, 1976.

107. Hala Sakakini, *Jerusalem and I: A Personal Record* (Amman: Economic, 1990), 118.

108. Letter to the *New York Times*, December 4, 1948, "New Palestine Party Visit of Menachem Begin and Aims of Political Movement Discussed."

109. Levy, *Nine Measures*, 343; quoted in Isseroff, "Deir Yassin."

110. HA 105/31; cited in Morris, "Historiography of Deir Yassin," 103n41.

111. See Morris, *Birth Revisited*, 91–96 for discussion of villages and towns seeking nonaggression pacts with the Haganah and Jewish officials.

112. CP III/3/110, Cunningham to Creech Jones, no. 1062, April 20, 1948; CP III/3/86, Kirkbride to Cunningham, no. 28, April 16, 1948.

113. Morris, *Birth*, 116.

114. *New York Times*, March 15, 1948; cited in Khalidi, *All That Remains*, 161.

115. Wilson, *Cordon and Search*, 187.

116. WO 261/223, Report on Negotiations over the Mishmar Ha'emeq fighting, Lt. Col. C. A. Peel commanding the Third King's Own Hussars.

117. Ibid.

118. Wilson, *Cordon and Search*, 188.

119. Morris, *Birth*, 116.

120. Ibid., 115.

121. Wilson, *Cordon and Search*, 188–89.

122. Morris, *Birth*, 116.

123. Jamil 'Abd al-Rahman Musa Muhsin, interviewed by author in Baq'a Camp, Jordan, August 22, 2001.

124. TNA WO 261/223, Report on the Negotiation over the Mishmar Ha'emeq fighting, Lt. Col. C. A. Peel, commanding Third King's Own Hussars, Ramat David, April 1948.

125. Morris, *Birth*, 117.

126. Yusif Muhammad Husayn al-Jammal, interviewed by author at al-Risafi, Jordan, August 8, 2001. Arab villagers mistook Zionist armored vehicles for tanks and identified as "war planes" small aircraft equipped with mounted machine guns from which Zionist forces threw make-shift bombs.

127. Morris, *Birth*, 117.

128. Sabbarin, Jamila Hatib, interviewed by author at Hittin Camp, Jordan, August 5, 2001.

129. The following Palestinians, each living in a different location and unknown to each other, recounted the Zionists' killing of elderly and others unable to leave their villages: Sabbarin, Jamila Hatib; Qaluniya, Hamdi Muhammad Matar; Bayt Mahsir, 'Aysha 'Ali Mahmud Tayim; Saris, Mahmud Ahmad Ziyad; and Hadatha, 'Abd al-Salam Abu al-Hayja.

130. TNA WO 275/65, Sixth Airborne Division, HQ Palestine, no. 58.

131. Ahmad 'Abdullah al-Swalma, interviewed by author at al-Husayn Camp, Jordan, September 11, 2001.

132. Eliezer Bauer (Be'eri) papers, Bauer to Galili, Moshe Mann, Baruch Rabinov, and Ya'akov Rifkin, April 14, 1948 cited in Morris, *Birth Revisited*, 243n610.

133. NACP 38/370/15/5/2, Current Development in Palestine Situation, Major Stephen J. Meade, April 20, 1948.

134. CP V/4/190, Cunningham to Creech Jones, April 12, 1948.

135. Ibid.

136. WO 261/222, Third King's Own Hussars, January–December 1947, QHR, Morale Report; LC, box 3/file 48, MacMillan interview.

137. NACP 84/350/63/11/5–6, Department of State to American Legation Beirut, January 12, 1948.

138. GP diary entry, April 22, 1948.

139. Milstein, *History of Israel's War of Independence*, 3:245.

140. Ibid., 251.

141. UN DAG 13/3.1.0:1, U.N. Palestine Commission, advance party, Azcárate to Bunche, April 1, 1948.

142. UN 0455-0013, Azcárate to Bunche, September 3, 1948.

143. Ibid.

144. CP V/4/101, MacMillan, General Position in Palestine, April 21, 1948.

145. CP III/3/80, Creech Jones to Cunningham, no. 1426, April 15, 1948.

146. CP V/4/101, MacMillan, General Position in Palestine, April 21, 1948; MacMillan Report, 11.

147. Milstein, *History of Israel's War of Independence*, 3:201.

148. Collins and Lapierre, *O Jerusalem*, 285. According to Collins and Lapierre, the British told the Arabs the date and hour of the convoy and assured them that they would be unhindered in the operation if they did not fire on British patrols.

149. LC box 3 file 35, Situation report on the Arab attack on the Hadassah Hospital convoy on April 13, 1948.

150. Ibid., MacMillan interview.

151. WO 275/64/6, Sixth Airborne Division Historical Section, HQ Palestine, no. 58, April 19–May 3, 1948.

152. NACP 84/350/61/34/4–5, Jerusalem Consulate, Wasson to Marshall, April 15, 1948.

153. FBIS, European Section, Near & Middle East—North African Transmitters, April 15, 1948.

154. LCP, MacMillan interview.

155. Pappé, *Ethnic Cleansing of Palestine*, 98–99.

156. Itzhak Levy, *Jerusalem in the War of Independence* (Hebrew), 207; cited in Pappé, *Ethnic Cleansing of Palestine*, 98.

157. TNA WO 261/193, appendix A to Second Infantry Brigade, QHR, June 30, 1948.

158. MacMillan Report, 11.

159. CP III/5/25, Cunningham to Creech Jones, no. 1217, May 1, 1948.

160. Collins and Lapierre, *O Jerusalem*, 304–8.

161. TNA WO 261/193, appendix A to Second Infantry Brigade, QHR, June 30, 1948.

162. Ahmad Tell, "The Battle of Old Jerusalem in 1948," part 1, www.jerusalemites.org/ahmad.html.

163. CP III/4/150, Cunningham to U.K. Delegation, Washington, no. 1306, April 30, 1948.

164. Ghada Karmi, "The 1948 Exodus: A Family Story," *Journal of Palestine Studies* 33.2 (1994): 35.

165. Ibid., 36.

166. NACP 38/370/15/5/2, Wasson to Marshall, no. 762, May 27, 1948.

167. Pappé, *Ethnic Cleansing of Palestine*, 99.

168. TNA WO 261/193, Second Infantry Brigade, April–June 1948. Wilson, *Cordon and Search*, 196. Many records covering the mandate's final quarter were reportedly lost or stolen during the withdrawal. Some are in the Israel State Archives.

169. CP III/3/25, Cunningham to Creech Jones, no. 1217, May 1, 1948.

170. Basheer K. Nijim, ed., and Bishara Muammar, researcher, *Toward the De-Arabization of Palestine/Israel, 1945–1977* (Dubuque, Iowa: Kendall Hunt, 1984), 58.

171. Fatima 'Ubayd al-Ababdah, interviewed by author at Baq'a Camp, Jordan, July 23, 2001.

172. 'Aysha 'Ali Mahmud Tayim, interviewed by author at Amman, Jordan, July 24, 2001; Khalidi, *All That Remains*, 276.

173. LHI publication Mivrak; cited in Pappé, *Ethnic Cleansing of the Palestinians*, 67.

174. Khalidi, *All That Remains*, 301–3, and Morris, *Birth*, 49–52.

175. 'Ali Mahmud Abu Ta'ih, interviewed by author at Amman, Jordan, August 12, 2001.

176. Ibid., Isma'il Salih al-Ta'ib, interviewed by author at Hittin Camp, Jordan, August 18, 2001.

177. Morris, "Historiography of Deir Yassin," 86n31.

178. Wadha Yusif 'Ammar, interviewed by author at Amman, Jordan, August 1, 2001.

179. Morris, *Birth*, 114, and Khalidi, *All That Remains*, 302–5.

180. Mahmud Ahmad Ziyad, interviewed by author at Amman, Jordan, July 24, 2001.

181. *Survey of Palestine*, 1:151. The Arab population of Tiberias was estimated to be 6,160 in 1948 by Abu-Sitta (*Palestinian Nakba*, 62).

182. Nafez Nazzal, "The Flight of the Palestinian Arabs from Galilee: A Historical Analysis," PhD diss., Georgetown University, 1974, Khalil al-Tabari interview, 243.

183. Ibid., Rev. Abdullah Sayigh interview, 247.

184. Nazzal, *Palestinian Exodus*, 28.

185. Morris, *Birth*, 56–57.

186. Nazzal, "Flight of the Palestinian Arabs from Galilee," Mahmud Sulaiman al-Turani, Amin al-Sari, Muhammad Salih Ghumairid interviews, 265–69. Al-Manshiyya's population figures are included with Khirbat Umm Juni, located 0.5 km. to the south; Khalidi, *All That Remains*, 532.

187. FO 816/117, Kirkbride to Bevin 23/4/48, no. 243, fol. 158.

188. Nazzal, "Flight of the Palestinian Arabs from Galilee." Khalil al-Tabari and Mustafa Sahtut said the attack on Nasir al-Din was April 10 (243–46), while Morris gives April 12 (*Birth*, 71), and Khalidi suggests April 11 or 12 (*All That Remains*, 534).

189. *Filastin*, April 13, 1948; quoted in Khalidi, *All That Remains*, 534.

190. Morris, *Birth*, xv, 73.

191. NACP, microfilm 1390, roll 1, Records of the Department of State Relating to Internal Affairs of Palestine, 1945–1949, Jewish Atrocities in the Holy Land, Memorandum to the U.N. Delegations, submitted by the AHC Delegation for Palestine, July 20, 1948.

192. Nazzal, "Flight of the Palestinian Arabs from Galilee," Khalil al-Tabari interview, 245; Wilson, *Cordon and Search*, 196–97.

193. Wilson, *Cordon and Search*, 196–97.

194. Tiberias Municipal Archive, "Written Testimony of Daniel Khidra, a resident of Tiberias,"

undated; cited in Morris, *Birth*, 71.

195. Palumbo, *Palestinian Catastrophe*, 107.

196. Ibid., NACP 84, Haifa 1948-840.4, n. 3.

197. Ibid., 108.

198. Nazzal, "Flight of the Palestinian Arabs from Galilee," Khalil al-Tabari interview, 244.

199. Ibid., Mustafa Sahtut and Rev. Abdullah Sayigh interviews, 248–49.

200. Ibid., Khalil al-Tabari interview, 245.

201. Palumbo, *Palestinian Catastrophe*, 107.

202. Ibid., TNA WO 275/66/60294, n. 2.

203. Ibid., Rev. Abdullah Sayigh interview, 249.

204. Ibid., Khalil al-Tabari, Mustafa Sahtut, and Rev. Abdullah Sayigh interviews, 243–51.

205. *Palestine Affairs: Research Department: American Zionist Emergency Council* 3.5 (1948): 67.

206. Nazzal, "Flight of the Palestinian Arabs from Galilee," Rev. Sayigh interview, 249.

207. CP III/4/23, Creech Jones to Cunningham, April 24, 1948; Ilan Va'shelah, 9; cited in Morris, *Birth*, 72.

208. TNA CO 537/3901, Implementation of UNO Decision: Reaction of Arabs, part 1, Sir Alec Kirkbride, Amman to FO, April 21, 1948.

209. Nijim and Muammar, *Toward the De-Arabization of Palestine/Israel*, 30–31.

210. Nazzal, "Flight of the Palestinian Arabs from Galilee," Husayn 'Ali Yusuf interview, 252–54.

211. Ibid., Husayn 'Ali Yusuf, Khalid al-Mu'ari, Muhammad Ibrahim Salih interviews, 252–59, Morris, *Birth*, 227.

212. Palumbo, *Palestinian Catastrophe*, 110.

213. Nazzal, *Palestinian Exodus*, 32. The Druze, an Arabic-speaking religious minority, sided with the Jews in 1948, and many were permitted to remain in Israel.

214. Salih Ramadan Shatawi Hamudi, interviewed by author at Hittin Camp, July 28, 2001.

215. Morris, *Birth*, xv.

216. Nazzal, "Flight of the Palestinian Arabs from Galilee," Ahmad Yusuf 'Ali, Ahmad Shahadah Muhammad interviews, 260–64.

217. Ibid., Said Salim Said, Hassan Mahmud Abu Qutun, Mustafa Qrayam interviews, 303–11.

218. Ibid., Mahmud Sulaiman al-Turani, Amin al-Sari, Muhammad Salih Ghumairid, Salih Suwaihil interviews, 265–74.

219. Morris, *Birth*, xv.

220. Ibid.

221. Isma'il Salih al-Ta'ib, interviewed by author at Hittin Camp, Jordan, August 18, 2001; Khalidi, *All That Remains*, 514.

222. 'Abd al-Salam Abu al-Hayja, interviewed by author at al-Wihdat Camp, Jordan, August 28, 2001.

223. Salah Ahmad Gharib, interviewed by author at Irbid Camp, Jordan, September 24, 2001.

Haganah forces attacking Palestinian Arab villages in Galilee, 1948

VII

The De-Arabization of Haifa

Kill any Arab you encounter; torch all inflammable objects and
force doors open with explosives.

Mordechai Maklef, Carmeli Brigade, Haifa

The mass exodus of Haifa's Arabs in April 1948 illustrates in microcosm how the Zionists used the cover of war to expel the Arabs during the mandate's final months. Economically and strategically, Haifa was the most important city in Palestine. Its port was the only one between Beirut and Egypt with quay-side facilities,[1] making it crucial for transport of men and materials—and thus essential to supplying the yishuv and an envisioned Jewish state and its military.[2] The Palestine Police observed in December 1947 that Zionist forces had plans "to ensure that, at all costs, the Ports of Haifa and Tel Aviv remain[ed] under Jewish control."[3] David Ben-Gurion was confident of Zionist military superiority. The Jews could "starve the Arabs of Haifa and Jaffa" if they wished to do so, he wrote in December 1947.[4] The climatic battle for Haifa came in late April, near the close of the mandate—the culmination of escalating intimidation, warfare, and population displacement.

Military and terror tactics were designed to make Palestinian Arabs flee Haifa. Arabs had been evacuating the city of Haifa and its subdistrict since November 27, 1947, principally as a result of Zionist terror and offensive operations. But this slow departure accelerated in April when the Haganah's offensive caused large-scale panic, flight, and deaths. The offensive sped up Arab evacuation, aided thereafter by British forces and pressed by Zionist intimidation tactics.

The assumption that Grand Mufti Haj Amin al-Husayni initially backed Arab violence in Haifa and ordered the Haifa Arabs to leave after the battle is proved false by the circumstances, contemporary evidence, and oral testimony.

Haifa was to serve as the main port for evacuating British stores and troops.[5] The mandate government's policy to preserve its evacuation routes at all costs and to avoid conflict with either community is painfully apparent in Haifa's fall. The British ignored civil and communal security while tacitly promoting partition policies that favored a Zionist takeover. Because Haifa was important to both the Zionists and the mandate government, the local British commander's decision in April to redeploy his forces furthered British and Zionist interests over those of the Arabs just before the battle of Haifa began.

Haifa Engulfed in Terror

Even before the civil war began, Haifa's Arabs worried whether they would be safe after British forces withdrew. The Jewish quarter was strategically situated halfway up Mount Carmel looking down on the historic Arab old town near the docks. Haifa's Jews numbered more than 74,000 in 1946.[6] The city's Arabs, almost equal in number at approximately 73,000, were predominately commercial shop owners and workers with little or no military experience. The British army government quarters were on Mount Carmel, between the Arab and Jewish populations.[7]

The British presence in Haifa had given the Arabs a sense of security. Ahmad al-Halil, the city's chief magistrate, stated that the Palestinian Arabs were "not prepared for any fight." They expected the Arab League's promised intervention and its relations with Great Britain and the United States to settle the partition dispute.[8] At the government's November 29, 1947, security conference, the Palestine Police's inspector general voiced his own concerns about the security of Haifa's Arabs during British withdrawal. Anticipating "friction" between the Arab and Jewish communities, he confirmed the need for police reinforcements.[9]

In the early hours of November 30, news of the U.N. vote favoring partition reached Haifa. It was "joyously received by the Jews and with distrust by the Arabs."[10] Susanna P. Emery, headmistress of the English High School in Haifa from 1934 to 1948, wrote that the 25,000 Christians Arabs were full of resentment "at the injustice of handing Haifa to the Jews."[11] The First Parachute Brigade reported that "bad feelings" between Arabs and Jews became "increasingly pronounced" during the first week of December 1947, and spasmodic fighting ensued, "initiated, in most cases, by the Jews."[12]

A wave of terror overtook Haifa during the initial phase of the civil war. Bombings, sniping, and shootings shocked cafes, restaurants, and the streets. Emery wrote on December 7 that although the Arabs were furious about partition and wished to prevent it if possible, "this present rioting has no backing or approval from the official Jews or from the Arab Higher Committee, who are trying their best to stop it." She noted that "the market is plastered with notices 'By order of the Arab Higher Committee,' saying, 'Don't shoot, don't riot. Keep calm.' Probably it is only a hundred or two on each side who are creating all this turmoil, but they upset the whole town."[13]

The First Parachute Brigade imposed a night curfew on the Arab quarter of Wadi Rushmiyya for December 8 and 9 to stem "continued and sustained shooting."[14] Those nights were fairly quiet, but trouble during the day increased, and British soldiers were being attacked. With police fully deployed and "fast approaching a breakdown," the government decided to end the curfew and to establish semistatic posts supported by armored-car patrols. Continued attacks on British troops, especially in the predominately Jewish Hadar Hacarmel quarter of Haifa, resulted in the imposition of a punitive curfew on the quarter's inhabitants in mid-December.[15] Internal security in Haifa at the end of December 1947 remained "delicate,"[16] according to the First Parachute Regiment.

Political and ethnic tensions were just part of the cause. British headquarters noted that "hooligans have taken the opportunity, created by partition, to settle old problems and to commit criminal offences."[17] Communal disorders grew, while the British military reported that "in practically every major incident, trouble was initiated by the Jews, and carried on by both sides."[18] This pattern of Zionist provocation and Arab response was repeated throughout the civil war. Emery noted at the end of December that despite some successful efforts to calm animosities, "Jewish terrorists are doing their best to prevent it, by wantonly attacking Arab villages."[19]

Haifa's Arabs were unprepared to fight partition. They "were not organized in any military sense," according to Colonel John Waddy of the Sixth Airborne Division. Even though defense committees were quickly established in each Arab neighborhood, the committees were poorly armed.[20]

For General Hugh Stockwell, charged with the security of northern Palestine from his headquarters in Haifa, the U.N. partition vote completely altered his mission. Before the vote, Stockwell viewed the military's responsibilities as civil duties. Their goal had been to keep "the Jews and Arabs apart" and to maintain Haifa and environs as a civil organization. In the wake of the partition vote, the British focus narrowed ever more strictly on evacuating the northern and southern sectors through Haifa Port.

After the United Nations adopted the partition plan, Arab and Zionist forces throughout the sector positioned themselves to take advantage of British departure. Both were intent on taking and holding territory after the British withdrew.[21] These competing objectives brought both communities' militias into conflict with British forces.

British officers in Haifa came to see Zionist activity as aggressive. Colonel Waddy, responsible for security in Haifa, recalled that after the partition vote, Jewish forces quickly went on the offensive against the Arabs "rather than solely against the British security forces." That effort had two aims, he reported: to gain strategic ground and to obtain control of Haifa harbor before or after the British left in order to disembark Jewish immigrants, and "to terrorize the Arab population and force them to leave." He concluded that in "certain areas . . . they were successful."[22] The mandate government realized that law and order could only be maintained in Haifa by deploying troops directly inside the strategic town.

The Zionist Revisionists did the most to escalate the violence at the end of December 1947. The clandestine Stern Gang (LHI) described its tactics as "intimidation attacks" to forestall "Arab anti-Jewish troubles." The British military characterized these attacks as "similar to those launched by Haganah and IZL but, in line with Stern habits and facilities, [they] are frequently more murderous and smaller in scope."[23]

A major IZL terrorist action disrupted the Haifa oil refinery on December 30, 1947. IZL coordinated this attack on refinery workers with Haganah forces as part of a plan to terrorize Haifa's Arabs into leaving.[24] Jewish and Arab workers operated the refinery together, overseen by British staff. At about 10:20 a.m., some IZL members threw two grenades from a car into a crowd of Arab laborers who were standing on the roadside awaiting casual employment. The explosion killed six people instantly and injured approximately 42 others. Ensuing events illustrate how the cycle of violence throughout the civil war was often sparked and escalated by dissident terrorist actions such as these.

News of the attack spread rapidly that morning. Rioting broke out throughout the installation. By 10:30 a.m., some 1,800 Arabs and 400 Jews joined a melee during which Arab workers attacked and beat Jewish workers to death with stones and sticks.

Khalid al-Khatib, an Arab refinery worker, recounted what he witnessed:

> I looked and saw 'Abd al-Rahim carrying his ax and 'Ali his shovel and the others their steel rods. It seemed that the indignation that had been growing inside all of us throughout the years played a unifying role and helped mobilize our efforts against the Jewish workers at the refinery. We no longer distinguished between the Palestinian Jews and those who came from outside. We didn't care whether a Jew supported the Arabs or the Haganah; his being Jewish was sufficient for us to attack.[25]

The Arab rioters killed 41 Jews and injured 48 others, leaving a scene that British military reported as "gruesome and bloody."[26] Waddy and members of the Sixth Airborne Division arrived from their camp north of Haifa about a half-hour after the riot ended. Waddy commented ruefully that "inevitably the British Army [was] blamed by the Jews . . . even though [the Jews] had instigated the incident."[27] A British officer with the 317th Airborne Field Security wrote that this incident may "perhaps teach" the dissidents that they were "mistaken in their theory that the Arab population, if shaken by a show of strength, will not present any further trouble to the future Jewish state—an opinion, incidentally, which is known to be widely held also among [the] Haganah."[28]

In reprisal for the oil refinery massacre, a Palmach force of 170 attacked the Arab village of Balad al-Shaykh and Hawsha (Hawassa) on December 31, where a number of refinery workers lived. Haim Avinoam, the local commander, was ordered to "encircle the village, kill the largest possible number of men, damage property, but refrain from attacking women and children."[29] During the three-hour attack on Balad al-Shaykh, they killed 60 Arab civilians, including women and children. Many others were injured.[30] Several dozen houses were also destroyed. The slaughter prompted a partial evacuation of the villages.[31] Again, the indiscriminate killing of women and children shocked the Arabs; many could not believe that Jews were capable of such atrocities. The Zionist use of terror and violence against civilians, including women and children, also shocked British sensibilities. Cunningham described Zionist reprisals against civilians as an "offense to civilization."[32]

Zionist Determination to Seize Haifa

British intelligence predicted the fall of Haifa to Zionist forces in a February 25 report. The brigade commander warned that disorder was likely to ensue "at any time" after March 15, 1948. He noted that the Jewish Agency believed its best course was to take offensive action "under the general immunity" from large-scale Arab "retaliatory action provided by the British security forces presence." Also, he noted, the Jewish leadership was concerned by a "growing belief" that the United Nations would either reconsider its partition recommendation or be unwilling to provide an international security force to implement partition. The U.S. representative to the United Nations had expressed doubts about the partition resolution in the U.N. Security Council on February 24.[33]

The commander warned that internal security would deteriorate as British forces decreased in strength, starting in early March 1948. Once control was lost, he cautioned, there would be "little likelihood of deploying the force necessary to restore the situation." He strongly advised establishing a Haifa enclave immediately for the withdrawal of British forces and transferring, at an early date, civil and military governance from Jerusalem, "over which it is obvious that we are no longer in a position to maintain effective control."[34] The commander was acutely aware that British weakness gave the Jewish Agency an opportunity to launch extensive offensive operations. Local commanders on the scene, along with the British government and military headquarters in Palestine, concurred that the current abandonment of the mandate enabled the lawlessness and violence of the civil war.

Escalation of Violence in Haifa

British abandonment of the mandate emboldened attacks and counterattacks between Zionist and Arab forces in the early months of 1948. Workers began to stay away from their jobs, the economy slowed and there was "no real hope of better things to come."[35] Haifa's Arabs began gradually to evacuate because the climate of terror caused by indiscriminate attacks, urban fighting, and food shortages created a sense of isolation and vulnerability. By April 1, the Arab population had fallen by nearly 50 percent.[36] Early evacuees, generally middle and upper class, sought safety in familial villages, Nazareth, or other outlying towns in Palestine, and in neighboring Arab countries. They hoped to return quickly when a political solution was reached.[37]

January through March 1948 was marked by "a continual increase in lawlessness" throughout Haifa. Initially, the First Parachute Brigade reported that escalating violence was caused "by Jews attacking Arabs," but after Arab reinforcements arrived in mid-March—some of them from Tiberias to prevent a similar occurrence in Haifa—their offensive operations in the area "reduced the Jewish population's morale by a series of attacks on outlying villages, and road and rail communications."[38] In the open country, British forces used "flag marches, displays of force, and punitive action" to deter fighting. In the towns, they dealt with communal violence by conferring with local leaders.

Zionist forces introduced truck bombs to communal violence, and Arab forces soon adopted the technique.[39] A large oil-bomb exploded outside the garden wall of the English High School on March 4. Headmistress Emery wrote an angry letter of protest to the Haifa Jewish Community Council, saying, "This cruel attack was made to terrify and probably to harm the people in the school."[40] The frequency of such explosions spurred the First Parachute Brigade to prohibit both communities from driving at night. By the middle of March, the brigade reported that Arab attacks on British road communications were so frequent that they needed to employ a Comet tank, which successfully prevented "further serious interference."[41]

The First Battalion Coldstream Guards, with thirty officers and 698 soldiers, took up positions throughout Haifa on April 4 to maintain security during evacuation. They were also deployed to keep open the main routes through town and ensure entry and exit of Arab and Jewish labor to the docks. The battalion's task became increasingly difficult because "tensions between Jews and Arabs in the town had been boiling up." For the first ten days of April, "all went well [for the British evacuation] in Haifa in spite of considerable shooting between Jews and Arabs in their respective quarters."[42] As shooting by night, sniping by day, and the blowing-up of houses by both sides accelerated, British liaison had less effect, so the battalion resorted to force in an attempt to control both communities.[43]

In one sense, British action in Haifa was different from elsewhere. The city's importance as a final evacuation center meant that the British military still employed its strength there, but only until they decided that their deployment could be limited to areas of Haifa important for withdrawal.

A Looming Battle

The battle for Haifa began in late April, but each side tells a different story of escalation. Arabs claim that they were on the defensive with a weak and poorly manned garrison. General Ismail Safwat warned the Arab League on March 23 that the relatively stronger garrisons in Jaffa, Jerusalem, and Haifa were attempting to prevent a Zionist takeover of the major cities. He wrote: "I doubt their ability to hold out against the Haganah, which is being held back only by fears of British intervention. As for the other smaller garrisons, they can be easily overrun if attacked by large Jewish forces. This weakness of our garrisons is not due only to the small number of fighters defending them, but also to the inadequacy of the weapons."[44]

In contrast, General Stockwell blamed the Arab Liberation Army (ALA) forces for precipitating the Haifa battle. In his report on Arab-Jewish clashes in Haifa, Stockwell stated that the ALA had strengthened its position in Haifa during April, adding Iraqi, Syrian, and ex-Transjordan Frontier Forces, along with a few Europeans. The ALA's goal, according to Stockwell, was to prevent the Jews—who had been awarded Haifa by the U.N. partition decision—from completely dominating the city.

Stockwell's characterization of the Arab operations as offensive does not diverge from Safwat's as much as it initially appears. Stockwell viewed ALA operations as politically offensive because they were designed to prevent a Jewish takeover of Haifa. Arabs saw this as a defensive aim. With weak forces at his disposal, Safwat attempted a feint. He ordered ALA forces in the Haifa region to attack Jewish targets on Mount Carmel and settlements around Haifa. His strategy was to draw Haganah forces back to defend those targets and to stop their unfettered attacks against Arab neighborhoods, attacks British forces made scant efforts to suppress.[45] Because ALA forces were unable to protect Haifa's Arabs, let alone defeat the Zionist forces—as events unequivocally show—Safwat tried diversionary tactics.

Realizing their dire situation, Haifa's leaders renewed their efforts in

March to secure a truce. Ben-Gurion and Haganah commanders refused, realizing that the military pressure on Haifa was causing the Arab exodus and that a truce might stop it. Ben-Gurion noted in his diary "that the Arabs are still leaving Haifa."[46]

Stockwell's decision not to halt the culminating Haifa battle reflected the noninterventionist policies of the British government and military. It also contributed to the partitioning of Palestine. In his summation of the battle, Stockwell wrote that from about April 12 or 13, the ALA had gone on the offensive in many quarters in Haifa, "to push forward from two salients, Wadi Nisnas and Wadi Salib, to get astride Herzl Street, the main Jewish thoroughfare in Hadar Hacarmel." The offensive, he also felt, was aimed to strengthen the personal positions of the two Arab military leaders in Haifa, Amin Bey 'Iz al-Din and Yunis Nafa'a, and to increase Arab morale generally.

Arab offensive or not, it was disastrous for the Arabs. The First Battalion Coldstream Guards situation reports indicate that between April 7 and 14, there were 37 Arab casualties and only one Jewish casualty. Further, by the week before the major battle, it was clear to the Third King's Own Hussars that the battle was imminent and that the Arabs were not favored: "The third week of April saw the preliminary moves prior to the Battle of Haifa, with the Jews gradually capturing the high ground from the Arabs."[47]

Considerable reinforcements of Palmach, Haganah, and IZL forces also arrived in Haifa, reflecting the full-scale mobilization undertaken by Zionist forces after the end of March. Stockwell estimated that 400 trained Jews were involved in the decisive Haifa battle, backed by an indeterminate number of reserves, and "some 2,000 Arabs were engaged."[48] Palestinian historian Walid Khalidi argues that there was no ALA garrison in Haifa, only citizen volunteers. The Lebanese ALA commander, Amin 'Iz al-Din, appointed by the military committee in Damascus, was the only trained commander in Haifa, and he had just taken up his post on March 27. The Haifa Arab garrison, according to Khalidi, numbered only about 450 men, armed mostly with World War I–vintage rifles and 15 submachine guns. On the other side, Haifa served as "home and recruiting base of the 2,000 strong Carmeli or Second Brigade," one of the seven brigades of KHISH, the Haganah's field army.[49]

Which scenario is accurate? Contemporary observers close to the field, including Stockwell's own subordinates, support Khalidi's appraisal of relative Arab weakness, both in quantity and quality. The British officer commanding the 257th Field Security Section, Captain T. Keen, noted in the battle's aftermath that the Haganah realized that their "success is substantially due to the scarcity of Arab fighting men in Haifa, and in many ways this [battle] was not an exhaustive test."[50] The U.S. consul in Haifa, Aubrey Lippincott, spent the night before the main battle with the Arab forces and their leaders. He observed that the Arab organization was hampered by "too many cooks" and was "much too remote from [its] higher command." They were "all amateurs," he said, including the Arab volunteers, who were lacking in essential discipline save for an "occasional trained man." They were "by no means numerous," and "their sense of organizational supply and tactics" was "almost nil." He wrote that "the Arab leaders and men proved poor and totally inadequate" to deal with Jewish forces. Lippincott also remarked that "the Haifa Arab[s]," particularly the Christians, were not the least bit interested in fighting the country's battles and were counting on outside Arab elements "to come in and settle this whole question for [them]."[51]

The military object of each side was "to capture vantage points" from which to control the town, according to a British northern sector report.[52] British forces deployed in Haifa had attempted to exercise some control for a while in mid-April by becoming intermittently engaged in clashes. These efforts proved futile. During the night of April 17, the troops used two-pounder guns and PIATs (antitank rocket launchers), firing all night, with varying results. British casualties rose, while suppression proved futile or only partially successful. Troops were ordered to remain in their positions by night and engage any snipers who were endangering them.

Smooth evacuation of British men and materiel ultimately remained the guiding British policy. Actions to quell clashes and restore order were to be made only at first light to permit the evacuation program to continue with minimum interference.[53] Stockwell reported that his tactics were partly successful, but security forces inflicted numerous Arab and Jewish casualties to prevent clashes, which might have interfered with the evacuation. Stockwell's dispositions remained thinly dispersed and dangerously vulnerable to determined assault by either side.

Stockwell tried persuasion. He visited the Arab and Jewish liaison offices in mid-April to impress on their leaders the "urgent necessity to soften their tactics." Both groups protested that they took no offensive action but only fired when fired on. Both communities vowed not to take offensive action, but Stockwell considered these to be "vague and useless promises."[54] On the afternoon of April 19, Abba Khushi of the Histradut, the Jewish trade union federation, and Harry Beilin of the Jewish Agency requested a meeting with Stockwell. Khushi, who had received orders from Tel Aviv, said that the situation in Haifa was no longer tolerable and that the Haganah would need to mount a major offensive to ensure the security of the Jewish quarter of Hadar Hacarmel, which he reported was threatened. Stockwell reported that he advised that "any such action at this stage would be most unwise." He suspected a full-scale battle was brewing and that Khushi was trying to determine what action Stockwell would take in the event of a Haganah offensive.

Stockwell's suspicions were soon confirmed. The Third King's Own Hussars reported that "the Jews intended to attack the Arabs in the near future, with a view of controlling the whole of Haifa."[55] Stockwell now believed it was only a matter of time before a major clash took place. He realized that "with the slender forces deployed in the town," he would "be unable to stop it." Consistent with general British policy, his overriding concern was that British troops be able to evacuate safely with minimal loss of British life.[56]

British Redeployment in Haifa

At this critical juncture, Stockwell concluded that three courses of action lay open to him: maintain his present dispositions in Haifa and eastern Galilee, concentrate the British eastern Galilee force in Haifa, or retain present dispositions in eastern Galilee and redeploy forces in Haifa to secure vital routes and areas to safeguard troops. The danger of maintaining his current deployment in Haifa was that British positions might be overrun and suffer considerable casualties in an attempt to stop a major Arab-Jewish clash. Haifa positions could not be reinforced with British forces redeployed from eastern Galilee before a clash took place, he determined; then, it would be difficult to extricate the troops. In addition, withdrawal from eastern Galilee might also precipitate Arab-Jewish clashes in that area. As for redeploying in Haifa town itself, Stockwell observed that "the obvious danger was the Arab-Jewish clash, but against this I should in a measure be able to safeguard my own interests and avoid estranging either community by engaging in a full scale battle."

Stockwell chose to redeploy inside Haifa but away from front-line positions to safeguard evacuation and to minimize British casualties. Over the northern sector, he would attempt "to exercise authority by negotiation." Whether Britain would suffer a "serious loss of prestige by abandoning the pretence of keeping law and order before the expiry of the Mandate" did not worry Stockwell, who regarded this as an "insignificant" concern compared to public outrage over heavy British casualties.[57] British troops in Haifa, wearied by futile attempts to maintain peace, adopted the attitude, "May the best side win and get it over."[58]

Stockwell thus decided to allow pent-up communal military tension to be released and open warfare to proceed. Given the relative strengths of the communities, this would amount to handing Haifa over to Zionist invasion and capture. The First Guards Parachute Battalion commander, Lieutenant Colonel Sir John Nelson, states in his memoir that "Haifa had virtually been handed over to the Jews . . . to ensure a secure embarkation port for the British withdrawal."[59]

The Zionist victory in the battle for Haifa has led some writers to contend that the British deliberately handed Haifa over to the Zionists. Walid Khalidi argues that Stockwell gave the Zionists exclusive foreknowledge of when he would withdraw.[60] This is a major issue in the historical and polemical debate over the period. A review of contemporary British records does not support the charge of direct Jewish-British collaboration, which given the timeline of reported events seems highly unlikely to have occurred.

On April 20, Stockwell gave orders for his forces to redeploy at first light on the next day to safeguard critical routes and areas. At 4:30 a.m., British forces began to pull out of their positions in town. By 6:00 a.m., they had assumed defensive dispositions on the outskirts "before either Jews or Arabs realized what was happening," reported the First Battalion Coldstream Guards.[61] Stockwell felt obligated to inform both Jewish and Arab leaders of his plans. Early on the morning of April 21, after the British redeployment, he sent first for the Jewish representative and then the Arab one. To each, he emphasized that the mounting Arab-Jewish clashes must cease and peace be maintained.

He reported that he impressed on each his intention to maintain certain "secure routes and areas essential" for the British evacuation from Haifa, and he outlined those routes and areas. Although he would not stand for interference with his dispositions or with any of Haifa's municipal services, he stated that he would be ready to assist either community in maintaining peace and order, since the British wished to leave Palestine with the best possible relationship with both communities.[62] Stockwell's version of the meetings states that he exhorted the two sides to keep the peace. He denied giving either party "the details and timing" of when he "was going to implement" the redeployment.[63]

One incident suggests that prior release of redeployment information to one side would have made little difference. When Stockwell called Chief Magistrate Ahmad al-Khalil to inform him of the withdrawal of British forces from the Arab areas of Haifa, an alarmed al-Khalil responded that this meant the "handover of Haifa to the Jews."[64] Stockwell reported that al-Khalil, the only remaining AHC member in Haifa, left by sea early the same day.[65]

It is always possible that partisan or careless British soldiers may have leaked some information to one or other community. Any such leaks, however, do not seem to have affected the events. The First Battalion Coldstream Guards' report corroborates that neither side knew of Stockwell's exact plans. Their movements in the early morning hours were "completed entirely without incident and practically without a shot being fired," suggesting there was little mobilization, or advance knowledge, by either community. The report concluded that "both the Jews and the Arabs were totally unaware of the withdrawal until well after it had been underway and many failed to realize that the two Coys [companies] had left the centre of the town until late into the morning."[66]

Khalidi's charge that Stockwell colluded with the Jews is also contradicted by the First Battalion Coldstream Guards' situation reports.[67] If, as Khalidi states, Haganah's Carmeli Brigade issued orders to begin moving into the vacated British positions at 10:30 a.m., it was even less likely that the Zionists had foreknowledge of the British withdrawal, because British redeployment was completed "in the early hours of the morning," around 6:00 a.m. Had the Haganah known in advance, they would have seized the positions immediately after the British withdrawal and not have left an opening of four and a half hours.[68]

Stockwell's decision to redeploy his forces in Haifa appears to have been a strategic maneuver to ensure security for British withdrawal from the port city. Stockwell's assessment prior to the Haifa battle strongly indicates that he was already sure Zionist forces would win the battle, pacify the city, and ensure a secure embarkation point for British forces.[69] Although Stockwell acknowledged, "I am probably starting a major conflict between Jews and Arabs which will result in considerable casualties to both sides," he nonetheless believed that, if the Jewish Agency forces won in Haifa, they would be strong enough to hold it.[70] While his political and strategic goals overlapped with Zionist political and strategic goals, operational collusion was unnecessary to achieve these results. He believed a Zionist victory was assured, and the timing of the British redeployment and the subsequent Zionist offensive were separated by several hours of daylight, during which Stockwell informed both sides and during which each could have discovered the redeployment for itself. Unsurprisingly, since the Haganah was better organized, it seized the opportunity faster and more effectively.

Stockwell considered other issues at the time of redeployment that also revolved around the British focus on safe withdrawal. Stockwell assessed the likelihood of continued operation of Palestine's utilities and oil installations, which were deemed vital to British communications and an orderly evacuation. The British were unable to maintain the utilities themselves because of the gradual depletion in the number of troops and civil administrators.[71] A Zionist success in Haifa would have seemed to solve this dilemma. After the battle, the Haganah were able to bring "slightly disrupted public utilities in control," with better-prepared Jewish staff running the post office, telephone service, and electricity.[72]

British oil installations in Haifa would also have been jeopardized without a de facto handover to an alternative administration. Cunningham wrote on March 5, 1948, that an Arab takeover would have been contrary to British interests: "So long as the installations do not pass under Arab control[,] existence and functioning of installations must be reckoned as of greater advantage to Jews than Arabs, so that Jewish authorities and [the] Haganah will doubtless exert pressure on dissidents [not to attack]. . . . The maintenance of [oil] output therefore depends entirely on the extent to which order can be maintained generally in Haifa."[73] The British priorities during evacuation— the port, railways, utilities, and oil installations—were equally important in Jewish Agency national planning. The British strategic interest in Haifa's oil installations paralleled the Jewish Agency's earnestly sought access to this crucial energy source.[74] (The subsequent regional conflict would nevertheless terminate Haifa's role as an oil center.) The Coldstream Guards reported this common advantage: The Zionist domination of Haifa "facilitated the control of the town of Haifa and the evacuation of troops and stores."[75]

The Unfolding of the Haifa Battle

As April 21 dawned, the center of Haifa was "completely uncontrolled." British troops had redeployed to the outskirts and were engaged in blocking all western, southern, and eastern entry and exit routes to the city. Haifa was now "left to carry on on its own," wrote the First Battalion Coldstream Guards.[76] During the day, Zionist forces quickly occupied the positions held by British No. 3 Company in Wadi Rushmiyya, while Iraqis with the ALA reportedly occupied No. 2 Company's posts at Prophets Stairs in Wadi

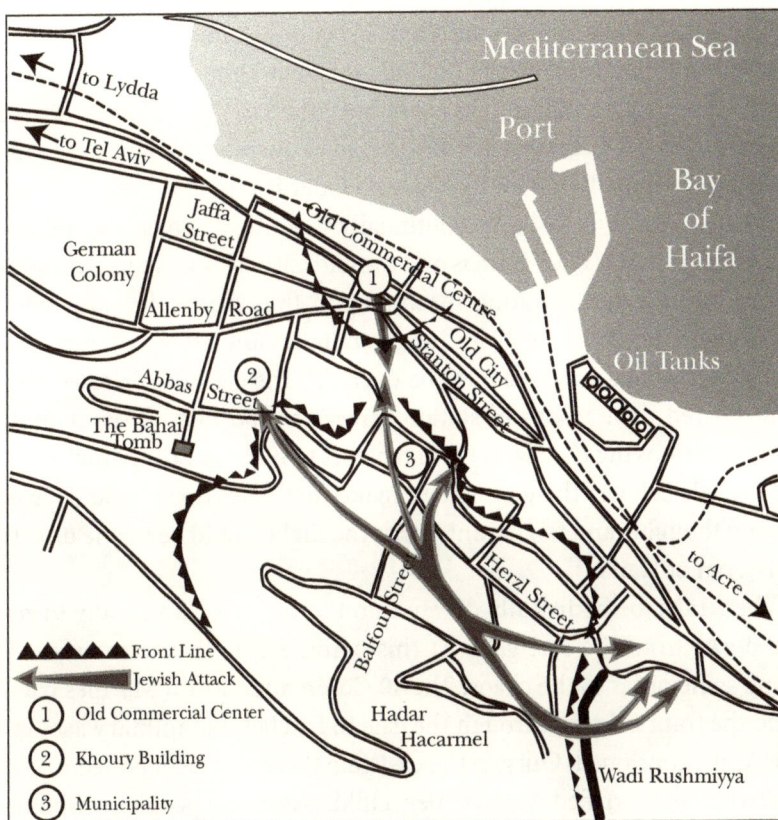

THE BATTLE FOR HAIFA, APRIL 1948

Nisnas.[77] The U.S. consul in Haifa wrote that the Zionist attack of April 21 met with an initial determined Arab resistance, which soon broke "in the face of superior Jewish organization, discipline, armament and strategic position."[78]

The fight did not start quickly. The morning of April 21 was fairly quiet, but heavy firing began in the afternoon and evening. The British stayed out of the battle, except when the firing fell anywhere near their disposi- tions. In such instances, they returned fire by two-pounder guns, PIAT, and small arms. Early on April 22, Zionist forces began a major advance into the city, and by daylight they controlled a large portion of the town.[79] Zionist forces securely held Haifa's key positions by 8:00 a.m., dominating the Arab quarters and capturing the main Arab headquarters. The old city, too, had fallen, along with Prophets Street, which overlooked all of Wadi Nisnas.[80] At this point, the souk (market) had not been attacked.

The British knew little of conditions in central Haifa in those early hours. "Appeals for help from Arabs not only for their fighting men, but also for their women and children, were sent out," the First Battalion Coldstream Guards reported. Later that day, British forces saw why civilians were calling for help. The First Battalion Coldstream Guards reported that "during the morning [Zionist forces] were continually shooting down on all Arabs who moved both in the Wadi Nisnas and the Old City. This included completely indiscriminate and revolting machine gun fire, mortar fire and sniping on women and children sheltering in churches and attempting to get out of Haifa through the gates into the docks."[81] The Carmeli Brigade officers had ordered their troops to station three-inch mortars on the mountain slopes overlooking the market and the port to bombard the panicked, flee- ing crowds below. "The plan was to make sure" the Arabs "would have no second thoughts and to guarantee that the flight would be in one direction only": out of Haifa.[82]

The Arabs, being literally driven into the sea, tried frantically to reach the docks from the east gate. At this point, a British unit intervened to bring some order to the chaos. The 40 Commando Royal Marines tried to send the frantic Arabs through the gate in batches, but military assault on the Arabs continued. Outside the east gate there was a congested mass "of hysterical and terrified Arab women, children and old people . . . whom the Jews opened up on mercilessly with fire." Arab casualties mounted. "Wom- en and children were entreating to be given help to evacuate themselves," the Coldstream Guards' unit reported.[83] Targeted mass civilian intimidation compelled evacuation from Haifa on April 22, 1948.

Truce Negotiations

Official discussions about the fate of Haifa's Arabs began soon after the April 21–22 Zionist offensive. Many subsequent historical works focus on decisions made then and how they affected Arab flight. Yet momentum for flight had already grown and many people had already fled during the violence of the preceding months and during the fighting and anti-civilian terror of the previous days and hours.

The Haifa Arab National Committee (ANC) delegation met with Stockwell on April 22 to protest his redeployment, which they viewed as "a flagrant violation of the declared policy of His Majesty's Government to be responsible for the maintenance of peace and order up to and including the 15th day of May, 1948."[84] The delegation asked Stockwell to reconsider his redeployment and guard areas where Arab-Jewish clashes were likely. Stockwell reasoned that he could not because, by stepping into the battle, he would be faced with "engaging the Jews in a full-scale battle." He also had issued orders, "in the interest of humanity, that no reinforcements should pass through his posts" into Haifa. By thereby stopping Arab reinforcements from marching into town, he believed that he prevented the inevitable "renewed flare up of full-scale fighting and further very considerable loss of life."[85]

The ANC delegation, acting on its own initiative, required a face-saving step to start negotiations. The delegates stated that, although not empowered to sue for a truce, they might negotiate one if Stockwell signed a memorandum stating that he "was unable and therefore not prepared to fight the Jews and put an end" to the violence. It should also note, they insisted, that Stockwell barred Arab reinforcements from entering Haifa.

Stockwell was aware that Zionist attacks had killed and wounded Arab civilians, even though Zionist forces had not yet attacked the souk. Should that happen, he was certain, more innocent Arabs would be killed or wounded. He feared that if he permitted the battle to resume, the souk would be attacked—an expectation that weighed greatly on his decision to deny entry to Arab reinforcements. About 300 to 400 Arabs attempted to reach Haifa from al-Tira village, he reported, and British forces turned them back.[86]

Stockwell examined the Zionist-proposed truce terms, amending them so that British rather than Jewish forces would have authority to disarm Arab forces and perform searches. He then arranged a truce meeting in the town hall at 1600 hours on April 22. When the meeting resumed, the five-member ANC delegation stated that they were not in a position to sign a formal truce. Their objections reveal that they had far less influence on events than subsequent history suggests. They noted that they were essentially powerless and without higher authorization, having "no control over the Arab military elements in the town," and thus being unable to "fulfill the terms of the truce, even if they were to sign." They lacked official Arab authorization because they were unable to obtain guidance from Arab League headquarters in Damascus.[87]

The intimidation "on the ground," in any event, overwhelmed what authority they may have had. Elias Koussa, a Haifa lawyer and member of the ANC, stated that "since the [Haifa] Arabs were panic-stricken and running away through the harbor area" and Stockwell "was unwilling to intervene," all the ANC could do "was to ask the General to take the steps necessary to ensure sufficient transport for these people and their household effects."[88] The exodus of the Haifa Arabs still remaining in April was thus driven by fear of direct attack on civilians by Zionist armed forces. The ANC's request for evacuation could only mitigate some of the danger by bargaining for a safe exit.

In a later interview, Elias Koussa summarized their predicament. The ANC's request, he said, was

> made absolutely at the initiative of the five persons concerned who were self-nominated, but were not acting under any orders or instructions from the Arab states or elsewhere. The British authorities had refused to interfere. We had no means of contacting personally the Arab authorities to obtain clear instructions. . . . Thus, on the spur of the moment we had to find a way out of the situation in which General Stockwell had placed us. We either had to accept the truce or have another 300 or 400 Arabs killed.[89]

The evacuation proposal may also have been a counterbluff. The ANC, Koussa reported, had hoped that Stockwell would feel compelled by the ANC's entreaty to resume control of Haifa to avoid supervising the Arab evacuation, saving ANC members from signing a truce without the mufti's authorization. Stockwell, however, called the bluff and acceded to the ANC's request to safeguard the evacuation.[90]

Stockwell's meeting minutes record a confrontational dialogue. Arab representatives told Stockwell that very few of the remaining 37,000 Arabs wanted to remain in Haifa. They had no gasoline and asked the military to provide it for evacuation. The Arabs wanted to take lots of luggage, but Stockwell protested that it would "take a fortnight" and "hold up" British movements.

The delegation blamed a growing "food problem" on continued Zionist shooting and occupation of Arab areas. British Commodore Allan Peachy, obviously annoyed by the distraction of evacuating the Arabs, retorted angrily, "If you sign your truce you would automatically get all your food worries over. You are merely starving your own people." The Arab representatives still refused to sign, declaring, "All is already lost and it does not matter if everyone is killed as long as we do not sign this document."[91]

In a follow-up meeting with the ANC and Jewish delegation on April 23, Stockwell announced the ANC's decision to accept a protected evacuation rather than sign the truce. Koussa noted that Mayor Shabtai Levy of the Jewish delegation was particularly moved by the Arabs' plight and appealed to the Arabs to reconsider.[92] Jewish leaders then assured the Arabs during the meeting that Arabs who evacuated could return safely to Haifa at a later date. Such assurances that Arabs could return to their "houses, business[es] and shops" may have contributed to the Haifa leadership's decision to evacuate Arabs who remained. In any event, by organizing an evacuation they did not intend to abandon homes, but rather to temporarily relocate people under the official promise of return.

The following meeting minutes were probably taken by GOC Stockwell and discuss the practicalities of evacuation:

Jews:	We will give every assistance possible.
GOC:	Question of restoring confidence.
Arabs:	Problem. Agreed to evacuate but that only depends on no shooting. If shooting does not stop we cannot evacuate.
Jews:	No shooting unless fired at.
GOC:	To Arabs must ensure that they can go back.

Jews:	Assist in every way to ensure this.
Arabs:	Can they go back to their houses, business and shops[?]
Jews:	Yes certainly.
Arabs:	We will not be shot at [during evacuation].
Jews:	Shoot only if shot at.

A joint Arab-Jewish committee, under Mayor Levy's chairmanship, was set up to tackle evacuation and food problems. British military and police assisted in evacuating wounded Arabs. The Coldstream Guards' described a scene of significant carnage and desperation: "Nothing was signed on paper but it was agreed that all fighting should cease, and that the Arabs should be allowed first to remove their dead, wounded, women and children, and then to leave Haifa themselves by boats organized from the docks and by convoys of trucks. All their arms would be taken from them by British Troops at the road blocks and these arms would be given over to the Jews after May 15th."[93]

The limited role of the controversial negotiations on April 22 and 23 in spurring the flight of Haifa's Arabs is illustrated by subsequent events. Despite the verbal agreement, Zionist intimidation continued. When a British officer, escorted by a troop of Staghound armored cars, took five ambulances down Allenby Road to remove Arab wounded, a Jewish sniper shot the officer in the arm. "It was clear that the Jews intended to prevent the ambulances from taking away the wounded Arabs," the troops reported.[94] British forces also engaged in fire with "Jews who were attempting to interrupt the flow of refugees through the main gate of the Port." Several British officers were wounded in these operations.[95] The "Arabs were in a state of considerable panic," fearing they would be killed by the continuous shelling. "Almost all inhabitants of Haifa headed to the port . . . thousands were on the seashore." The port was the sole exit from Haifa because "Jews had blocked the eastern and western sides" of the city.[96] Sailboats, steamers, and motorboats departed and returned each day. Fifty-person boats were overcrowded with 300 to 400 people. Some of the fleeing population fell into the water and drowned. During the next few days, C Squadron King's Own Hussars escorted Arab refugees overland to the frontiers of Lebanon and Transjordan.[97]

At the Port of Haifa, British police attempted to organize the Haifa Arabs and to ship them to Acre by Royal Navy Z craft.[98] The refugee flow continued through April 24. The Third King's Own Hussars reported that it was "difficult to assess where the refugee problem finishes and organized evacuation starts."[99]

Meanwhile, an incensed Arab League secretary general, Azzam Pasha, contacted the high commissioner on April 25 to denounce Zionist violence against Haifa's Arabs. Although the Arab League head said that "Jews had stopped mutilating women and children," he charged that "they were shooting them down in large numbers and pretending that this was merely an unfortunate result of battle."[100]

Casualty figures from fighting in Haifa vary widely among British officials. Stockwell estimated casualties at 16 to 20 Jews killed and 30 to 40 wounded; and 100 Arabs killed and 150 to 200 wounded.[101] His figures may reflect only military casualties. Cunningham's report on Haifa implies that Stockwell's casualty figures included only combatants. He wrote, "Not yet known number of casualties among women and children who were involved in the battle." Cunningham stressed, however, that there was "no question of [a] massacre."[102] Other British sources closer to the scene report many more civilian casualties. The Palestine Police estimated that as many as 2,000 Arabs had been killed.[103] Haganah forces also reported many dead and wounded. The Carmeli Brigade reported on April 22 that "the Arab hospitals are full of dead and wounded. Corpses and wounded lie in the streets and are not collected for lack of organization and sanitary means; panic in the Arab street is great."[104]

The high commissioner's report to his political superiors downplayed the violence, but his account may have been self-serving. A figure of 2,000 Arabs killed, including women and children, would support the Arabs' assertion of catastrophic British failure. The mandate government, criticized for inaction after the Dayr Yasin massacre, was not apt to admit another debacle.

The Arab evacuation to the docks continued throughout April 24. The Zionist advance now turned to looting, despite an ostensible cease-fire. British troops noted that Haganah forces "went through very many of the Arab houses in Haifa and much looting went on."[105] It was not clear if this was officially countenanced: the British were uncertain whether Haganah leaders had full control of their forces. The Haganah finally dropped leaflets "warning looters that they would be shot on sight," but the warning seemed to have had little effect on the dissident groups. The Coldstream Guards noted that IZL forces seemed to want "to promote a further rush of armed forces into the suk [souk] and other places where Arabs were still living in order to force the issue by creating more refugees and a new wave of terror. Looting of Arab property by [the] IZL took place."[106]

Two weeks after Dayr Yasin, the IZL flag was flying from four different houses in Haifa, further intimidating the Arabs who remained in Haifa.[107] Haganah efforts to stem the looting occasionally turned serious, as when an IZL man was shot by the Haganah in Wadi Nisnas.[108]

The climate of terror was sustained throughout the battle and afterward. The Arabs were "still very stunned," the British reported, adding that Arabs who now remained in Haifa were "too terrified to leave their homes."[109] But a great many managed to reach the docks. There conditions were horrible, recalls a police officer. Husbands could not find wives; frantic and crying mothers searched for their children. He described a desperate scene, confirming British reports and suggesting that high-level negotiations about evacuation did little to help the refugees.

> They were all running towards the port. They ran away with only their lives, and left behind everything they possessed: money, shops, clothes, goods and houses. The available boats could not take all those people at one time. Therefore, they slept on the streets of the harbor for three days in the cold and rain. It was raining heavily for the first time in April in Haifa. People were sleeping in this rain without any cover. . . . Some of them were barefoot and some of the women were without enough clothes to cover them. They left everything behind, even their shoes.
>
> They were in a horrifying condition. . . . How could anyone leave all that behind without feeling a pressing danger, against his life and the life of his children?[110]

Feeding all the Arabs waiting for a ship, he said, was a "considerable problem" for the British.[111]

Evaluating the Arab Exodus

The momentum of the attack and its excesses had set off a spontaneous evacuation of Haifa's remaining Arabs. They continued to leave the city "unceasingly with the least possible delay," and British military observers realized that few were likely to remain. Convoys of Arabs left for Acre escorted by the First Battalion Grenadier Guards, but 300 Arabs remained in the Haifa port outside the east gate and refused "to move until escorted to Lebanon."[112] The wisdom, acceptance, and implementation of an organized evacuation of the Arab remnant consumed the town's leadership for days after the major assault, just as it has consumed much subsequent historiography on Haifa's Arab depopulation. Contemporary observations, however, reveal that the momentous exodus was spurred by violence and abuse by Zionist military forces, both official and dissident, and that the negotiations over evacuation were simply ad hoc crisis management with little fundamental impact.

Certainly, the Arab depopulation was abetted by the failures of Arab military and political leadership to secure Haifa's Arab areas while provoking violence from the other side. Many officials and commanders contributed to intensifying overall violence in the city and then abandoned Haifa at the crucial stage of the battle. Stockwell reported that the Arab commanders Amin 'Iz al-Din and Yunis Nafa'a left town on April 21 and April 22, respectively. Khalidi asserts that Captain 'Iz al-Din went straight to Damascus to alert the Arab League military committee of Stockwell's plan to withdraw from Haifa after the April 21 meeting. He had, meanwhile, handed over the Arab garrison command to Yunis Nafa'a, a Palestinian sanitary engineer "with no military experience whatsoever."[113] Stockwell's information was that the ALA command in Damascus had ignored continual requests from the Palestinian Arabs for reinforcements.[114]

The chief secretary of Palestine, Sir Henry Gurney, observed that the Zionist offensive had been provoked by the Arabs: "It became clear today that the Jewish offensive at Haifa was staged as a direct consequence of four days' continuous Arab attacks." Nevertheless, Gurney also believed that the offensive was part of overall Zionist designs. "Not that it [the offensive] is contrary to Jewish policy. The Arabs have played right into their hands. We have seen this coming for some time but with one or two exceptions, our requests that the Arab States should hold their hands have been largely ignored."[115]

Lippincott, the U.S. consul, provided a local perspective: "If the present situation goes on, there will be a Jewish state in all of Palestine and not only in the areas proposed by the partition scheme. Certain British officers who have observed the whole situation here are deeply impressed by Jewish organization, training, and discipline. They feel that there is no force in the Arab world today which is capable of dealing with them."[116]

Debate over the Arab Exodus

The historical and related political debate over the Arab exodus from Haifa reflects the conflicts' two distinct political camps. Palestinians insist they were violently forced out. Zionists claim that the mufti, represented by the Haifa Arab leadership, told the Arabs to leave while Jews pleaded with them to remain. Although the contemporary record can be selectively cited to support either view, the sequence of events constructed from eyewitness accounts shows that the Palestinian narrative is more accurate.

The Zionist narrative alleging that the Arabs left on Arab orders took root early. On April 23, the Jewish Agency said in the *Times* of London that "this exodus has been carried out deliberately by the Arabs to besmirch the Jews, to influence the Arab Governments to send more help, and to clear the ground for an attack by regular Arab forces later."[117]

British and U.S. contemporary reports and conclusions do state that the Arab leadership advised the Arabs to leave, an interpretation derived from the failed truce negotiations. The ANC delegation had admitted to Stockwell in those negotiations that they were not empowered to sign a truce. The leaders opted instead for a British-supervised evacuation. In this regard, the ANC's decision appears to have been leader-inspired flight.

But the simplistic assumption of Arab-initiated exodus neglects the fact that the organized evacuation measures accepted by a nearly powerless body followed months of anti-civilian violence, culminating in the Zionist offensive in April. A mass stampede to the harbor by the terrorized and panicked Haifa Arab population was well under way when negotiations began. Additionally, the British had political motives to blame the evacuation on Haifa Arab leaders' decision making. Stockwell and the British military were angered by the Arab leadership's refusal to sign a truce and eager to vindicate their own abandonment of the city to the subsequent chaos, population flight, and warfare. The mass evacuation of Haifa Arabs also created a logistical burden for British forces, affecting their own evacuation. Responsibility for all of this had to be cast away from the British or the Zionists to whom they had effectively turned over the city's fate.

Certainly, the Arab leadership's refusal to sign a truce, as Lippincott wrote, "left Jews with no way to meet Arabs," and therefore, there was "no organization of Haifa, no thorough disarming of Arabs and no curfew imposed."[118] The apparently sincere appeal by Mayor Levy asking the Arabs to reconsider their evacuation substantiates a claim of Arab-initiated abandonment. Further, the Zionist leadership had a real incentive to limit flight, both for the sake of international appearances and because it feared that the departure of Arab labor might "slow down to [the] danger point" all essential port and industrial activity, as Lippincott observed.[119] The Haifa refinery did partly close under Arab threats to cut the pipeline if the Jews attempted to supply labor.[120] Thus, incentive to limit Arab flight from Haifa existed, and Jewish leaders took stabilizing measures over the ensuing days.

Nevertheless, the Haganah and dissident Zionist groups had clearly propelled the enormous rush of panicked refugees after intimidating much of the city's Arab population into evacuating earlier. The Haifa Arab leaders' decision to request a protected evacuation had limited consequences because it was not enforceable against Arabs who did not wish to go, and because it affected only the proportionally small and fleeing population that remained. Farid Sa'ad, head of the Arab Bank and an ANC member who participated in the truce negotiations, said no "order" was given to evacuate. When Lippincott questioned Sa'ad about the Arab exodus on April 28, the latter replied, according to Lippincott, that "no order had been given to the Arab population telling them to leave. . . . those members of the National Committee who remained in Haifa were telling people to use their own judgment as to whether they should stay or leave."

Sa'ad cited Zionist pressure on the population: "People were in a panic after the unexpectedly easy Jewish victory," and "subsequent Jewish looting and attacks on refugees had simply added to the panic." In September 1947, there were approximately 80,000 Arabs in Haifa. Departures due to "unsettled conditions," including the atmosphere of directed violence, had reduced the number to about 40,000 by April 1, 1948. Approximately 35,000 fled thereafter, during the April 21–23 fighting, leaving "not more than 5,000 Arabs in Haifa," Sa'ad reported. He believed fewer than 1,000 Arabs remained in Haifa by May 1, 1948.[121]

One eyewitness account illustrates why the population's flight was beyond Arab leaders' control. The Haifa resident Fatima Husayn al-Jawabri said the Zionists "shot people in the streets. They killed many people in their stores." In statements corroborated by contemporary British reports cited earlier, al-Jawabri said some people left Haifa in fear while others remained frightened but hidden: "[The Jews] sprayed people in the streets with machine-gunfire. They did not differentiate between women and children or men. . . . They destroyed some houses in Haifa over the heads of the people. . . . We did not have a choice, either run away or turn ourselves over to them." Al-Jawabri recalled the ultimate cause of the exodus: "We looked death in the face."[122] No official evacuation or truce decision by an ad hoc authority during such chaotic conditions was likely to override widespread panic and intimidation.

Experienced contemporary observers also blamed the flight on persistent intimidation and terror. Colonel Waddy described the Arabs' plight as resulting from "acts of terrorism," which included "mortaring of [the Arab] area." Many Arabs evacuating the town headed for safety in "private car, lorry and bus[,] . . . loaded up with all sorts of their household belongings, carpets, mattresses, cooking material," a stream of humanity leaving for safety in Lebanon. In Waddy's assessment, the flight was "what the Jews wanted them to do."[123]

Many families had been split up during the battle and wanted to reunite in safer areas. Haifa's Arabs eventually fled to Syria and Lebanon, as well as to Nazareth and other outlying Arab towns in Palestine.[124] Haifa's Arabs had become aware that they could not defend themselves, nor could the Arab forces defend them. In the final period, during and after the Haganah assault of April 21–22, they found that the British would not protect them. Violence and intimidation through a variety of tactics, from psychological to actual warfare, and the Arabs' awareness that they were defenseless, were the decisive factors impelling the Arabs' exodus from Haifa.

No leader, local or foreign, could calm this fear. As the Haifa resident Hasib Sabbagh of the Arab Abbas quarter put it, when "the final Jewish onslaught came . . . there started a panicky flight."[125] One leader, the Haifa National Committee member George Mu'ammar, "upset by the flight of Haifa's residents," stood on his balcony, "haranguing the crowds . . . pleading with them not to leave." His efforts proved fruitless.

Benny Morris vastly overstates one factor in the Haifa exodus by concluding that the departure of the Arab military and political leadership was a major cause.[126] While the leaders' departure did contribute to a decline in order and morale, Haifa's Arabs evacuated because of war-induced panic, believing they were fleeing for their lives. No local informant cited the premature departure of town notables and commanders as a reason for flight.

Haifa after the Zionist Takeover

As time passed and the violence ebbed in Haifa, tension grew between demographically oriented Zionist military intimidation and attempts by some Jewish leaders to stem the continued flight for economic and humanitarian reasons. When manual labor shortages became acute, Haifa's Jews set up relief-committee liaison offices and did "a considerable amount to induce the Arab labor to stay," as more Jews were being forced into manual labor in the docks. A pamphlet written in Arabic and signed by the chief of Haganah stated:

> To All Arab People in Haifa
> All those who have gone from Wadi Nisnas and the Wadi Salib areas
> must return to their homes immediately, open their shops and start work.
> We will ensure they are safe.[127]

Yet Zionist repressive measures continued to spur the Arabs' evacuation and block return. The Coldstream Guards observed that Zionist looting continued and that Arabs were not allowed "to move anything from their houses."[128] These actions heightened anxieties already reigning among the Arabs and augmented their "terror of returning to their homes."[129] Haganah members also arrested "many Arabs who were reputed to have had anti-Jewish feelings and ideas."[130] These and similar menacing actions did "much harm towards any attempt to induce Arabs to remain in Haifa," the Coldstream Guards observed.[131] The U.S. consul also reported there was "considerable Jew[ish] looting in evacuated Arab areas." Two churches were desecrated, and an Arab doctor's clinic was stripped of equipment and furnishings, then demolished. Jewish leaders and Arabs attempted joint measures to stop the looting, with the main action being a curfew imposed on the Arab area for all Jews.[132]

Looting was eventually stopped, primarily because private property appropriated was to be transferred to Zionist central command. On Ben-Gurion's initiative, Moshe Dayan, the officer for Arab affairs, was sent to Haifa to administer "abandoned Arab property." Dayan "ordered that everything the army could use be transferred to Zahal warehouses," and everything else be distributed among Jewish agricultural settlements. Golda Meir agreed to this policy "as a form of reparation for the settlements that had suffered from Arab terrorism."[133]

U.S. Consul Lippincott wrote that Jewish leaders eventually "organized a large propaganda campaign to persuade Arabs to return." The Arabs, however, did not trust the efforts, "particularly after the looting of the past few days and in view of Jewish control of the whole Arab area of the city."[134] Haifa's Arabs were predominately Christian, and the Jewish Agency was apparently willing to allow some of them to remain in certain areas. Nonetheless, the remaining Arabs, Colonel Waddy said, were expecting that, at any time, another all-out Zionist attack would completely overrun the Arab quarter. The British were impotent to stop it, according to Waddy: "[Zionist forces] could have by passed the British Army Post, we were very thin on the ground and if they had taken the Arab quarter we couldn't have done anything about it, except mount [an] immediate operation and start up a minor war."[135] Thus, despite a measure of stabilization, continuing Zionist repressive measures prompted further evacuation and discouraged Arabs from returning.

Some Arab families apparently returned from Acre, where they had sought safety. But the Israeli Communist Party charged on May 10 that the Arabs lacked basic services such as running water, electricity, and garbage collection. Looting continued, and the curbs on freedom of movement resulted in "a prison regime" existence.[136] Like those in Jaffa, Acre, and other cities and towns, Arabs in Haifa were forced into ghetto-like areas. The approximately 4,000 who remained were transferred to the Wadi Nisnas neighborhood and to Abbas Street in early July. The Israeli government seized thousands of Arab homes and settled new immigrants there.[137]

Political Fallout from the Zionist Victory

The fall of Haifa to Zionist forces created a brief political firestorm in London, but it failed to change British evacuation policy. A member of Parliament demanded to know whether the secretary of state for war had issued the announcement on April 22 that "he was unable" and therefore "not prepared to fight [the] Jews in order to stop massacre of Arabs in Haifa but was prepared to prevent [the] entry of armed Arabs coming to the defense of their nationals."[138] The strife in Haifa was quite embarrassing for the British government, which had repeatedly pronounced that it would remain responsible for law and order in Palestine until the mandate's termination.[139] The minister of defense said "the steps taken to meet the threat [in Haifa] had very important political implications," and there was no doubt that the chiefs of staff should have advised the ministers before a decision was taken.[140]

Although Stockwell's decision was politically unpopular in London, Cyril Marriott, the British consul general designate in Haifa, defended his actions. Marriott wrote that by the time he arrived in Haifa, the "tension between Jews and Arabs had grown so acute and both sides appeared so confident" that Stockwell had to consider action to safeguard British troops and their evacuation.[141] Marriott also blamed the lack of security in Haifa on the civil administration, which for at least two months had been "more interested in the liquidation of their own private affairs and with the detail of winding up their own offices than with the maintenance of law and order."[142] The British military indignantly complained that "after [the Arab] defeat at Haifa [and] in order to excuse their own ineptitude[,] Arab leaders accused us of helping Jews and hindering Arabs[,] although it [defeat] was actually due to inefficient and cowardly behavior of Arab military leaders and their refusal to follow our advice to restrain themselves."[143]

Cunningham quickly drafted an official report, reinforcing Stockwell's account of the battle and forcefully countering every Arab argument of British connivance. He indignantly telegrammed London that the Haganah attack at Haifa resulted from Arab attacks on Jews over four days, and he denied a "massacre." Cunningham said "the Arabs in Haifa were thus themselves responsible for this outbreak in spite of our repeated warnings." Justifying Stockwell's decision, he emphasized that "as always" the army was "completely impartial" and any suggestion that it was taking sides was "not only untrue but deeply resented."[144] To protect himself politically, Cunningham needed to explain away the disaster, but he also contradicted Stockwell's and his own admissions of the need to preserve Zionist rule in Haifa.

The Arab League political committee strongly resented Cunningham's version of events leading up to the Zionist occupation of Haifa. Committee members claimed that Haifa Arabs constituted less than half of the population and were weakly armed, cut off by the Jews from the rest of the country, and on the defense. It was unfair to accuse the Arabs of aggression, particularly "considering the Arab restraint in spite of Jewish conduct at Dayr Yasin and Tiberias," where Zionist dissident forces had massacred and Haganah forces expelled the populations.[145] The Arab states protested vigorously to the Foreign Office that the British withdrawal in Haifa was "contrary to [the] understanding under which Arab states decided to refrain from intervening in Palestine until after May 15," and they claimed that the sudden British exit from Haifa, for which the Arabs were unprepared, had given considerable advantage to the Zionists.[146] The Foreign Office's Eastern Department was also disturbed by the events in Haifa. Its head, Bernard Burrows, said that he was "surprised and somewhat mystified" by developments in the city, where the British military appeared "to have acted as though it were May 15."[147]

The Haifa battle and forced exodus of the population caused the Arab states to escalate threats to intervene before May 15. The Arab League secretary general, Azzam Pasha, told the British colonial secretary on April 23 that he was convinced the Haifa "massacre" was "part of [a] Jewish military plan designed to terrorize the Arab population inside the Jewish state so that by May 15th they would be released of having to deal with any fifth column and be able to concentrate their whole energy on action against regular Arab forces which they believed would then enter Palestine from outside."[148] Azzam Pasha threatened that "if these massacres continued and British Forces were unable to give protection," public opinion would force the Arab states to intervene militarily," in which case, the Arab states "could hardly be accused of an act of aggression."[149] Two days later, Azzam Pasha tried persuasion to convey the Palestinian Arabs' desperate plight in facing a "fully mobilized Jewish force," whose activities the British were "completely unable to control." A counterbalancing Arab force, he argued, "could only come from outside." He pessimistically (and presciently) predicted that if the British maintained their policy of resisting Arab incursions by force until May 15, Zionist forces would have "occupied all the strategic positions they required and the Arabs would find themselves at a grave disadvantage."[150]

Azzam Pasha held the British responsible for the events in Haifa. He had written to GOC Gordon MacMillan, "warning him that the Arabs at Haifa were in a defenseless position," and had requested reassurance that "adequate warning would be given in order to prepare for their defense." He characterized Cunningham's statement that the Arabs had provoked the

Haganah attack and occupation of Haifa as "devoid of truth." There had been street fighting for two months, but "there were not enough [Arab] men or arms to make an attack." On several occasions, Haifa's district commissioner, Husayn al-Khalidi, had also sought reassurances from the British military authorities that civilian Arabs would be protected in case of a sudden British withdrawal. Al-Khalidi's last request was reportedly made just three hours before the order was given for British forces to redeploy to the port area. "The bad faith of the British," Azzam Pasha bitterly complained, "was overwhelmingly apparent." He was appalled at the Haganah's treatment of the civilian population. It was "clearly indicative of what the status of the Arabs would be under Jewish authority," he remarked.[151]

Anti-British reactions to the Haifa situation were "fairly strong" in the Arab national capitals, especially after the Dayr Yasin massacre. In Cairo, Damascus, and Baghdad the slogan was "Down with [the] British and the Zionists."[152] After the Arab defeat in Haifa, the Arab states threatened to send armed forces into Palestine immediately. The British minister in Transjordan, Sir Alec Kirkbride, reported that the king and the regent were "under tremendous public pressure to intervene immediately in Palestine." Amman was crowded with Palestinian refugees, making the situation there especially difficult. Both men, however, were "apprehensive" about embarking on a military campaign in Palestine "against forces [of] unknown strength."[153]

British policy grew more concerned with preventing the Arab states' entry into the conflict. MacMillan told the high commissioner on April 23 that he was "no longer in a position to take any steps to prevent such [a military] incursion." Moreover, MacMillan warned that the "Jewish Agency already know[s] that he can no longer undertake any major operation against either community." As far as the Arab states' threats were concerned, Cunningham judged the only major Arab force immediately available to intervene was the Arab Legion, and he assumed it would be possible to prevent King Abdullah from sending in the Legion before the mandate terminated. He had no doubt, however, that the Haifa affair would "result in strong pressure" on King Abdullah to act earlier.[154] In the end, Arab pressure failed to alter British policy, in part because threats were not followed by action. As of April 27 there were "no present intention[s of] Arab armies to move into Palestine before May 15." On the contrary, Kirkbride said that Arab leaders were using the existence of the mandate as an "excuse not to move" and to

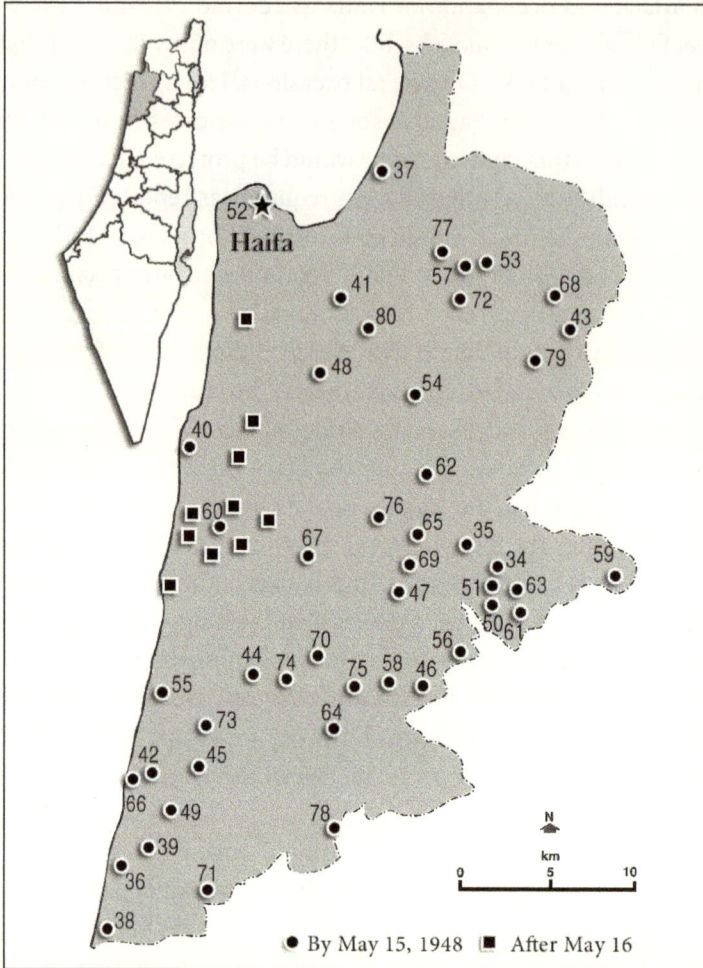

● By May 15, 1948 ■ After May 16

HAIFA SUBDISTRICT DEPOPULATED TOWNS AND VILLAGES

34. Abu Shusha
35. Abu Zurayq
36. 'Arab al-Fuqara'
37. 'Arab al-Ghawarina (Jidru)
38. 'Arab al-Nufay'at
39. 'Arab Zahrat al-Dumayri
40. 'Atlit
41. Balad al-Shaykh
42. Barrat Qisarya
43. Bayt Laham
44. Burayka

45. Khirbat al-Burj
46. Al-Butaymat
47. Daliyat al-Rawha'
48. Khirbat al-Damun
49. Al-Dumayri
50. Al-Ghubayya al-Fauqa
51. Al-Ghubayya al-Tahta
52. Haifa (Arab)
53. Hawsha
54. Al-Jalama
55. Kabara

56. Al-Kafrayn
57. Khirbat al-Kasayir
58. Khubbayza
59. Khirbat Lid (Lid al-'Awadin)
60. Khirbat al-Manara
61. Al-Mansi ('Arab Baniha)
62. Khirbat al-Mansura
63. Al-Naghnaghiyya
64. Qannir
65. Qira wa Qamun
66. Qisarya (Caesarea)
67. Khirbat Qumbaza
68. Khirbat Ras 'Ali

69. Al-Rihaniyya
70. Sabbarin
71. Khirbat al-Sarkas
72. Khirbat Sa'sa'
73. Khirbat al-Shuna
74. Al-Sindiyana
75. Umm al-Shawf
76. Umm al-Zinat
77. Wa'arat al-Sarris
78. Wadi 'Ara
79. Waldheim (Ummal 'Amad)
80. Yajur

shift "popular Arab feeling against His Majesty's Government."[155]

Chief Secretary Gurney viewed the growing anti-British feeling among the Arabs, largely resulting from Haifa's fall and the flight of its refugees, as a significant problem. His conclusion was to redouble the existing policy of nonintervention, as he felt Britain was unable to do anything further. The danger that this animosity would spread was another reason why the mandate government and garrison should extricate itself with haste "from an impossible position in Jerusalem." Gurney wrote on April 27 that it was "not as though we could now conceivably do any good by staying."[156] In contrast to the hesitancy of the Arab states, Gurney believed that the Zionist forces, "full of confidence and optimism," would "go for an all-out offensive against the Arabs in Jerusalem and Jaffa," to demonstrate their superior military strength and, "in the case of Jerusalem, to cut the remaining roads by which the Arab Legion could come into Jerusalem or Palestine."[157] In the aftermath of the Zionist victory in Haifa, the Zionists had "become very full of their importance," even circulating rumors abroad that they completely controlled Haifa (where British forces were still deployed). Two ships of illegal Jewish immigrants arrived in Haifa with this understanding.[158]

Intimidation of the Arabs in the suburbs of Haifa followed. The Haganah requested access to Haifa airfield and permission "to attack certain Arab villages." The British believed these requests confirmed Jewish Agency intentions of conquering and controlling the entire area surrounding Haifa in order to maintain access to the northern Jewish colonies. Furthermore, the First Battalion Coldstream Guards reported that it was a Haganah goal to terrorize the population on Haifa's outskirts to flee by employing tactics similar to those used in the town. The battalion considered it likely that the Haganah would "continue mortaring and shelling round Haifa to create an evacuation of the population," which they considered essential "to maintain control of all the villages and ground around Haifa."[159] Haganah forces attacked and occupied the satellite Arab village of Balad al-Shaykh on the Nazareth road on April 24 and al-Tira village on April 26, forcing the Arab villagers to flee.[160]

Depopulated Villages and Towns of Haifa Subdistrict

Zionist military action and intimidation continued in the area surrounding Haifa around the time the city fell. The Haifa subdistrict of the Palestine mandate was administratively the same as the Haifa district. In 1945, subdistrict lands were 44.6 percent Arab-owned, 35.3 percent Jewish-owned, and 20.1 percent public property. The population was 53.5 percent Arab and 46.5 percent Jewish. Seventy-two Arab villages existed in 1948. Fortyseven villages, or 65 percent, were forcibly depopulated before the mandate ended and eventually demolished. Some village demolition preceded the mandate's end.[161] Palestinian refugee recollections included here recount how the inhabitants of some of these villages were expelled.

The depopulation policy can be traced in Zionist documentation. By January 1948, Joseph Weitz, the director of the Jewish National Fund's Lands Department—"the principal Zionist tool for the colonization of Palestine"[162]—was considering how to remove Arab tenant farmers. In 1940 he wrote in his diary, "The only solution is to transfer the Arabs from here to neighboring countries. Not a single village or a single tribe must be let off."[163] Weitz believed that the Zionists had a "right to transfer the Arabs," and "the Arabs should go!"[164] Like Ben-Gurion, he viewed the civil war and anarchy in early 1948 as a historic opportunity to clear the Arabs from the land. Regarding the tenant farmers of Daliyat al-Rawha' (pop. 325), he wrote in his diary: "Is it not now the time to be rid of them?"[165]

Psychological warfare tactics were used to intimidate the villagers at Daliyat al-Rawha'. 'Alya Muhammad Hasan, a woman from the village, said that when the war started, neighboring Jews came to the fields and threatened them, saying, "We cannot secure your lives because we cannot stop the Haganah from killing." The villagers left on March 3, 1948, because of such threats. "We were frightened as a small village situated between four Jewish settlements," Hasan said. They left for Ijzim, where they stayed for four months, hoping to return. Her uncle returned to Daliyat al-Rawha' after 15 days and found the houses destroyed. When Zionist forces attacked Ijzim later in July 1948, the villagers of Daliyat al-Rawha' fled a second time with Ijzim's inhabitants.[166]

Hawsha (pop. 464) was attacked by Zionist forces and depopulated on April 15. According to Rafik 'Urabi Mahmud Hamdan Fahmawi, of the neighboring Umm al-Zinat village, "Jews stabbed pregnant women in [Hawsha] and killed many people; even a mute boy from our village was shot in his eyes and killed in that massacre. His name was Hasan Khalid. Hawsha (Hawassa) was occupied before [Umm al-Zinat] and we heard all its details."[167] Details of Fahmawi's account are partially corroborated by the *History of the Haganah,* which states that Hawsha saw fierce fighting, sometimes with knives. The *New York Times* reported that "many Arabs were killed."[168] Salman Abu-Sitta lists Hawsha as the site of a massacre.[169]

Asad Nimir Dib Sidik said that after the villagers of Rihaniyya (pop. 278) shot one of two Jewish infiltrators, they were attacked from neighboring Jewish camps and settlements. With only two or three guns in the entire village, the villagers decided to leave on April 30: "We decided to leave our village because it was small and we did not have guns to defend it. They kicked everybody out from the surrounding villages. We thought we would remain outside [the village] for a week, then [it became] a month, then seven months." The villagers took their belongings with them to Umm al-Zinat. When Zionist forces attacked that village, "without any provocation,"[170] Rihaniyya's villagers "left Umm al-Zinat with nothing but our clothes on," Asad Sidik remembers. The villagers next sought refuge in Ijzim, along with inhabitants of 'Ayn Ghazal: "In our village nobody was killed, but when they attacked Umm al-Zinat some of our villagers were shot along with people from Umm al-Zinat. Jews closed all the roads so we could not go back to our village. . . . We heard about the Tantura massacre [May 22–23] where young men were shot after being lined up against the wall." The villagers remained in Ijzim for six months. Zionist forces then attacked Ijzim "and kicked everybody out," Sidik said. The villagers of Rihaniyya then sought refuge in Umm al-Fahim.[171]

Amina Ahmad Dabbur, of Umm al-Zinat (pop. 1,705), said that some Jews warned the villagers that the Haganah would attack. The men tried to barricade the main street of Umm al-Zinat with stones. When Haganah forces attacked the village during Operation Hametz, they destroyed the barricade, "entered the village and killed three men." Zionist forces previously had attacked the village unsuccessfully three times, being unable to penetrate the barricade. The mukhtar left for Nazareth before the attack, and other villagers left in fear after him. Nevertheless, Dabbur said "the majority of the village stayed until the Jews attacked" on May 15.[172]

Rafik 'Urabi Mahmud Hamdan Fahmawi, of Umm al-Zinat, said they had no guns to defend the village.

> The Jews forced the people out of the village. They killed Isma'il al-Khalil and Muhammad al-Salim and a man called 'Abd al-Ghani, who was killed in his house. . . . They killed a man called Yusif 'Ulayan and Husayn Abu Zayni and Muhammad Hasan Salih, and they beheaded Ali Saffuri. Those people were killed because they did not leave the village. This was a sudden attack, and nobody resisted.

> The Jews opened a road to the village of Daliyat al-Druze and let the people pass to that village. Some people went to the village of Ijzim. Then people were forced to leave Ijzim after its fall and were then rounded up in Daliyat al-Druze, where Jews forced them into buses. The buses passed by our village, and we saw them robbing the houses. The buses left us in an area called Wadi al-Milih. Then [the Jews] took our possessions and money.

Of the elderly who remained in Umm al-Zinat, "[The Jews] put them on donkeys saying 'go to King Abdullah.'"[173]

Villagers fleeing from the village of Balad al-Shaykh told 'Alya 'Ali 'Abdullah of Yajur (pop. 708) that the Jews had "killed and massacred the people [in Balad al-Shaykh] with axes and machine guns. . . . We were in the village at that time, and fear filled our hearts, especially because there were two Jewish settlements near us. So some families left for 'Isfiya." After a visit from the Jewish mukhtar, all the villagers left for 'Isfiya together. Some of the villagers returned to the village to harvest their crops and sell them in Haifa. "One day the Jews ambushed them, killed the horses, and massacred the men and the women." Yajur villagers stayed in 'Isfiya for four months, then "the Jews came and with the help of the Druze expelled us from 'Isfiya." The villagers were not allowed to take anything with them.[174]

IZL forces attacked a number of villages while British troops were still stationed in the countryside, including Burayka, Khubbayza, Sabbarin, al-Sindiyana, and Umm al-Shawf. Some villagers fled under heavy mortar fire, while others, signaling their surrender with white flags, "were instantly exiled." Because Sabbarin villagers attempted to defend themselves, Zionist forces confined the old men, women, and children for days in barbed-wire cages.[175]

In the course of "cleansing" occupied villages, Zionist forces carried out routine "search-and-arrest" operations. Young boys and men were lined up, and those on a "wanted" list—for any number of reasons—were identified by an informant wearing a cloth headsack with eyeholes cut out. Some villagers were shot on the spot.[176] Others became prisoners. Males, aged ten to 50, were held in large temporary pens throughout the countryside until they were transferred to prisons.[177]

After Haifa's occupation, Israeli intelligence units searched for "returnees," exiled Arabs attempting to return to their homes after the fighting had subsided. The returnees, even those residing in their own homes, would be rounded up and taken to the interrogation center in the Hadar neighborhood on Mount Carmel. Prisoners were tortured; even Israeli high command "expressed reservations about the brutality" used against Palestinians interned at Haifa.[178]

Other detainees were sent to forced-labor camps. They were used "in any job that could help to strengthen both the Israeli economy and the army's capabilities."[179] A survivor of the massacre at Tantura village (pop. 1,728)—near Haifa, where the Haganah's Alexandroni Brigade murdered between 200 and 250 villagers—testified about his prison camp life.[180] He worked in the quarries carrying heavy stones, lived on one potato in the morning and half a dried fish at noon. "There was no point in complaining as disobedience was punished with severe beatings," he said.[181] 'Adil Muhammad al-'Ammuri and Mahmud Nimr 'Abd al-Mu'ti, from Tantura, both teenagers at the time, testified that they were forced to harvest Arab fields for the Jews. They were aware that "a number of those that went to work didn't come back."[182] Red Cross officials reported that Israelis exploited the prisoners to "strengthen the Israeli economy."[183]

A Pattern of Zionist Intimidation and British Nonintervention

The Palestinian Arab exodus from Haifa and surrounding rural areas represents in microcosm the pattern of events throughout Palestine during the civil war. British security forces, legally bound as the mandate authority to maintain law and order, were reduced too quickly to be able to act as protectors or pacifiers. Consistent with GOC MacMillan's nonintervention policy, the local Haifa commander, General Stockwell, decided to step back from fighting he knew was imminent, thereby creating a vacuum into which superior Zionist forces quickly moved. The battle provided the cover to implement the Jewish Agency's ideologically and strategically rooted practice of forced population "transfer." Similarly, in rural areas surrounding Haifa, Zionists systematically intimidated peaceful Arab villages through direct attack, atrocities, and psychological warfare, forcing villagers to leave their lands, driving them farther from their homes.

The Haifa episode also illustrates why British nonintervention policy during troop evacuation was so widely accepted in British circles: it was successful. Before Stockwell redeployed, his forces had suffered "an enormous number of casualties . . . totally unnecessary for the British soldier, achieving absolutely nothing," he said. After he redeployed and avoided intervention, there were no more casualties.[184] Redeployment left the Zionist and Arab forces facing each other, with the British confident that the Zionists would emerge victorious and preserve the necessary public services during the final period of evacuation. As a result, British troops were no longer occupied with holding the two warring sides apart, utilities would operate uninterrupted, and the Haifa refinery would be protected.

The British policy of nonintervention to safeguard evacuation was crucial to enabling the Zionist offensives in Haifa. Stockwell attested to this himself: "While endeavoring at all times, with the power at my disposal, to maintain the peace in my sector, I have had in mind the primary essential of a smooth and rapid evacuation of the British forces through the Port of Haifa."[185] Although Stockwell's decision enabled the destruction of Palestinian society, the expulsion of Arabs, and the violent partition of Palestine, the Haifa enclave was secure for the British exit from the country.

1. NACP 84/350/61/34/03, American Consulate Haifa to Marshall, April 23, 1948.
2. TNA CO 537/3899, HQ Palestine Police Force, CID, December 9, 1947, Jewish mobilization plans, intelligence summary, no. 15/47.
3. Ibid.
4. Israeli State Archives Publications, *Political and Diplomatic Documents of the Zionist Central Archives and Israeli State Archives*, December 1947–May 1948, Jerusalem 1979 (Hebrew), doc. 45, 14, December 1947, 60; cited in Pappé, *Ethnic Cleansing of Palestine*, 47n15.
5. TT, Gen. Gordon MacMillan interview.
6. *Survey of Palestine, Supplement*, 12.
7. TT, Col. John Waddy interview.
8. TT, Ahmad al-Halil interview.
9. CP IV/1/98, Minutes of Security Conference, November 29, 1947.
10. TNA WO 261/211, HQ First Parachute Brigade, QHR, October–December 1947.
11. MP, S. P. Emery to her mother, November 30, 1947.
12. TNA WO 261/211, HQ First Parachute Brigade, QHR, October–December 1947.
13. MP, S. P. Emery to her mother, December 7, 1947.
14. TNA WO 261/211, HQ First Parachute Brigade, QHR, October–December 1947.
15. Ibid.
16. TNA WO 261/399, 2/3 Battalion, Peninsular Barracks Haifa, Parachute Regiment, QHR, December 31, 1947.
17. TNA WO 261/574, HQ Palestine G Branch Historical Record April 1–June 30, 1948, Report on Operations in Haifa, November 30–December 15, 1947, HQ Sixth Airborne Division G (Ops) (3), December 6, 1947.
18. Ibid.
19. MP, S. P. Emery to her mother, December 20, 1947.
20. TT, Col. John Waddy interview.
21. TT, Gen. Sir Hugh Stockwell interview.
22. TT, Col. John Waddy interview.
23. TNA WO 275/83, Sabotage to Oil Installations March–December 1947, Sixth Airborne Division.
24. Pappé, *Ethnic Cleansing of Palestine*, 59.
25. Maysson Fadel Soukarieh, "For the Sake of Remembrance: A Reader in English for Ninth Graders in the Palestinian Camps in Lebanon," MA diss., American University of Beirut, 2000, Khalid al-Khatib interview.
26. TNA WO 261/211, Report on Rioting at CRL Refinery on December 30, 1947, HQ First Parachute Brigade, December 30, 1947; WO 275/83, Sabotage to Oil Installations, March–December 1947, Sixth Airborne Division; WO 261/223, Third King's Own Hussars, QHR, June 30, 1948.
27. TT, Col. John Waddy interview.
28. TNA WO 275/83, Sabotage to Oil Installations, March–December 1947, Sixth Airborne Division.
29. Pappé, *Ethnic Cleansing of Palestine*, 59.
30. Ibid.; Khalidi, *All that Remains*, 153–54; Morris, *Birth Revisited*, 101; MacMillan Report, Diary of Events 1948, 21, MacMillan reported 14 Arabs killed and 11 injured.
31. Khalidi, *All That Remains*, 154.
32. TNA CO 537/2643, Cunningham to Creech Jones, December 15, 1947.
33. John, *Palestine Diary*, 2:312.
34. TNA WO 275/486, Sixth Airborne Division Historical Section Operations and Incidents, January–May 1948.

35. MP, S. P. Emery to her mother, January 3, 1948.
36. NACP 84/350/61/34/3, American Consulate Haifa to Secretary of State, April 29, 1948, memorandum of conversation with Farid Sa'ad, Arab National Committee member, Haifa, April 28, 1948.
37. Ibid.
38. TNA WO 261/212, HQ First Parachute Brigade, Mount Carmel, January–March 1948.
39. Ibid.
40. JEM, LXXI/2, Palestine Disturbances 1947–49: Correspondence, December 1947–May 1948.
41. TNA WO 261/212, HQ First Parachute Brigade, Mount Carmel, January–March 1948.
42. TNA WO 261/297, First Battalion Coldstream Guards, QHR, June 31, 1948.
43. Ibid.
44. Safwat Report, 71.
45. Safwat's Report, March 23, 1948, to chairman of the Arab League Palestine Committee, in Segev, *Behind the Screen*, 93, 100–101; cited in Morris, *Birth Revisited*, 107n257.
46. DBG-YH 1, 290 and 326, entries for March 10 and 30; cited in Morris, *Birth Revisited*, 107n258.
47. TNA WO 261/223, Third King's Own Hussars, QHR, June 30, 1948.
48. TT, Gen. Sir Hugh Stockwell interview.
49. Khalidi, "Selected Documents on the 1948 Palestine War," 87.
50. SP 6/25, Reaction to events of April 21–23, 1948, in Haifa, OC 257 FS Section, Capt. T. Keen, April 24, 1948.
51. NACP 84/350/61/34/3, Lippincott to Marshall, April 23, 1948.
52. SP 6/13, Report on Arab-Jewish Clashes in Haifa, April 21–22, 1948, North Sector Palestine to Troopers, April 20, 1948.
53. MacMillan Report, Extracts from Report by GOC North Sector Major Gen. H. C. Stockwell, Leading up to, and after the Arab-Jewish Clashes in Haifa, April 21–22, 1948, appendix F(i).
54. Ibid., 2.
55. TNA WO 261/223, Third King's Own Hussars, QHR, June 30, 1948.
56. MacMillan Report, appendix F(i), 3.
57. SP 6/13, Report on Arab-Jewish Clashes in Haifa, April 21–22, 1948, North Sector Palestine to Troopers, April 20, 1948.
58. TNA WO 79, Sixth Airborne Division, 257 and 317 FS Section, weekly report no. 2, April 21, 1948.
59. NP, "Always a Grenadier," Major Gen. Sir John Nelson, 64. Nelson served with the First Battalion Grenadier Guards from 1950 to 1952.
60. Walid Khalidi, "The Fall of Haifa," *Middle East Forum*, December 1959, 26; Khalidi, "Selected Documents on the 1948 Palestine War," 88.
61. TNA WO 261/297, First Battalion Coldstream Guards, TAC HQ, no. 15, April 21, 1948; WO 261/297, First Battalion Coldstream Guards, QHR, June 31, 1948.
62. MacMillan Report, Extracts from Report by GOC North Sector Major Gen. H. C. Stockwell, leading up to, and after the Arab-Jewish Clashes in Haifa, April 21–22, 1948, appendix F(i), 4.
63. TT, Gen. Sir Hugh Stockwell interview. Morris states that a pro-Arab British officer informed the head of the ANC of the impending British deployment, and suggests that similar informal notice may have been given to the Haganah; Morris, *Birth*, 75n38.
64. TT, Ahmad al-Halil interview.
65. MacMillan Report, appendix F(i), 4.
66. TNA WO 261/297, First Battalion Coldstream Guards, TAC HQ, no. 15, April 21, 1948.
67. Khalidi, "Fall of Haifa," 26. See also, Khalidi, "Selected Documents on the 1948 Palestine War," 88.
68. Ibid.
69. SP, Appreciation of the situation by Major Gen. H. C. Stockwell, April 20, 1948, at Haifa.
70. Ibid.
71. NACP 84/350/61/34/3, U.S. Consulate, Haifa Palestine to Secretary of State, no. 29, April 22, 1948.
72. Ibid., no. 33, April 23, 1948.

73. TNA AIR 23/8342, Deployment Palestine, Cunningham to Creech Jones, March 5, 1948.

74. TNA WO 275/113, Organization and Administration of Arab Legion, November 1947–March 1948, HQ First Parachute Brigade 606/G, December 16, 1947.

75. TNA WO 261/297, First Battalion Coldstream Guards, QHR, June 31, 1948.

76. TNA WO 261/297, First Battalion Coldstream Guards, TAC HQ, no. 15, April 21, 1948.

77. Ibid., nos. 15 and 16, April 21, 1948.

78. NACP 84/350/61/34/3, Lippincott to Marshall, April 23, 1948.

79. Ibid.

80. TNA WO 261/297, First Battalion Coldstream Guards, TAC HQ, no. 16, April 22, 1948.

81. Ibid.

82. Pappé, *Ethnic Cleansing of Palestine,* 96n21, 273; Zadok Eshel, ed., *The Carmeli Brigade in the War of Independence,* 147.

83. TNA WO 261/297, First Battalion Coldstream Guards, TAC HQ, no. 16, April 22, 1948.

84. Khalidi, "Selected Documents on the 1948 Palestine War," 90. See also TNA WO 261/223, Third King's Own Hussars, QHR, June 30, 1948.

85. Khalidi, "Selected Documents on the 1948 Palestine War," 93.

86. MacMillan Report, Extracts from Report by GOC North Sector Major General H.C. Stockwell, Leading up to, and after the Arab-Jewish Clashes in Haifa, April 21–22, 1948, appendix F(i), 5.

87. Khalidi, "Fall of Haifa," 32.

88. *Jewish Observer,* September 18, 1959; quoted in Khalidi, "Fall of Haifa," 32.

89. Ibid.

90. Ibid.

91. SP, truce meeting minutes handwritten in pencil, presumably by Stockwell.

92. *Jewish Observer,* September 18, 1959; quoted in Khalidi, "Fall of Haifa," 32; CZA S25-10.584, "Report by Harry Beilin on the Conquest of Haifa," April 25, 1948; and Moshe Carmel, *Ma'arachot Tzafon* [Northern Battles] (Tel Aviv: IDF-Ma'arachot, 1949), 107; cited in Morris, *Birth,* 82.

93. TNA WO 261/297, First Battalion Coldstream Guards, TAC HQ, no. 17, April 24, 1948.

94. Ibid.

95. MacMillan Report, Extracts from Report by GOC North Sector Major Gen. H. C. Stockwell, Leading up to, and after the Arab-Jewish Clashes in Haifa, April 21–22, 1948, appendix F(i), 6.

96. TT, Police officer Abu M. interview.

97. TNA WO 261/223, Third King's Own Hussars, QHR, June 30, 1948.

98. Ibid.

99. Ibid.

100. CP III/4/45–46, Creech Jones to Cunningham, no. 1652, April 25, 1948.

101. MacMillan Report, Extracts from Report by GOC North Sector Major Gen. H. C. Stockwell, Leading up to, and after the Arab-Jewish Clashes in Haifa, April 21–22, 1948, appendix F(i), 4.

102. CP III/4/15, Cunningham to Creech Jones, no. 1094, April 23, 1948.

103. SP 6/17, Sixth Airborne Division, February 26–May 5, 1948, April 23, 1948.

104. IDFA 7353/49/46, Unsigned but Carmeli, Summary of Information on the Enemy 22.4.48, undated but from afternoon of 22 April 1948; HA 80/54/1, "Yosef: The Conquest of Haifa"; cited in Morris, *Birth Revisited,* 191n202.

105. TNA WO 261/297, First Battalion Coldstream Guards, TAC HQ, no. 17, April 24, 1948.

106. Ibid., no. 18, April 24, 1948.

107. Ibid., no. 20, April 30, 1948.

108. Ibid., no. 18, April 24, 1948.

109. Ibid.

110. TT, Abu M. interview.

111. TNA WO 261/297, First Battalion Coldstream Guards, no. 18, April 24, 1948.

112. Ibid., no. 20, April 30, 1948.

113. Khalidi, "Selected Documents on the 1948 Palestine War," 89.

114. MacMillan Report, appendix F(i), 4.

115. GP folio 1/1, April 22, 1948.

116. NACP 84/350/61/34/3, Lippincott to Marshall, April 23, 1948.

117. "Mass of Refugees on the Move," *Times* (London), Jerusalem, April 23, 1948.

118. NACP 84/350/61/34/3, Lippincott to Marshall, no. 40, April 25, 1948.

119. Ibid.

120. NACP 84/350/63/11/5–6, Haifa to American Legation Beirut, relay from Haifa, Marshall, no. 40, April 22, 1948.

121. NACP 84/350/61/34/3, Lippincott to Marshall, April 29, 1948.

122. Fatima Husayn al-Jawabri, interviewed by author in Baq'a Camp, Jordan, July 19, 2001.

123. TT, Col. John Waddy interview.

124. NACP 84/350/61/34/3, Lippincott to Marshall, April 29, 1948.

125. Hasib Sabbagh, *From Palestinian Refugee to Citizen of the World,* ed. Mary-Jane Deeb and Mary E. King (Washington, D.C.: Middle East Institute, 1996), 34.

126. Morris, *Birth,* 97.

127. TNA WO 261/297, First Battalion Coldstream Guards, no. 19, April 29, 1948.

128. Ibid.

129. Ibid.

130. Ibid.

131. Ibid.

132. NACP 84/350/61/34/3, Lippincott to Marshall, April 29, 1948.

133. Shabtai Teveth, *Moshe Dayan: The Soldier, the Man, the Legend,* trans. Leah Zinder and David Zinder (Boston: Houghton Mifflin, 1973), 134–35.

134. NACP 84/350/61/34/3, Lippincott to Marshall, April 29, 1948.

135. TT, Col. John Waddy interview.

136. ICP, The Situation in Haifa Two Weeks after the Conquest of the Arab Parts of the City by the Haganah, May 19, 1948; ISA AM 20 aleph, Cisling [Zisling] to Cabinet, May 20, 1948; cited in Morris, *Birth Revisited,* 206.

137. Morris, *Birth Revisited,* 389n288.

138. TNA WO 275/119, Internal Security Incidents and Reports, May–June 1948, Middle East to Military Palestine; *Times* (London), April 22, 1948.

139. TNA CO 537/3926, Chiefs of Staff Committee Confidential Annex, COS (48) 56th Meeting, April 23, 1948.

140. Ibid.

141. Marriott Report, May 10, 1948, appended to MacMillan Report, appendix F (ii).

142. Ibid.

143. PP, Cipher from Middle East to Troopers, April 29, 1948.

144. CP III/4/15, Cunningham to Creech Jones, no. 1094, April 23, 1948.

145. "Arab League and Haifa Incident," *Times* (London), April 25, 1948.

146. NACP 84/350/63/11/5–6, London to American Legation, Beirut, Douglas, no. 10, April 23, 1948.

147. Ibid.

148. CP III/4/6, Creech Jones to Cunningham, no. 1599, April 23, 1948.

149. Ibid.

150. CP III/4/45–46, Creech Jones to Cunningham, no. 1652, April 25, 1948.

151. NACP 84/350/61/34/4-4, Jerusalem Consulate General, enclosure no. 1 to dispatch no. 361, April 28, 1948, American Embassy, Cairo, Egypt. Memorandum of conversation between Azzam Pasha, Arab League secretary general and Philip W. Ireland, first secretary, U.S. Embassy in Cairo.

152. GP, diary entry, April 24, 1948.

153. NACP 84/350/63/11/5–6, London to American Legation Beirut, no. 13, April 28, 1948.

154. TNA PREM 8/860, Cunningham to Creech Jones, no. 1101, April 23, 1948.

155. NACP 84/350/63/11/5–6, London to American Legation Beirut, no. 13, April 28, 1948.

156. GP, diary entry, April 27, 1948.

157. Ibid., April 24, 1948.

158. TNA WO 261/297, First Battalion Coldstream Guards, no. 20, April 30, 1948.

159. Ibid., no. 19, April 29, 1948.

160. Ibid., nos. 17 and 18, April 24, 1948.

161. Nijim and Muammar, *Toward the De-Arabization of Palestine/Israel,* 45.

162. Pappé, *Ethnic Cleansing of Palestine,* 17.

163. Ibid., 62n48, Yosef Weitz, *My Diary,* 2:181, December 20, 1940, manuscript in Central Zionist Archives. Hebrew to English translations of Weitz's diary entries vary slightly by source.

164. Ibid., 23n39, Weitz, *My Diary,* 2:181, December 20, 1940.

165. Weitz, *My Diary,* vol. 3, January 11, 1948; cited in Morris, *Birth,* 55.

166. 'Alya Muhammad Hasan, interviewed by author at Irbid Camp, Jordan, September 20, 2001.

167. Rafik 'Urabi Mahmud Hamdan Fahmawi, interviewed by author at al-Risafi, Jordan, August 6, 2001.

168. Avigur et al., *History of the Haganah,* 1567; and *New York Times,* April 17, 1948; cited in Khalidi, *All That Remains,* 163.

169. *Palestine 1948,* in Abu-Sitta, *Palestinian Nakba.*

170. HA, Village Files, 105/255 files from January 1947; cited in Pappé, *Ethnic Cleansing of Palestine,* 20n33.

171. Asad Nimir Dib Sidik, interviewed by author in al-Risafi, Jordan, August 8, 2001.

172. Amina Ahmad Dabbur, interviewed by author in Baq'a Camp, Jordan, August 27, 2001.

173. Rafik 'Urabi Mahmud Hamdan Fahmawi, interviewed by author in al-Risafi, Jordan, August 6, 2001.

174. 'Alya 'Ali 'Abdullah, interviewed by author in Irbid Camp, Jordan, September 24, 2001.

175. Pappé, *Ethnic Cleansing of Palestine,* 108n49.

176. HA, Village Files, 105/255 January 1947; HA 194/7, 1–3, interview of December 19, 2002; cited in Pappé, *Ethnic Cleansing of Palestine,* 21–22n34, 35.

177. IDF 50/2433, file 7, Minorities Unit, Report no. 10, February 25, 1948; cited in Pappé, *Ethnic Cleansing of Palestine,* 201n3.

178. IDF 50/2433, file 7, Operation Comb, undated; cited in Pappé, *Ethnic Cleansing of Palestine,* 200n1.

179. G59/I/GG, Red Cross, February, 6, 1949; cited in Pappé, *Ethnic Cleansing of Palestine,* 203n10.

180. For testimony by Tantura survivors, see www.palestineremembered.com; see also Nimr al-Khatib, *Palestine's Nakba* 116 (Damascus, 1950); cited in Pappé, *Ethnic Cleansing of Palestine,* 203n12.

181. Nimr al-Khatib, *Palestine's Nakba,* 116 (Damascus, 1950); cited in Pappé, *Ethnic Cleansing of Palestine,* 203n12.

182. Testimony by Tantura survivors, www.palestineremembered.com.

183. G59/I/GG, Red Cross, February, 6, 1949; Pappé, *Ethnic Cleansing of Palestine,* 200n1.

184. TT, Gen. Sir Hugh Stockwell interview.

185. MacMillan Report, Extracts from Report by GOC North Sector Major Gen. H. C. Stockwell, Leading up to, and after the Arab-Jewish Clashes in Haifa, April 21–22, 1948, appendix F (i), 7.

Fifteen hundred Palestinians fleeing the
Zionist bombardment of Jaffa, April 1948

VIII

"Cleansing" Jaffa and the Coastal Plain

*The village [al-Batani al-Sharqi] was burned, we were expelled
everywhere—to the mountains and under the trees.*

Muhammad 'Ali 'Abd al-Qadir Muslih, May 1948

Arabs from most communities along the coastal plain of western
Palestine—from Mount Carmel south of Haifa to the Egyptian
frontier—would be driven out before the mandate ended, as would
those in the Mediterranean port city of Jaffa. As elsewhere, the decisive
factor in the forced depopulation of these locales was violent intimidation
by Zionist forces. The same process would displace Arab communities in
the four neighboring coastal subdistricts of Jaffa, Tulkarm, al-Ramla, and
Gaza. Zionist psychological warfare and military attacks were followed
by policies and actions to prevent the Palestinian Arabs from returning
home.

Al-'Imara, the only known village in the vast southern Beersheba subdistrict to be depopulated during this period, is also discussed in this
chapter. The pattern of attack and expulsion was repeated with numbing
similarity from village to village.

Spontaneous Violence in Jaffa

The U.N. partition plan assigned Jaffa to the Arab state, creating an Arab
enclave encircled by the Jewish state. With a population of approximately
77,000, it was the largest Arab city in Palestine. Even though Jaffa bordered southern Tel Aviv, it was not originally considered an immediate

strategic threat to Zionist military planners. All approaches to Jaffa were commanded by Jewish settlements, so it could be easily blockaded. The Haganah was confident that a frontal attack on Jaffa was unnecessary, because the town could be brought to its knees by a siege.[1]

Jaffa's mayor, Yusuf Heikal, and the city's merchant class recognized the city's strategically precarious position and focused primarily on maintaining Jaffa's security to prevent disrupting the economically important citrus harvest. To this end, Mayor Heikal and Tel Aviv Mayor Yisra'el Rokach signed a nonaggression agreement on December 9, 1947. The mufti rejected the agreement, and the Haganah district commander was doubtful that the Arab moderates would "succeed in their efforts" to control extremists; nor was he certain that the Haganah could control Zionist dissidents.[2] Events proved him correct on both counts.

Jaffa suffered the initial spontaneous violence that greeted the United Nations' vote for partition. "Disturbances" immediately broke out that night in Jaffa's al-Manshiyya quarter and Abu Kabir suburb, leading to "wholesale destruction, burning of property and numerous Arab and Jewish casualties."[3] Beginning December 2, only a day after the countrywide Arab strike protesting partition, British police and military forces were fully occupied "keeping the peace between Arabs and Jews."[4] The British military depended for manpower on Arab and Jewish civilian workers, many of whom lived in Jaffa and Tel Aviv. To transport these civilians to and from military installations, convoys escorted by British troops made the daily run between the two cities. The armed escort accompanying every military driver proved a further drain on British manpower.[5]

The initial disturbances escalated into a more general confrontation in Jaffa and its surrounding area. "Fierce fighting" broke out between the Jewish settlement of Hatikva and the Arab village of Salama, east of Jaffa, resulting in a number of Jewish houses being gutted by fire. The First Battalion King's Own Scottish Borders established a rifle company in each locale to stop further disorder and to prevent the spread of violence to other villages and settlements. British troops were quickly stretched thin. By December 24, the whole battalion was committed to maintaining law and order in the troubled curfew areas of al-Manshiyya and Abu Kabir.[6] The increase in Jewish casualties and the desire to maintain Jewish traffic to the south along the Tel Aviv to Jerusalem road made the conquest of Jaffa a high priority for both the IZL and the Haganah.[7]

During non-curfew hours, both Arabs and Jews living in the areas bordering the fighting "carried on wholesale evacuation." As the conflict escalated, the economy deteriorated. Many Arabs relocated internally to different parts of Jaffa. Others moved to their families' ancestral villages or other towns they perceived as more secure, particularly in areas designated in the partition plan as part of the Arab state. Although this seemed to be a voluntary political choice, the initial exodus was a result of "relentless pressure" by Zionist militias "together with the random but deliberately orchestrated bombardment of the largely civilian population," according to the Palestinian nationalist academic Ibrahim Abu-Lughod, a Jaffa native.[8]

The proximity of Tel Aviv intimidated most of the evacuating Arabs, who expected a fierce Zionist assault.[9] Many who departed during this period were affluent. The Arab National Committee (ANC) of Jaffa attempted to stem these departures by levying a tax on Jaffans who insisted on leaving.[10] By January 1948, a large sector of the al-Manshiyya quarter, the "front line district," was deserted, a virtual "no-man's-land" and "snipers' paradise." British forces were stretched to their limits trying to enforce security while being sniped at by both sides. The police were "patrolling the streets by day and enforcing the curfew by night."[11]

The conflict escalated dramatically in Jaffa on January 4. Members of the IZL penetrated the city disguised as Arabs and parked a large truck bomb between Barclays Bank and the Jaffa municipality or *saraya*, a former palace of the Ottoman governor. The powerful explosion was aimed at terrorizing and killing civilians as it destroyed a wing of the bank, the municipality, and other buildings and houses in central Jaffa, including a children's social welfare center that tended to the poor and handicapped. William Fuller, the Lydda district commissioner supervising the rescue work, remarked that it looked as "if a buzz bomb struck here."[12] Twenty-eight Arabs were killed and 60 injured in the blast; many were trapped under the rubble. The Arabs became "hysterical" and "showed marked anti-British feelings." The IZL bombing caused the Haganah to call off a military operation that it had planned despite the nonaggression pact between Tel Aviv and Jaffa.[13]

By January 6, "it was apparent that the hooligans of Jaffa were losing their heads and openly flouting the Security Forces," the Third Infantry Brigade reported.[14] Unauthorized roadblocks were established throughout

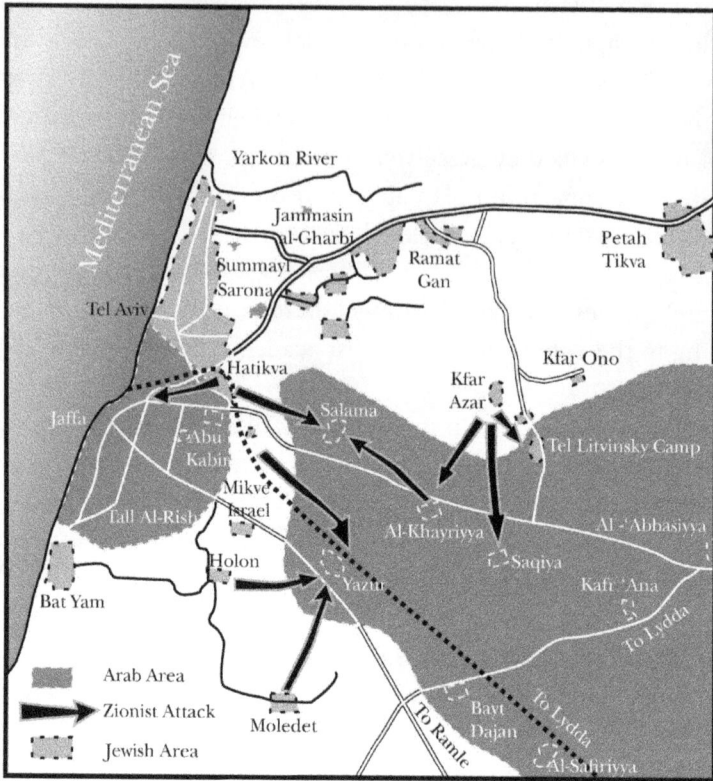

THE BATTLE FOR JAFFA, APRIL 1948

the city. Arab fears were accentuated by a report that Jews who had fired on a roadblock in the center of Jaffa were wearing British uniforms. Civilians began carrying rifles and automatics and "took it upon themselves" to stop, search, and identify British civilians and troops "as a precaution against the Jews infiltrating into Jaffa dressed as [British] soldiers."[15] At this point, the local Arab defense committee decided to work to stem the flight of Jaffa's Arab population. The committee erected a roadblock on the only road out of Jaffa, a measure designed to enhance security. Only those demonstrating business, medical, or military justification were permitted to leave.[16] But these measures did little to stem the exodus.

The Arab League was so concerned by the violence in the city that at the end of January, Arab League Secretary General Azzam Pasha requested that the British station Arab Legion units in Jaffa "to guard against the possibility of a Jewish *coup de main*." Brigadier Clayton, head of the British Middle East Office in Cairo, replied that such action was impossible. Evacuation of troops and stores remained the primary British concern, and Clayton said that Arab Legion units "were employed in a purely defensive role as guards on stores, etc." He added that the two British companies stationed in Jaffa should be sufficient to "allay" the inhabitants' fears.[17]

Arab League members grew fearful that a power vacuum was developing that the Zionists could exploit as the British evacuated. The League's political committee saw this as a consequence of British assistance to the Jews "both before and after the war [World War II,] which contributed to the formation of their Haganah force and another terrorist army." Azzam Pasha protested that the British had extended "no assistance of any kind" to the Palestinian Arabs "to help them defend their towns and villages or form an armed force to undertake such defense." He complained that the British had "completely disarmed them during the 1936–39 period," thereby exposing the "defenseless Arabs to the wiles and horrors of the Jewish terrorists."[18]

Unconvinced by Brigadier Clayton's reassurances, Azzam Pasha requested information for the Arab League's March meeting regarding measures the British intended "to enable the Arabs to defend themselves during and after the withdrawal of the British forces" and details about the administration's handover of authority.

Zionist Motives for Attacking Jaffa

Jewish military and civilian positions encircled Jaffa. Zionist forces were concentrated to the south, and Tel Aviv lay to the north. British forces were stationed between the two sides with tanks trained on the Jewish town of Holon. Zionist forces remained stationary in these positions until implementing Operation Hametz on April 27, aiming to isolate Jaffa and open a road to Lydda airport, which had been assigned to the Jewish state in the partition proposal.[19] Shmuel Toledano, a Jewish intelligence officer, said Zionist forces "had to capture Jaffa and the surrounding Arab villages as quickly as we could," because they feared that Arab armies would invade, "and having the enemy [Palestinian Arabs] within the country would have been serious for us."[20] Zionist military orders to capture Arab locales included the expulsion of the Arabs to reduce the non-Jewish population, advancing the political goal of a homogenous Jewish state.

The Jaffa to al-Ramla road was an important communication route for British evacuation. As fighting escalated in the district, maintaining this line became increasingly difficult, and its almost daily repair required infantry escorts.[21] A British commander forewarned Haganah members of British interest in keeping this route open, warning them "not to move into Jaffa until May 14th." However, the IZL, commanded by Menachem Begin, disregarded British warnings; having learned from a British police informant of the military's pullout date from Jaffa and witnessed British behavior in Haifa, the IZL did not expect British interference in its attack on the city.[22]

The Zionists began to move against Jaffa with IZL forces mortaring British positions. The British interpreted this as a part of "the softening-up process" prior to an all-out attack on Jaffa. Chief Secretary Sir Henry Gurney underscored British awareness of these actions by noting that the attack on Jaffa was "another expected development." The IZL intensified mortaring and sniping of British positions on April 22. The Haganah "were quick and loud in disowning" the IZL's attack on Jaffa as "an act of aggression," even as the Haganah was simultaneously launching similar mortar attacks in Haifa.[23]

The first determined IZL effort to gain ground in the al-Manshiyya quarter of Jaffa began on April 25. Zionist units sabotaged the road at Mikve settlement to prevent the British army from assisting the Arabs.[24] Several prominent Jaffa citizens frantically called District Commissioner Crosby and demanded to know "if the British had already decided to surrender Jaffa as they seemed to have done with Haifa."[25] The situations in the two cities differed remarkably: British forces had redeployed in Haifa to permit Zionist forces to pacify a marginally Jewish-majority city assigned to the Jewish state. But Jaffa was a wholly Arab city assigned to the Arab state, located along an important British line of communication. The deteriorating situation in Jaffa prompted the British brigade commander to reinforce and protect the British garrison—rather than redeploy—with Cromwell tanks, armored cars, and additional forces.[26]

On April 26, Jaffa's inhabitants were subjected to widespread terror. IZL mortars began to shell Jaffa at 8:00 a.m., destroying numerous civilian Arab homes.[27] The main attack on the city came from the south, north, and west: from Tall al-Rish, al-Jabaliyya, and al-Manshiyya. General Horatius Murray reported that Jewish units started "systematically to mortar Jaffa," continuing for 48 hours. Rows and blocks of houses were blown up.[28] 'Abd al-Ghani Nasir, who worked for the British military in Jaffa, recalls that the attack on Jaffa consisted of artillery shells aimed at crowds in places like the central market. Bombing would start and then cease until civilians ran to the site frantically looking for friends and family; then bombing would recommence more intensely with the aim, Nasir said, "to inflict the maximum killing that they could."[29] The Zionist record corroborates the indiscriminate slaughter of civilians that the Palestinians recall, as well as the intent to remove the Arab population. One of the objectives of the mortar barrage, according to the instructions of the IZL commanding officer, Amihai Paglin, was "to cause chaos among the civilian population in order to create a mass flight."[30] (Paglin also masterminded the 1946 terror attack on the King David Hotel.)

Meanwhile, indirect intimidation and direct force were applied against Arab communities in the Jaffa area. While the IZL was bombarding Jaffa, the Haganah moved against outlying Arab villages east of Jaffa. These towns included al-Khayriyya, Salama, Saqiya, and Yazur and constituted a phase of Operation Hametz. Benny Morris, relying on data from Zionist sources, concluded that the Haganah attacked these villages but took them "without a fight."[31] Palestinian accounts better capture why the inhabitants left their villages. "Without a fight" did not mean without violence or intimidation.

Khadra Muhammad Mustafa Abu al-Rus, from al-Khayriyya (pop. 1,647), said Haganah forces approached from Saqiya and Kafr 'Ana villages. The Jews surrounded al-Khayriyya, "attacked the village on April 25, and started to shoot immediately." Al-Rus recalls that the Haganah attacked people [sleeping] in their beds and "mutilated their bodies. . . . Some women hid in a house. They were discovered and killed. [The Jews] killed people who did not resist from the first moment. They continued shooting until we reached Wadi Bayt Dajan. Some people were imprisoned, and we still do not know anything about them. People from Salama, Kafr 'Ana, and al-'Abbasiyya were running with us." While some villagers managed to escape, al-Rus said, "others were surrounded and killed in the village." Only ten families escaped from al-Khayriyya, and all houses were destroyed except one on the hill. "None of the people who stayed in the village remained alive," she said.[32]

The men of Salama (pop. 7,807) were already very involved in the war, having fought around Tel Aviv and in the attack on Natir settlement. 'Abd al-'Aziz Kamal al-Minawi accused the Zionists of starting the fighting by repeatedly attacking the town and killing many inhabitants. The effects of reports of the Dayr Yasin massacre and other atrocities, combined with the approach of Zionist forces, can be seen in the villagers' actions. "People started abandoning their homes," he said. "The town elders were advising people to leave. They were afraid we would be massacred by the Jews, or suffer other evil things at their hands. We escaped our village as the Jews got close to Kafr 'Ana. After Salama, we first went to Kafr 'Ana." People ran in different directions. Furniture, cattle, everything was left behind on April 25. "When you are running for your life, how much can you carry with you?" said one villager.[33]

Zionist snipers were positioned on a high building between Yazur (pop. 4,675) and Bayt Dajan, recalled 'Uthman Yusif Abu Nubus. From there, they shot and killed many people. "They would also come at night to the village and bomb one or two houses, in order to force people to leave." They "attacked small and weak villages," said Abu Nubus. The villagers had 14 guns among them. Yazur was depopulated on May 1: "One night the Jews attacked the village, exploding about 20 houses around the town, and bombed and mined several places. They would send people during the day to assure the mukhtars that they would do no harm, and at night they would kill and destroy.... They kept provoking us for three months before May 15, 1948.... The Jews attacked the town with tanks [armored cars]. They entered the town with the help of the British."[34]

What really was the British role? Although British deserters did participate in fighting on both sides, Palestinian refugees who were interviewed believe to this day that the British assisted the Zionists in conquering their villages. British archival sources and Palestinian recollections, however, confirm that Zionist forces often disguised themselves as British or even Arab forces to confuse the Arabs and preserve the element of surprise. 'Arif al-'Arif, an Arab nationalist historian, reported that Zionist forces employed this tactic specifically at Yazur.[35]

Abu Muhammad, from Saqiya village, said that Arab Liberation Army (ALA) commander Hassan Salamah's forces were divided among the villages, and some were stationed in Saqiya (pop. 1,276). The villagers of Saqiya did not have weapons, because they could not afford them. The price of a gun was 100 dinar, and "that was a fortune at that time," Abu

Muhammad and others said.

On April 25, Haganah forces attacked Saqiya.

> Jews entered the village and started shooting women, men, and old people. They arrested girls, and we still do not know what happened to them. They came from the settlement that was near the village. . . . All the people were in the village when the Jews attacked. They used Bren guns. Then armored vehicles entered the center of the village. Fourteen were killed that day. . . . Two women could not run, so they were killed in the village. . . . Others managed to escape.

> The villagers ran together in the direction of al-Lid [Lydda]. After that families started to leave separately. . . . We left everything in the village. . . . We thought it would be a short trip and we would come back. We left al-Lid after Jews attacked it [in July 1948].[36]

Palestinian accounts make clear that Zionist forces had been harassing these towns and villages for some time with snipers, raids, kidnappings, and other forms of psychological warfare. Despite being poorly armed, inhabitants usually remained in their villages until the climate of terror exploded after an escalation of violence culminated in a direct attack. The final Zionist onslaught on an Arab locale included barrel bombs, indiscriminate killing of civilians, close-range assassinations, and firepower intent on driving the panicked Arab families from their homes.

Temporary British Military Intervention in Jaffa

While the IZL attack on Jaffa raged, "the long delayed merger between [the] Haganah and IZL," as the Sixth Airborne Division described it, was announced. The Haganah now found itself forced "to account to world opinion for an act of unwarranted aggression" by trying "to convince the world that the attack was only undertaken with the object of stopping alien Arab machinations in that area."[37] Lydda District Commissioner William Fuller concluded that the Jewish Agency used the IZL "to commit acts of aggression, or even terrorism, which the Agency could then disclaim." Alternatively, Fuller posited that the Jewish Agency organized aggressive acts itself—such as the attack on Jaffa—knowing it could pass blame to the IZL.[38] Menachem Begin confirmed British suspicions of the Jewish

Agency's complicity in IZL terror attacks:

> In the month preceding the end of the Mandate, the Jewish Agency de-
> cided to undertake a difficult mission as prelude to taking over the Arab
> cities before the evacuation of British forces and the dispersal of their Arab
> population. The Jewish Agency came to an agreement with us [the IZL]
> that we should execute these arrangements, while they would repudiate
> everything we did and pretend that we were dissident elements, as they
> used to do when we fought the British. So we struck hard and put terror
> into the hearts of the Arabs. Thus we accomplished the expulsion of the
> Arab population from the areas assigned to the Jewish state.[39]

As the attack wore on, the rapidly disappearing mandate government
decided to reassert itself, if only briefly, for two reasons: Jaffa's strategic location for British withdrawal and the city's great importance to the Arabs.
Gurney acknowledged that the Arabs attached "more value to Jaffa on historical and sentimental grounds than to any other Palestine town except
Jerusalem." More immediate political pressure came from the mandate's
widely criticized inaction in Haifa a few days earlier and the catastrophe
that befell the Arabs there. Gurney warned that "there must be no repeti-
tion there [Jaffa] of what happened last week at Haifa."[40]

In an April 28 letter to London, High Commissioner Cunningham concurred:

> Jews have launched heavy attacks on Jaffa today. Any success here will
> have much greater effect on the Arab States than Haifa. I have asked the
> Army and the Air Force to take full action against the Jews and attack has
> gone in this afternoon, result as yet unknown. I would however suggest
> that in any approach made to Americans with the object of restraining
> the Jews, the stopping of attack on Jaffa should be stressed as strongly as
> prevention of attacks in Jerusalem.[41]

Cunningham emphasized to the Jewish Agency that its request for the
British to restrain the Arab states was "extremely inconsistent with attacks
by Jews on a wholly Arab town which can only inflame the [Arab] states
still further."[42] Meanwhile, Azzam Pasha lodged a protest with the British
ambassador in Cairo on April 28. He reminded the ambassador of his own
letter that had requested that Arab Legion troops be stationed in Jaffa to

prevent "an expected Jewish coup." Azzam Pasha reported receiving hourly appeals for help from Jaffa, and he renewed his request to the British to allow Arab Legion units in to protect Jaffa until May 15.[43] The mandate's diplomatic efforts to halt the Zionist attack on Jaffa proved ineffective.

Chief Secretary Gurney took direct action. He sent a "strong letter" to the Jewish Agency on April 29, "making it clear" that if attacks on Jaffa did not cease immediately, the army and the Royal Air Force (RAF) "would take full action against those areas of Tel Aviv and other places from which they were launched." An angry General Murray sent for the Jewish liaison officer and told him "this is blatant aggression" and "unless [the Jews] stop mortaring Jaffa, I shall shell Tel Aviv."[44] The threat did not prove idle. In a very rare such instance, British forces intervened during the mandate's evacuation to quell Arab-Jewish fighting. On April 29, a tank troop of Fourth/Seventh Dragoon Guards and a troop of the 41st Field Regiment Royal Artillery fired 120 rounds on IZL mortar positions in Tel Aviv, inflicting heavy casualties.[45] Shelling soon stopped, and the British action "quickly halted the Jewish advance and caused the Jews to ask for a truce" at 2:00 p.m., to which the British agreed.[46] Jewish casualties were about 15 killed and 40 wounded, while Arab casualties were estimated at 23 killed and 60 wounded.[47]

General Gordon MacMillan maintained that the Jaffa intervention was in line with his policy of limiting British military intervention in Arab-Jewish fighting only to situations where British evacuation was threatened. The attack on Jaffa threatened British communications with Sarafand, the largest and most important military installation in Palestine. He did not, however, overlook the political motives to intervene, observing dryly that the IZL attack caused "a certain stir at home."[48]

London had suffered international embarrassment from British passivity toward the Dayr Yasin massacre and the fall of Haifa, so it initially refused to accept the fall of Jaffa to the Zionists. Emboldened by British inaction at Haifa, the Zionists had expected no British opposition to their takeover of Jaffa. In this case, they miscalculated, at least initially, the effect of London's loss of prestige and MacMillan's policy of nonintervention in Arab-Jewish battles.

Orders had come directly from Whitehall and the commander-in-chief of Middle East forces that Jaffa was to be "retaken at all costs . . . and handed back to the Arabs." By the time London's orders, troop reinforcements, and two navy ships arrived in Palestine, General Murray, commanding the First Infantry Division located in Sarafand, "had already dealt with Tel Aviv['s]" aggression by bombarding the Haganah's and IZL's mortar positions.[49] General Murray had received cabled orders from Chief of the Imperial General Staff (CIGS) Field Marshal Bernard Montgomery ordering the Jewish army's expulsion "from *all* parts of Jaffa," including the solely Jewish suburbs bordering Jaffa, probably north of al-Manshiyya.[50]

Eventually, the relative autonomy of local British commanders prevailed. MacMillan had anticipated and partly complied with London's orders to relieve Jaffa's strife, but he also partly ignored the instructions to drive Zionist forces from solely Jewish areas bordering Jaffa. District Commissioner Fuller abetted MacMillan by advising General Murray to ignore Montgomery's punitive instructions because such action would have caused "great problems without achieving anything of any value."[51] MacMillan's relative autonomy to choose a military course of action, though in this case at odds with London's policy, had been evident in his intervention in Jaffa even before London's orders arrived. That autonomy was also evident when he halted further British aggressive action against Tel Aviv.

Mass Arab Exodus from Jaffa

General MacMillan considered British military action against Jaffa successful mainly because it did not cause many British deaths. The action was completed "at the cost . . . of about five British casualties." Jaffa was "quite quiet again," MacMillan reported, and he was baffled by the Arab residents wanting "to get out of Palestine as quickly as possible."[52] General Murray's forces remained between Jaffa and Tel Aviv after the operation and confirmed MacMillan's assessment of Jaffa's Arabs frantic desire to leave.

The morning after British intervention had stopped the Zionist shelling and attacks of the previous days, Murray recalled "a scene which I never thought to see in my life."

> It was the sight of . . . all the people of Jaffa pouring out onto the road carrying in their hands whatever they could pick up, awfully well-dressed people, women, children, men, no transport, just they were heading south

as fast as their legs could carry them and it was a case of sheer terror. You couldn't do anything about it . . . the infantry which had been attacking . . . Tel Aviv, had been put into Jaffa to stop looting and you went in there and it was just as if the pied piper had been there.

There wasn't a soul. Gas stoves were still burning in the houses, the shops were full of goods, the houses, which had obviously had been left in a great hurry, a city of the dead and . . . it remained so until the mandate terminated.[53]

The Arab exodus from Jaffa happened in a matter of four hours, according to Murray. District Commissioner Fuller said that although "the Arabs knew that we would protect them" until May 15, "they were terrified at the thought of their treatment by the Jews after that date."[54] After a month of British passivity at Dayr Yasin, Tiberias, and Haifa, one might ask if Jaffa's Arabs still had any confidence in British protection. Even before the IZL mortar attack, some 5,000 Arabs had already left Jaffa because of the uncontrolled fighting and deteriorating living conditions.

The high commissioner estimated that roughly 30,000 of Jaffa's original 77,000 Arab inhabitants left. They fled mainly by sea to Gaza southward and to Beirut in Lebanon to the north. Others went over land eastward to Ramallah and Nablus.[55] The Arab exodus described by Murray and witnessed by many can be portrayed, and has been, as mass hysteria or voluntary departure. A critical examination of the circumstances shows that Zionist intimidation drove the Arabs from Jaffa.

Shafik al-Hout, a veteran Palestinian Liberation Organization (PLO) leader in Lebanon, described the motivation and the experience of flight by Jaffa's families. Escape by land was difficult, because the only road was "closed and also dangerous," and the Haganah "had taken positions all over the place." Al-Hout's family "had no choice but the sea" for escape.[56] All available boats were used. "The flight was random. There were many families whose members were distributed on different boats, going in different directions" and even to different Arab countries. At the chaotic port, al-Hout—then 16 years old—remembered that "thousands of *Yafawites* [Jaffans] were elbowing their way through the crowd." Such chaos was not an organized evacuation—its impetus was the prior bombardment, the lack of British protection, and a shared desire "to get away from death," al-Hout recalled. He and his family fled to Beirut.[57]

Most of Jaffa's National Committee and municipal leaders had left Jaffa, but a small core remained, including Mayor Yusuf Heikal and two city councilors. One of them, like Heikal, had returned from neighboring Arab states after hearing of the IZL's bombardment.[58] Basil Ennab, a Jaffa native, reported that after the April 29 ceasefire, the ANC "lost all control of the situation."[59] As in Haifa, Jaffa's Arab leaders were opposed to evacuating the population and it was only after they had lost control of the exodus that they asked the British to arrange for the Arab civilians to depart by sea.[60]

Indiscriminate bombardment and other terrors hastened the evacuation. Iris Shammout, then 12 years old, was among those crowded into the port area. She remembers snipers firing on weeping and screaming civilians,[61] which was also recorded by the British military: "Refugees [were] fired on by Jewish snipers as [the refugees] moved off."[62] Zionist snipers had also shot at fleeing Arabs and ambulances during Haifa's evacuation, further heightening the Arabs' terror. An unknown number of Palestinian Arabs also drowned during the exodus by sea.

Intimidation targeted the entire civilian population. Shukri Salameh, a Palestinian attorney, reported a Zionist clandestine radio broadcasting constantly in Arabic, "urging the population of Jaffa to escape with their families before their houses were blown over their heads." The radio broadcaster reminded the Arabs ominously of the Dayr Yasin slaughter. Salameh left Jaffa by car with his wife, eight months pregnant, and baby daughter along the main highway to Jerusalem. As he passed the Neter Jewish Agricultural Settlement, he saw a large group of Jewish settlers gathered at the entrance "gazing at all the fleeing cars and trucks and laughing."[63]

While the British had not tried to prevent the Arab evacuation of Jaffa, they did provide some protection to the fleeing exiles. Jewish artillery officer Ephraim Shorer reported that a British officer warned his unit that British armored cars would be positioned "all along the road to the south, with their guns aimed at you from both sides," and told them not to interfere with Arabs evacuating Jaffa. Shorer recalled that "all of a sudden, trucks and horse-drawn cars and people on foot [were] on one side. And if you looked at the other side—to the sea—boats, all moving toward the south, toward Gaza."[64]

As the exodus proceeded, the British forced the Haganah to open an overland route on the main Jaffa to Jerusalem road for people who had not yet escaped by sea.[65] General MacMillan said a great deal of effort was exerted "giving the Arabs safe conduct out from Jaffa right up to the north of Palestine and over the border."[66] 'Abd al-Ghani Nasir, who worked for the British, left Jaffa by truck, heading along the Jerusalem road. There he saw trucks and cars filled with Palestinian Arabs extending for two kilometers near Neter settlement, frantically trying to leave. Nasir also saw Jewish and British officers standing together along the road, which led him to misconstrue the British evacuation assistance and believe the British were assisting the Jews in expelling the Palestinian Arabs. A number of the Jaffa refugees sought refuge in al-Lid and al-Ramla. Some al-Lid locals accused the refugees of being "cowards," Nasir recalled.[67] In July 1948, the Israeli Defense Forces (IDF) would attack and expel the Arabs, about 27,000 civilians, from both towns.

Why the Refugees Left

Benny Morris claims that "military assault" was the decisive reason the Arabs abandoned Jaffa, which suggests that military assaults had no intention of intimidating civilians into fleeing. Contemporary, on-site, professional British military observers state clearly that the IZL attack sought not to secure a military goal but to expel civilian Arabs by creating panic and through intimidation. The IZL documentary record also supports this interpretation. Cunningham emphasized this in a May 3 telegram to Colonial Secretary Arthur Creech Jones: "It should be made clear that IZL attack with mortars was indiscriminate and designed to create panic among the civilian inhabitants. It was not a military operation."[68]

Arabs evacuated Jaffa mainly because of the terror induced by three days of large-scale, indiscriminate IZL bombing of civilians and their homes. As Arabs fled, continual sniper attacks on civilians and looting of Arab homes and businesses fed Arab panic. When the attacks stopped after British intervention, the terrorized population was able to flee more safely—and it was then that mass evacuation ensued and local leaders saved face by requesting that the British protect the evacuation.

According to Morris, the British believed "one of the major causes of the exodus from Jaffa," as well as from Haifa and Tiberias, to be "the flight of the city leaders before and during the battle." While most Palestinian

Arab leaders did reportedly leave before or during battles, the British did not view their flight as a precursor to general flight,"[69] as Morris suggests (in fact, some leaders even returned at the last minute). Cunningham observed that the leaders' departure demoralized the townspeople, but he did not suggest that it was one of the major causes for evacuation. In the high commissioner's words, "You should know that the collapsing Arab morale in Palestine is in some measure due to the increasing tendency of those who should be leading them to leave the country."[70] Cunningham actually viewed the Zionist attacks as the proximate cause of the exodus, writing that "a serious refugee problem has arisen as a result of the Haifa and Jaffa engagements."[71]

Shmuel Toledano, a Haganah intelligence officer, supports Cunningham's evaluation. The Arab population left Jaffa for two reasons, he said: (1) shelling that was "making the Arabs very much afraid," and (2) rumors "based on the Etzel's (IZL's) reputation." Due to these factors, "many Arabs were under the impression that the minute the Jews entered the town, the inhabitants would all be slaughtered."[72] Psychological warfare reminded Jaffa's citizens that their attackers had committed atrocities against Arabs earlier that month in Dayr Yasin, Nasir al-Din, Tiberias, and Haifa.

Michel Issa, ALA commander of the Palestinian-Arab Ajnadin Battalion, who arrived in Jaffa on April 29 from Jerusalem, offered a similar assessment. Fawzi al-Qawukji, another ALA commander, sent the battalion to the city in response to the Jaffa National Committee's desperate pleas for assistance. The collapse of the Jaffa garrison, Issa said, was due to continuous shelling by the Zionists, "which caused inhabitants of [the] city, unaccustomed to such bombardments, to panic and flee."[73] Shafik al-Hout also affirms Issa's analysis. "Signs of defeat started to become transparent" after 'Abd al-Qadir al-Husayni died in the battle of al-Qastal, he said. News about massacres and the fall of Palestinian villages reached Jaffa daily. The population "grew restless after hearing such news. This restlessness turned into fright after the Jews started shelling Jaffa's squares and streets haphazardly. . . . News about the Dayr Yasin massacre reached Jaffa causing a wave of anger and fright in the city. . . . a spontaneous decision was taken to evacuate the children, the women and the elderly from the city until the Arab troops would enter it and until things went back to normal."[74]

By May 3, Jaffa "was practically empty." Those remaining—about

5,000—were mostly "ill, poor, handicapped, and old."[75] British troops were holding a line in the al-Manshiyya quarter against Zionist forces. Only the truce to which they had earlier agreed prevented the Zionists from simply walking in and taking the town. The Jewish Agency stated on May 3 that if the Iraqi and other "foreign troops" who remained in Jaffa were withdrawn, there would be no further attack on Jaffa.[76] The Iraqi field commander Major Adil Najm al-Din and the bulk of his troops and allied Yugoslavs (Bosnian Muslims) had already left Jaffa by sea without a formal handover of the Jaffa garrison. Only about 80 ex-Transjordan Frontier Force soldiers remained, along with a few local Arab irregulars and a few ALA fighters "who either couldn't or wouldn't join in the general desertion."[77] Haganah forces relieved the IZL forces on the line opposite the British troops—an exchange reminiscent of the attack on Dayr Yasin, where the IZL and LHI committed the massacre and the Haganah gave them cover to prevent British retribution.[78]

Some remaining Arabs then evacuated. During a May 3 meeting, an Arab delegation expressed its fears to British government officials that after May 15, any Arab who remained in Jaffa would be massacred by the Jews.[79] "We are in a weak position," Cunningham wrote, "in attempting to discourage evacuation because whatever counter-operation we might take against the Jews we cannot guarantee safety of Arabs in a fortnight's time."[80]

Arab leaders continued their efforts to protect the rights of the Jaffans. On May 12, three Jaffa Arab Emergency Committee (AEC) members—Amin Andraus, Salah al-Nazar, and Ahmad Abu Laban—went to Tel Aviv to meet with Haganah Fourth (Kiryati) Brigade officers to discuss terms of Jewish takeover. The committee members were officially assured that the Jaffans would be able to return to their homes. The Arabs of Haifa had been made the same promise.

> Andraus asked: "What about those who recently left Jaffa and wish to return. Will they be allowed to return . . . ?"
>
> OC Michael Ben-Gal replied: "We agree that every citizen of Jaffa who wishes to return, we will check the matter in consultation with [the AEC] and in line with municipal records [proving that the person in question] was in fact an inhabitant of the city. If there is no special reason to think him dangerous, we will not prevent his return."[81]

In a follow-up meeting the next day, Ben-Gal reiterated, "We wish to help the residents of Jaffa who wish to return but in this matter there will be a need to make some arrangement so that they will be able to return. The intention of the clause is that inhabitants will be able to return."[82]

In the signed agreement, Ben-Gal committed the Haganah to abiding by the "Geneva Conventions and all International Laws and Usages of War." The Arab signatories endorsed the "Instructions to the Arab Population by the Commander of the Haganah, Tel Aviv District given on 13th May 1948." These included handing over all arms and punishing those not complying, screening all adult males, and interning "criminals or persons suspected of being a danger to the peace." Ben-Gal said that "adult males wishing to return would be individually screened, implying that women and children could return to Jaffa without such screening."[83]

Despite the Haganah's written pledges to honor international law, the Israeli occupation of Jaffa—uncontested by the inhabitants—was brutal. Red Cross representative reports depict a "collective abuse of basic rights."[84] The occupying Israeli troops intimidated, screened, beat, tortured, and concentrated the remaining inhabitants, about 4,100, in one or more areas encircled by barbed wire. Private property was looted, vandalized, robbed, and destroyed. Some prisoners were used as forced labor. Atrocities continued after the occupation under the military governorship of Yitzhak Chizik. Fifteen Arab men were found shot dead on May 25 in the al-Jabaliyya neighborhood. A 12-year-old girl was raped by Israeli soldiers on May 14 or 15, and numerous other attempted rapes occurred.[85] Chizik himself was appalled by the troops' brutality. "They do not stop beating people," he wrote in one uncensored Israeli archive report.[86]

Jaffa's AEC was asked to cooperate with the resettling of Jewish immigrants in Arab homes. The Arab leaders "energetically" opposed any Jewish settlement in Jaffa. Despite their protests, remaining Arabs were evicted from their homes and forcibly transferred in mid-August 1948 to the 'Ajami neighborhood, south of the city center, to free the rest of Jaffa for Jewish resettlement. The Russian-born Moshe Erem, head of the Minority Affairs Ministry's Department for Promotion and Ordering of Relations between Jews and Minorities, protested the operation. He was one of the few officials who attempted (unsuccessfully) to block the destruction of some Arab villages. He complained that the barbed wire fence that was going to be set up between the Arab and envisioned Jewish neighborhoods, creating a ghetto, raised "among us [Jews] many awful associations." The Arabs would also be prohibited from access to the sea "for security reasons." Erem warned that Israel was "planting poisonous seeds, unnecessarily and without cause or purpose."[87]

Arab property was officially looted by order of the Israeli government. British wholesale stores of sugar, barley, wheat, and rice, kept for the Arab population, were seized and sent to Jewish settlements. Reporting to David Ben-Gurion on the confiscation in July, Chizik wrote, "As for your demand, sir, . . . I will make sure 'that all the commodities required by our army, air force and navy will be handed over to the people in charge and taken out of Jaffa as fast as possible.'"[88]

Looting by Haganah and IZL soldiers was endemic. Patrolling troops on the roads stole valuables such as watches, rings, and cash. Palestinian refugees frequently testified that they were robbed while being driven out. "There is not one house or shop which was not broken into," Ahmad Abu Laban protested to Israeli officials. "The goods were taken from the port and stores. Food commodities were taken from the inhabitants."[89] Vandalization of property was widespread in Jaffa; house robberies took place in broad daylight. Furniture, clothes, and other household goods useful for new Jewish immigrants were stolen from Arab homes. U.N. observers believed the plundering was also to prevent the Palestinians from returning.[90]

One Jewish official reported on May 25: "During the whole day I walked about the streets. . . . I saw soldiers, civilians, military police, battalion police, looting, robbing, while breaking through doors and walls." Despite the fact that many soldiers were caught stealing, the military governor believed that not one was ever prosecuted.[91]

Even Jewish authorities' pledges to safeguard buildings belonging to religious communities were not honored. Mosques and churches, monasteries, convents, and schools were also looted and vandalized.[92] The greater Jaffa area had 17 mosques, but only one survived.[93] Nothing was safe. Institutional and individual looting was so widespread throughout Palestine that it was either officially sanctioned or uncontrollable. In either case, the effect was to further terrify the already traumatized Palestinian Arabs.

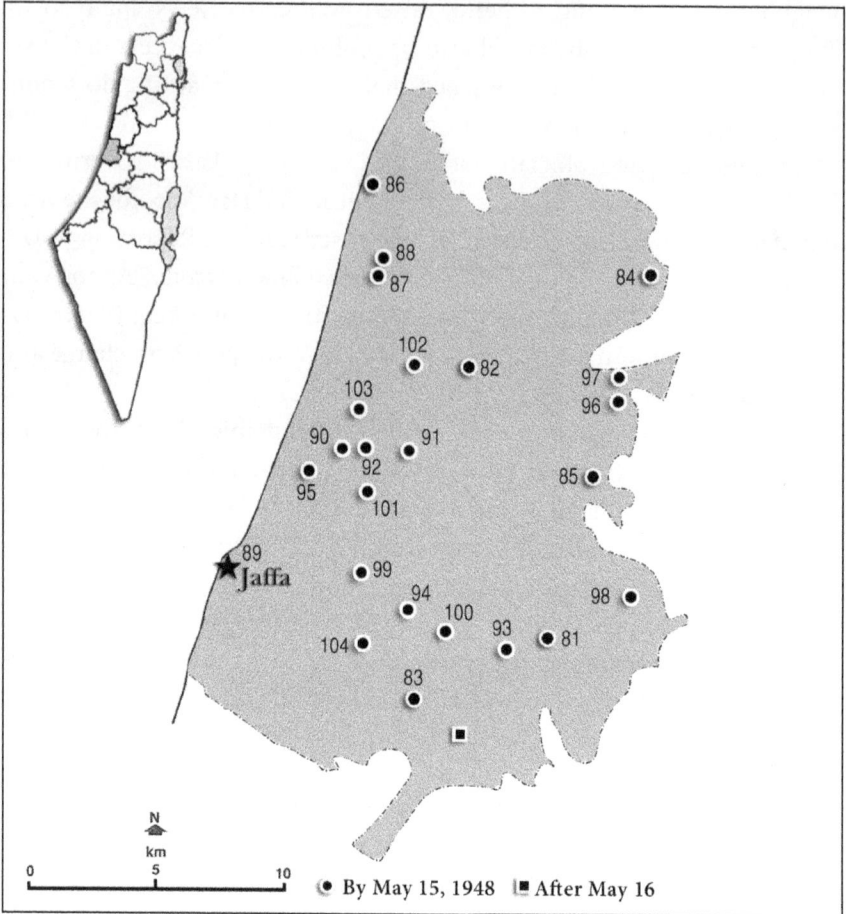

● By May 15, 1948 ■ After May 16

JAFFA SUBDISTRICT DEPOPULATED TOWNS AND VILLAGES

81. Al-'Abbasiyya (Al-Yahudiyya)
82. Abu Kishk
83. Bayt Dajan
84. Biyar 'Adas
85. Fajja
86. Al-Haram (Sayyiduna 'Ali)
87. Ijlil al-Qibliyya
   (Jalil al-Qibliyya)
88. Ijlil al-Shamaliyya
89. Jaffa
90. Al-Jammasin al-Gharbi
91. Al-Jammasin al-Sharqi
92. Jarisha

93. Kafr 'Ana
94. Al-Khayriyya
95. Al-Mas'udiyya (Summayl)
96. Al-Mirr (Al-Mahmudiyya)
97. Al-Muwaylih
98. Rantiyya
99. Salama
100. Saqiya
101. Sarona
102. Al-Sawalima
103. Al-Shaykh Muwannis
104. Yazur

Exiling the Jaffa Subdistrict's Arabs

Under pressure, Arabs began to flee not just from Jaffa but from throughout its subdistrict. Jaffa was the smallest of Palestine's subdistricts, and the only one with a Jewish majority—29.3 percent Arab and 70.7 percent Jewish in 1945. Arabs, however, still dominated as landowners. The lands were 52.9 percent Arab-owned, 38.6 percent Jewish-owned, and 8.6 percent public property. By the end of the civil war, 92 percent of Arab villages and towns were forcibly depopulated—24 of the 26 locales, including the city of Jaffa. Of the three villages that fell to the Zionists after the mandate ended—Rantiyya, al-Safiriyya, and Wilhelma (a Lutheran agricultural colony)—the village of Rantiyya was attacked in April 1948 and its inhabitants forced out, but they apparently returned, until they were definitively expelled in July 1948. All 25 Palestinian villages in the Jaffa subdistrict and portions of the city itself were destroyed by Zionist forces to prevent the Arabs from coming back.

Zionist tactics compelled villagers to leave. The town of al-'Abbasiyya (pop. 6,554) had endured several IZL attacks, including a car bombing, indiscriminate shootings, and house demolitions as early as December 1947.[94] Nijma Shawarab, who was then 16 years old, married, and had a son, said the townspeople of al-'Abbasiyya had been frightened by Zionist attacks on the nearby village of al-Tira.[95] When IZL forces attacked al-'Abbasiyya at 4:30 a.m. on May 4, the women "ran away," while the men stayed to protect the town, according to Shakir al-Musa.[96] Shawarab said that during the attack many people were killed in their houses, and survivors were intimidated into flight: "[The Jews] chased the people who were running away and shot at them. We hid in a school. They attacked the school, too. The school was completely destroyed."[97] The defenders fought until they ran out of ammunition about sunset. "We were trapped," al-Musa lamented. Al-'Abbasiyya changed hands several times before it finally fell on July 10.[98]

Hamzi Abu Hatab, from Abu Kishk (pop 2,204), said that the villagers had lived peacefully until learning of the murder of Kunaishat clan members, who had had relatives in Abu Kishk. "The Jews had rounded them up and killed them," Abu Hatab said. The villagers believed that the Kunaishat were killed because they lived near a Jewish settlement. The village leader told his villagers to leave because he expected skirmishes with the Jews. "So we left," said Abu Hatab, on March 30, before the wheat fields were ready to harvest. The family sought refuge in Kafr Kassam. "We were afraid for our daughters," he said. Not all the villagers left at once; the fate of villagers who remained is unknown.[99]

The inhabitants of Bayt Dajan (pop. 4,454) were poorly armed. Every six or seven families owned one rifle. One townswoman said their weapons "were no match for the tanks bombing the village," which "killed three or four people."[100] The townspeople decided to leave, and most left as a group on April 25 during Operation Hametz. Roads were closed; some people fled toward Aboud, others went to al-Lid and al-Ramla. "Some people stayed, but then the Jews forced them to leave, just as they were, without their belongings," she said.[101] The inhabitants of Bayt Dajan left because of direct Zionist attacks and expulsion.

Fajja (pop. 1,392), an isolated farming village, received little information about the war because it had no radios. Although skirmishes occurred between Zionist forces and the villagers, Amina 'Umran Zahran recalls that "the Jews attacked us suddenly" on May 15:

> We left Fajja for Qulia and then for Qalqiliya. Everybody was afraid and careful because the Jews and armored scout vehicles were shooting at the village. The Jews did not enter Fajja, but people left because some villagers were killed. People made their own decision to leave. . . . rumors about rapes and killings made people afraid. . . . The attacks of the Jews reached all villages in order to put fear in the hearts of villagers and push them to leave.[102]

The villagers fled for Qulia en masse, running from their homes barefoot with no possessions, and thereafter for the village of Aboud, encountering others fleeing from Jaffa en route. Fajja's villagers remained in Palestine for about a year, wandering from village to village; some were able to return clandestinely to Fajja. Many others feared for their lives and decided not to return.

Villagers of al-Jammasin al-Gharbi (pop. 1,253) were unarmed and could not defend themselves, according to resident Abu Sami: "We were surrounded by Jewish settlements: in the west, Tel Aviv, in the south, Ramat Gan, and in the east, Ramal Tan. Where should we go? They shot at the village from Ramat Gan. They attacked us three or four times, [and] after that we left. . . . In 1948, they shot at the village to intimidate us."[103] Wealthier villagers began to leave in January 1948. Remaining villagers complained to the Jaffa municipality about the exodus, but they received no response. Others began to depart. After a final attack, the villagers left on March 17 and traveled to al-Shaykh Muwannis, then to Abu Kishk. When the inhabitants of Abu Kishk evacuated, al-Jammasin al-Gharbi's villagers fled again, seeking refuge in al-Lid, from which they were expelled in July 1948 by Haganah forces.[104]

Al-Jammasin al-Sharqi (pop. 847) was about 35 kilometers from al-Jammasin al-Gharbi. Abu Sami said al-Sharqi villagers had fought against the Jews for three days, until they ran out of ammunition. "Many people were killed in al-Sharqi. While the men shot one bullet, Jews were shooting 50 bullets," he said. By the time Zionist forces entered the village, women and children had already left.[105] The villagers were driven out at gunpoint on March 17, the same day as the al-Jammasin al-Gharbi expulsion.

Rasmi Mahmud, of Kafr 'Ana (pop. 3,248), had heard that "all the women in Dayr Yasin were raped." In Kafr 'Ana, she said, Zionists killed 14 villagers, after which "[the Zionists] tied [their bodies] to the tanks and dragged them." According to Mahmud, Zionist forces surrounded the village and shot at anyone who left his or her house, a siege lasting for two weeks. Mahmud 'Abd al-'Aziz Khayr said the village mukhtar and a delegation sought British help, but they were told, "We are done with Palestine. It is not our business anymore."

Khayr recalled that Kafr 'Ana was hit with mortars while the women were winnowing wheat and explosions beheaded some of them.

Some shots hit children. [The Jews] did not spare any house from their shooting. They did this all day long from sunset until dawn for two months before they attacked the village, until the night when they expelled us. Before that they did not have enough force to enter the village, but when they got it, they fired on the village with mortars. . . . What could we do? We had no one outside to help us. We begged for bullets. We used to buy each [bullet] for a quarter lira to defend ourselves. . . . We all defended our village, but we did not have enough weapons. What could we do against their might?

We feared for our honor. They started doing horrifying things to women in many villages, even in Kafr 'Ana; they did even worse. We feared that [rape]. We didn't fear being slaughtered.[106]

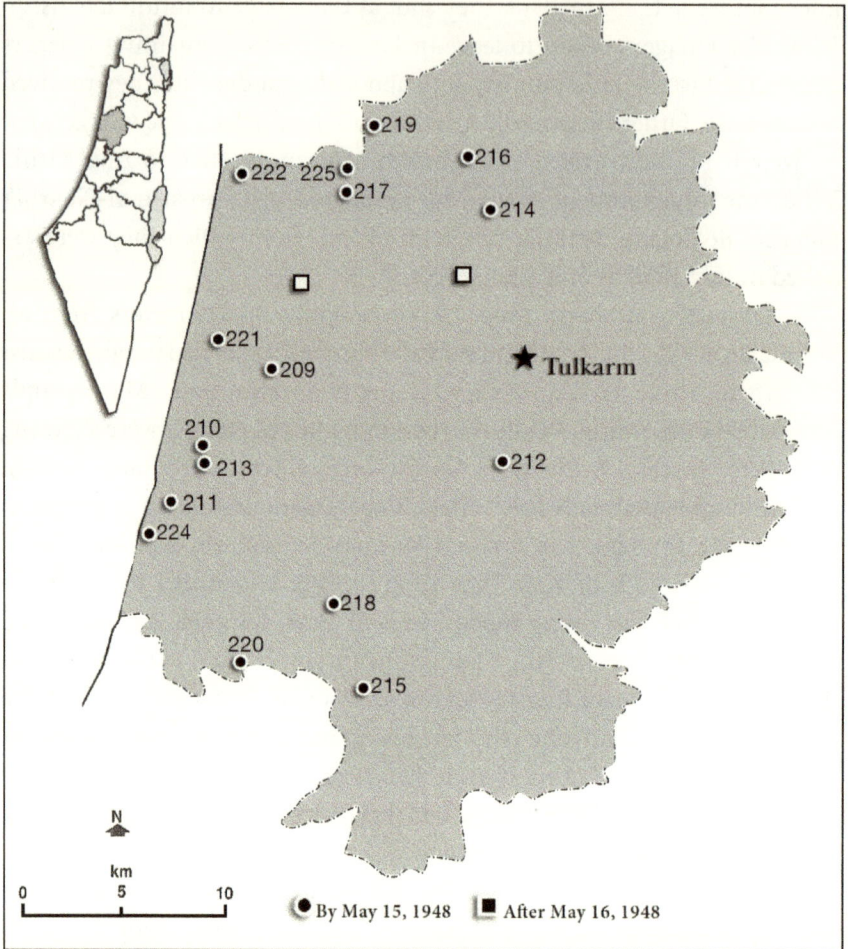

TULKARM SUBDISTRICT DEPOPULATED TOWNS AND VILLAGES

209. Khirbat Bayt Lid
210. Bayyarat Hannun
211. Birket Ramadan
(Wakf Khirbat Rahman)
212. Fardisya
213. Ghabat Kafr Sur
214. Khirbat al-Jalama
215. Kafr Saba
216. Khirbat al-Majdal

217. Khirbat al-Manshiyya
218. Miska
219. Raml Zayta (Khirbat Qazaza)
220. Tabsur (Khirbat 'Azzun)
221. Umm Khalid
222. Wadi al-Hawarith
223. Wadi Qabbani
224. Khirbat Zababida
225. Khirbat Zalafa

Mahmud said Zionist forces shot at villagers while they fled.[107] Zionist forces drove out the population of Kafr ʻAna at gunpoint on April 25 during Operation Hametz.

In the village of al-Masʻudiyya (pop. 986), Yasra Ibrahim recalled being expelled: "Jews ordered people to leave. They were terrorists. We were frightened of them. The old people said that we had to leave because Jews might attack the village at night. We had no weapons to fight. We left for Yibna." When Abu Jabara, who was the mukhtar and the wealthiest man in the village, decided to leave, others soon followed. "What the old people told us was that Jews ordered them to leave or else they would bomb us." Villagers stayed in Yibna under trees for about ten days; they then fled to al-Majdal, where they were not welcomed. Still, no one tried to return to al-Masʻudiyya, because Zionist forces had occupied it, and the roads to it were closed.[108]

Zionist-Arab nonaggression agreements did not ensure a village's safety. The Haganah had a truce with al-Shaykh Muwannis (pop. 2,239), according to Muhammad Hamid Haddad, a farmer from the town. Nevertheless, at the end of March, IZL forces infiltrated al-Shaykh Muwannis and kidnapped five of its leaders, prompting an exodus.[109]

> For us, we left our village without any fight. . . . We heard at the time that Syria, Iraq, and Egypt were preparing to send an army to liberate Palestine. . . . We were afraid that if the Arab armies entered our village they would think that we were traitors and maybe kill us. Then the British army said that they are leaving on May 15, and if anyone wants to leave before the Jews take over, this is the time to do it. The British said this to the older people and the mukhtar.[110]

Haddad's family left for Biyar ʻAdas (pop. 338), most of whose inhabitants had already gone. ALA forces were bunkered in Biyar ʻAdas, from where they sniped at a nearby settlement. Zionist forces attacked Biyar ʻAdas at 8:00 or 9:00 a.m. from the east and west. Haddad said only fighters remained in Biyar ʻAdas, as most of the villagers had already gone. Haddad's family was eventually forced to flee again in July, when the Haganah attacked Lydda. "A lot of people died trying to return to obtain personal items," he said.[111] Zionists routinely mined depopulated villages and shot Palestinians attempting to return to their homes.

Tulkarm Subdistrict's Arabs Driven Out

Zionist forces depopulated about half of Tulkarm subdistrict's Arab villages before the mandate ended, a third of them during March 1948. The
Tulkarm subdistrict, north of Jaffa, included part of the Mediterranean
coastal plain and the central Palestinian highlands. The subdistrict area
was 77.9 percent Arab-owned and 16.9 percent Jewish-owned in 1945;
the population was 82.7 percent Arab and 17.3 percent Jewish. In 1948,
34 Arab villages existed; 17 were forcibly depopulated, and a total of 16
villages were demolished during the war.[112] Original accounts reported
here are the only known histories of the depopulation of Khirbat Bayt Lid,
Ghabat Kafr Sur, Raml Zayta, and Umm Khalid.

The farming village of Khirbat Bayt Lid (pop. 534) was located on the
plain 20 kilometers from Bayt Lid. Its villagers grew fearful on hearing
news of fighting and left their village for Bayt Lid, where they had family, believing that they could return in several weeks. According to Husni
'Abd al-Latif 'Atawat, "They left all their belongings in Khirbat Bayt Lid.
The Jews occupied it, and they could not return."[113]

Salim Abu Sayf said that on the night the Zionists attacked the Bedouin
village of Ghabat Kafr Sur (pop. 858), his uncle's wife was shot. The villagers left for al-Tira, where they stayed for a week, until the Zionists forced
its villagers out on May 15.

> When the Jews attacked al-Tira, we fled to Qalqiliya. We were not allowed
> to carry guns. Even knives were forbidden by the British. So we had noth-
> ing with which to defend ourselves. [The Jews] were shooting at us from
> both sides, and the Jews' [massacre] at Dayr Yasin . . . made us leave.

> We stayed in Tirah Bani Sa'ab for more than a week until the Jews attacked.
> The village [Tirah Bani Sa'ab] fought bravely, but in the end nobody could
> fight tanks and planes with guns.

> The Jews followed us to Qalqiliya and blew up the school with mines.
> Many people were killed there. We kept going from village to village. .
> . . Nobody could return after that to the village, because the Jews settled
> there in mobile houses transferred by tractors. We walked barefoot and
> hungry from village to village. . . . . Fearful stories about massacres made
> people run away.[114]

Zakiya Abu Hammad said that Zionist forces besieged Raml Zayta (pop. 162) for about two weeks; the villagers had no food. Hungry and frightened, they huddled in their homes for protection before the attack on March 15. "[The Jews] started going into people's homes and forcing them out. They told us, 'You either leave or we'll kill you.' Some people were killed on the roads, as they abandoned their homes. . . . They followed us. Those who were lucky, escaped with their lives, others did not." Zionists completely "ethnically cleansed" the village of Arabs; no one was permitted to stay: "The Jews took it over, the whole town, from east to west. Everyone was forced out of Zayta and the surrounding villages. They let no one stay. People abandoned their homes, but a few stayed trying to defend their homes. Some were killed, and others escaped with their lives."[115]

Jewish colonists had extended settlements very close to Umm Khalid (pop. 1,125). According to Ahamad 'Uthman, Zionists surrounded and blockaded the village in 1947, and this continued into 1948.

> [The Jews] did not allow anyone to enter or leave the village. They did not allow us to sell or buy anything from outside the village. . . . After a month of the Jewish blockade, some families left. We left in groups on camels and donkeys. The people went to their relatives in other villages. Others, however, remained in the village until 1948. My family went to Tulkarm. . . . We had been awaiting the end of the blockade, but it would not end unless the people left. . . . They were shooting, but not heavily. They shot from outside the village to make the villagers afraid.
>
> No one returned to Umm Khalid. We were not allowed to return. . . . Jews killed many people in Mlabis and in many other places. . . . What did they do in Dayr Yasin? . . . I thank God we left before they entered the village.[116]

The villagers abandoned the village on March 20 due to the siege and the sniping.

In another village, Tabsur (pop. 1,000), people had fewer than 12 guns. Before it was attacked, Mose Natur, a Jewish settler, visited as a "friend" and told the villagers that they must flee to save themselves. Natur returned three days later with Haganah forces and "forced everybody to abandon"

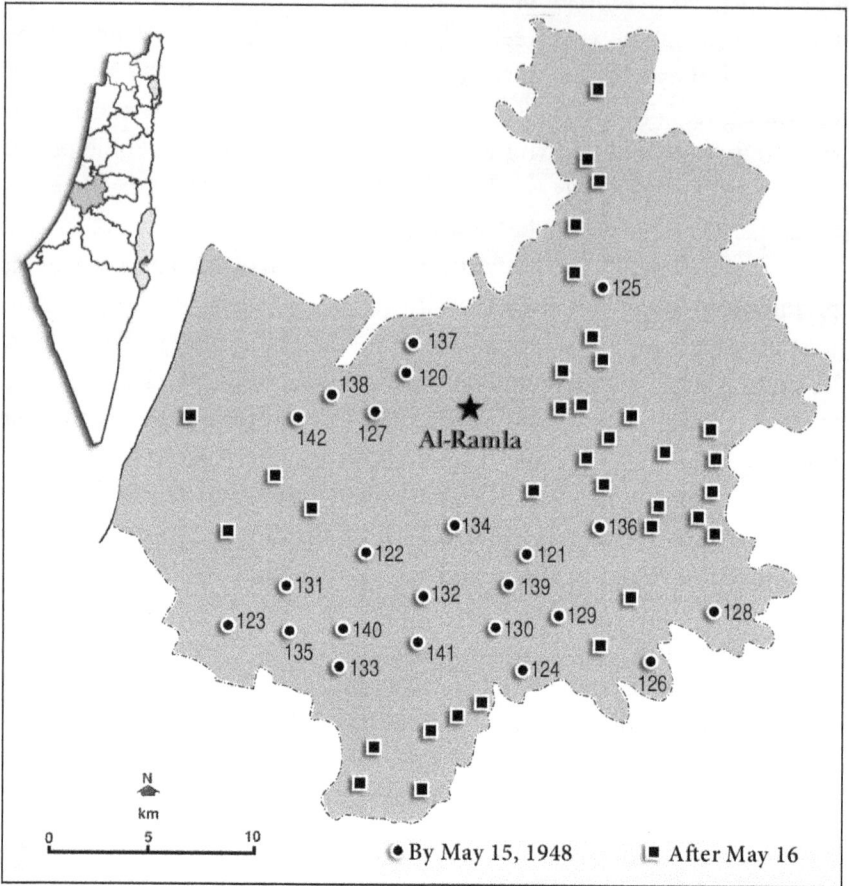

AL-RAMLA SUBDISTRICT DEPOPULATED TOWNS AND VILLAGES

120. Abu al-Fadl
   ('Arab al-Satariyya)
121. Abu Shusha
122. 'Aqir
123. Bashshit
124. Khirbat Bayt Far
125. Bayt Nabala
126. Bayt Susin
127. Bir Salim
128. Dayr Ayyub
129. Dayr Muhaysin
130. Khulda

131. Al-Maghar
132. Al-Mansura
133. Al-Mukhayzin
134. Al-Na'ani
135. Qatra
136. Al-Qubab
137. Sarafand al-'Amar
138. Sarafand al-Kharab
139. Saydun
140. Shahma
141. Umm Kalkha
142. Wadi Hunayn

the village, taking nothing along. The Haganah expelled all remaining villagers on April 3.[117] Only three villagers remained in Tabsur, hidden nearby and in the orange orchards. They resisted until June, when they too fled.[118]

Arabs Expelled Completely from Al-Ramla Subdistrict

Zionist forces systematically forced out the Arabs from the al-Ramla subdistrict during the war and after. Al-Ramla subdistrict, extending the length of the coastal plain southeast of Jaffa, was important for its transportation routes and fertile land. The area was 78.8 percent Arab-owned, 14 percent Jewish-owned, and 7.1 percent public property in 1945; with a population 76.9 percent Arab and 23.1 percent Jewish. Fifty-six Arab towns and villages existed. Before the mandate ended, Zionist militias forced Arabs to leave from 23 villages, or 41 percent of preexisting locales. All Palestinian villages and towns in the al-Ramla subdistrict have since been destroyed, in an effort to wipe out all traces of the Arabs' existence.[119]

Operation Barak (Lightning) was launched in the area on May 9, in part to create "general panic" and break the Arabs' morale by attacking villages to cause the inhabitants to leave. OC Shimon Avidan, of the Haganah's Givati Brigade, had great discretion in implementing the operation's guidelines.[120] He was able to determine, in consultation with Arab affairs advisers and intelligence officers, the villages in his zone that "should be occupied, cleaned up or destroyed." Avidan moved to attack and expel as many Arabs as possible before the mandate ended.

Palestinians describe how they were targeted by Haganah forces.[121] 'Abd al-Rahman Salih Abu Shraykh recalls that a number of skirmishes occurred near Abu Shusha (pop. 1,009). Jews came to the village disguised as Transjordanian army personnel to collect information about the number of weapons in the village, he said. They left after promising to return later to install artillery to protect the village from attacks. After a siege of about a week, Zionist forces attacked the village on May 14, between 3:00 and 4:00 a.m., surrounding and occupying it after killing 80 villagers. Abu Shraykh recalls the atrocities committed in his village by Haganah forces: "They shot my grandfather in his mouth. He was 95 years old or more. Bullets came out of his head when they shot him. . . . The Jews generally killed the old people who could not escape, after they took the villages."[122] Haganah forces also reportedly terrorized the population with the threat of rape, and at least one soldier attempted to rape a 20-year-old woman.[123] Abu Shraykh said, "They kidnapped two young girls from the village in Abu Shusha. The army took them and kept them for three days until the elderly people went to their [Jewish] leader and managed to get them back. They went to the camp and told them, 'We are Muslims, you should not do this. This is dishonoring, rape is not good.' Honor is very important for Muslims. People left in '48 because the honor of women was very important."[124] The villagers tried to defend themselves, but were unable. After they were expelled from Abu Shusha, no one returned, said Abu Shraykh's wife.

The people of Saydun had sought refuge in Abu Shusha after leaving their village on April 6 because of direct attack and atrocities. They likely fled again with the villagers of Abu Shusha on May 14 when it was attacked and the inhabitants expelled.

The town of 'Aqir (pop. 2,877) was surrounded by Jewish settlements. 'Abd al-Fatah al-Asmar said Zionist forces attacked from the settlements and besieged 'Aqir. After they cut the road to al-Ramla, the townspeople could not obtain supplies. Finally, Zionist forces entered 'Aqir and ordered the inhabitants to leave their houses, separating men from women and children beneath a large lotus tree. "They did not allow anyone to move. They wanted to kill the people, but the British [unit that arrived] did not allow them" because the town had not resisted, al-Asmar said: "There were two people who died during the ambush on 'Aqir, one from the family of al-Jamal and the other was called al-Khatar. During the attack, these two were on the school's rooftop and did not hear the order to leave the houses. When they came down they were killed. Their bodies were brought to us while we were waiting underneath the tree. The bodies were mutilated with knives, so we were all so scared." The village was depopulated on May 6. Terrified by the atrocities, the villagers fled to al-Maghar, and fled again when Zionist forces attacked Bashshit (pop. 1,879) on May 13.[125]

Latifa Muhammad Hamdan of Bashshit said that ten days after the first attack on her village, the Haganah attacked it again in the early morning from the west: "We resisted them until night and the following night. After that, people started to escape toward the valleys. We had resisted until the Jews entered the village. They killed 15 people, including Muhammad Khalid and 'Arif Hindawi. They killed Muhammad by shooting him through the forehead while his mother was watching. Jews burned and

destroyed all the houses in the village. When we returned in the morning, we found that the entire village was destroyed." Some villagers left for
Yibna, others for Dayr Nakhas. When Yibna was attacked, the villagers
from Bashshit left for Dayr Nakhas to join the others.[126]

Hasan al-'Ashawi said villagers of Bayt Nabala (pop. 2,680) had "no
military training [and] no weapons." They had taken part in skirmishes
around the village, in which some villagers were killed, before they left.
Al-'Ashawi's narrative suggests that Bayt Nabala was evacuated in mid-
July, approximately the same time as al-Tira, Dayr Tarif, and Rantiyya. In
any case, Zionist attack was the primary reason for evacuation. The village
was unlikely to have been completely evacuated on May 13, as other accounts state.[127] Some of the following narrative appears to refer to events
after May 15, when the Arab Legion entered the war.

> Our town was attacked from the west. Al-'Abbasiyya had fallen, and
> Salama, then al-Tira, and Rantiyya. People [in town] did not know what
> was going on. The fighting started, and we were attacked. A plane came
> and dropped a large bomb near the school, by the main road. People ran
> away. They had no experience with war.

> We were in the town, going up the mountain near town. We were told
> to leave our town for three to four days, then come back. The Jordanian
> army was to go after them [Jewish forces]. They [Arab Legion] would
> have chased them to Tel Aviv. Instead, they were ordered to withdraw to
> Butrus. People ran away, and the invasion continued. The people followed
> the streams, concealing themselves underneath the trees.[128]

Bayt Susin (pop. 211) was a small, poor village. "Fifty dinars would not
be found among all the people," said a villager. The Jewish settlement of
Jafourja was nearby, but the villagers had no communication with it be-
cause it was newly built, in 1947, and surrounded by a fence. The villagers
knew Zionist forces were attacking the villages around them: al-Bariyya,
Khulda, Abu Shusha, al-Na'ani, and Saydun, yet they did not leave Bayt
Susin. They left on May 15, only after they were attacked directly and civilians were killed, according to a village woman identifying herself only as
Wardi: "We were not afraid; we stayed in Bayt Susin until Jews occupied
Bayt Susin and fired on the village with tanks. Because the Jews killed
many people, we left for Bayt 'Umar. After that we left for Ariha [Jericho],

and we stayed there because they built refugee camps."[129]

The farming village of Dayr Ayyub (pop. 320) was strategically located in Bab al-Wad on the road to Jerusalem, the scene of frequent fighting between Arab and Zionist forces. Fatma Muhammad ʿAli ʿAmmar said the women helped the men to hide munitions. Village gunmen attacked Jewish convoys traveling to Jerusalem numerous times. In one incident, ʿAli ʿAmmar recounts, Zionist forces rounded up the villagers and held them on the outskirts of the village until sunset. The final impetus for departure came when the ALA commander ʿAbd al-Qadir al-Husayni came to nearby Bayt Mahsir. Shortly afterward, she said that Jewish fighters returned to the village and "blew up my uncle's house. Before it was blown up, [the village men] sent us to Yalu. [The Jews] blew up [houses in] the village twice." After this, skirmishes between Arab and Zionist forces around Dayr Ayyub began in earnest and increased after the British evacuation. "The Jews shot at Dayr Ayyub many times," ʿAli ʿAmmar said. "The women left for Yalu at night and returned in the morning. The men stayed in the village, but the women and children could not stay because of nightly shootings."[130] The villagers of Dayr Ayyub did not leave en masse despite the frequent attacks; in fact, they returned after each skirmish. "We left many times for Yalu and returned after the shooting ended." ʿAli ʿAmmar said the villagers were fearful after Dayr Yasin. Dayr Ayyub apparently changed hands several times during the war before finally falling to Zionist forces after May 15.[131]

Tahsin Shahadi said the villagers of al-Maghar (pop. 1,740) had been frightened by accounts of Dayr Yasin. Yet when Zionist forces began shooting at his village, they rallied to defend themselves.

> The Jewish army had armored cars outside the village. The army crept into the village from four sides and started shooting while it was advancing. Because our village was very high, [the Jewish soldiers] could not attack it easily. The people from the village killed many Jews before, and we used to attack Jewish convoys in 1948. The Jews were very angry with us. Because of that, they left our village for last, until they had occupied Bashshit, Qatra, and ʿAqir. . . . Before the attack, we sent the women and children to Qazaza and Hebron. The fighters stayed in the village. There were 40 or 50 fighters in the village. But they could not defeat the tanks and mortars.

Those villagers who could not run were killed.

When [the Jews] entered the village, they found it empty except for some old people who could not run. They killed them. They killed a blind old man in his house. . . . They burned the people they found in the village [set fire to their homes]. They entered the village like madmen. They shot Khadar Sada [a villager] and threw him into the orchard. They killed another very old man from the Abu ʻAbdu family. Also, I saw three or four other people killed in their houses, and they were very old people. The youngest and strongest people ran away. [The Jews] usurped the land. . . . They were aggressors. . . . Many people came to our village [for safety] because it was high, and they thought that the Jews would not attack. They left with us. We left May 15.[132]

Ziyad ʻAbdullah al-Wihdat, of al-Mukhayzin (pop. 300), said relations with local Jews were very good until foreign Jews arrived. The first attack on al-Mukhayzin was toward the end of 1947. Darwish al-Wahidi started to train village young people to defend the community. The Jewish mukhtar from Qatra settlement told him "not to tire himself training people, because this is useless. We are going to take your lands." The village was attacked twice; the first time, the villagers managed to protect themselves; the second time, they could not. Al-Wihdat said:

The Jewish mukhtar of the nearest settlement was negotiating with us. He told us the orders are to leave or fight. They surrounded the village from three sides and left the east one for us to leave.

When they attacked the village, they immediately bombed the houses. The houses were bombed while people were leaving. All the people left together. It was 6:00 p.m. in the evening. We took nothing with us except blankets and covers. Abu ʻUmar's house was bombed in the village. They robbed some houses before they bombed them.[133]

Muhammad Khamis Muhammad Hasanayn said al-Naʻani (pop. 1,705) had a good relationship with local Jews. "We were like brothers," he said. "We had a radio in the village. We used to hear the news by radio, and from people who traveled between villages. We heard about Abu Shusha and Dayr Yasin. [The Jews] started rumors about al-Aʻrd [women's honor, i.e., rape] to make people leave without fighting." The unarmed village was attacked. Unable to defend themselves, the villagers feared rape and other atrocities. Because Arab forces were in al-Ramla, small groups of villagers gradually decided to go there for protection.

> We left without resisting, because of honor. We went to al-Ramla because we were surrounded by Jewish settlements. We knew we could not resist against the Jews. . . . They attacked the village three or four times, but they could not enter the village. People who had guns guarded the village at night. [The Jews] would attack the village from nearby settlements, like Hulda. In these skirmishes, seven or eight people were killed. Other villagers were killed with knives, like in Dayr Yasin and Abu Shusha.

Finally, it appears, Zionist forces were able to enter and oversee the village's evacuation.

> Groups of five families left together. The Jews were in the streets watching us while we left and searching for guns in peoples' belongings. Unlucky were those people Jews found with weapons. We saw a man killed because he carried his gun. They knew who he was. They called him to come with his things. Then they took him to the orchards and shot him. There were many spies who told the Jews about the gunmen. The villagers departed over a period of four months. The mukhtar was the last one to leave. The majority of the villagers went to al-Ramla.[134]

Despite repeated attacks, psychological warfare, and extended evacuation, some villagers apparently remained in al-Na'ani, only to be "ordered to leave or intimidated into leaving" on June 10.[135]

In al-Qubab (pop. 2,297), the townspeople had no contact with the Jewish settlements around them. Aziza Mahmud Nababti's family said that when Zionists forces attacked, the inhabitants fled in fear. Nababti said they "were afraid Jews would kill their young and rape their daughters. People were afraid for the honor of the women," so they ran away. The villagers from Abu Shusha who had sought refuge in al-Qubab fled alongside.

> They attacked us. They took over everything. God help us. The Jews surrounded the village. . . . We ran away on a road south of the village. My father heard the Jews in the streets. He went out and heard Abu Muhammad. He saw them kill him, our neighbor. . . . My father stayed in the

village to harvest. They attacked us in May in the middle of the sesame and wheat season. . . . After two or three days, some people came back to the village after the Jews left and gathered the bodies of the dead in the mosque and buried them. They were 15. Even old men were killed. Those who were wounded, they killed them. Two to three days after we left, those who stayed were shot.[136]

Amina 'Abd al-Qadir Hammad left Sarafand al-'Amar (pop. 2,262) with her family to al-Lid [Lydda], due to a fear of being killed or tortured: "We left Sarafand in fear, without any fighting, after the Jews stole the British [Sarafand] camp. Dayr Yasin was the cause of our leaving." Hammad's family camped in an olive orchard for three months near Lydda. "When [the Jews] attacked al-Lid, they expelled us."[137]

The villagers of Sarafand al-Kharab (pop. 1,206) left as a group for al-Ramla. Surrounded by the Jewish settlements of El Jaj, El Mentara, and Jeta, they felt threatened. Zaynab Hasan 'Anbar said, "We heard about the Jaffa massacre. We were a small village. We had no guns." The villagers left for al-Ramla, using the only way out. "Jews surrounded the other directions," she said. Some villagers tried to return to retrieve their belongings and check their houses, but Zionist forces killed them.[138] When Zionist forces attacked al-Ramla in July, they killed many from Sarafand al-Kharab, while others escaped. Villagers from both Sarafand villages had left because of intimidation created by attacks and reports of atrocities.

Thurayya Shahin, of Shahma (pop. 325), said that her village related well with neighboring Jews, until attacks began. "Jews had attacked Shahma many times. They did not kill anyone. They just came and shot in the air and left." Shahma's villagers departed because of violent intimidation and repeated attacks. During subsequent stays in other towns, they experienced terror and intimidation.

First, we left the houses and lived in the farms. During the day we were in the village, and in the night we moved to the farms. We continued this for weeks, then we moved to al-Maghar. We were in the village during the day and returned to al-Maghar at night. Then [the Jews] bombed al-Maghar and destroyed the schools. We then left for al-Mukhayzin. Three old people were killed in our village; we could not carry them, and one of them was my grandmother. My grandmother was trying to leave when they killed her. The day we left, Jews were shooting everywhere. In al-

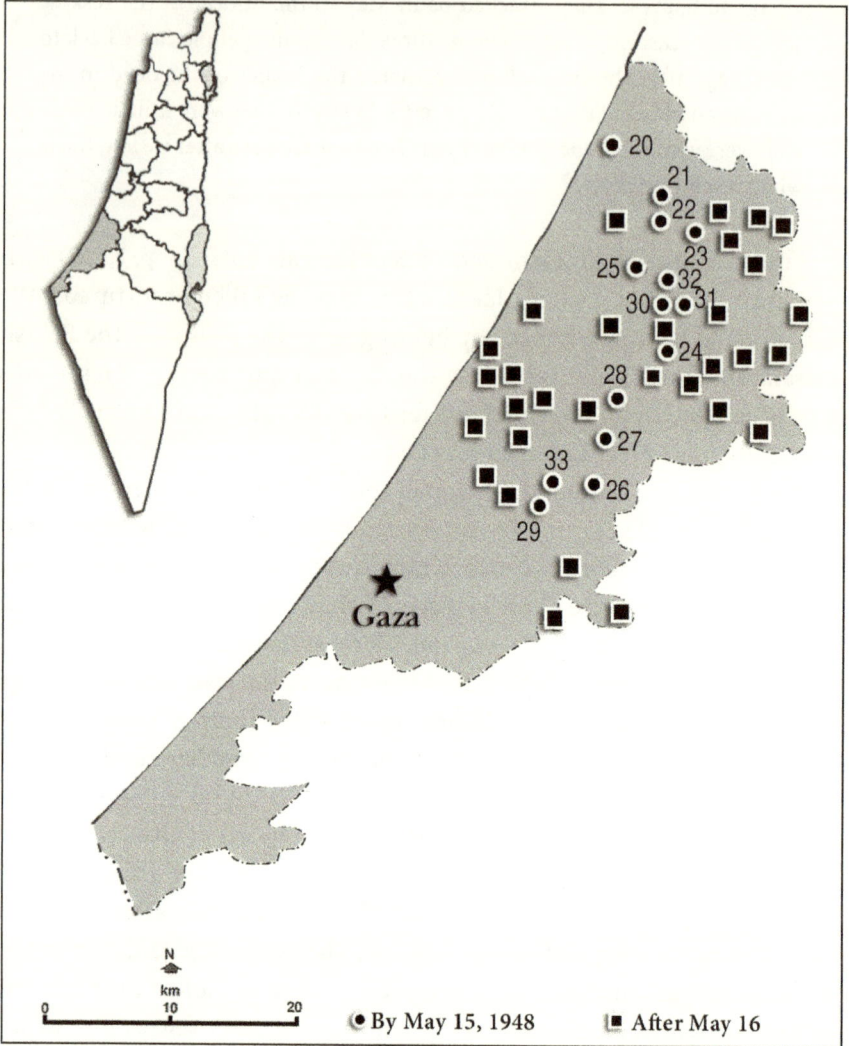

● By May 15, 1948   ■ After May 16

GAZA SUBDISTRICT DEPOPULATED TOWNS AND VILLAGES

20. 'Arab Suqrir
21. Barqa
22. Al-Batani al-Gharbi
23. Al-Batani al-Sharqi
24. Bayt 'Affa
25. Bayt Daras
26. Burayr

27. Hulayqat
28. Kawkaba
29. Najd
30. Al-Sawafir al-Gharbiyya
31. Al-Sawafir al-Shamaliyya
32. Al-Sawafir al-Sharqiyya
33. Simsim

Mukhayzin, we continued to go to our village during the day, but [the Jews] attacked the village and did not allow anyone to return.

After that, our trip to nowhere began. We moved to Amuria, then to Ajjur, Bayt Jibrin, and so on. We have stayed in 100 villages. We left together with the people of al-Mukhayzin.[139]

Gaza Subdistrict: "We Were Expelled Everywhere"

The Gaza subdistrict lies in the south of Palestine bordering the Mediterranean. Part of the subdistrict was included in the proposed Arab state; the land was 74.8 Arab-owned and 4.4 percent Jewish-owned in 1948. The population was 97.9 percent Arab and 2.1 percent Jewish. In 1946, there were 46 Arab villages, all of which the Zionists demolished. Before the mandate ended, Zionist forces expelled the villagers from 14 of these, and four were within the proposed Arab state.[140]

Despite repeated attempts by King Abdullah, the AHC, the national committees, and Arab League Secretary General Azzam Pasha to stem the exodus from May 5 to 15, Palestinian Arabs continued to depart in panic.[141] Many villages were captured and their populations driven out during Haganah's Operation Barak, which sought to destroy Arab villages around Burayr and to create a "wave of panic and flight in the satellite villages" before Egypt's military intervened from the south, which the Jewish Agency expected after May 15.[142]

The following Palestinian accounts explain why the villagers left the Gaza area.

The farming village of 'Arab Suqrir (pop. 452) was first attacked on January 9.[143] Thurayya Shahin said 'Arab Suqrir, like Shahma, was burned and attacked. Its villagers left for what is now the Gaza Strip on May 10.[144]

Umm Khalid said Zionist forces attacked and entered al-Batani al-Gharbi (pop. 1,137) from the north and west, surrounding the unarmed villagers. Women and children began to flee on May 13. The fighting intensified after two days, and the men were also forced to flee. The villagers continued to flee from one village to another in the Gaza subdistrict as Zionist forces attacked each community and drove out the population. "We would rest under trees and see the attack on the next village and continue to run with the people from that village,"[145] said Umm Khalid.

Muhammad 'Ali 'Abd al-Qadir Muslih, from al-Batani al-Sharqi (pop. 754), said the first attack in his village's area was on Bayt Daras. The neighboring villagers rallied to support that village with their armed men. The attack on al-Batani al-Sharqi itself was from the north and the west on the night of May 13, as Muslih recalls:

> People who had remained in the village were rounded up while Jews searched the houses, as well as burned the houses. Four houses were burned before people left. Because not enough people were expelled, [the Jews] sprayed them with bullets while they were running. Some people were killed while leaving, and others were injured. I was with the fighters between the trees. As I remember, 25 people were killed that day. Some of them were from other villages that came to support us. [The Jews] left open the route for us to take. It was toward Tall al-Safi. The same day the village was burned, we were expelled everywhere—to the mountains and under the trees.[146]

Muhammad Sa'id Muhammad Jabir said Bayt Daras (pop. 3,190) was attacked three times, but Zionist forces were unable to enter it. Finally, they attacked with overwhelming numbers, because they realized that once they defeated Bayt Daras, "all the surrounding villages would become frightened and run away." The attack began with encirclement, Jabir said.

> The fourth time they attacked us from everywhere—the sea side and the airport side. . . . In the early morning, we discovered that tanks and soldiers surrounded the village. The whole village had 20 guns, and the people were very poor.

> They surrounded the village on four sides and left a small exit for people to leave. They started shooting from early morning until sunset. All of the people were inside the village. After they were sure the fighters had finished their bullets, they entered the village.

> The village was full of fires. When Jews entered, people started to leave. Fifty people were killed that day. The shooting was from all sides. We had support from al-Majdal and Hamama [villages]. It was a very big battle. When Bayt Daras fell, the villages that were nearby fell the next day, because these villages were small and did not have weapons.[147]

The village was pillaged and burned. Many civilians were killed: "When Jews entered the village, they looked for people in the houses. The people who were hidden in the houses were killed. [The Jews] were angry at our village. We were tough people who had stubborn minds. They stayed two weeks in the village. Most of our sheep were gone. We left for Isdud. The road to Isdud was very dangerous. They placed Bren [guns] on the roads. If any one was seen, he was killed."[148] The villagers left together after the fourth attack. Some went to Hamama, some to al-Majdal, and some villagers snuck back into Bayt Daras to retrieve belongings and food. "The Haganah surrounded Bayt Daras after we left. They were the kind of people who never sleep. Many people [villagers] were killed while they were sneaking back."[149]

The main asphalted street in Burayr (pop. 3,178) was the only access road to 37 Jewish settlements. Jews came and went near the town well, where the women of Burayr drew water. Apparently fearing for their women's safety, the town closed its street to Jews. The British suggested a compromise of letting Jews pass through at 7:00 a.m. and after sunset—restrictions that, according to 'Abd al-Rahman al-'Alawi, sparked Jewish shooting at Burayr. Finally, Zionist forces besieged the town and blocked entry and exit. Al-'Alawi said:

> We had closed the street for six months, so Jews started to shoot at the village. Two days before the British evacuation, Jews had attacked the village at night. They surrounded the village from midnight until morning. We had some weapons, but not too many. We had Syrian and Egyptian fighters in the village.
>
> [The Jews] opened one way for people to escape. People started leaving. In the morning we found 100 young people were killed while resisting against the Jews. When the village fell into Jewish hands, many people left. Jews caught people who could not run away and killed them in the village.[150]

Palestinian assertions of Zionist atrocities in Burayr are corroborated by the Israeli record. The Haganah's Ninth Armored Battalion troops "killed a large number of villagers, apparently executing dozens of army-age males." They also raped and murdered a teenage girl.[151]

Al-'Alawi's family left for Najd but was forced to flee again. "In Najd, people ran away under fire and bombing. They did not have as many killed as we had in Burayr." From Najd, they went to the small village of al-Iraq al-Gharbi. No one returned to Burayr, because "Jews were on the roads." Some villagers attempted to sneak back into the village at night to retrieve their belongings; some were successful, but others were killed. "Jews destroyed everything in Burayr, houses and everything. When they entered the village they burned it."[152] The casualties reported by al-'Alawi are corroborated by Salman Abu-Sitta, whose research reports Burayr as the site of a massacre.[153]

The villagers of Hulayqat (pop. 487) attacked British-protected Jewish convoys, whose passengers, according to villager Ibrahim Salim, provoked the villagers with curses and threats. The men from Burayr, the largest village in the area, helped to defend smaller villages nearby, such as Hulaykat, Kawkaba, and Buytamat, whose residents were afraid of Jewish convoys passing through. The Jews were clearly arming the nearby settlement of Hud, while their Arab neighbors were poorly armed. The villagers of Hulayqat fled after the Palmach's Negev Brigade attacked Burayr on May 13.[154] Hulaykat and Kawkaba villagers fled to al-Jiyya and Hiribiya, where they stayed until Zionist forces attacked Hiribiya, al-Majdal, and Bayt Tima. Villagers were killed by Zionist forces as they tried to return home for food and belongings: "Anybody who was caught was shot immediately, and they would even booby-trap bodies with mines and explosives so that when his relatives would come to take him, they would also be killed. Many people were killed this way."[155]

Jamila 'Abd al-Qadir Ahmad said many of villagers of Kawkaba (pop. 789) sold their wives' dowries to purchase rifles, but there were no skirmishes before Zionist forces attacked Kawkaba on May 12.

> The Jews soon attacked, and they had two tanks with them. As they started shooting, the people of the village started running for their lives and left the village. That same night, villagers who had rifles went back to fight the Jews. Fifteen villagers were killed that day, along with a Jewish settler called Shlomo. . . . Initially, we fled the village to nearby vineyards. The Jews followed us and shot at us. We fled then to al-Majdal and later, after the Jews withdrew, returned to the village to bury our dead. While [we were] in al-Majdal, Jewish planes attacked us. The same night we fled the village.

It took Ahmad several days to reunite with her family in al-Majdal, "as people fled in different directions."[156]

Abu Muhammad said that Najd (pop. 719) was poorly armed. The village, along with Burayr and Simsim, drew fire from Zionists who came from a nearby settlement. Abu Muhammad recalls how Najd's villagers were expelled on May 13:

> [The Jews] entered Najd with armored vehicles and they shot people. . . . They bombed Burayr badly. When we heard they had entered Najd, we were frightened. We ran away from the village. They had attacked Najd many times the same month, but we did not leave. But after what happened in Burayr, all the people left Najd.
>
> We walked from Najd to Dimra to Bayt Lahya [and] to many villages. We did not stay in any of them because of Jewish attacks. After days of walking, we arrived at Bayt Lahya because it was far away from war. People tried to sneak into Najd to bring some belongings and food—wheat and lentils. The people who were seen were killed or imprisoned by Jews.[157]

His wife, Umm Muhammad, recalls: "We were frightened when they said the Jews had started to attack, in view of the massacres they did in other villages. My cousin was killed in Burayr. He was my aunt's only son. She asked them to spare him, but they refused her pleas and shot him in front of her. Another cousin was killed in Simsim. Many people were killed while leaving from Dimra to Bayt Hanin and on the roads."[158]

The three al-Sawafir villages "were as one village," said Ramadan 'Abdullah al-Bahsi. The valley of al-Qurayjiyya separated al-Sawafir al-Gharbiyya (pop. 1,195) from al-Sawafir al-Sharqiyya (pop. 1,124), and meters away was al-Sawafir al-Shamaliyya (pop. 890). The three farming communities shared a school and a mosque. Haganah attacks on al-Sawafir al-Gharbiyya and al-Sawafir al-Sharqiyya occurred concurrently on May 10 during Operation Barak.[159]

Shakyh Ramadan said al-Sawafir al-Shamaliyya's relations with the Jewish settlement of Tabeh were good before the announcement of partition. Skirmishes started afterward when settlers began shooting at the village.

> We left the night after the Jews entered the village and shot people. The villagers were not well armed and could not defend themselves. . . . They surrounded the entire village and opened one entrance for us to leave.

They shot many times, I think ten times, at the village [before the final attack]. Once they came at sunset and shot at the village with a cannon [mortar]. That day we resisted them and killed some Jews. . . . Before the heavy attack, no one had left the village. We returned to the village from al-Sawafir al-Sharqiyya, but they shot at us, which made us leave again.

The villagers tried to reenter the village to obtain food and belongings, but Zionist forces shot at and killed some of them.

We left for al-Sawafir al-Sharqiyya, but we could not stay. They continued advancing and shooting until [villagers from] al-Sawafir al-Sharqiyya also left. We did not take anything with us. We wanted to protect ourselves. They wanted to occupy our land. The last British tank was evacuating from Palestine when we were attacked. We were living normally, harvesting and planting as usual, when they attacked. They destroyed the stone basin where we used to store the crops. They destroyed everything in the village; even the graves were destroyed, but not immediately.[160]

Zionist desecration of graves and destruction of cultural centers such as schools, churches, and mosques sought to obliterate any traces of Palestinian Arab society and existence, another component of the ethnic cleansing of Palestine.

Al-Bahsi said the villagers of al-Sawafir al-Sharqiyya had only five guns among them, which they purchased after Zionist attacks from Tabeh settlement, east of the village. He said Zionists attacked three times; the third and final attack came, he said, because of the ALA's presence in the village, although the ALA was disorganized and could not unite the village men to defend themselves. The attack came from the east and the rear of the village on May 10. "[The Zionists] killed many people in the village," Al-Bahsi said. "Some people managed to escape; others did not. People who could not escape—and most of them were old people—were killed. The final time [attack], the ALA was in the village. When [the Jews] attacked, they started to kill people everywhere." After the Zionists occupied al-Sawafir, some villagers fled to the mountains, others to al-Faluja, Hata, and Qaratiyya. "Everybody ran away."[161] Al-Bahsi said Zionist forces pursued the villagers, attacking and killing a number of people: "Jews flew small planes to throw 'kayazin' [petrol] bombs above our heads while we were escaping. . . . We stayed in Barqusiyya one month; then Jews attacked

Barqusiyya, so we left for Bayt Jibrin, Iraq al-Manshiyya, and al-Faluja."
Al-Bahsi said many villagers attempted to return to al-Sawafir to retrieve
food or clothing. "However, most of those who tried to return were killed."
The Zionists destroyed al-Sawafir one month after the attack.[162] Even
though all three al-Sawafir villages were attacked and subjected to systematic killing, available Zionist records provide information only on the
depopulation of al-Sawafir al-Sharqiyya, which it attributed to "fear."[163]

"Cleansing" Operations: Reliability of Zionist Records Examined

Zionist records of military operations in Arab areas, which Benny Morris
relied on almost exclusively to determine why Palestinians left their homes
during the 1948 war, either remain suppressed or do not fully disclose the
Zionist "cleansing" tactics employed. Graphic testimony by Palestinian
refugees—particularly on the question of expulsion and atrocities—leads
one to surmise that Haganah and dissident forces self-censored their
campaign reports or released documentation that was sanitized or only
partially declassified.

Morris assigned the decisive causes for the Palestinian Arabs' abandonment of towns and villages in his study to the following categories:

E   Expulsion by Jewish forces
A   Abandonment on Arab orders
F   Fear of Jewish attack or of being caught up in the fighting
M   Military assault on the settlement by Jewish troops
W   Haganah/IDF "whispering" campaigns (i.e., psychological
    warfare geared to obtaining an Arab evacuation)
C   Influence of fall of, or exodus from, neighboring town[164]

He states that the lines between F, M, and C "are somewhat blurred," as is
the distinction between M and E. By logical inference, all lines between
Morris's categories of the motives for flight are blurred to some extent.

In numerous cases, Morris's conclusions as to why Arabs abandoned
towns and villages are not supported by the evidence, including, at times,
the evidence he himself offers. Frequently, when he attributed villagers'
evacuation to fear, the fall of neighboring villages, or psychological warfare, Palestinians testified that they left because of intimidation, direct

attack, and expulsion. This was true with Bayt Dajan, Fajja, al-Jammasin al-Ghabri, al-Jammasin al-Sharqi, Kawkaba, al-Mas'udiyya, Na'ani, and Shahma, among others.[165]

Even when Morris concludes that villages were depopulated as a result of military attack, the actual intensity of violent intimidation against civilians and deliberate use of atrocities to terrify the villagers is not apparent from his designations. Morris attributes the abandonment of Burayr, which suffered a massacre and where at least one rape occurred, to "military attack," which fails to adequately indicate the level of violence directed against the villagers. [166]

Morris has admitted that his descriptions are imprecise and that his work relied almost exclusively on Israeli sources, particularly Zionist military field and intelligence reports. Therefore the fact that the decisive causes he assigns are weighted toward the Zionist view of events is unsurprising, especially since he has also wondered whether "today's Middle East would be a healthier, less violent place" if Ben-Gurion had "engineered a comprehensive rather than a partial transfer in 1948."[167]

To correctly determine the factors that impelled Palestinian Arab flight, other available sources should be included, most especially the refugees themselves. Palestinian eyewitnesses are the best-informed sources to explain the circumstances that motivated their exodus. These accounts highlight the limitations of the Zionist sources and Morris's categorizations to explain Palestinian departures. By including Palestinian testimony, as well as British, Zionist, and other documentary sources, the decisive causes for the Arab population's evacuation can be more fundamentally recharacterized. These detailed categories more accurately describe the reported experiences that caused the Palestinian Arab exodus during the civil war.

The range of causes I see is organized in descending order by intensity of violent intimidation:

1   On-site massacre, atrocities, rape, expulsion by Zionist forces
2   Expulsion orders or transported out by Zionists
3   Direct mortar attacks on civilians, siege, shooting at fleeing Arabs
4   Terror raids, house demolitions, sniping, hostage-taking, looting, destruction of crops and livestock
5   Psychological warfare to promote Arab evacuation: verbal threats of

violence, threatening broadcasts, loudspeakers, leaflets, etc.

6 Attack or atrocity in neighboring village or community
7 Fear of impending attack, or fall of neighboring town or village
8 Victims' or witnesses' reports of atrocities, attack, and expulsion
9 Evacuation on Arab orders

A detailed comparison of the causes of depopulation for each locale by subdistrict is provided in appendix 1.

Beersheba Subdistrict's Villages Demolished

The remote Arab Bedouins of the Negev were not spared from the Zionist drive to cleanse southern Palestine of its non-Jewish inhabitants. Because of the Arab character of the Negev, it was to be included in the Arab state delimited by the U.N. partition plan, but the Zionists wanted it for the Jewish state. The southern part of Palestine is strategically important as a link between the Mediterranean and the Red Sea. Chaim Weizmann (the first president of Israel) met with U.S. president Harry Truman on November 19, 1947, to impress on him the importance of allocating the Negev to the Jews. Truman agreed to the request. The "president [was] as good as his word," Weizmann wrote in his memoirs.[168]

The Beersheba subdistrict, comprising 49 percent of Palestine, consisted largely of the Negev Desert. In 1948, the subdistrict was 99.7 percent Arab and 0.3 percent Jewish; Arabs owned 96.7 percent of the land. Nonetheless, the greater part was included in the Jewish state envisioned by the partition plan. The IDF demolished the 26 Arab villages that existed in 1948 and drove out numerous Bedouin tribes during the war.[169] (The Israeli government continues its efforts to "transfer" the remaining Bedouins from the Negev by a variety of discriminatory laws and practices.)[170]

Even though the partition resolution assigned 55 percent of Palestine to the Jewish state, Jews only owned about 5.8 percent of it. But Ben-Gurion was confident that war would provide new lands for Jewish development. That Ben-Gurion intended to seize Arabs' lands in the Negev by conquest was clear from his pronouncements. He assured the Mapai Council on February 7, 1948, that "the war will give us the land. The concept of 'ours' and 'not ours' are only concepts for peacetime, and during war they lose their meaning."[171] He told Joseph Weitz, the (Russian-born) Jewish Na-

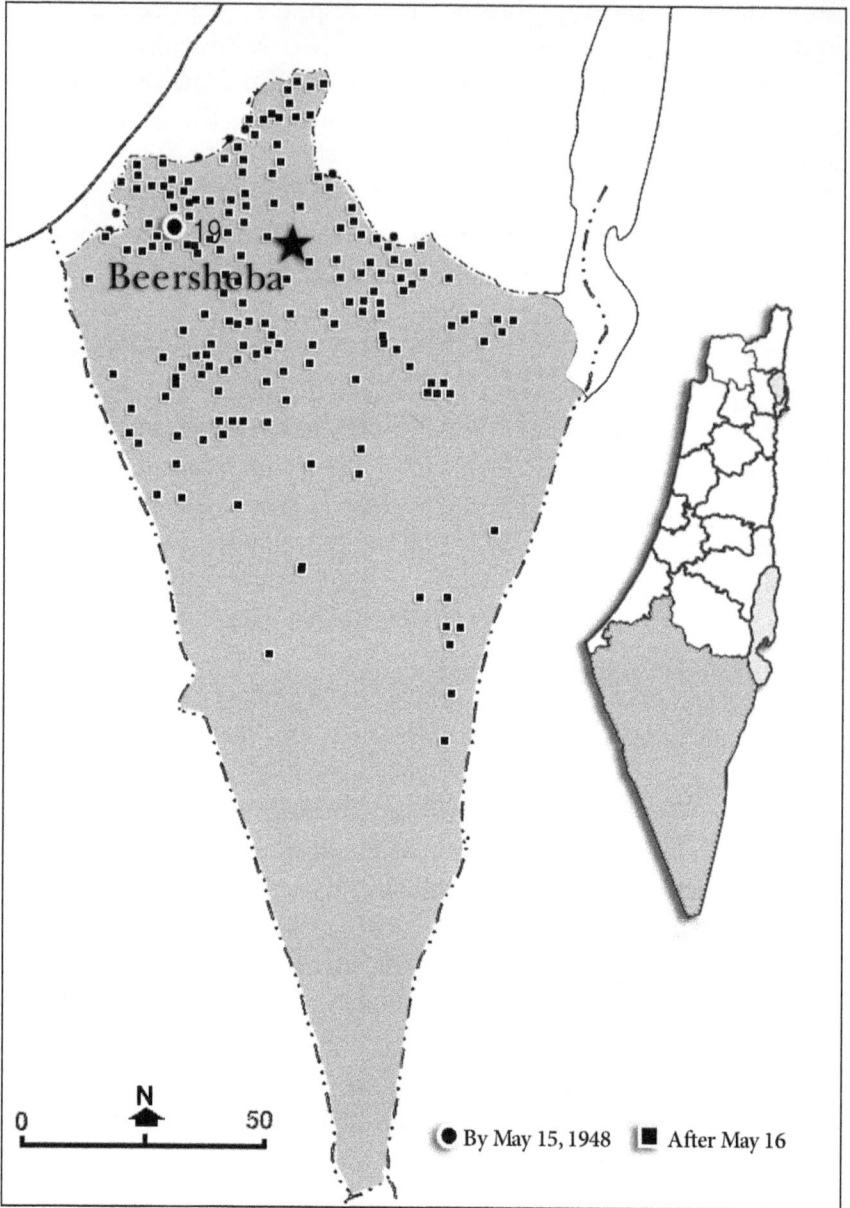

BEERSHEBA SUBDISTRICT DEPOPULATED TOWNS AND VILLAGES

19. Al-'Imara

tional Fund (JNF) director and chairman of the Negev committee, and Avraham Granovsky (Granott), (the Ukrainian-born) JNF chairman that, "Our army will conquer the Negev, will take the land into its hands and will sell it to the JNF at £P 20–25 per dunum. And there is a source . . . of millions [of Palestine pounds]."[172]

In the Beersheba subdistrict, al-'Imara village was the only known settled population center that Zionist forces attacked and depopulated before the mandate ended. While detailed information is scant about the fate of Beersheba's other villages and Bedouin settlements, the expulsion of the Bedouins, begun by Israeli forces in the autumn of 1948, was completed in December 1948. Ninety percent of the Arabs whose families had lived on their lands for centuries in the southernmost part of Palestine—about 90,000 tribesmen were expelled.[173]

Al-'Imara (pop. 119) was located about one kilometer from a British police station. Such stations were strategic targets that the Jewish Agency intended to occupy before the end of the mandate. Zionist forces attacked al-'Imara about a month before the villagers were forced out, killing a young girl. The final attack came as the British military was pulling out of the areas. Muhammad Abu Susin, from al-'Imara, stated that "Jews attacked the village and then expelled the people who were around the village" on May 13.

> The freedom fighters started to collect themselves in the village after we had been attacked many times. Many people were killed by Jewish attacks. They attacked us with tanks. The Bedouins started to leave the village. Our family, Abu Susin, stayed in the village until the Jews attacked. Jews followed us until we reached the valley. Jews attacked us while we were still in our houses. Jews attacked and burned the houses while the people were running away. First, the Jews surrounded the clan. . . . The Jews kept saying: "Go to [King] Faruq [of Egypt]."

The entire clan left al-'Imara together for the al-Shalalah Valley. Two days later, after the mandate ended, Zionist forces attacked the villagers in the valley, forcing them to flee to Khan Yunis in what is now the Gaza Strip. "The same thing happened in Khan Yunis," said Abu Susin. The villagers took nothing with them except for blankets and covers. Some villagers were killed by Zionist forces while attempting to return to al-'Imara to collect food and belongings. Abu Susin said none of the villagers had left before the Zionist attack: "No one would leave his home because of fear. . . . We also did not know that Jews would do this to us. We did not even conceive of it occurring."[174]

Abu Susin's sentiments echo those of many Palestinian Arab refugees interviewed—they could not believe that they could be forced from their homes. No Palestinian Arabs decided voluntarily to emigrate or to abandon their homes or lands. All were intimidated into leaving by physical attack or psychological terror evoked by fear of massacre and—especially—of rape. In numerous cases, the elderly, infirm, disabled, or wounded who could not escape Zionist attack were killed. This was ample warning to Palestinian Arabs of what fate they would suffer if they dared attempt to return.

A pattern of intimidation marked the civil war. Indiscriminate killings, including outright massacres, instilled in Arab villagers an all-consuming terror for their safety at the hands of advancing Zionist forces. The pattern began with an attack or series of attacks on Arab populations, killing civilians and destroying houses, sometimes augmented by verbal warnings to leave. When a final three-flank attack came, an escape route was deliberately left open to direct and facilitate escape. Random killings and other violence drove Arab villagers toward the available exit, with attackers often in pursuit. Following the terrorized departure of most villagers, threats to or killing of stragglers and returnees would send an unmistakable message to villagers and to those who gave them refuge that their homes would not be safe for the foreseeable future.

❀

1. Avigur et al., *History of the Haganah*, vol. 3, part 2, 1475–5; cited in Morris, *Birth*, 95n99.

2. Uri Milstein, *History of Israel's War of Independence*, vol. 2, *The First Month*, trans. and ed. Alan Sacks (Lanham, Md.: University Press of America, 1997), 62.

3. TNA WO 261/197, Third Infantry Brigade, January–March 1948.

4. TNA WO 261/322, First Battalion King's Own Scottish Borders, January–March 1948, QHR, October 25, 1947 to December 31, 1947, Domestic Camp, Lydda.

5. TNA WO 261/173, HQ South Palestine District, QHR, September 30, 1947.

6. Ibid.

7. Banks, *Torn Country*, 120; Dan Kurtzman, *Genesis 1948: The First Arab-Israeli War* (New York: World, 1970), 169.

8. Ibrahim Abu-Lughod, "After the Matriculation," *Al-Ahram Weekly*, www.allthatremains.com.

9. Abdel Qader Yassin, "Ghost City," *Al-Ahram Weekly*, May 3–6, 1998, www.allthatremains.com.

10. Ibid.

11. TNA WO 261/197, Third Infantry Brigade, January–March 1948.

12. "Children Are Victims," *New York Times*, January 5, 1948.

13. Milstein, *History of Israel's War of Independence*, 3:85–88; Shukri Salameh, "Cleansing Jaffa: Detailed Eyewitness Account," www.allthatremains.com.

14. TNA WO 261/197, Third Infantry Brigade, January–March 1948.

15. Ibid.

16. TT, Basil Ennab interview; quoted in Palumbo, *Palestinian Catastrophe*, 84.

17. TNA CO 537/3901, Sir John M. Troutbeck, Middle East Office, Cairo to Bevin, March 4, 1948.

18. Ibid., Abdul Rahman Azzam to Brigadier I. N. Clayton, British Middle East Office, Cairo, February 28, 1948.

19. Banks, *Torn Country*, 121.

20. Ibid., 122.

21. TNA WO 261/173, HQ South Palestine District, QHR, September 30, 1947.

22. Banks, *Torn Country*, 124.

23. TNA WO 275/64, Sixth Airborne Division HQ Palestine, December 20, 1947, no. 58, HQ British Troops in Palestine, April 19–May 3, 1948.

24. GP, diary entry, April 25, 1948.

25. Shukri Salameh, "Cleansing Jaffa."

26. TNA WO 261/381, Second Battalion Royal Irish Fusiliers, QHR, January–June 1948.

27. TNA WO 275/66; cited in Palumbo, *Palestinian Catastrophe*, 86.

28. Ibid.

29. 'Abd al-Ghani Nasir, interviewed by author in Zarka, Jordan, September 22, 2001.

30. Haim Lazar, Kibush Yaffo [Conquest of Jaffa], 142, 126; cited in Morris, *Birth*, 96.

31. JI IZL Papers, kaf-4, 8/I, Kibush Yaffo [Conquest of Yaffo]; cited in Morris, *Birth*, 100.

32. Khadra Muhammad Mustafa Abu al-Rus, interviewed by author in Amman, Jordan, August 15, 2001.

33. 'Abd al-'Aziz Kamal al-Minawi, interviewed by author in Hittin Camp, Jordan, July 29, 2001.

34. 'Uthman Yusif Abu Nabus, interviewed by author in Amman, Jordan, August 7, 2001.

35. 'Arif al-'Arif, *Al-Nakba*; cited in Khalidi, *All That Remains*, 261.

36. Abu Muhammad, interviewed by author in Amman, Jordan, September 12, 2001.

37. TNA WO 275/64, Sixth Airborne Division Historical Section HQ Palestine, December 20, 1947, no. 58, HQ British Troops in Palestine, April 19–May 3, 1948.

38. FP, Random Notes, June 1979, W. V. Fuller, district commissioner of Lydda, 36.

39. Musa Alami, "The Lesson of Palestine," *Middle East Journal* 3.4 (1949): 381–82n1, *Al-Hayat* (Beirut), December 20, 1948.

40. TNA WO 261/381, Second Battalion Royal Irish Fusiliers, QHR, January–June 1948.

41. TNA DEFE 7/389, Cunningham to Creech Jones, no. 1180, April 28, 1948.

42. CP III/4/119, Cunningham to Creech Jones, no. 1180, April 28, 1948.

43. CP III/4/106, His Majesty's Ambassador, Cairo to Cunningham, no. 37, April 28, 1948.

44. TT, Gen. Horatius Murray interview.

45. TNA WO 261/183, First Infantry Division, QHR, June 30, 1948.

46. TNA WO 261/381, Second Battalion Royal Irish Fusiliers, QHR, January–June 1948; WO 261/183, First Infantry Division, HQ QHR, June 1948 and December 1948, June 30, 1948.

47. GP, diary entry April 29, 1948.

48. TT, Gen. MacMillan interview.

49. Ibid.

50. FP, Fuller's handwritten transcription of diary notes, 36.

51. Ibid., 20.
52. TT, Gen. MacMillan interview.
53. TT, Gen. Horatius Murray interview.
54. FP, Report on Certain Officers in Lydda District, District Commissioner Lydda District, [n.d.].
55. CP III/5/43, Cunningham to Creech Jones, no. 1232, May 3, 1948.
56. Soukarieh, "For the Sake of Remembrance," Shafik al-Hout interview.
57. Ibid.
58. CP III/5/43, Cunningham to Creech Jones, no. 1232, May 3, 1948.
59. TT, Basil Ennab; cited in Palumbo, *Palestinian Catastrophe*, 87.
60. CP III/5, Cunningham to Creech Jones, no. 1218, May 1, 1948.
61. TT, Iris Shammout interview.
62. TNA WO 275/66; cited in Palumbo, *Palestinian Catastrophe*, 90.
63. Salameh, "Cleansing Jaffa," www.allthatremains.com.
64. Banks, *Torn Country*, 123.
65. See Khalidi, "Selected Documents on the 1948 Palestine War," 101.
66. TT, Gen. MacMillan interview.
67. Jaffa, 'Abd al-Ghani Nasir, interviewed by author in Zarka Camp, Jordan, September 22, 2001.
68. CP III/5/43, Cunningham to Creech Jones, no. 1232, May 3, 1948.
69. Morris, *Birth*, 97.
70. CP III/4/71, Cunningham to Creech Jones, no. 1148, April 26, 1948.
71. CP III/5/25, Cunningham to Creech Jones, no. 1217, May 1, 1948.
72. Banks, *Torn Country*, 124.
73. Khalidi, "Selected Documents on the 1948 Palestine War," 105.
74. Soukarieh, "For the Sake of Remembrance," Shafik al-Hout interview.
75. Morris, *Birth Revisited*, 218n383.
76. Khalidi, "Selected Documents on the 1948 Palestine War," 103; CP III/5/43, Cunningham to Creech Jones, no. 1232, May 3, 1948.
77. TNA WO 261/297, First Battalion Coldstream Guards, QHR, May–December 1948, situation report, no. 22, May 3, 1948.
78. Ibid.
79. FP, Fuller Diary Notes while District Commissioner of Lydda with HQ in Jaffa, 9.
80. CP III/5/43, Cunningham to Creech Jones, no. 1232, May 3, 1948.
81. IDFA 321/48/97, Protocol of a Meeting between the Commander of the Haganah in Tel Aviv and His Aides and Representatives of the Inhabitants of Jaffa, Tel Aviv, May 12, 1948; cited in Morris, *Birth Revisited*, 219n390.
82. Ibid., n. 391, IDFA 321/48/97, Second Meeting between the Haganah OC in Tel Aviv and the Representatives of the Jaffa Emergency Committee in Tel Aviv on May 13, 1948 at 10:45 hours.
83. Ibid., n. 392, HA 55/31, Texts of Agreement and Instructions.
84. Pappé, *Ethnic Cleansing of Palestine*, 204.
85. ISA FM 2406/2 Second Memorandum Submitted by the Emergency Committee of Jaffa Protesting against the Irregular Activities of the Jewish Forces in Jaffa Area, May 28, 1948; ISA FM 2564/9, Chizik, Minutes of a Meeting Held on the 31.5.48 between the Military Governor of Jaffa and Mr. Robert Gee [sic] of the International Red Cross; IDFA 321/48/97, Military Governor's Office, Jaffa, Summary 15.5.48; cited in Morris, *Birth Revisited*, 220nn397–98.
86. Yossef Ulizki, *From Events to a War* (Hebrew) (Tel Aviv: Haganah Publication of Documents, 1951), 53; cited in Pappé, *Ethnic Cleansing of Palestine*, 205-6n19.
87. ISA FM 2564/9, Erem to Shitrit, August 11, 1948; cited in Morris, *Birth Revisited*, 386n259.
88. Quoted in Pappé, *Ethnic Cleansing of Palestine*, 204n15.

89. Dan Yahav, *Purity of Arms: Ethos, Myth and Reality, 1936–1956* (Hebrew) (Tel Aviv: Tamuz, 2002), interview with Abu Laban, 223–30; cited in Pappé, *Ethnic Cleansing of Palestine*, 206–7n22.

90. Ibid., 205.

91. Morris, *Birth Revisited*, 220n406.

92. Pappé, *Ethnic Cleansing of Palestine*, 221.

93. Ibid., 102.

94. Khalidi, *All That Remains*, 232.

95. Nijma Shawarib, interviewed by author in Baqʻa Camp, Jordan, July 19, 2001. The al-Tira mentioned could have been al-Tira, Haifa; or al-Tira Dindan, al-Ramla. Both villages were attacked.

96. Shakir al-Musa, interviewed by author in Amman, Jordan, July 19, 2001.

97. Nijma Shawarib, interviewed in Baqʻa Camp, Jordan, July 19, 2001.

98. Avigur et al., *History of the Haganah*; cited in Khalidi, *All That Remains*, 233.

99. Hamdi Abu Hatab, interviewed by author in Hittin Camp, Jordan, July 29, 2001.

100. Anonymous elderly woman interviewed by author in Hittin Camp, Jordan, July 29, 2001. The woman refused to state her name for fear of Israeli retribution against her or her family living in the occupied West Bank and Gaza Strip. In many interviews, refugees identify Zionists' armored cars as "tanks."

101. Ibid.

102. Amina ʻUmran Zahran, interviewed by author in al-Husayn Camp, Jordan, September 11, 2001.

103. Abu Sami, interviewed by author in al-Husayn Camp, Jordan, August 12, 2001.

104. Ibid.

105. Ibid.

106. Muhammad Abu al-ʻAziz Khayr, interviewed by author in al-Wihdat Camp, Jordan, July 21, 2001.

107. Rasmi Mahmud, interviewed by author in al-Wihdat Camp, Jordan, July 21, 2001.

108. Yasra Ibrahim, interviewed by author in Hittin Camp, Jordan, August 11, 2001.

109. Khalidi, *All That Remains*, 260.

110. Muhammad Hamad Haddad, interviewed by author in Hittin Camp, Jordan, August 7, 2001.

111. Ibid.

112. Nijim and Muammar, *Toward the De-Arabization of Palestine/Israel*, 49.

113. Husni ʻAbd al-Latif ʻAtawat, interviewed by author in Zarka, Jordan, August 8, 2001.

114. Salim Abu Sayf, interviewed by author in Souf Camp, Jordan, September 19, 2001.

115. Zakiyya Abu Hammad, interviewed by author in Hittin Camp, Jordan, July 28, 2001.

116. Ahamad, interviewed by author in Amman, Jordan, August 27, 2001.

117. Morris, *Birth,* 53, 188.

118. Salah Shihadeh, e-mail correspondence with author, March 24–25, 2001.

119. Nijim and Muammar, *Toward a De-Arabization of Palestine/Israel*, 54.

120. Avrahon Eilon, ed., *Havitat Givati Bemilhemet Hakomemiut* [*The Givati Brigade in the War of Independence*] (Hebrew) (Tel Aviv: Maʻarachot/Defense Ministry Press, 1959), 485, 527–28; cited in Morris, *Birth*, 125–26.

121. Ibid., 485; cited in Morris, *Birth*, 125–26n219.

122. ʻAbd al-Rahman Salih Abu Shraykh, interviewed by author in Baqʻa Camp, Jordan, July 23, 2001.

123. HA 105/92 aleph, "Doron" (Maoz) to HIS-AD, "The Interrogation of Women Prisoners in the Village of Abu Shusha," June 24, 1948; cited in Morris, *Birth Revisited*, 257n763.

124. ʻAbd al-Rahman Salih Abu Shraykh, interviewed by author in Baqʻa Camp, Jordan, July 23, 2001.

125. 'Abd al-Fatah al-Asmar, interviewed by author in Hittin Camp, Jordan, July 29, 2001.

126. Latifa Muhammad Hamdan, interviewed by author in Baq'a Camp, Jordan, August 26, 2001.

127. Ibid., 67.

128. Hasan al-'Ashawi, interviewed by author in Hittin Camp, Jordan, July 28, 2001.

129. Wardi, interviewed by author in Baq'a Camp, Jordan, August 26, 2001.

130. Fatma Muhammad 'Ali 'Ammar, interviewed by author in Amman, Jordan, August 30, 2001.

131. Ibid.

132. Tahsin Shahadi, interviewed by author in Jabal al-Amir Faysal, Jordan, August 9, 2001.

133. Ziyad 'Abdullah al-Wihdat, interviewed by author in Baq'a Camp, Jordan, August 26, 2001.

134. Muhammad Khamis Muhammad Hasanayn, interviewed by author in Amman, Jordan, August 18, 2001.

135. Morris, *Birth*, 127, xvii.

136. Aziza Mahmud Nababti, interviewed by author in Baq'a Camp, Jordan, July 23, 2001.

137. Amina 'Abd al-Qadir Hammad, interviewed by author in Baq'a Camp, Jordan, July 23, 2001.

138. Zaynab Hasan 'Anbar, interviewed by author in Hittin Camp, Jordan, September 11, 2001.

139. Thurayya Shahin, interviewed by author in Baq'a Camp, Jordan, August 26, 2001.

140. Nijim and Muammar, *Toward a De-Arabization of Palestine/Israel*, 70.

141. HHA-ACP, 10.95.10 (4), "Our Arab Policy in the Middle of the War," Aharon Cohen, May 10, 1948; HHA-ACP, 10.95.11 (8), "In Face of the Arab Evacuation," Aharon Cohen, summer 1948; KMA-PA 100 MemVav Dalet/3-158, Haganah Intelligence Service Information, May 13, 1948; CZA S24-9045, Information about the Arabs of Palestine (from Arab broadcasts, May 10–11), and Information about the Arabs of Palestine (from Arab Broadcasts, May 14–15); KMA-PA 100/Mem/VavDalet/3, Haganah Intelligence Service Information, May 13, 1948; cited in Morris, *Birth*, 69n20.

142. Ibid., 126, and Khalidi, *From Haven to Conquest*, appendix 7, 856.

143. Khalidi, *All That Remains*, 80.

144. Thurayya Shahin, interviewed by author in Baq'a Camp, Jordan, August 26, 2001.

145. Umm Khalid, interviewed by author in Zarka, Jordan, August 9, 2001.

146. Muhammad 'Ali 'Abd al-Qadir Muslih, interviewed by author in Jarash Camp, Jordan, September 3, 2001.

147. Muhammad Sa'id Muhammad Jabir, interviewed by author in Jarash Camp, Jordan, September 3, 2001.

148. Ibid.

149. Ibid.

150. 'Abd al-Rahman al-'Alawi, interviewed by author in Hittin Camp, Jordan, August 8, 2001.

151. Moshe Giv'ati, *In the Path of Desert and Fire: The History of the Ninth Armored Battalion, 1948–1984* (Hebrew) (Tel Aviv: Ma'arachot/Defense Ministry Press, 1994), 45–47; Rami Rosen, "Col. G. Speaks Out," *Ha'aretz*, September 16, 1994. Morris, *Birth Revisited*, 258n777.

152. 'Abd al-Rahman al-'Alawi, interviewed by author in Hittin Camp, Jordan, August 8, 2001.

153. *Palestine 1948*, in Abu-Sitta, *Palestinian Nakba*.

154. Khalidi, *All That Remains*, 104. Some villagers from Hulaykat returned briefly to their homes and farming after Egyptian forces recaptured the area on July 8, but IDF forces expelled them again in October 1948.

155. Ibrahim Salim, interviewed by author in Hittin Camp, Jordan, August 7, 2001.

156. Jamila 'Abd al-Qadir Ahmad, interviewed by author in Hittin Camp, Jordan, August 7, 2001.

157. Abu Muhammad, interviewed by author in Hittin Camp, Jordan, August 11, 2001.

158. Umm Muhammad, interviewed by author in Hittin Camp, Jordan, August 11, 2001.

159. Ramadan 'Abdullah al-Bahsi, interviewed by author in Hittin Camp, Jordan, August 11, 2001.

160. Shaykh Ramadan, interviewed by author in Hittin Camp, Jordan, August 11, 2001.

161. 'Abdullah al-Bahsi, interviewed by author in Hittin Camp, Jordan, August 11, 2001.

162. Ibid.

163. Morris, *Birth*, xvii, 126–27.

164. Ibid., xiv.

165. Ibid., xvi.

166. Ibid., 128, 182–83.

167. Benny Morris, "A New Exodus for the Middle East," *Guardian*, October 3, 2002.

168. Chaim Weizmann, *Trial and Error* (London: East and West, 1950), 561–63.

169. Nijim and Muammar, *Toward a De-Arabization of Palestine/Israel*, 74; Abu-Sitta, *Palestinian Nakba*.

170. Jonathan Cook, "Bedouins in the Negev Face New Transfer," May 3, 2003, www.merip.org/mero/mero051003.html; www.adalah.org.

171. David Ben-Gurion, *Be-hilahem Yisrael* (As Israel Fights) (Tel Aviv: Mapai, 1952), 71; cited in Morris, *Birth Revisited*, 360n118.

172. Ibid., entries for February 3 and 4, Weitz, *Diary*, 3:232–33. A dunum is 1,000 square meters. £P is a Palestine pound, the currency used in mandate Palestine.

173. Pappé, *Ethnic Cleansing of Palestine*, 194; Abu Sitta, *Palestinian Nakba*, 44.

174. Muhammad Abu Susin, interviewed by author in Gaza Camp, Jordan, September 3, 2001.

PALESTINIAN CHILDREN IN THE JEWISH-DESIGNATED
"ARAB QUARTER" OF HAIFA, 1948

IX

The Shattering of Arab Palestine

If the Jews continue to attack Arab positions in Palestine, some action by Arabs outside Palestine will be almost inevitable.

Colonial Secretary Arthur Creech Jones, April 1948

As the British finalized their exit from Palestine, hastening to abandon all mandate responsibilities, the full-scale civil war raging after March 1948 threatened to escalate into a multistate conflict. Arabs in other countries clamored for leaders to "save Palestine," stem the tide of refugees, prevent more atrocities, and thwart the establishment of a Jewish state. Meanwhile, the Zionist leadership set its sights on capturing additional Palestinian cities and territory. The predominately Arab cities of Acre (Akka) and Safad were their next targets. During the final weeks of the mandate, both cities and their suburbs suffered the now established pattern of escalated violence followed by a siege and a decisive military attack, forcing Palestinian Arabs to evacuate. Unhindered by weakened British security forces, the Zionists escalated their use of military force against civilian Arabs.

Villagers and townspeople of the Safad, Baysan, Acre, and Nazareth subdistricts attest in oral recollections that they were in most cases compelled by intimidation to leave their homes. As village after village fell, the Palestinian Arab exodus swelled. By the time the mandate ended, more than half of all Palestinian Arabs who would become refugees during the 1948 war were already displaced.

When the British administration terminated on May 15, the former governors were impressed by the Zionist forces' effectiveness but appalled by

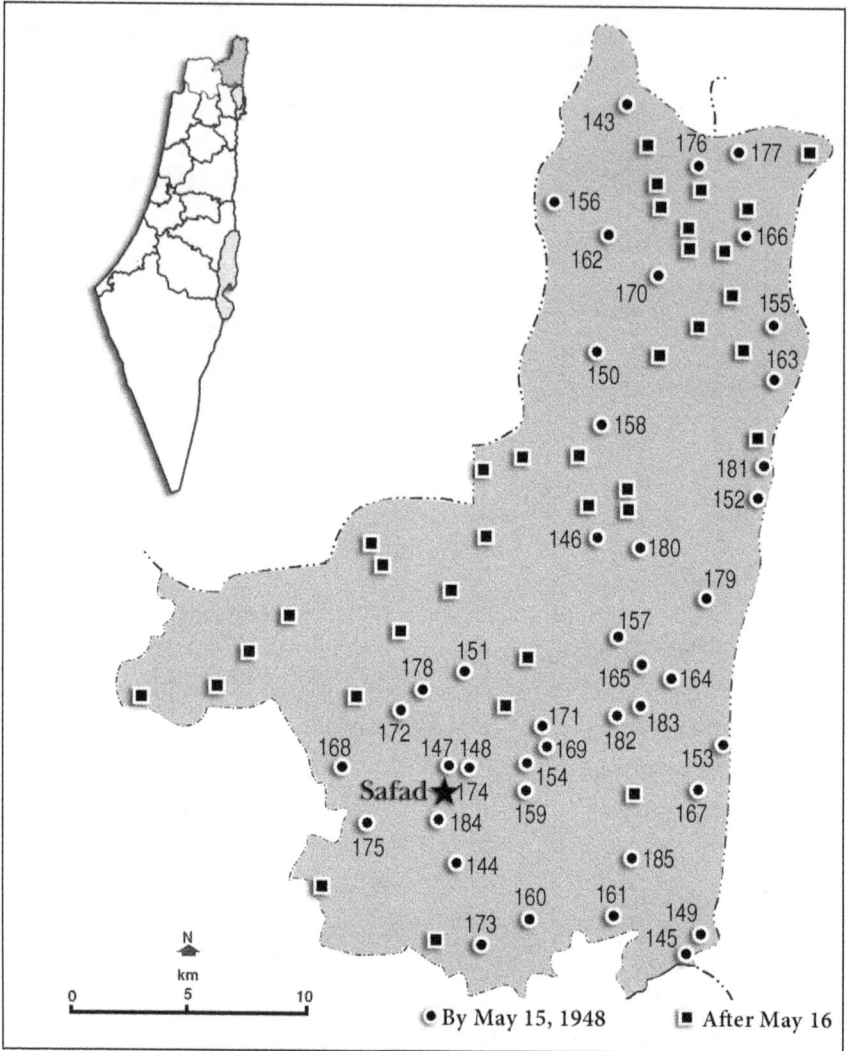

By May 15, 1948 ■ After May 16

SAFAD SUBDISTRICT DEPOPULATED TOWNS AND VILLAGES

143. Abil al-Qamh
144. 'Akbara
145. 'Arab al-Shamalina
146. 'Arab Zubayd
147. 'Ayn al-Zaytun
148. Biriyya
149. Al-Butayha
150. Buwayziyya (includes Meis)
151. Dallata

152. Al-Dirbashiyya
153. Al-Dirdara (Mazari' al-Daraja)
154. Fir'im
155. Al-Hamra'
156. Hunin (Hula and Udeisa)
157. Al-Husayniyya
158. Jahula
159. Al-Ja'una
160. Jubb Yusuf ('Arab al-Suyyad)

161. Khirbat Karraza
162. Al-Khalisa
163. Khiyam al-Walid
164. Kirad al-Baqqara
165. Kirad al-Ghannama
166. Madahil
167. Mansurat al-Khayt
168. Mirun
169. Mughr al-Khayt
170. Al-Na'ima
171. Qabba'a
172. Qaditta
173. Al-Qudayriyya
174. Safad (Arab)
175. Al-Sammu'i
176. Al-Sanbariyya
177. Al-Shawka al-Tahta
178. Taytaba
179. Tulayl
180. Al-'Ulmaniyya
181. Al-'Urayfiyya
182. Al-Wayziyya
183. Yarda
184. Al-Zahiriyya al-Tahta
185. Al-Zanghariyya (Zuhluq)
186. Al-Zuq al-Tahtani

the deliberate ruthlessness of the violence employed against Arab civilians to achieve political goals. The following narratives—mainly Palestinian Arab eyewitness recollections—describe the forced exodus from towns and villages in the mandate's final days. I also assess the positions and predicaments of key participants as British rule over the Holy Land ended.

Safad Subdistrict Arabs Nearly Obliterated

The Arab communities in Safad subdistrict were almost completely wiped out during the 1948 war. Safad was the northernmost subdistrict in mandate Palestine, bordered by Lebanon to the west and Syria to the east, and strategically important for its water resources. In 1948, the subdistrict land was majority Arab-owned and populated. The land was 68.2 percent Arab-owned, 17.4 percent Jewish-owned, and 14.3 percent public property, with a population 86.2 percent Arab, 21.5 percent Jewish, and 1.5 percent other.[1] Of the 83 Arab villages in Safad subdistrict, Palestinian Arabs were displaced from 44 villages and towns, or 53 percent of the subdistrict's population centers, by the mandate's end. The exodus from these locales was spurred by direct Zionist attacks and psychological warfare.

By the end of the 1948 war, Zionist forces depopulated and demolished 78 locales, or 94 percent, of Safad's Arab villages, the majority during Operation Yiftah, launched by the Haganah on April 28 "to purify Eastern Galilee of Arabs," according to Plan D.[2] Only five Arab villages remained intact, and these were predominately non-Muslim: al-Rihaniyya (Circassian and Muslim), Jish (Christian and Muslim), Hurfeish (Druze), Tuba

(Bedouin), and 'Akbara, which was attacked but only its Muslim inhabitants driven out. Zionist forces used 'Akbara as a transfer and collection site for Galilean Arabs who had remained in their villages,[3] and who would be resettled in selected sites or expelled from here.[4]

The fate of villages with mixed ethnic groups or religions further undermines the "accident of war" theory of Arab displacement. The selectivity based on religion and race underscores that expulsion was carried out by design and guided by political principles. Further, ample evidence shows that passive villages, or portions of them, were depopulated gratuitously and selectively by demographic group. Benny Morris uses Israeli sources to allege that Zionist forces did not expel or uproot the Arabs of non-resisting villages. The population of one of the villages he cites, Alma, was in fact uprooted and expelled. As another example, Morris cites the mixed Muslim-Christian village of Jish, which suffered a massacre.[5] Apparently Zionist forces permitted Christians, Druze, and Circassians to remain in some villages. David Ben-Gurion singled out these minorities for "favored treatment."[6]

The "Cleansing" of the Galilee

The deterioration in eastern Galilee communications compelled the British to pull back isolated military detachments to avoid having their evacuation routes cut off.[7] Their withdrawal left the Haganah free to implement Operation Yiftah, its campaign to conquer the region. The Haganah implemented this part of Plan D during the second half of April and the first half of May 1948. It involved securing the eastern Galilee border where Syrian forces were expected to cross into Palestine and "cleansing" the area of its Arab inhabitants.[8]

Yigal (Paicovitch) Allon, the Palmach officer commanding (OC), determined that the border would best be secured by clearing all Arab forces and inhabitants from the area.[9] Toward the end of April, Zionist attacks on Arab villages near Lake Hula compelled many Arab inhabitants to flee. Allon's forces also employed psychological warfare, known as "whispering campaigns," initiated at the command level. In such tactics, Jewish town or settlement mukhtars would threaten their neighboring Arab villages with attack to induce fear and flight. Allon himself described the tactic in a well-known passage from the *History of the Haganah*: "I gathered the

Jewish *mukhtars* . . . and I asked them to whisper in the ears of several Arabs that giant Jewish reinforcements had reached the Galilee and were about to clean out the villages of the Hula [and] to advise them, as friends, to flee while they could."[10] Although this tactic was successful in some cases, Palestinian refugees attest that direct military assault and atrocities had a far greater impact in precipitating evacuation.

The fall of a number of Safad-area villages, ascribed to "the influence of the fall or exodus from a neighboring village,"[11] were actually depopulated by Zionist attack and expulsion. For example, on March 13, al-Husayniyya (pop. 394) suffered what the Sixth Airborne described as a "particularly brutal and unnecessary attack by [the] Haganah." Palmach forces killed several dozen villagers, including women and children; another five were missing, presumed dead, and four were seriously wounded.[12] A number of houses were also blown up, precipitating an evacuation. A subsequent Palmach attack on March 16 killed another 30 villagers.[13]

Ahmad Ashkar recounts how Zionist forces attacked Kirad al-Ghannama (pop. 406) in the dead of night on April 22.

> Dread overtook us. We were not prepared, and we had not expected this. The soldiers ordered us to leave the village that very night and threatened that if we did not leave, they would do to us what was done to the inhabitants of al-Husayniyya village. We knew that the Jews had slaughtered dozens of inhabitants of that village like sheep. We were absolutely panic-stricken and did not argue with them. Our goal was to get out of there as fast as possible and reach a safe place.
>
> On the way to the unknown, we all wept. Men, women, and children were all choking on silent tears.[14]

The twin village of Kirad al-Baqqara (pop. 418), only separated by a small *wadi* [stream] to the east of Kirad al-Ghannama, probably suffered the same fate, as it was depopulated on the same date.

The Siege and Expulsion of Arab Safad

At an elevation of 2,750 feet, the city of Safad was the unproclaimed Arab capital of the Galilee. Safad was also the linchpin of Operation Yiftah. The city's population was estimated by the British in 1944 at 11,000 Arabs and 3,500 Jews.[15] In late 1947, anxiety and apprehension were prevalent among the vulnerable Jewish settlements of the district's northern Hula area, as well as in the Jewish community of Safad itself, which had suffered a massacre during Arab attacks in 1929.[16] Strong Haganah forces were concentrated in Safad "to deal with any trouble in the town itself . . . and also to act as a mobile force for the defense of the Hula settlements."[17] In preparation for the anticipated war, Haganah forces "conducted wide-ranging exercises called the 'War before the War.'"[18] Moshe Kalman, commander of the Safad battle, attests to the importance given to its conquest: "Safad was the nerve-center and the focal point of all enemy activities in the Galilee region, and to some extent it was a symbol for all the Arabs in the country. It was clear that once we succeeded in conquering Safad, it would undermine the whole basis for the secure existence of Arab settlement in Galilee, and the control over the entire eastern part of that region would come into our hands very easily."[19]

According to the Sixth Airborne Division, and consistent with a pattern of escalation throughout Palestine, sniping between Jews and Arabs began in Safad in mid-December 1947 after Menahem Mizrahi, a Haganah intelligence agent patrolling the market in an Arab neighborhood, was killed. The Haganah's provocative "aggressive reconnaissance incursions" into Arab areas triggered skirmishes.[20] Firing was intense, and casualties occurred on both sides. When Palestine Police requested assistance, Transjordan Frontier Force troops moved in to restore order. The army imposed a curfew and brought in a company from the Eighth Parachute Battalion. From mid-December on, a British infantry company stationed in the town attempted to maintain law and order. Major R. Dare Wilson, who served with the division, wrote that "for its size, Safad probably gave [us] more trouble than any other town in Palestine."[21] According to Jewish sources, some British forces in Safad, particularly First Battalion Irish Guards, secretly assisted and cooperated with Zionist operations but provided no military assistance to Arab forces, or actually hindered their efforts.[22]

After March 1948, the forced Judaization of Safad reached its climax. Israeli records confirm that the Jewish Agency leadership contemplated expelling the population. Arab recollections verify that the Zionists intimidated civilians. After the British garrison evacuated Safad on April 16, Arab forces occupied the city's strategic positions: the citadel, the government house, and the Mount Cana'an police post. Palmach OC Yigal Allon reviewed the military situation after the British withdrew and recommended a series of operations to prepare for "the expected Arab invasion." One was the "harassment of Arab Safad in order to speed up its evacuation," as it was considered a sensitive border town, being only 12 kilometers from Syria.[23]

Despite receiving news of war raging elsewhere in Palestine, Safad's Arabs remained confident. Fayiz Qadurah, a Safad businessman, said, "We were the majority, and the feeling among us was that we would defeat the Jews with sticks and rocks." Even after hearing about the fall of Tiberias and the Dayr Yasin massacre, Qadurah believed Safad was safe. Only after Palmach forces attacked and occupied the Arab villages of 'Ayn al-Zaytun, Biriyya, and others along the Tiberias to Safad road did Safad's Arabs feel threatened.[24] These attacks appear to have been part of Allon's plan to harass and intimidate the inhabitants of Safad into evacuating.

A Palmach force of about 200 attacked 'Ayn al-Zaytun (pop. 951) on the night of May 1 from the east and south. OC Kalman terrorized the Arabs by blowing up the village buildings one by one during daylight so Safad's Arabs on the opposite ridge "could see what was in store for them."[25] Barrel bombs rolled down onto 'Ayn al-Zaytun, followed by grenade and mortar attacks. Ahmad Hussain Hamid heard that "Jews were killing civilians and expelling the rest." Nevertheless, the villagers had decided among themselves to remain. He said the Jewish settlements of Ayn Zeitim and Rosh Pinna had harassed 'Ayn al-Zaytun

> because they wanted to connect the settlements with the Jewish quarter of Safad. . . . The Jews ordered the villagers to assemble in Mahmud Hamid's courtyard and then separated the men from the women. At about sunset, they forced our women and children out of the village, firing over their heads to make them run. Later during the night, the Jews came and ordered us to leave, threatening death to those deciding to stay. . . . They kept 37 young men as hostages.[26]

Those taken hostage were never seen again by the villagers. At least one villager was killed while trying to return. Palmach sappers blew up the villagers' homes on May 2 and 3 to bar their return and to demoralize Safad's Arabs.[27] OC Elad Peled described the frenzied destruction: "At noon, our men began blowing up the village. The intoxication of victory blinded them and they went berserk, breaking and destroying property."[28]

The Israeli historian Uri Milstein reports that the Arab youths taken hostage were massacred.[29] In fact, Israeli archives report two massacres at 'Ayn al-Zaytun. A soldier named Aharon Yo'eli testified that Zionist forces first captured 23 Arabs, stole their watches, "led them over the hills and killed them. The rest were expelled in the direction of the Germak that same evening, and to make them go fast, we shot at them." A soldier named Yitzhak Golan reported the second massacre. Thirty Arab prisoners were taken for interrogation at Har Kna'an. The hostages were then to be taken to Rosh Pinna police station: "On the way [the Arabs] attempted to escape, so we shot at them. There was no alternative. The danger was that they might reach Safad and would tell there how few weapons and manpower we had. . . . Next morning a platoon was sent to bury them."[30]

This "shot while escaping" explanation is challenged by the veteran's subsequent admission that "it is possible [the Arab prisoners] were chained."[31] Netiva Ben-Yehuda, a Palmach sabotage officer who participated in the attack on 'Ayn al-Zaytun, testified in detail to events. After rounding up the prisoners, "they took all these, tied their hands and feet and threw them down into the deep *wadi* under Ein Zeitun ['Ayn al-Zaytun] and left them lying there for two days." After foreign agencies learned of the atrocities, soldiers were asked to untie the massacred prisoners' hands and legs. Ben-Yehuda obeyed and described the scene: "I had never before seen such a thing . . . a bloodbath, a real bloodbath . . . how could they have finished them all off?"[32]

Despite the atrocities, the expulsion of the village women, children, and men, and the detention and later massacre of the male prisoners, Morris ascribes the abandonment of 'Ayn al-Zaytun solely to military assault, even after acknowledging in his narrative discussion that a massacre occurred.[33] In this case, and in numerous others, Morris's conclusions as to why Arabs abandoned towns and villages are not supported by the evidence, including at times the evidence he himself offers.

The news of the 'Ayn al-Zaytun and Dayr Yasin massacres terrified the farming village of Fir'im (pop. 858). Still, its inhabitants remained until Zionist forces attacked with mortars on May 1. They left on May 2 under attack, unable to defend themselves.[34] Zionist forces entered Fir'im and burned it to the ground. While Palmach forces were shelling Fir'im from the east, they also shelled the Arab villages of Mughr al-Khayt (pop. 568) and Qabbaʻa (pop. 534). Villagers began to flee north to the Palestinian Arab villages of ʻAmmuqa, Dallata, al-Rihaniyya, Saliha, and Yarun, as well as to Bint Jubayl in Lebanon.[35]

Soon after Zionist forces occupied the Rosh Pinna police fortress, some villagers from Jaʻuna (pop. 1,334) panicked and fled, but the majority remained.[36] Unarmed and incapable of self-defense, most villagers left together on May 1 to save their lives, their "honor," and their children. Talib Tamim said, "We were afraid that the Jews would do what they had done in Dayr Yasin and ʻAyn al-Zaytun. Why should we take a chance?"[37] Zionist forces shot at least one villager who attempted to return. Those remaining in Jaʻuna were expelled and "dumped on a bare, sun-scorched hillside near the village of ʻAkbara."[38] The Palmach's conscious purpose in shelling Firʻim, Mughr al-Khayt, and Qabbaʻa was "that in the end the Arabs would flee from them," said Haganah member Yosef Ulitsky.[39] Those who did not flee or who attempted to return were often expelled as in Jaʻuna, or killed.

After isolating Safad from its satellite villages, Haganah forces besieged the city on May 2. For almost a week, Fayiz Qadurah reported, they heavily shelled Safad "from all directions."[40] Although the Palmach ground attack on May 6 failed, a second attack quickly followed on May 9 and 10.[41] Zionist forces used their "secret weapon," the Davidka mortar, to expel the Arabs of Safad. The shrieking shells and the deafening detonations caused shock and panic among the Arabs. Kalman's explicit aim was to create panic by firing mortar bombs. He said, "I gave the order to send a Davidka shell every few hours after nightfall over the Arab quarter in order to create panic and rouse the fears of the residents." Peled confirmed that the purpose of the terrific noise was "to sow panic among the civilian population."[42]

According to the sources of a United Press correspondent, Zionist forces were ordered to conquer the entire city of Safad at all costs before May 15, "as this would give the Haganah a strategic position from which to defend the Hula valley against any Arab invasion."[43] The Arab garrison and ALA forces in Safad numbered between 800 and 1,000, with various arms and limited ammunition. The ALA officer Sari Fnaish knew that the Arab forces could not defend the city. It was rumored that Fnaish had requested assistance from King Abdullah, who "was ready to have the Jews occupy Safad rather than see the mufti form a government in the city." Lacking reinforcements, and warned of the impending attack, Fnaish left the city the night before the battle. Arab commander Adib Shishakli and the local militia trainer, Ihsan Kamlamaz, also vanished before the battle. Fayiz Qadurah believed the ALA's presence lessened the inhabitants' sense of responsibility for their own defense. "The feeling was why die if there were people to do your work for you?" Nevertheless, he said, the ALA did not fight well, did not know the area, and, most important, were not well armed or unified.[44]

People panicked as rumors spread during the battle that the ALA had begun to retreat. Rain poured down and no one knew what was happening. "We knew we could not sustain the defense of our city alone," said Usamah al-Naqib, and "so by midnight, we decided to retreat." Safad's Arabs feared living under Zionist control. They also believed that if they chose exile, in only four days the "Arab armies would enter Palestine and push the Jews out of our homes."[45] As the Arabs fled, Palmach forces "intentionally left open the exit routes" to "facilitate" their exodus, following a pattern often seen elsewhere.[46] Most Arabs left together on foot in the darkness on May 10 and 11, with only the clothes they were wearing. Muslim Safad Arabs who remained, mostly the ill and elderly, were rounded up and "were later transported by the Jews to the Lebanese frontier," clearing Safad of all its Arab inhabitants, reported Usamah al-Naqib.[47] Remaining Christian Arabs were later transferred to Haifa on June 13 and not permitted to return to Safad.[48]

Thousands of shell-shocked Safad residents wandered the outskirts of the city and hid in nearby wadis, according to the Palmach's Third Battalion. To prevent Arabs from returning to their homes, Kalman ordered airplanes to bomb the area to induce the Arabs to flee: "To speed the flight, we asked for piper planes to drop a few bombs on groups of retreating residents and we also fired a few mortar shells in the direction of the wadis to chase away those who still remained."[49]

Jewish civilians also sought to prevent the exiled Arabs' return. Safad's Jewish notables appealed directly to the Israeli cabinet in early June 1948 to bar the Arabs' return. They feared retribution, especially because "most of the Arab property in Safad has been stolen and plundered since the Arabs left." If Jews were not quickly settled in the city, they advised Jewish leaders that "the Arab houses . . . be destroyed and blown up lest the Arabs have somewhere to return to."[50] The members of the Transfer Committee shared this strategic thinking. Ezra Danin, a committee member, wrote that to prevent a refugee return, the Arabs "must be confronted with faits accomplis," including "destruction of Arab houses, settling Jews in all the areas evacuated, and expropriating Arab property."[51]

The leaders of the Arab states angrily protested the Zionist attack on Safad. Arab League Secretary General Azzam Pasha told the British oriental secretary in Damascus that the "Arabs could not accept any truce proposal while Jews are forcing Palestine Arabs out of their homes."[52] Damascus was full of rumors—believed by the Syrian government—that the Jews had turned Safad into a second Dayr Yasin.[53] The British government feared a disaster in Safad would cause the Arab states to intervene militarily in Palestine before the mandate ended. London therefore authorized General Gordon MacMillan "to use all practicable means, including air action, to restore the situation,"[54] but MacMillan did not waiver from his noninterventionist policy, once again tacitly implementing partition. Like Haifa, Safad was assigned to the Jewish state.

A day after Safad fell, Palmach forces attacked 'Akbara (pop. 302). Many villagers had already left after the 'Ayn al-Zaytun massacre, taking the old men, women, and children to the neighboring villages of al-Farradiyya and al-Sammu'i. The 20 haphazardly armed men remaining to protect the villages were then forced to join their families in al-Farradiyya, the only route left open by Zionist forces.[55] Palmach troops entered the village, and "destroyed a few houses and part of the village mosque." They then left "with our livestock," Mahmud Rashid recalled.[56]

The townspeople of al-Khalisa (pop. 2,134) were terrified by Safad's fall. They moved their families for safety to Hunin village, bordering Lebanon, on May 12, as advised, but not ordered, by the ALA. None of the inhabitants took anything along, because the roads were hilly and they could not carry possessions in addition to their children while walking. About 100 armed men remained in al-Khalisa; shelling from El Manara settlement and from the main Safad to Metulla road forced the men to retreat. The people of al-Khalisa remained in Hunin waiting for the Arab armies to rescue them and return them to their homes.[57]

The village of Qaditta (pop. 278) and the neighboring Jewish settlements had several skirmishes during the civil war. After the villages of 'Ayn al-Zaytun and Mirun were occupied and Safad fell, the villagers of

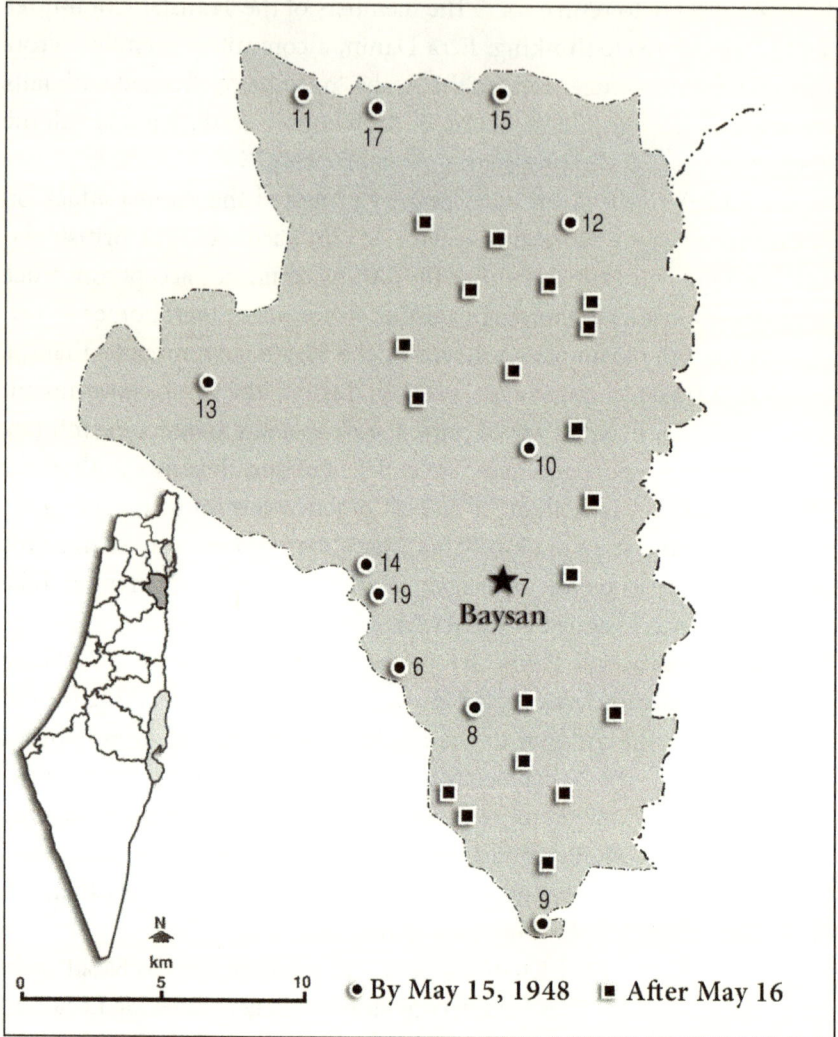

● By May 15, 1948   ■ After May 16

BAYSAN SUBDISTRICT DEPOPULATED TOWNS AND VILLAGES

6. Al-Ashrafiyya
7. Baysan
8. Farwana
9. Al-Fatur
10. Al-Hamidiyya
11. Kafr Misr
12. Khirbat al-Taqa

13. Qumya
14. Al-Sakhina
15. Sirin
16. Tall al-Shawk
17. Al-Tira
18. Zab'a

Qaditta were terrified they would be attacked next. The villagers went to Bint Jubayl in Lebanon for a while and then returned to settle in Jish village, near the Palestine-Lebanon border. When Zionist forces attacked and massacred villagers in Jish and in Safsaf in late October 1948, the people of Qaditta fled once again to Lebanon.[58]

The villagers of Taytaba (pop. 615) also were terrified by the 'Ayn al-Zaytun massacre and the fall of Safad. Many of them decided to move their families to the fields on the outskirts of the village between Taytaba and al-Ras al-Ahmar on May 11. Only armed men remained in Taytaba. The villagers stayed in the fields until driven out by Zionist forces in October 1948, when all of the Galilee fell into Jewish hands.[59] As one inhabitant of Taytaba explained, "We were afraid that the Jews would come and do to us what they had done at Dayr Yasin. We did not want a massacre in our village."[60]

The inhabitants of al-Zahiriyya al-Tahta (pop. 406) moved their families to safety in 'Ayn al-Wuhush after 'Ayn al-Zaytun was attacked. The mukhtar suggested that the villagers retreat and join their families in 'Ayn al-Wuhush after Safad fell. At dawn on May 11, some went south to al-Farradiyya village and others went east to al-Sammu'i village. Men and women who tried to return to the village were reported killed by land mines placed by Zionist forces.[61]

As Palestinian Arab narratives show, villagers attempted to remain in the Galilee by moving from village to village seeking safety. But as Zionist forces attacked wherever Arabs sought refuge, the villagers were forced farther and farther from their home village and beyond the borders of Palestine. Although the villagers tried for months to return, the armed forces of the new State of Israel employed violent tactics to prevent this, including looting, land mines, demolishing villages, burning harvests, killing or stealing livestock, shooting returnees, and taking prisoners.

The Expulsion of the Baysan Arabs

Baysan's proximity to the Transjordan frontier made it a target for Zionist forces. Palmach commander Yigal Allon wanted to clear Arab population centers along probable Arab Legion entry routes into Palestine. He targeted the Arab town of Baysan, with a population of 6,000, for harassment "in order to increase the [Arab] flight from it."[62] Although surrounded by

Jewish settlements, Baysan's inhabitants did not think they would be attacked. These same settlements further pressured the local Haganah command "to push out the Arabs" from Baysan and the rural hinterland.[63] Even though Baysan had been attacked several times, the townsmen still did not expect the last attack and were not prepared for it.[64] Baysan's Arabs were defended by approximately 160 to 175 men, 60 to 70 of whom were ALA.[65]

The inhabitants were worried, but remained hopeful because of their proximity to Transjordan. Wealthy families did flee Baysan, after the townspeople had heard about Dayr Yasin and then learned that "the Jews had captured Tiberias and forced its Arab inhabitants out." Some of Jaffa's and Haifa's escaping residents had taken refuge in Baysan and told the inhabitants "horrible things."[66]

The Golani Brigade laid siege to Baysan at the end of April 1948 during Operation Gideon, the goal of which was to clear the Baysan Valley of its Arab population.[67] Zionist forces attacked from all directions and captured Tall al-Hussun, a hill overlooking the city from the north. Muhammad Suraidi recounted, "Once the hill was occupied, the Jews controlled the situation. They ordered the city to surrender, giving us until morning to do so."[68] The remaining national committee members wanted to travel to Nablus to obtain instructions on capitulation, but this was refused by Palti Sela, the Haganah commander.[69] On May 12, Baysan surrendered to Zionist forces, who ordered the inhabitants to leave the following day.[70] "Some were transferred to Nazareth . . . some to Jenin," but the majority were "driven across the nearby Jordan River on the opposite bank."[71] As the Baysan Arabs evacuated the town, they passed three checkpoints and were searched by "Jewish girls, dressed in uniforms," who stole the refugees' money and jewelry.[72] The walk to the Jordan River took four hours, but before Marsila Abu Khalil's family crossed to safety "the Jews picked four teen-aged boys" and took them prisoner.[73]

Baysan resident Ma'susih 'Abd al-Rahman al-Naqqash's account of the expulsion corroborates other accounts of atrocities. She said Zionist forces

> put young people into cars and made them take off their clothes, and then they killed them. My mother refused to leave. She stayed in Baysan until they started killing people inside [their] houses. They killed my neighbor

by beating him with a gun. They killed his sheep and took them. . . . We stayed 20 more days, then Jews came and ordered us to leave. They said Baysan was a military area and "you must leave." They gave my uncle two choices: leave or be killed.

As people were leaving, Jews stopped them on the roads and took their money and gold. They did not allow anyone to stay in Baysan. There was a Christian woman who refused to leave. However, they forced her to move to Nazareth. They told people this is a military area—"Go and dine with King Abdullah." They killed many in Baysan.[74]

The local Haganah commanders finally sought and received permission to evict all the remaining Arab population. Most were expelled on May 14 or 15 across the Jordan River. The remaining 250 to 300 Christians were given the choice of going to Transjordan or to Nazareth. Most were trucked to Nazareth on May 28.[75] Some refugees managed to slip back across the Jordan River to Baysan, but they were able to remain only "until mid-June, when the Israeli army loaded the people at gunpoint onto trucks and drove them across the river once again."[76]

Some members of the left-wing Mapam party criticized Allon's using the slow-shuffling columns of refugees for strategic purposes. Their misery conjured images of Jewish suffering. Meir Ya'ari, the party co-leader, said: "Many of us are losing their [human] image. . . . How easily they speak of how it is possible and permissible to take women, children, and old men and to fill the roads with them because such is the imperative of strategy. And this we say, the members of Hashomer Hatza'ir [Youth Guard] who remember who used this means against our people during the [Second World] war . . . I am appalled."[77]

The Baysan Subdistrict: Terror, Expulsions, and Looting

The Arab-majority Baysan subdistrict suffered the same violent depopulation as other parts of Palestine. Located in southern Galilee and bordering Transjordan, the subdistrict was 44.9 percent Arab-owned, 34 percent Jewish-owned, and 21.1 percent public property in 1948, with 70.3 percent Arab and 29.7 percent Jewish residents. Thirty-one of the 33 Arab villages and towns would be forcibly depopulated and demolished during the war. Thirteen of these, or 42 percent, would be depopulated before the mandate ended, mostly during the Haganah's Operation Gideon. A number of Arab villages around Baysan were depopulated immediately before the siege of Baysan or after its capture on May 12, including al-Ashrafiyya, Farwana, al-Fatur, al-Hamidiyya, al-Sakhina, and Tall al-Shawk. The following accounts of the fate of these towns are based on Palestinian refugee recollections.

The mukhtar of Kafr Misr (pop. 372), who was regarded as a collaborator with the Jews, advised the poor and unarmed villagers to leave for Nazareth to avoid being attacked and massacred. Zionist militia had raided the village at least once previously. The villagers left for Nazareth as advised.[78]

Ayshi Mahmud Khalid recalls that all the families of Qumya (pop. 510) fled together on March 26: "Some left for Nazareth and some for Jordan. We were afraid of Jewish attacks. . . . On our way we passed by Ma'oz settlement. Jewish women came to search us and stole our money. . . . The Jews stole even our livestock." The villagers of Qumya sought refuge in Baysan, from which they were expelled along with the town's inhabitants in May 1948.[79]

The Golani Brigade occupied the farming village of Sirin (pop. 940) on May 12.[80] Some villagers apparently had left already, fearing atrocities and not, as Morris suggests, on Arab orders. Fatima al-Mahir recalls:

> We left the village because we noticed that villagers were leaving every day. Every morning we woke up and saw a neighbor leaving—even the Christians were leaving. So we decided to leave. . . . We were afraid that the Jews would kill our children. . . . This is why we left. . . . Nobody returned. The elderly people, like the mukhtar and others, convinced people to leave. Only the priest remained in the church. All the Christian families left for Nazareth and Haifa.[81]

Zionist troops ordered the remaining villagers, both Christians and Muslims, to cross over the Jordan River. They then demolished the mosque, the church, the monastery, and all the houses to prevent a return.[82]

The Siege and Depopulation of Acre

The seacoast walled city of Acre was included in the proposed Arab state in the U.N. partition plan. After the U.N. vote, Acre's Arabs established the Acre National Committee to attend to political, social, administrative, and military affairs. In 1948, Acre had a population of 14,000 that was 86 percent Arab. Acre's Arabs did not believe the Zionists would attack and were therefore poorly prepared to defend themselves or the city. Once they heard Zionist forces had attacked and expelled Arabs from Tiberias, Haifa, Safad, and Baysan, they became terrified that they would be next. Jewish convoys were traveling through and around Acre going to and from Haifa and the scattered northern Jewish settlements.

For Matti Bouri, life in Acre remained relatively normal until the first few months of 1948, when two incidents occurred. The first was the Haganah's ambush of 'Abd al-Rahman al-Mukthar's bus, which was traveling from Haifa to Acre; the second, a few days later, was the Zionist forces' targeting of an Arab convoy carrying weapons and ammunition along the same route. Further incidents resulted in the closing of the road to Haifa. The Arabs felt isolated and fearful. To restore their self-confidence, the Orthodox Club retaliated against the Jews by attacking a convoy traveling from Nahariya settlement. They succeeded in "killing some Jews, burning a vehicle and confiscating another one" before a British patrol intervened.[83]

Acre had strategic importance as a road junction in northern Galilee. The Arab city remained an obstacle to Zionist control of the entire northern area. The British had permitted Jewish convoys to pass through Acre to the Jewish settlement of Nahariya during much of the civil war. Musa al-Najami, the head of the local National Guard, had expected an attack once the British departed, because the Jews insisted that Acre be declared an open city so their convoys could continue to travel north. "We could not reach an agreement," al-Najami said, "and so the Jews prepared to seize the city as soon as the British withdrew."[84]

The Arabs wanted to stay and defend their city, but they lacked the wherewithal to do so. Salih Hakim, a Palestinian judge, said Acre lacked "responsible leadership. . . . We tried to do as much as we could do. When the British left Acre, there were no preparations to regulate the city. A national committee was formed in Acre, but it was not very effective, and we could not stop the people from leaving, including the mayor. We did not have much to offer them in terms of protection." This would appear to be one case where the departure of leadership demoralized Palestinian Arabs. But Hakim attributes large-scale departures instead to Zionist attacks and Arab fear of atrocities. "Many began to leave as early as 25 April, when the Jews first attacked the city," he said.[85] Matti Bouri's uncle rented trucks to transport their families to safety in Lebanon, but Bouri himself refused to leave Acre. His uncle shouted angrily at him, "Do we need to wait for them to kill the men and the youth and rape our women in order to leave?"[86]

The national committee's first priority was to fortify Napoleon Hill because of its strategic location overlooking Acre. Whoever controlled the hill would indisputably control the city. The Orthodox Club began purchasing rifles, holding weapons and first-aid training, and arranging guard duty of the hill. The first rifles were French, "most of which turned [out] to be useless," Matti Bouri said.[87] Acre was protected by only 45 armed men, about 30 ALA volunteers and 15 volunteer villagers.[88]

When Haifa fell on April 23, its refugees poured into Acre, filling the schools, churches, and mosques, exacerbating security and humanitarian conditions, and swelling the population to approximately 40,000. Many of the refugees were starving, British field security forces reported.[89] The people of Acre were disheartened by the condition of the Haifa refugees, who, according to Chief Secretary Gurney, were "spreading the wildest and most untrue stories of events in Haifa."[90] Bouri described the situation prevailing in 1948 Acre as "countless protests, a terrible sense of loss, hopelessness and terror." Of the Haifa refugees, he said, "They all talked about the terrifying deeds the Haganah, the Stern and the Irgun had committed in the towns they had conquered. It was this same fear that urged a large number of people to abandon their plans to settle in Acre just two days after arriving, and instead to head for the Lebanese borders. They were so panic-stricken that they generated sudden terror in the hearts of Acre's people, forcing them to escape."[91]

Two days after Haifa fell, and while the British were still in Acre, Haganah forces mortared the city, then attacked and seized Napoleon Hill and the Muslim cemetery. This induced great terror and panic in the population. Bouri recalled that "we put up a good resistance in collaboration" with the ALA, which had moved to Acre after Haifa's capture.[92] But although they fought and prevented the Haganah's advance, the Arabs were unable to force the Jews to retreat. British forces intervened after the Acre National Committee delegation asked for protection. They directed Acre's Arab defenders to leave their positions near Napoleon Hill. As they retreated, the British fired several mortar shells, forcing the Haganah to retreat. British troops moved in to calm the situation in Acre and the outlying Arab village of al-Tira, where fighting had flared up during the night of April 25. The fighting at al-Tira also ceased after the British fired a few rounds of high explosives.[93] The brief British intervention in Acre likely was intended to protect northern evacuation routes and Acre's inclusion in the proposed Arab state.

Because of the siege and the influx of refugees, food and medicine were in short supply. The situation was aggravated on May 5, when Zionist forces blew up the Ottoman-built aqueduct, which provided Acre's water from the Kabri Springs, located about ten kilometers north of the city.[94] Typhoid broke out and spread throughout Acre, but the highly infectious disease was not due to the crowded, unhygienic conditions. Even before the Haganah implemented Plan D, an IZL radio broadcast in Arabic on March 27 "warned 'Arabs in urban agglomerations' that typhus, cholera and similar disease would break out 'heavily' among them 'in April and May.'"[95] Hisham al-Dahan, one of a group of Lebanese doctors providing medical aid, told the Arabs of Acre that the "city's water was polluted." He accused the Haganah of poisoning the Kabri Springs and advised the residents not to drink the water.[96] About 70 civilian casualties were reported.[97]

British intelligence initially attributed the outbreak to the poor living conditions in the hot weather, until about 55 British soldiers and Palestine Police also became ill.[98] Only then did they suspect that the epidemic was due to Zionist sabotage of the aqueduct.[99] Brigadier Arthur Beveridge, chief of British medical services, told Maximilian de Meuron, the International Committee of the Red Cross (ICRC) delegate, that this was "the first time this [typhoid] happened in Palestine." De Meuron, who investigated the sudden outbreak, independently verified the assertion of biological warfare in a series of reports written from May 6 to 19. He identified deliberate contamination of the water supply as the sole explanation.[100]

Independent evidence and Israeli records suggest that Acre was not the sole location where Zionists used germ warfare to terrify and remove the local population. Egyptian intelligence forces apprehended two Jews disguised as Arabs attempting to inject typhoid and dysentery viruses into Gaza artesian wells in May.[101] Ben-Gurion acknowledged in his diary the saboteurs' capture.[102] He was very interested in using science and technology to thwart Israel's enemies. Uri Milstein, the Israeli military historian, confirms that the typhoid epidemic in Acre was due to the Haganah's actions and designed to prevent the return of the Palestinian Arabs.[103]

The full extent of Israel's prestate use of biological warfare during the 1948 war is unknown. In February 1948, Ephraim Katzir, a physical chemist, and his brother Aharon were developing biological weapons, with "good results" to cause blindness in people.[104] In April 1948, Ben-Gurion asked a Jewish Agency operative to recruit East European scientists expert in biological weapons.[105] The Israeli reporter Sara Leibovitz-Dar wrote that "rumors about secret BW [biological weapons] operations in Palestinian villages and towns have persisted for years,"[106] although any Israeli records on their use remain classified.

Despite the demoralizing effect of biological warfare, military attack was still the crucial factor in Acre's evacuation. Most Arabs "started to leave the city soon after the Jews attacked on April 25, including the mayor," according to Farid Abu Nasab, an officer in the British police corps.[107] Those who left at this point believed they would return to their homes after the Arab armies won back their city. The Arabs knew that they could not depend on the departing British forces for their security.

Acre National Committee members turned to the Arab Higher Committee (AHC) and to neighboring Lebanon for assistance in defending their city. A delegation, traveling to Beirut on May 14 to ask the mufti for additional arms, was forced to travel the long route through Kafr Yasif and al-Rama because Zionist forces already occupied the coastal road. After a three-day wait, they were told that "there were no additional arms," and that they "must wait until May 15 when the Arab armies would defend the city." Disappointed by the mufti's response, the delegation also met with the Lebanese chief of staff and asked "if the Lebanese army could intervene and fire a few bombs at Napoleon Hill to prevent the Jews from capturing the city." Again, the delegation was told to wait "for the entry of the Arab armies."[108] They were, however, *not* told by Arab leaders to leave Acre—indeed, they were told the opposite.

The Haganah offensive in western Galilee called Operation Ben-Ami began on May 13 and ended on May 17 with the capture of Acre. The final attack on the city began the night of May 16 with a mortar barrage from positions on Napoleon Hill: "As the Carmeli Brigade units advanced into the town, an armored car mounting a loudspeaker, in a psychological warfare ploy, broadcast the imminent fall of the town and declared that the choice before the inhabitants was either surrender or suicide."[109] From the sea, Haganah boats indiscriminately machine-gunned Acre, a tactic that had been employed effectively in Haifa and Jaffa to terrorize fleeing Arab civilians. Panic took hold, and resistance collapsed. "The armed men were able to leave," said Musa al-Najami, "however, those who decided to remain in the city could not break the siege and had to surrender."[110] Matti Bouri described the final fall of Acre: "The Haganah occupied Napoleon Hill, and a few days later they also occupied New Acre's police station, turning it into their headquarters. As we lost all hope to win or resist, a group of the town's notables . . . went to negotiate a cease-fire with the Haganah. The conditions set by the Haganah's leader were to open the doors of the old city to his army, to surrender all the weapons, and evacuate all of New Acre."[111]

The following day, the Zionist military commander forced all of Acre's males over 16 years old to gather in the square facing the central prison, where they were taken for interrogation. Every house was searched, weapons were confiscated, and men were arrested, Matti Bouri recalled.[112] Acre was emptied of all men except the elderly. Bouri lamented that "seeing the Haganah moving freely in my town's streets scared me, hurt me, killed me and made me wonder: Is this really my city—Acre—where I used to happily stroll the streets tens of times each day?"[113]

Immediately after the Zionist conquest, Arabs in Acre lived under a "regime of terror," according to the Red Cross representative.[114] At least one known rape and murder of a girl and the murder of her father are recorded.[115] The Haganah ordered the Arab residents to evacuate New Acre, which the Zionists deemed off limits to Arabs, according to eyewitnesses. Months later, a U.N. observer also noted that Israelis killed many Arabs living in the new city who had "refused to move into the portion of the old city that was being used as an Arab ghetto."[116] The Haganah's intimidation tactics, as well as their record in Haifa and elsewhere, were sufficient to compel Acre's population to leave during and after the attack. The Arabs' exit was a direct result of the Haganah's siege, harassing mortar attacks, psychological and biological warfare, indiscriminate shooting of civilians, and wholesale looting.

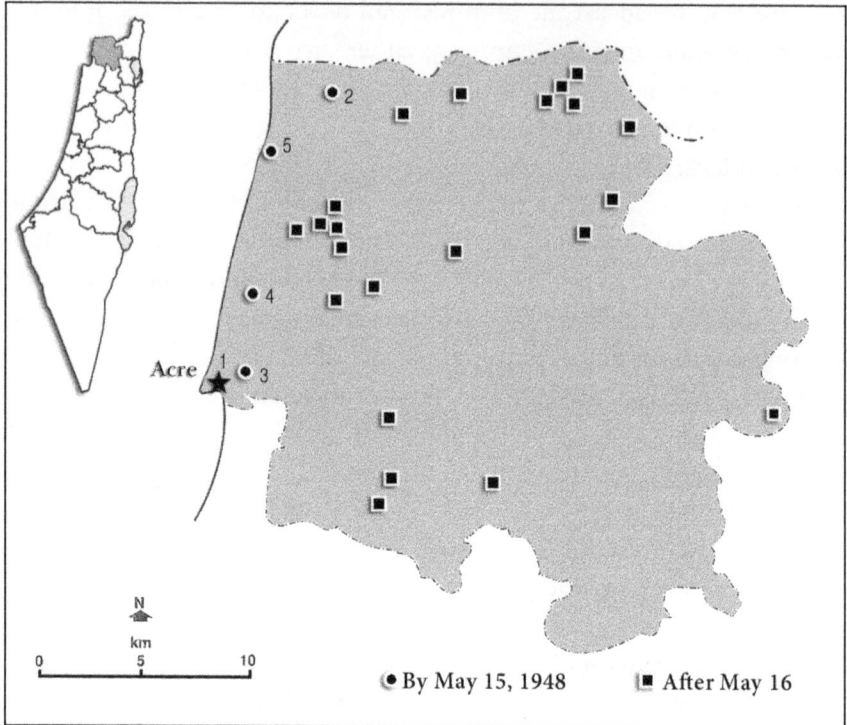

ACRE SUBDISTRICT DEPOPULATED TOWNS AND VILLAGES

1. Acre
2. Al-Bassa
3. Al-Manshiyya

4. Al-Sumayriyya
5. Al-Zib

The Acre Subdistrict's Forced Depopulation

The Acre subdistrict, even though mostly included in the proposed Arab state, suffered the fate of other regions. Bordered by Lebanon in the north and by the Mediterranean on the west, it extended over the northwest corner of Palestine. In 1948, the land was 87.3 percent Arab-owned, 3.1 percent Jewish-owned, and 12.5 percent public property, its population 85.5 percent Arab, 4.3 percent Jewish, and 10.2 percent other. Of the 64 Arab towns and villages in the subdistrict, 29 locales—45 percent—were demolished by Zionist forces.[117]

During the Haganah's Operation Ben-Ami and afterward but before the mandate ended, Zionist forces attacked and drove out those living in the Arab coastal villages of al-Bassa, al-Manshiyya, al-Sumariyya, and al-

Zib, situated along the Acre to Beirut road. These four villages fell within the area designated by the partition plan as the Arab state. The following Palestinian refugee accounts explain why they actually left.

The terrified townspeople of al-Bassa (pop. 3,422) sent their families to Lebanon, some immediately after the April 12 Dayr Yasin massacre. Among those remaining were the elderly and about 40 armed men. On the morning of May 14, a Haganah infantry unit attacked al-Bassa from the southeast. Town defenders repelled the attack, but a Zionist armored unit disguised as Arabs approached from the west and shelled the village. The remaining townspeople retreated north, the only escape route open. A couple who remained the day al-Bassa fell remembers that "Jewish soldiers ordered all those who remained in the village to gather in the church. Simultaneously, they took a few young people . . . outside the church and shot them dead. Soon after, they ordered us to bury them. During the following day, we were transferred to al-Mazra'a."[118] In addition to executing youths, Haganah forces also raped or molested a number of women in al-Bassa, as well as in the neighboring villages of al-Sumayriyya and al-Zib.[119] Zionist forces also shot and killed villagers who tried to return to collect their belongings or retrieve food.

The villagers of al-Manshiyya (pop. 940) were farmers who lived peacefully and had significant interaction with their Jewish neighbors. But fighting in Acre and the news of Dayr Yasin frightened them. Maryam 'Ali Wardi recalled the May 14 dawn attack coming from the hill overlooking the village. The villagers, with bullets whizzing over their heads, ran toward the east "because all other sides were surrounded by the Jews." Wardi recounted that when the villagers returned to remove the bodies, they found the village strewn with mines. Her father returned to al-Manshiyya about ten days after the attack and found it completely destroyed.[120]

Some families began to evacuate al-Sumayriyya (pop. 882) to safer areas after Dayr Yasin. The repeated promises by leaders of Arab states to intervene encouraged the villagers to resist Zionist attacks until the Arab armies arrived. Haganah forces attacked al-Sumayriyya at dawn on May 14 from the northwest. While the villagers were repelling the attack, a Carmeli brigade armored unit, disguised in the traditional red-and-white Arab *kaffiya* or head scarf, approached from the south along the main road from Acre and shelled the village. Forty to 45 men who guarded the village with assorted old rifles could not prevail against the two-pronged

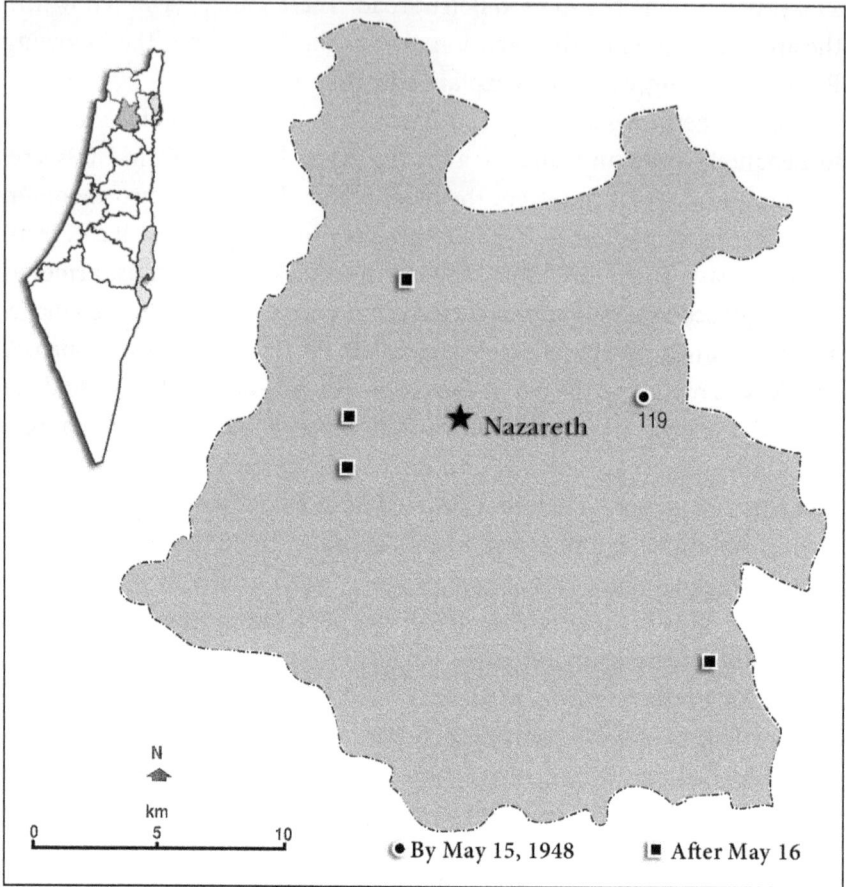

NAZARETH SUBDISTRICT DEPOPULATED TOWNS AND VILLAGES

119. 'Arab al-Subeih

attack,[121] so they retreated at sunrise to al-Ghabisiyya, leaving behind many killed and injured. Al-Sumayriyya's villagers fled once again when Haganah forces attacked and expelled the population of al-Ghabisiyya on May 19. Villagers from al-Sumayriyya who had sought refuge in Acre were forced out again when Acre was attacked.[122]

At dawn on May 14, Haganah forces also attacked al-Zib (pop. 2,216) from the south. An armored unit disguised as Arabs approached and shelled the town from the Acre to Beirut road. Anticipating the attack and terrorized by reports of the Dayr Yasin and Nasir al-Din massacres, residents had moved the elderly, women, and children from the town. The 35 or 40 remaining defenders could not withstand the attack and retreated north, the only possible escape route. Within a month, Zionist forces had destroyed most of the southern and eastern sections of al-Zib to prevent residents from returning and expelled remaining elderly townspeople to al-Mazra'a.[123]

Depopulated Villages and Towns of the Nazareth Subdistrict

Nazareth subdistrict was divided in the proposed partition plan between the Jewish and Arab states. The subdistrict was 52.9 percent Arab-owned, 27.6 percent Jewish-owned, and 19.5 percent public property. The population was 83.5 percent Arab and 16.5 percent Jewish in 1945. Although the largely Arab Christian town of Nazareth was included in the proposed Arab state, the newly declared State of Israel occupied Nazareth in July, during the 1948 war's first armistice. Four other Arab villages—Saffuriyya, Ma'lul, al-Mujaydil, and Indur—were occupied and demolished before the war ended.[124]

One Arab village in the Nazareth subdistrict, 'Arab al-Subeih, was depopulated on April 19. Morris attributes this to the fall of a neighboring village.[125] But according to Palestinian refugees, Zionist forces attacked the village and committed atrocities. S'ada al-Subeih said the villagers of 'Arab al-Subeih had lived on good terms with their Jewish neighbors, who "were Arabs like us." After a Haganah attack, however, some villagers left the area. During the "battle of Shajara," Zionist forces attacked 'Arab al-Subeih at dawn from an eastern settlement. The village defenders, together with men from other villages, fended off the attack, during which seven Jews were killed. Al-Subeih said that the Jews

> gathered their forces with people from outside [foreigners] and attacked again, this time to win. While leaving al-Subeih, the families of 'Ali and Husayn Nimr were all massacred by the Jews. Even the breast-feeding child was stabbed and killed. They were a family of 18, only one girl survived. . . . Later, the Jews killed many people.

> My family went [to the village] and saw the bodies. It was horrible. So the people of al-Subeih left the village and ran to Nazareth. The Jews entered many tents and homes and killed people, and even when people were running, the Jews shot at them. . . . Nobody returned to the village after the attack.[126]

The End of the British Mandate

In the spring of 1948, the world watched helplessly as the U.N. General Assembly futilely tried to calm a civil war unleashed by its partition vote and to prevent the Arab states from entering Palestine to stop Zionist expansion, atrocities, and expulsions. But the U.N. deliberations were outrun by events. In Palestine, the British government was wrapping up its own affairs and preparing its final departure from the quagmire that Palestine had become in just five months.

A fortnight before the mandate ended, High Commissioner Sir Alan Cunningham wrote candidly of his impressions about the Palestine situation. His disdain for the increasing Zionist attacks and tactics against civilians was prominent. Cunningham viewed many of the military operations, "based on the mortaring of terrified women and children," as simply gratuitous anti-civilian violence. He criticized the intimidating nature of the Zionist media and the yishuv's behavior. Military successes had "aroused extravagant reactions in the Jewish press" and "a spirit of arrogance" among the Jews themselves that "blind[ed] them to future difficulties." The "Jewish broadcasts both in content and in manner of delivery," he wrote, were "remarkably like those of Nazi Germany." Jewish newspapers claimed the Haganah controlled Haifa, imposed curfews, and decided "on what terms the Arabs may or may not live in the town." On the roads, the Haganah's armored cars were "increasingly impudent and intrusive," and in the plains areas, Jewish settlers began "to domineer over the local *fellahin*" (peasants).[127]

Cunningham also commented on the Jewish Agency's policy of intimidating the Arabs, as well as its single-minded drive to establish a Jewish state in Palestine at virtually any cost.

> This is all part of the Jewish policy of doing their utmost to consolidate territorial holdings and to cow neighboring Arabs into a state of subjection in which they will be unwilling to offer further resistance themselves or to give help or encouragement to foreign Arab elements. The Jews in fact are implementing the useful theory propounded by Mrs. Myerson [Golda Meir] some months ago of "aggressive defense," and it is clear that they will go to almost any lengths to achieve their aim.[128]

Finally, he observed that "the Arabs" reacted emotionally, resulting in an irresponsible backlash to the Zionist onslaught. Such a response provided the Jewish leadership with "the excuse" to pursue its ideological goals through military means under the cover of war.

> The Arabs of the large towns, who have borne the brunt of recent Jewish offensive action, are much more bitter against the British; fear breeds recrimination, and they are perhaps willfully blind to the fact that for months past they and their press have clamored for the entry of the foreign Arab guerrilla bands which, having successfully stirred up the Jews (and incidentally provided them with the excuse that they are merely defending themselves against Arab aggression), are now proving quite unable to protect the local Arabs from the Jewish reaction.[129]

According to Hazem Nuseibeh, a Palestinian attorney and political scientist, the Palestinian Arabs' ineptitude and undisciplined responses were principally due to poor leadership or the lack of any leadership at all. Throughout the war, the mufti remained in exile and the rest of the Palestinian Arab "leadership was afraid to act without his consent."[130]

The Arabs were completely unprepared for the dissolution of the British mandate government and for the battle that was taking shape. Nuseibeh, who was working in Jerusalem for Palestinian Broadcasting in 1948, described the way the British terminated the mandate as "one of the biggest acts of immorality committed by any people." The British in Palestine, he said, "were simply disintegrating like salt in water. . . . One day you had a British force here. The next day, it was a no-man's-land. There was a total breakdown of law and order, almost deliberate. It was chaos. . . . [The British] could have avoided it." The chaos enabled Zionist forces to occupy many Palestinian towns and villages even before the mandate ended. When the Arab armies finally decided to aid the Palestinians, most of the main cities and many towns and villages had already fallen. "Palestine was a trust in the hands of the British," Nuseibeh said. "It was a sacred trust! They should have kept this sacred trust. They did not."[131]

The series of reversals in April 1948 lowered the morale of Arabs, who began to suspect that the British were helping the Jews to defeat them. In reality, the Palestinian Arabs were losing the war because they were unprepared and virtually leaderless. The U.S. consul general in Jerusalem, Thomas C. Wasson, wrote on May 3 that Arab resistance had been ineffective and that GOC MacMillan and others believed that the "Jews will be able [to] sweep all before them unless regular Arab armies come to [their] rescue."[132] However, these same British authorities also blocked the possibility of rescue. To prevent Arab state intervention, MacMillan reiterated his warning to the Arab states in early May that "he would attack relentlessly any regular force entering Palestine before 15 May."[133]

Arab Forces Unlikely to Enter Palestine before May 15

After a succession of defeats, Palestinian Arabs awoke to the fact that their leaders were impotent and the ALA was ineffective. They placed their trust in Arab League promises and depended on Arab states' forces to prevent their total domination by the Zionists. But Arab leaders—despite their warlike rhetoric—were fundamentally indecisive, lacking a strategy, and most reluctant to intervene in Palestine before the British withdrew. Egypt's prime minister, Nokrashi Pasha, also opposed the Arab states' forces entry into Palestine before May 15, because he feared U.N. repercussions. Furthermore, he believed that a resounding defeat by Zionist forces risked invalidating the Egyptians' contention that they could defend themselves without foreign assistance, an important factor in Egypt's determination to remove the permanent British bases around the Suez Canal. He also feared that an ineffective military effort by the Arab states would permanently damage the Palestinian Arab cause.[134]

Many Arab leaders believed that the establishment of a Jewish state was inevitable.[135] Arab League Secretary General Azzam Pasha believed events in Palestine indicated the Jewish Agency's intention to present the world with a Jewish state as an irreversible fait accompli.[136] The U.S. ambassador to Iraq, George Wadsworth, reported that Arab armies would have entered Palestine prior to May 15 if their leaders had concluded that military action could have effectively blocked the promulgation of a Jewish state.[137] The Arab League had hoped that U.N. action could prevent the need for the Arab states to fight. According to the Lebanese prime minister, Riad al-Solh, the Arab states would have accepted a truce provided that the entry of Zionist reinforcements, arms, and ammunitions were stopped, and that Arab areas seized by Zionist forces were returned. He insisted the situation had reached the "absolute low for Arabs," and the Arab states were being forced to take violent action. He warned that "any steps by [an]

Arab leader to slow down action would result in his assassination." The Arabs, he said, "could not accept domination by Jews and would have to fight to the end."[138]

U.S. military intelligence reported on April 27 that both Jews and Arabs had informed the United Nations that "each would set up an independent state embracing the whole of Palestine upon the termination of the mandate."[139] The British Colonial Office believed the Zionists were anxious to secure as much territory as they could, particularly in Jaffa, but the Jewish Agency was exercising restraint "for U.N. reasons." Nevertheless, the Colonial Office described Jewish forces exhibiting "an arrogance of strength and an overweening pride of victory" that emboldened them "into new aggressions against Arabs and militaristic oppressions of their own people." The Jewish Agency had in fact impounded all Jewish passports to discourage any Jewish attempts to leave Palestine. "Thousands of Jews want[ed] to get out."[140]

The Jewish and Arab states were already in existence by May 4, the British concluded, and the only "real bone of contention between the two forces" was Jerusalem. At this point, 23,000 British troops remained in Palestine, with 5,000 in and around Jerusalem. MacMillan remained seriously concerned that he would have to fight his way from Jerusalem to Haifa against the Palestinian Arabs, who held the British responsible for the "Jewish invaders."[141] His fears were not unrealistic. The Palestine government undersecretary, Sir John Fletcher-Cooke, believed that the "Jews were stalling for time until the Mandate ended in order not to tie their hands." He was also concerned that the "Jews might attempt [to] provoke Arabs into [a] fight by another incident similar to Deir Yassin." The Arabs would thus "be obliged [to] avenge such outrage and might throw in their forces without proper preparations."[142]

Zionist Policy: Expel the Arabs

International observers viewed Zionist tactics as increasingly aggressive. British Foreign Office Undersecretary Michael Wright considered the onslaught against Jaffa and Jerusalem as "particularly flagrant."[143] Wright believed that after the British withdrew, it was a question of when, not if, the Arab states would enter into the conflict. Wright asserted that the British government was doing "its utmost to restrain [the] Arab states" and expressed his hope that the U.S. government would similarly exert "every effort to restrain [the] Jews." But British admonitions to the Arab states were becoming "less and less effective in the face of present aggressive tactics of Jews."[144]

Many Israeli scholars argue that Zionist military operations displacing Arabs were primarily defensive and carried out to secure borders. The contemporary documentary record and Palestinian testimony demonstrate, to the contrary, that Zionist attacks on Palestinian Arab civilians communicated only two options: "leave or perish." Further, some Zionist participants in the war contradict the claim of "defensive" purpose. Aharon Cohen, director of the Mapam party's Arab department, wrote in a critical May 10, 1948, memorandum that the forced transfer of the Palestinian Arabs was "being done out of certain political objectives and not only out of military necessities, as they [the Labor leaders] claim sometimes." He observed: "The 'transfer' of the Arabs from the boundaries of the Jewish state is being implemented. . . . the evacuation/clearing out of Arab villages is not always done out of military necessity. The complete destruction of villages is not always done only because there are 'not sufficient forces to maintain a garrison.'"[145] Cohen insisted that the forced transfer of the Palestinian Arabs "was in part due to the official Jewish policy" of transfer, and he concluded that the exigencies of war could not alone account for the destruction of villages.[146] "Will our state be built on the destruction of Arab settlements?" Cohen asked.[147] The answer—apparently—was yes.

Other Jewish leaders also protested the brutality used to force Arabs' evacuation. Minister of Agriculture Aharon Zisling, a native of Russia, was tormented by reports of atrocities and declared: "I couldn't sleep all night. . . . This is something that determines the character of the nation. . . . Jews too have committed Nazi acts."[148] Zisling also complained about the destruction of Arab villages. In the cabinet meeting of June 16, he differentiated between "destruction during battle," citing al-Qastal, and destruction afterward. Destruction during battle, he warned, "is one thing. But [when a site is destroyed] a month later, in cold blood, out of political calculation . . . that is [an]other thing altogether . . . This course [of destroying villages] will not reduce the number of Arabs who will return to the Land of Israel. It will [only] increase our enemies."[149] Zisling held Ben-Gurion personally responsible for the wholesale destruction of Arab villages.

Experienced contemporary British commanders in Palestine have corroborated Cohen's and Zisling's assessments. Colonel John Waddy, of the Sixth Airborne Division, stated that one goal of Jewish offensives against the Arabs was "to terrorize the Arab population and force them to leave."[150] Chief Secretary Gurney observed that IZL mortar attacks in Jaffa were "aimed at civilian targets and were designed to create panic among the population."[151] Cunningham denounced Zionist "mortaring of terrified women and children" and stated unequivocally that "it was the Jews who were trying to frighten the Arabs and drive them into the sea."[152] This was not merely a figure of speech: as in Haifa and Jaffa, Zionist forces literally drove Arabs to the docks and into the sea where many drowned. British diplomats, including Sir Alec Kirkbride in Amman, also observed that Palestinian Arabs were forced into leaving. Kirkbride agreed that the Arabs of Tiberias had been expelled.[153] Analysts in the Cairo-based British Middle East Office concluded that "Jewish terrorism and Arab panic" were "persuading the Arabs of Palestine to leave their homes."[154]

U.S. military intelligence also recognized that "one of the objectives of the Zionists" was the expulsion of "a substantial portion of the Arab population from Palestine."[155] Finally, consistent and detailed civilian Palestinian testimonies of attack, intimidation, and atrocities, many originally researched and reported in this book, bear witness to systematic Zionist tactics of expulsion and destruction. Cohen's and Zisling's assertions that the Zionist leadership's policy advocated expelling the Palestinian Arabs and preventing their return are corroborated by the survivors themselves.

Massacres, Psychological Warfare, and Obliteration

The Zionist leadership reaped clear military and demographic benefits from deliberate and tactical employment of terror and atrocities. Terror's use, as explained by American military psychologist Lieutenant Colonel Dave Grossman in his general study of warfare, *On Killing*, "quite simply scares the hell out of people. . . . The raw horror and savagery of those who murder and abuse cause people to flee, hide, and defend themselves feebly, and often their victims respond with mute passivity."[156]

The violent removal of Palestinian Arab inhabitants—reported by them and by other contemporary independent observers—is corroborated by the Israeli archives. Aryeh Yitzhaki, an Israeli historian who served as director of the Israeli Defense Force (IDF) archives, researched massacres during the 1948 war. In almost every conquered village, he attests, Zionist forces committed war crimes such as indiscriminate killings, massacres, and rapes. Palestinian testimony confirms atrocities in numerous villages, including Nasir al-Din, Burayr, Hawsha, and 'Ayn al-Zaytun. Yitzhaki's research records at least ten major massacres, which he defines as more than 50 victims each. He also acknowledges the enormous impact of massacres in precipitating Arab flight. Palestinian researcher Salman Abu-Sitta alleges 33 known massacres (which he does not define) during the entire 1948 war, 16 of which occurred during the civil war period.[157]

Massacres sometimes occurred during the heat of battle and others while Zionist forces "cleansed" a captured area after battle. In some cases, atrocities occurred after the villagers had surrendered, such as in 'Ayn al-Zaytun, al-Bassa, and Baysan. Yitzhaki said the Zionist forces' use of massacres on the battlefield spread, but "there were no explicit orders to exterminate."[158] He described typical Zionist military tactics in 1948 as follows: A village would usually be subjected to heavy artillery from a distance. Soldiers would then assault the village. Arab resisters would withdraw while attempting to snipe at advancing Zionist forces. Some villagers, mainly the elderly and women, would not flee and would remain in the village, and in the course of "cleansing," Zionist forces "used to hit them [sic]."[159] Oral testimonies in this study and in others confirm the pattern Yitzhaki adduces from the Zionist military field records.

Official approval of the pattern of terror was apparent in the operational indifference to the reckless killing of noncombatants. No established procedure seems to have existed to check for civilians before soldiers blew up or burned houses.[160] Yet Zionist forces must have known that people were in the houses they blew up, as they generally attacked before daybreak while villagers slept. Official approval of violent measures against Arab civilians can also be assumed from the prevailing impunity for indiscriminate killing, terrorization, and population expulsion. Such tactics were often reported by the participants without consciousness of wrongdoing, despite the Haganah's formal "purity of arms" ethics code.[161]

Israeli sources confirm that expulsions and atrocities impelling Arab flight were authorized and sanctioned by Jewish Agency leaders and Haganah high command. Responding to complaints from kibbutzniks about "the prevalence of an attitude that everything of [the Arabs'] should be murdered, destroyed and made to vanish," Ezra Danin, a Syrian-born Haganah intelligence officer, expressed high-level approval of terror tactics: "If the commanders believe that by destruction, murder and human suffering they will reach their goal more quickly—I would not stand in their way."[162] Jewish leaders and soldiers' pervasive acceptance of terror tactics was verified by the savage October 29, 1948, massacre at the town of al-Dawayima (pop. 4,304) in the Hebron subdistrict, where the IDF's 89th Battalion Eighth Brigade, OC General Yitzhak Sadeh (the Russian-born Isaac Landsberg), murdered an estimated 80 to 100 men, women, and children. Soldiers killed children by smashing their heads with sticks. Civilians, including the elderly, were locked into houses without food and water, and then sappers blew up the houses. One rape and murder of a woman was reported. Soldiers killed about 75 old people praying in the Darawish Mosque, and many others were machine-gunned from two sides after being lined up and ordered to walk.[163] The mukhtar counted 455 people missing, including 170 women and children.[164] One soldier—described by a Mapam party member as "one of our people, an intellectual and 100 percent reliable"—attributed the debasement to the Jewish leadership's principle of liquidating Arabs. He said that "cultured officers . . . had turned into base murderers and this not in the heat of battle . . . but [through] a system of expulsion and destruction. The [fewer] Arabs remained—the better. This principle is the political motor for the expulsion and the atrocities."[165]

Some soldiers may have been disciplined for their part in atrocities, but Ben-Gurion ensured that "no one was actually jailed for taking part in the atrocities," writes Benny Morris. In fact, Ben-Gurion defended and protected Zionist forces against all external criticism and investigation. "Maltreatment of civilians and POWs [prisoners of war] went almost completely uninvestigated and unpunished," Morris concludes, noting that trials and punishment were avoided to conceal atrocities to preserve the reputation of Israel and the IDF. The Jewish leadership's greater fear, Morris suggests, was that officers and soldiers could implicate the chain of command in the civil war's atrocities—from regional commanders such as Moshe Kalman, who expelled the Arabs from the Safad area, or Moshe Carmel, who uprooted the Arabs of the Galilee, to Ben-Gurion himself.[166]

The Israeli journalist Guy Erlich described a typical battle report about the conquest of a village. One Zionist soldier reported that "we cleansed a village, shot in any direction where resistance was noticed. After the resistance ended, we also had to shoot people so that they would leave or who looked dangerous."[167] Assessing the extent of massacres in 1948, the Israeli historian Uri Milstein corroborates Yitzhaki's findings and adds that "even before the establishment of the state, each battle ended with a massacre."[168] Such evidence confirms that Palestinian Arab oral histories draw from real recollections, whatever inevitable errors of memory or embellishments of the record may occur from time to time.

Palestinian Arab refugee recollections match up with the Zionist military record in another way. According to refugee testimony, Zionist forces would relentlessly pursue fleeing Arabs from village to village, forcing them farther and farther from their homes. Yitzhaki attests to the regularity of this Zionist "cleansing" tactic, which even had its own term: *mezanvim baborchim* or "tailing the fugitives."[169] Another corroborated method of ejection was barring Arabs from returning to their lands by creating conditions to prevent return. Once the villagers were expelled, Zionist forces might mine or demolish village houses, schools, mosques, and other public buildings; rob, loot, and destroy possessions; and burn crops, and steal or kill animals. In other cases, Jewish settlers quickly assumed possession of Arab lands, and new Jewish immigrants were settled in Arab villages and urban neighborhood areas.

In addition to military attack and atrocities, Zionist forces employed several psychological tactics to clear a village, including "whispering campaigns." Al-Mukhayzin and Abu Kishk villagers evacuated in response to this tactic. Palestinian Arabs who left believed their choice was to flee or die. Such fears were not irrational; aside from reports of actual atrocities like Dayr Yasin, which Palestinian refugees often cited, those villagers who remained behind—usually the aged, disabled, infirm, or wounded—were often killed by Zionist forces or forcibly expelled, according to numerous oral accounts.[170] The dead were sometimes booby-trapped, causing additional casualties when families returned to villages to retrieve bodies for burial.

In some cases, expulsions were selective, and frequently occurred along sectarian lines. Zionist forces deliberately expelled Muslim Arabs, while sometimes permitting Christian Arabs, Druze, and Circassians to remain, as was the case in Haifa, the Nazareth area, and al-Rama. In other cases, villagers or townsmen were expelled from their respective village, town, or quarter to another area under Zionist control. This occurred most famously in the Christian villages of Kafr Bir'im and Iqrit late in the 1948 war, but also in the cities of Haifa, Safad, and Acre during the civil war period.

The ethnic cleansing of Palestine reached beyond the indigenous Arabs themselves. Zionist forces had operational orders to destroy villages, eradicating the memory of the Palestinian Arabs' presence on the land.[171] Mosques, churches, schools, and graveyards were desecrated and destroyed. Homes were blown up or burned down; whole villages were erased from the Palestinian landscape overnight. This served not only to terrorize the population, but also prevented a return to their homes. Even place names were changed in an attempt to erase the Palestinians' existence.

Moshe Dayan reminded one audience in 1969 that

> there is not one single place built in this country that did not have a former Arab population. . . . Jewish villages were built in the place of Arab villages. You do not even know the names of these Arab villages, and I do not blame you because geography books no longer exist; not only do the books not exist, the Arab villages are not there either. Nahlal arose in the place of Mahlul; Kibbutz Gvat in the place of Jibta; Kibbutz Sarid in the place of Huneifis; and Kefar Yehushu'a in the place of Tal al-Shuman.[172]

Unanimous Predictions of Zionist Victory

The greatest menace to Zionist forces during the civil war was the threat of Arab states' direct military intervention. Such intervention was deterred until May 15 by repeated British threats of punitive force, strong international pressure, and the Arab states' own reluctance and unpreparedness to fight. The critical six-month civil war period enabled Zionist forces to gain the initiative, consolidate territorial gains, expel the Arab population from the seized lands, and brace themselves for the possibility of the Arab states' military action. General Ismail Safwat warned the Arab League in March 1948 that the regular Arab armies had "many logistical deficiencies," and that unless these were promptly addressed and mobilization took place, they would be unprepared to act when the mandate expired, and would "lose the race against time," as they had "lost it in the past."[173] The British chiefs of staff conceded that while the issue of Palestine might unite the Arabs in opposing the Jews, they believed that "jealousy over the spoils of Palestine, whether it be the partitioned portion or the whole of Palestine," was likely to prevent any coordinated action "other than negative, such as fighting the Jews."[174]

Chief Secretary Gurney severely criticized the Arab states and their poor performance during the civil war period: "This is what the Palestine Arabs get from the assistance provided by the Arab States. Perhaps our warnings to the states not to indulge in such premature military action were not always strong enough. True it is that this ill-organized and stupid intervention, in defiance of all our protests, has cost the Palestine Arabs dearly, and one could almost say that it is all over bar the shouting and the re-opening of the Jewish road to Jerusalem."[175]

A fortnight before the mandate ended, effective intervention by the Arab states still appeared unlikely. The U.S. secretary of state, General George C. Marshall (chief of staff during World War II), observed that the Arab countries' internal weakness made it difficult for them to take action. He predicted a dismal military showing if they entered the conflict at all.[176] As a caveat, Marshall predicted that in the face of the Arab world's hostility, a Jewish state could survive as a self-sufficient entity over the long term only with a major power benefactor: "If Jews follow counsel of their extremists who favor contemptuous policy toward Arabs, any Jewish state to be set up will be able [to] survive only with continuous assistance from abroad."[177]

Despite the Arab states' weakness and reluctance to intervene, U.S. military intelligence predicted that popular domestic pressure whipped up by Arab military defeats, and the influx of Palestinian Arab refugees, could prompt the Arab states—particularly Egypt, Syria, and Transjordan—"to employ some of their armed forces in Palestine." Rising passions among Arab populations were particularly inflamed by reports of Jewish forces violating Arab women.[178] U.S. military intelligence viewed the Arab armies' entry into Palestine as legally justified by the Zionists' attack on the Arab city of Jaffa, designated as the Arab state's port in the partition plan.[179] On all the principal fronts, as of May 18, "Jewish forces were fighting in Arab territory," and Arab irregular forces numbering some 13,000 "had made only two relatively light efforts to enter Jewish areas," U.S. intelligence reported.[180]

On the eve of the mandate's expiration, it was evident to the high commissioner of Palestine that "with the possible exception of the Arab Legion, the Jews were perfectly able to defend themselves," against the Arab armies. He conceded that the British "just did not know how well organized or how well trained the Haganah really was. . . . they were jolly good."[181] Cunningham stated that during the final period of the mandate the Zionists were consciously implementing a determined and ruthless policy to expel the Palestinian Arabs from their homeland. As he explained to the journalist Larry Collins years later, "In the end, it was clear that it was the Jews who were trying to frighten the Arabs and to drive them into the sea. . . . They were being pretty ruthless in their attacks and it was clear it was being done by conscious design."[182]

⚶

1.   Nijim and Muammar, *Toward the De-Arabization of Palestine/Israel,* 25–26.

2.   Khalidi, *From Haven to Conquest,* appendix 7, 856.

3.   Nijim and Muammar, *Toward the De-Arabization of Palestine/Israel,* 25–26. A majority of Palestinians from the Safad subdistrict fled to Syria and Lebanon, the only route open to them.

4.   Morris, *Birth,* 242–43.

5.   ISA MAM 302/114, "Villages that surrendered and [villages that] conquered [after resistance] outside the State of Israel," November 17, 1948; cited in Morris, *Birth,* 226n23. See also, Laila Parsons, "The Druze and the Birth of Israel," in Rogan and Shlaim, *War for Palestine,* 60–78.

6.   Morris, *Birth Revisited,* 492–93.

7.   CP V/4/100, Addendum to Statement on the Military Situation in Palestine, March 28, 1948, dated April 2, 1948.

8.   KMA-PA 170-44, "Sasha" (Allon) to Yadin and "Hillel" (Galili), April 22, 1948; cited in Morris, *Birth,* 121n201, 102.

9.   Ibid.

10.   *Sefer Hapalmah II,* 286; cited in Morris, *Birth,* 122.

11.   Morris, *Birth,* 123–24.

12.   TNA WO 275/78, Sixth Airborne, March 16, 1948; Morris, *Birth Revisited,* 344.

13.   Khalidi, *All That Remains,* 456–57.

14.   Kirad al-Ghannama, Abu Salim Khawalid interview by Ahmad Ashkar of the National Committee for the Defense of the Rights of the Uprooted in Israel, Minority Rights Group International [n.d.].

15.   *Survey of Palestine,* 1:151.

16.   TNA WO 275/60, Sixth Airborne Division, intelligence summary no. 61, October 23, 1947.

17.   Ibid.

18.   Mustafa Abbasi, "The Battle for Safad in the War of 1948: A Revised Study," *International Journal of Middle East Studies* 36 (2004): 23.

19.   Ibid., 31n55, Kalman, Haganah Archives, file no. 65/13, 9.

20.   Pappé, *Ethnic Cleansing of Palestine,* 97.

21.   Wilson, *Cordon and Search,* 158; Abbasi, "Battle for Safad," 25.

22.   Abbasi, "Battle for Safad," 34.

23.   KMA-PA 170-44, "Sasha" (Allon) to Yadin, "Hillel" (Galili), April 22, 1948; cited in Morris, *Birth,* 101.

24.   Nazzal, "The Flight of the Palestinian Arabs from Galilee," Fayiz Qadurah interview, 312.

25.   Abbasi, "Battle for Safad," 30.

26. Ibid., Ahmad Hussain Hamid interview, 276. See also Nazzal, *Palestinian Exodus,* 33–37.

27. Morris, *Birth,* 102; Nazzal, "Flight of the Palestinian Arabs," 'Ayn al-Zaytun interviews, 276–84.

28. Abbasi, "Battle for Safad," 34.

29. Guy Erlich, "Not Only Deir Yassin," *Ha'ir* [Hebrew daily], May 6, 1992. Aryeh Yitzhaki lecturer at Bar Ilan University, Tel Aviv. He served as the director of the IDF archives in the 1960s.

30. Ibid.

31. Ibid.

32. Abbasi, "Battle for Safad," 35.

33. Morris, *Birth,* 102.

34. Nazzal, "Flight of the Palestinian Arabs," Salim Nimir Abdullah interview, 292–94.

35. Ibid.

36. Ibid., Yunis Muhammad Hussain Tamim interview, 285.

37. Ibid., Talib Tamim interview, 287–89.

38. *Ha'aretz,* August 7, 1949; and ISA JM5667 gimel/25, "In the Name of the Oppressed," Sheikh Attiya Jawwad to the justice minister, June 9, 1949; cited in Morris, *Birth,* 242.

39. HHA 5.18 (2), "Operation Yiftah for the Liberation of the Galilee," Yosef Ulitzky; cited in Morris, *Birth,* 121n204.

40. Nazzal, "Flight of the Palestinian Arabs," Fayiz Qadurah interview, 312.

41. Morris, *Birth,* 102–3.

42. Abbasi, "Battle for Safad," 41.

43. TNA WO 261/237, 41st Field Regiment Royal Artillery, QHR, January–December 1948, "Safad Lost to Arabs," Sam Souki, United Press correspondent.

44. Nazzal, "Flight of the Palestinian Arabs," Fayiz Qadurah interview, 312.

45. Ibid., Usamah al-Naqib interview, 315.

46. *Sefer Hapalmah II,* 285; cited in Morris, *Birth,* 104.

47. Nazzal, "Flight of the Palestinians," Fayiz Qadurah, Usamah al-Naqib, Issa 'Abid al-Khadrah interviews, 313–19.

48. ISA MAM 310/33, "A Meeting in Safad," July 29, 1948, and DBG-YH II, 494, entry for June 7, 1948; cited in Morris, *Birth,* 105. Pappé, *Ethnic Cleansing of Palestine,* 98; Abbasi, "Battle for Safad," 41.

49. Abbasi, "Battle for Safad," 41.

50. Morris, *Birth Revisited,* 316.

51. Danin to Weitz, May 18, 1948, Yosef Weitz Papers, Institute for the Study of Settlement (Rehovot); cited in Morris, *Birth Revisited,* 312n11.

52. NACP 84/350/61/34/4–5, Jerusalem Consulate, U.S. Embassy London, no. 71, May 9, 1948.

53. Ibid.

54. TNA AIR 23/8345, Report on the Evacuation of the Royal Air Force from Palestine, Air Vice Marshal W. L. Dawson, Air Officer Commanding, Levant, 7, no. 1869, CO to HQ Palestine.

55. Nazzal, "Flight of the Palestinian Arabs," Mustafa Ahmad Ma'ari interview, 326. See also Nazzal, *Palestinian Exodus,* 43–45.

56. Ibid., Mahmud Rashid interview, 329.

57. Ibid., Said al-Abdullah interview, 337–38.

58. Ahmad Dakkur, interviewed by author in 'Ayn al-Hilwi Camp, Lebanon, August 16, 2001.

59. Nazzal, "Flight of the Palestinian Arabs," Ali Hussain interview, 332–34.

60. Ibid., Musa al-Haj Muhammad al-Rifai interview, 336.

61. Ibid., Mir'i Hassan Salamah interview, 320.

62. KMA-PA 170-44, "Sasha" (Allon) to Yadin, "Hillel" (Galili), April 22, 1948; cited in Morris, *Birth,* 101, 106.

63.   CZA A246-13, 2373, entry for May 4, 1948; cited in Morris, *Birth,* 106.

64.   Nazzal, "Flight of the Palestinian Arabs," Ma'mun 'Abdulrahman Darwish 'Ahmad, Marsila Abu Khalil interviews, 355, 350.

65.   Ibid., Muhammad Ahmad Shuraidi interview, 348.

66.   Ma'susih 'Abd al-Rahman al-Naqqash, interviewed by author in Hashmiyya, Jordan, August 8, 2001. Naim S. Ateek, "Remembering al-Nakba," Westminster Cathedral Sermon, London, May 2, 1998. Ateek was born in Baysan.

67.   Nijim and Muammar, *Toward the De-Arabization of Palestine/Israel,* 34–35.

68.   Nazzal, "Flight of the Palestinian Arabs," Muhammad Ahmad Shuraidi interview, 347.

69.   Pappé, *Ethnic Cleansing of Palestine,* 102.

70.   Ephraim Talmi, *Lexicon Melhemit ha-Itzmaout* [A Lexicon of the War of Independence] (Tel Aviv: Davar, 1970), 36–38; cited in Nazzal, *Palestinian Exodus,* 17.

71.   Pappé, *Ethnic Cleansing of Palestine,* 102n31, interview with Palti Sela in the Haganah Archives, File 205.9, January 10, 1988.

72.   Nazzal, "Flight of the Palestinian Arabs," Nadir Shakhshir interview, 357.

73.   Ibid., Marsila Abu Khalil interview, 350–52.

74.   Ma'susih 'Abd al-Rahman al-Naqqash, interviewed by author in Hashmiyya, Jordan, August 8, 2001.

75.   Morris, *Birth,* 105–7.

76.   Pappé, *Ethnic Cleansing of Palestine,* 102.

77.   Morris, *Birth Revisited,* 434n107.

78.   Nazzal, "Flight of the Palestinian Arabs," Kafr Misr interviews, 360–67.

79.   Ayshi Mahmud Khalid, interviewed by author in Irbid Camp, Jordan, September 24, 2001.

80.   History of the Haganah, 1420; cited in Khalidi, *All That Remains,* 60.

81.   Fatima al-Mahir, interviewed by author in Irbid Camp, Jordan, September 24, 2001.

82.   Pappé, *Ethnic Cleansing of Palestine,* 106n46.

83.   Soukarieh, "For the Sake of Remembrance," Matti Bouri interview.

84.   Nazzal, "Flight of the Palestinian Arabs," Musa al-Najami interview, 394.

85.   Ibid., Salih Hakim interview, 390–91.

86.   Soukarieh, "For the Sake of Remembrance," Matti Bouri interview.

87.   Ibid.

88.   Nazzal, "Flight of the Palestinian Arabs," Farid Abu Nasab interview, 392.

89.   TNA WO 275/64, Sixth Airborne Division HQ Palestine, fortnightly newsletter, 257 and 317 Field Security, weekly report no. 3, April 28, 1948.

90.   GP, diary entry April 29, 1948.

91.   Soukarieh, "For the Sake of Remembrance," Matti Bouri interview.

92.   Ibid.

93.   TNA WO 261/223, Third King's Own Hussars, QHR, June 30, 1948.

94.   TNA WO 275/62, Intelligence Report 5/6 May.

95.   Childers, "Other Exodus."

96.   Soukarieh, "For the Sake of Remembrance," Matti Bouri interview.

97.   Salman Abu-Sitta, "Traces of Poison," *Al-Ahram Weekly,* February 27–March 5, 2003, no. 627; ICRC reference G59/1 GC, G3/82.

98.   TNA WO 275/64, Sixth Airborne Division HQ Palestine, fortnightly newsletter, 257 and 317 Field Security, weekly report no. 4, May 5, 1948.

99.   TNA WO 275/62, Intelligence Report 5/6 May.

100.   Abu-Sitta, "Traces of Poison."

101.   Ibid.

102. Ibid.; Ben-Gurion's war diary, May 27, 1948.

103. Avner Cohen, "Israel and Chemical/Biological Weapons: History, Deterrence, and Arms Control," *Nonproliferation Review* 8 (Fall–Winter 2001): 29–30; cited at www.nti.org. "Israel has not signed the 1972 Biological Weapons Convention, nor explained the reasons behind its refusal to sign."

104. Pappé, *Ethnic Cleansing of Palestine*, 73–74.

105. Avner Cohen, "Israel and Chemical/Biological Weapons"; cited at www.nti.org.

106. Sara Leibovitz-Dar, "Haydakim Besherut Hamedinah" ("Microbes in State Service"), *Hadashot*, August 13, 1993; cited at www.nti.org.

107. Nazzal, "Flight of the Palestinian Arabs," Farid Abu Nasab interview, 391–93.

108. Ibid., Salih Hakim interview, 390–91.

109. Morris, *Birth*, 109.

110. Nazzal, "Flight of the Palestinian Arabs," Musa al-Najami interview, 394.

111. Soukarieh, "For the Sake of Remembrance," Matti Bouri interview.

112. Ibid.

113. Ibid.

114. Morris, *Birth Revisited*, 231.

115. Ibid., 231n519.

116. Palumbo, *Palestinian Catastrophe*, 119. Lieutenant Petite was a U.N. observer from France who visited Acre to investigate Arab charges of mistreatment under Israeli rule.

117. Nijim and Muammar, *Toward the De-Arabization of Palestine/Israel*, 41.

118. Nazzal, "Flight of the Palestinian Arabs," Hussain 'As'ad Khalil interview, 385. See also "The Cleansing of al-Bassa," www.allthatremains.com/acre/al-bassa/story 103.html.

119. Morris, *Birth Revisited*, 253n725, "Hiram" to HIS-AD, May 19, 1948, HA 105/aleph.

120. Maryam 'Ali Wardi, interviewed by author in 'Ayn al-Hilwi Camp, Sidon, Lebanon, August 16, 2001.

121. Nazzal, "Flight of the Palestinian Arabs," Ibrahim Tahir Sa'ayah interview, 374.

122. Ibid., Ahmad Ibrahim Yusif and Hussain Khalil Awad interviews, 369–76.

123. Ibid., Muhammad 'As'ad Qiblawai interview, 379.

124. Nijim and Muammar, *Toward the De-Arabization of Palestine/Israel*, 34–35.

125. Morris, *Birth*, xv.

126. S'ada al-Subeih interviewed by author in Irbid Camp, Jordan, September 20, 2001.

127. CP III/4/152–53, Cunningham to Creech Jones, no. 1211, April 30, 1948.

128. Ibid.

129. Ibid.

130. Hazem Nuseibeh, interviewed by author in Amman, Jordan,
     September 30, 2001.

131. Ibid.

132. NACP 84/350/61/34/4–5, Wasson to Marshall, no. 530, May 3, 1948.

133. Ibid.

134. Ibid.

135. CP III/2/104, Creech Jones to Cunningham, no. 1153, March 27, 1948.

136. NACP 84/350/61/34/4–5, U.S. Embassy Cairo, Pickney S. Tuck to Marshall, no. 435, April 28, 1948.

137. Ibid., Wasson to Wadsworth, no. 307, May 2, 1948.

138. NACP 84/350/63/11/5–6, London to American Legation Beirut, May 3, 1948, no. 16.

139. NACP 319/270 6/15/4, G2 Intelligence Report, for Chiefs of Staff, Current Situation in Palestine, April 27, 1948.

140. NACP 38/37/15/5/2, Lewis W. Douglas, London Embassy to Marshall, no. 1926, May 4, 1948.

141. Ibid.

142. NACP 38/370/15/5/2, Wasson to Marshall, no. 597, May 13, 1948.

143. NACP 84/350/63/11/5–6, London to American Legation Beirut, no. 16, May 3, 1948.

144. Ibid.

145. Memorandum titled "Our Arab Policy during the War," in Giv'at Haviva, Hashomer Hatza'ir Archives, 10.10.95 (4). The Mapam party was founded in Jerusalem in 1948. Its members included Haganah commanders Yisrael Galili, Yigal Allon, Yitzhak Rabin, and Moshe Carmel; cited in Masalha, *Expulsion of the Palestinians,* 181.

146. Memorandum to the Political Committee of Mapam, October 12, 1948, Aharon Cohen Personal Archive, Giv'at Haviva, Hashomer Hatza'ir Archives, 11.10.95; cited in Masalha, *Expulsion of the Palestinians,* 181, and Morris, *Birth,* 160.

147. HHA 66.90 (1), Protocol of meeting of Mapam Political Committee, August 19, 1948; cited in Morris, *Birth Revisited,* 355n84.

148. KMA-ACP 9/9/3, Transcript of Cisling's statement at cabinet meeting, November 17, 1948; cited in Morris, *Birth Revisited,* 488n159.

149. Morris, *Birth Revisited,* 350.

150. TT, Col. John Waddy interview.

151. GP, diary entry, May 2, 1948.

152. LCP, Sir Alan Cunningham interview; CP III/4/152–53, Cunningham to Creech Jones, no. 1211, April 30, 1948.

153. TNA CO 537/3901, Partition: Implementation of UNO Decision: Reaction of Arabs, Part 1, Sir Alec Kirkbride, Amman to FO, April 21, 1948.

154. TNA FO 816/139, BMEO to FO, August 3, 1948.

155. NACP 218/190/1/19/4–5, Report by the Director, Joint Staff, to the Joint Chiefs of Staff on Force Requirements for Palestine, March 31, 1948, 69. See also chap. 3.

156. Dave Grossman, *On Killing: The Psychological Cost of Learning to Kill in War and Society* (Boston: Little Brown, 1995), 206–7.

157. *Palestine 1948,* in Abu-Sitta, *Palestinian Nakba.* Sites of massacres during the civil war period according to Abu-Sitta's research include: al-'Abbasiyya, Abu Shusha, 'Ayn al-Zaytun, Balad al-Shaykh, Bayt Daras, Burayr, Dayr Yasin, Haifa, Hawsha, al-Husayniyya, Khubbayza, Mansurat al-Khayt, Nasir al-Din, Qisariya, War'a al-Sawda, and Wadi 'Ara.

158. Erlich, "Not Only Deir Yassin."

159. Ibid.

160. Pappé, *Ethnic Cleansing of Palestine,* 75. Pappé writes that "In Jaffa, houses were randomly selected and then dynamited with people still in them," as part of Yigael Yadin's plan for "deep invasions" inside Palestinian areas.

161. Erlich, "Not Only Deir Yassin."

162. ISA FM 2570/11, Avira to Danin, July 29, 1948, and Danin to Avira, August 16, 1948; cited in Morris, *Birth Revisited,* 356n96.

163. Khalidi, *All That Remains,* 213–315; KMA-AZP 6/6/4, Kaplan to Peri, November 8, 1948; cited in Morris, *Birth Revisited,* 470n47.

164. Pappé, *Ethnic Cleansing of Palestine,* 196.

165. KMA-AZP 6/6/4, Kaplan to Peri, November 8, 1948; cited in Morris, *Birth Revisited,* 470n47.

166. Morris, *Birth Revisited,* 486 and 503n165; Pappé, *Ethnic Cleansing of Palestine,* 6.

167. Erlich, "Not Only Deir Yassin."Ibid.

168. Ibid.

169. Morris, *Birth,* 501n122. Moshe Carmel, OC Carmeli Brigade, recalls seeing civilians killed in

Sa'sa' village, including cripples, after the village was conquered, Emmanuel Yalan (Vilensky) reported.

170. Pappé, *Ethnic Cleansing of Palestine*, 88.

171. Moshe Dayan speech to the Haifa Technion, *Ha'aretz*, April 4, 1969.

172. Safwat Report, 72.

173. TNA DEFE 5/10, COS(48) 45 (O) 26/2/48, annex.

174. GP, diary entry, May 5, 1948.

175. NACP 319/270 6/15/4, G2 Intelligence Report, for Chief of Staff, Situation in Palestine, April 27, 1948.

176. Ibid.

177. NACP 84/350/63/11/5–6, Department of State to American Legation Beirut, May 5, 1948, no. 214.

178. NACP 319/270/ 6/15/4, G2 Intelligence Report for Chief of Staff, Situation in Palestine, April 27, 1948.

179. NACP 319/270/6/15/4, G2 Intelligence Reports, Memo for Chief of Staff: Intelligence Division Special Briefing, the Palestine Situation, May 18, 1948.

180. LCP, Sir Alan Cunningham interview.

181. Ibid.

PALESTINIAN CIVILIANS HELD PRISONER BY THE
HAGANAH IN ACRE, 1948

X

A Pattern and Practice of Intimidation and Violence

Until we succeed in securing the goodwill of the Arabs, a dark portentous shadow remains over the National Home.

Jewish commentator, May 13, 1948, *Times* (London)

The civil war phase was critical to the final outcome of the 1948 Palestine war. By the end of the British mandate on May 15, 1948, the Jewish Agency had achieved its key ideological goals. The bitter conflict and the expulsion of the Arabs enabled the Agency to declare a Jewish-majority State of Israel, without specifying borders. And although the Jewish state was not completely homogeneous, the non-Jewish community had been vastly reduced. Zionist forces would succeed in capturing the Galilee area bordering Lebanon, Syria, and Jordan; most of the coastal strip; and a number of areas designated as part of the Arab state in the U.N. partition plan. The Jewish Agency viewed removing the Arabs there as necessary to securing the new state's declared ethnic character.

The Haganah, aided by the IZL and LHI, successfully implemented the Agency's policy of Arab population transfer through a deliberate and systematic practice of intimidation and military violence. Without a militarily significant opponent during the civil war, Zionist militias were able to expel the indigenous Palestinian Arabs unhindered. The British policy of abandoning effective governance and not interfering in communal fighting enabled violence to escalate and expulsion to occur under the cover of war.

The majority of Palestinian Arabs were displaced during the civil war. By May 15, about 55 percent of the total number of Palestinians who would become refugees by the war's end in January 1949 had already been forced into exile.[1] Furthermore, Zionist forces prevented them from returning to their homes, even before the mandate ended, by razing houses and entire villages, mining fields and villages, looting personal and public property, and destroying crops, animals, and other means of livelihood. They also pursued a great number of terrified Arab civilians from village to village, forcing them ever farther from their homes and frequently beyond the borders of Palestine into neighboring Arab states.

Displaced Palestinian Arabs often took nothing with them because they were not permitted to do so, or they were so terrorized by sudden attack that they left under fire without any preparation. Civilian flight was clearly a goal of Zionist attackers, as demonstrated by the frequency of three-pronged assaults on Arab population centers, permitting panicked civilians only one escape route. In areas bordering Arab countries, this exit would typically be directed toward the frontier, emptying the country of its native population. In many cases, fleeing Arabs believed that they would return home after a brief period, after the Arab armies marched in to reclaim their lands for them. This passive and unrealistic outlook (in contrast to that of the yishuv and its leadership) resulted from the politically and socially underdeveloped Palestinian Arabs having been drawn into a war virtually leaderless, effectively disarmed, and mostly disorganized.

The population transfer implemented by the Jewish Agency during the civil war gave the Jews numerous political, economic, territorial, and military advantages. The Zionist leadership seized unfettered control over the Palestine state apparatus built by the British, which greatly facilitated Israeli state building and development. Most, if not all, of the strategic and well-fortified British police stations had fallen into Zionist hands. Former British military camps, the ports of Acre, Jaffa, and Haifa, the airports, prisons, radar stations, warehouses, utility infrastructure, and many Palestine government offices also were taken.[2] This strategic advantage meant that by the time Arab military detachments entered Palestine on May 15, they were unable to reverse the Zionists' territorial gains. The uprooting of the populace created additional logistical challenges for the forces of Arab states: a large number of Arab refugees and the absence of a self-sustaining friendly local population. This situation was created on the orders of the Zionist leaders: evict the villagers "so that they would become an economic liability for the general Arab forces."[3]

British Policy during Withdrawal

The role of British action, or rather deliberate inaction, during 1947 and 1948 clearly accelerated the spiral into civil war, with its attendant Arab dispossession. Across Palestine, the inaction was sometimes inconsistent; on a local and ad hoc basis, British withdrawal included occasional interventions that tacitly aided the implementation of partition or were designed to mitigate damage to British prestige. These were limited interventions in certain Arab-Jewish battles, notably Jaffa, and the relinquishing of government offices to one side or the other, typically to the community designated in the U.N. partition plan.

More consistently, with a focus not on maintaining order but strictly on avoiding British casualties and salvaging military stores, the British evacuation from Palestine enabled the civil war's outbreak and escalation and facilitated the creation of the Palestinian Arab refugees. The policy of reckless nonintervention nurtured an anarchy the British proved unable and unwilling to stop. Some reasons for nonintervention were practical, such as the self-fulfilling fear that once hostilities started it would be even harder to reverse course.

The end of March 1948 proved decisive. The security situation was so bad that by March 28, the military pressed London to evacuate Palestine before May 15. Knowing they could no longer maintain order, commanders feared that the young and inexperienced British soldiers serving in Palestine would be unable to extricate themselves from the conflict as the situation deteriorated. British troops were reduced by two-thirds from April 1 to May 1, leaving the Palestinian Arabs vulnerable to Zionist forces.[4] The rapid withdrawal continued unabated even after the United Nations suspended the partition plan in March, demonstrating Britain's single-minded determination to abandon the mandate regardless of the chaos and conflict this would unleash.

Contributing to the rapid British withdrawal and resulting vacuum were initial Arab hostilities. The British military issued its withdrawal plan on December 6, 1947, and carried it out generally unaltered, albeit accelerated. The plan relied on Arab promises "not to make trouble" for the British. While Arab forces generally kept that promise by not directly attacking them, except at times to obtain weapons, they still entered the fray and advanced the intercommunal conflict inside Palestine.

Despite the Arab Higher Committee's (AHC) initial attempts to prevent clashes with the British and to cool the flames, localized Jewish-Arab hostilities and the intervention of foreign Arab fighters intensified the tension. British decision makers grew annoyed that the Arabs did not keep to the spirit of their promises to check warfare. As a result, the security situation rapidly deteriorated, while the British felt ever more justified in their passivity.[5]

In an effort to avoid further British casualties in an increasingly dangerous environment, and in an unsuccessful attempt to maintain good relations with both communities, General Officer Commanding (GOC) Gordon MacMillan laid down a firm policy of British nonintervention in intercommunal fighting, except where British lines of communication or personnel were threatened. With varying reservations, London and High Commissioner Sir Alan Cunningham acquiesced in the policy.

MacMillan was confident that he could evacuate his troops and still control any conflict between British security forces and either Arabs or Jews. However, he did not think his troops would be able to engage militarily with both communities at once, even though this situation never materialized. The direct conflict between Arabs and Jews proved to be the greater risk, even as threats to safe British evacuation from both communities remained a constant menace.

Another detrimental aspect of Britain's exit was the government's refusal to hand over formal authority for Palestine to the United Nations, to any other government, or to the proposed Arab or Jewish states before withdrawal. Even though the British military foresaw civil war if there was not a prior handover of institutional authority, the policy was designed to protect Great Britain's geopolitical interests in the Middle East by not legitimizing the partition plan, which the Arab states had denounced. The mandate government further obstructed any orderly transfer of authority by delaying the U.N. commission's arrival in Palestine until just two weeks before the mandate ended.

London's directive relieving British forces of the responsibility to maintain internal law and order before their physical departure contributed to disorder; so did the ban on British subjects' accepting positions in the governments of the envisioned Arab and Jewish states. The British military also ceased aggressively interdicting illegal Jewish immigrants in early February 1948, which permitted the immigrants to enter the country and become combatants, thereby increasing Zionist fighting strength.

Arab League Miscalculations and British Inconsistency

Arab local leaders in Palestine were unprepared for and fearful of warfare, but Arab League actions forced their hand. Arab rioting and burning of the Jewish commercial center in Jerusalem, largely unhindered by the British police and military, was the first major violent incident after the partition vote. The rioting was, however, a largely spontaneous response to Jewish celebrations viewed as provocative by Palestinian Arabs. The Zionists argued nonetheless that such actions justified their usually indiscriminate reprisals, further escalating the situation. Palestinian Arab leaders initially attempted to quiet the fury. Husayn al-Khalidi, a member of the Arab Higher Executive (AHE), warned after the riots that "the Jews are looking for trouble. They are trying to provoke us." Al-Khalidi advised being prepared "to hit them back if they hit us," but added that "anyone who wants to start trouble" must be stopped.[6] Another AHE member, Emile al-Ghoury, and the rest of the Palestinian Arab leadership realized "the time had not yet come to resort to violence." The AHE recognized "the dangers of becoming involved with the British, and also the tactical mistake of staging a premature uprising."

The Palestinian Arab leaders' efforts "directed towards controlling their unruly elements," provoked initially by Jewish triumphal demonstrations after the partition announcement, never really succeeded. Palestinian Arab leaders finally "abandon[ed] their efforts [at control] as more and more irregulars infiltrated into the country from the Arab states," according to Major R. D. Wilson of the Sixth Airborne Division.[7]

The Arab League directly helped to escalate the civil war by introducing mediocre and ill-disciplined guerrilla fighters into a situation they had reason to know would lead to an expanded and fruitless war. In October 1947, the Arab League military committee had already concluded that the Zionists possessed the requisite political and military organization to establish a Jewish state immediately. Even though the Arab League viewed the Palestinian Arabs' situation as dire by December 1947, the leaders remained intent on not placing themselves "in the position of aggressors" by intervening with their regular military forces in Palestine. Their ill-considered strategy was to wage war on the Zionists in the form of clandestine armed resistance[8]—which not only escalated the conflict but provided the better-prepared Zionists an opportunity and justification—under the guise of self-defense—to launch aggressive counter-offensives to achieve long-held territorial and demographic aims, to the detriment of the Palestinian Arabs.[9]

British policy led not only to civil strife but also gave a clear advantage to superior Zionist forces. The Palestinian Arabs entered the civil war greatly limited in power and will to fight. The British had effectively disarmed most of them during their brutal suppression of the Arab rebellion of 1936–39. The mandate government also banished their leadership, leaving the Palestinian Arabs in disarray. Once civil war broke out, the Arab states had hoped to arm and train the Palestinian Arabs to defend themselves, but the British curbed open assistance by relaying the message that "such action would be regarded as an 'unfriendly act' against the Mandatory government."[10] The Egyptian foreign minister protested that Britain's prohibition against Arab states' military aid to the Palestine Arabs "acted as encouragement to [the] Jews in their present actions." He also argued that British prevention of an open Arab volunteer presence worked to the Arabs' detriment and demonstrated British partiality toward Palestine's Jews, regarded by Arabs collectively as an "external aggressor."[11] The British, however, were not taking strong measures against the infiltrating Arabs, while noting that the Arab guerrillas were politically and militarily counterproductive for the Palestinians.

As Palestinian Arab population centers began falling to Zionist forces, and particularly after the Dayr Yasin massacre in early April, the Arab League states increasingly threatened to send their armies to protect civilians from Zionist aggression by filling the vacuum created by the evacuating British forces. Even though the Arab League's vociferous threats were more likely posturing than planning, and their forces (with the exception of the Arab Legion) lacked a qualitative edge over those of the Zionists, credible threats from the Arab states to deploy their regular forces might still have influenced Zionist decision making and international opinion before the mandate's end.

Overall, British policy contributed to Arab dispossession through the mandate's relatively scrupulous external maintenance of international law for Palestine, particularly by preventing early external Arab regular army intervention, while at the same time abandoning domestic law in mandate Palestine. High Commissioner Cunningham himself questioned the propriety of British policy toward the Arabs. He realized that, owing to Zionist operations prior to May 15, the Arabs could lose decisively and the Jews could "win everything" because of Britain's policy to block the Arab states' armies entry into Palestine.[12]

The Aggressive Zionist Posture

The Zionists' campaigns of psychological terror, territorial seizure, and ethnic cleansing constituted the main offensive violence of the conflict. Since 1945, terrorism perpetrated by dissident Zionist groups had destabilized Palestine. The horror and fear evoked in the Palestinian Arab population by the IZL's bombing of the King David Hotel in 1946 was, as Edward Marroum of Jerusalem recalled, akin to the psychological trauma induced by the terror attacks in the United States on September 11, 2001.[13]

As of September 19, 1947, those killed in dissident Zionist terror attacks included 141 British, 44 Arabs, and 25 Jews. Palestinian Arabs' distrust of Zionist Jews had steadily mounted as a result of "the flood of Jews into Palestine," and the loss of Arab life and property due to terrorist attacks.[14] The acceptance of rule by a Jewish national government led by the perpetrators of terrorist attacks was inconceivable to the Palestinian Arabs.

Aggressive goals were not universal among the Jews of Palestine, or among all Zionist activists. However, the official Zionist leadership of the yishuv, including the more influential decision makers, along with armed dissident groups and much of popular opinion were decisively driven in that direction. Ben-Gurion said perhaps only 20 percent of Jewish leaders were prepared to fight to expand the Jewish state area "regardless of what the Arabs did."[15] Yet he and his military commanders were confident that Arab reaction to Zionist political steps could prove provocative enough to give the more expansionist Zionists an opportunity to achieve their goals. The U.N. partition decision was the spark that ignited reckless Arab reactions and opened the way to civil war. "Arabs could not accept domination by Jews and would have to fight to the end," summarized Lowell Pinkerton, U.S. consul in Lebanon.[16] By deciding to fight partition, Ben-Gurion observed, "the Arabs came to our aid," enabling the achievement

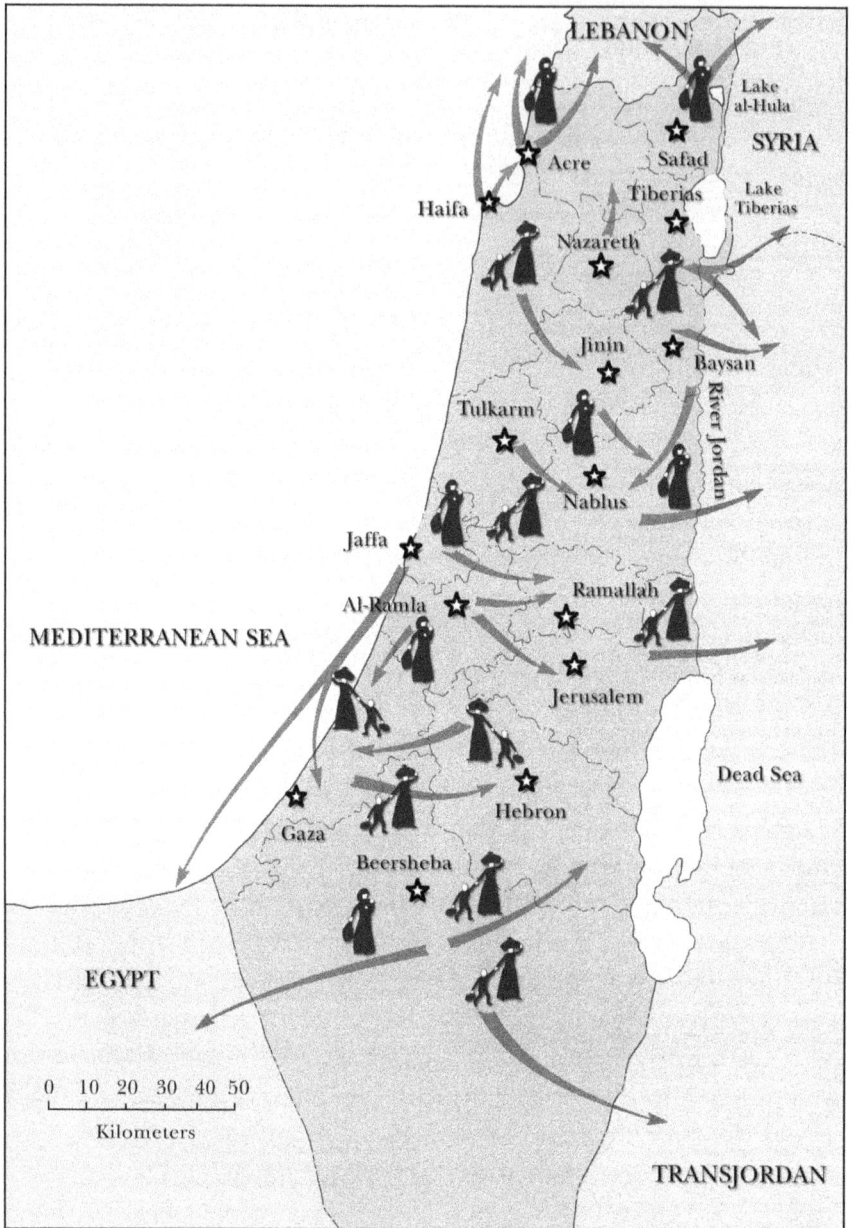

LEBANON

Lake
al-Hula

SYRIA

Acre

Safad

Haifa

Tiberias

Lake
Tiberias

Nazareth

Jinin

Baysan

Tulkarm

Nablus

Jaffa

Al-Ramla

Ramallah

MEDITERRANEAN SEA

Jerusalem

Dead Sea

Gaza

Hebron

Beersheba

EGYPT

0   10   20   30   40   50
Kilometers

TRANSJORDAN

DIRECTION OF PALESTINIAN FLIGHT FROM TOWNS AND VILLAGES

of Zionist goals: "At almost every moment in our history the Arabs have helped us by attacking us; they helped us make important achievements that otherwise might have [been] missed. But the greatest error the Arabs ever made on our behalf was refusing the U.N. decision."[17]

Although Ben-Gurion viewed the partition plan's specific terms as unfavorable for the Jews—Jerusalem internationalized and "the state cut up into those three parts"—he rationalized that "when the Arabs refused [partition] that changed everything for us." By refusing partition, he believed the Arabs "gave us the right to get what we could." He decided definitively that "from now on what our state will be will depend on arms; it's going to depend on arms not [on] the U.N. whether we will win this place or that place."[18] And he assiduously used his official and charismatic power as Jewish Agency chairman and head of the defense committee to carry out that aim.

The Zionist leadership pressed the civil war forward with steadily increasing ferocity, and by the crucial month of March 1948, it had opted for full-scale war waged mostly against civilians. The decision was based on immediate factors: the United Nations' stepping away from partition with no substitute regime; Arab irregular activities, especially the blockade of Jews in Jerusalem; and Britain's final rapid evacuation over the ensuing weeks.

The anti-Arab demographic aims of the Zionist offensives were obvious. In fact, the Zionist leaders had already planned for a state bureaucratic and defense apparatus in which Arab citizens would not participate. An explicit blanket decision to expel the Arabs from the Jewish state area was apparently not formalized by the Zionist leadership, at least in any record known to date, but at a minimum, as Benny Morris states, it "was understood by all concerned that . . . politically, the fewer Arabs remaining in the Jewish state, the better."[19]

The Phases of "Ethnic Cleansing"

The initial and proportionately small departures from Palestine's main cities by middle- and upper-class Arabs and Jews beginning in December 1947 through early March 1948 were caused by indirect forms of intimidation such as urban fighting and terrorist bomb attacks, as well as by direct attack, sniping, and related psychological terror. Dissident and sometimes official Zionist attacks against ordinary public places and urban civilians had particularly devastating effects. More general war factors, such as economic privation, took their toll as anarchy spread and mandate authorities completed their tasks with official indifference.

Urban families were confused and desperate. Amina Rifai, an Arab Jerusalemite, said, "We were just ordinary people literally fighting for our survival."[20] Many urban families relocated from the centers of fighting to cities or towns in the designated Arab state or to their ancestral familial villages. Others traveled to Amman, Beirut, and Cairo, where many had family members. This exodus was not part of any Arab organized evacuation; the Palestinian Arab leadership, in fact, tried to stop the movement by banning departures from cities—using diplomatic contacts with neighboring Arab states to ban Palestinian Arabs' entry and to send those fleeing back to Palestine. The Jewish Agency, however, was more successful in preventing Jewish departures by confiscating passports and other repressive force.

The April 1948 Zionist escalation, attendant on the diminished strength of British forces after March, unleashed the full force of offensive military operations formulated under Plan D. Haganah brigade- and battalion-level commanders received carte blanche to clear areas they determined to be vital and to expel Arab villagers they deemed hostile. Except for brief forceful interventions to protect lines of communication and evacuation routes in the Shaykh Jarrah quarter of Jerusalem, Jaffa (Sarafand Camp), the Haifa port and oil facilities, and Acre, British forces maintained a policy of nonintervention in the intercommunal battles of the final, full-fledged combat phase of the civil war. This left the Palestinian Arabs virtually defenseless. Meanwhile, London repeatedly warned the Arab states to "stand off" with their regular forces or suffer Great Britain's full diplomatic and military response.

The Main Causes of Palestinian Displacement

The driving force in the exodus from the main towns and cities in the mandate's last month and a half—which constituted the bulk of the civil war exodus—was direct military attack by Zionist forces. These operations typically included several days of mortaring, siege, psychological warfare aggravated by reports of specific atrocities, and a final multi-pronged assault. British documents confirm that Zionist forces regularly provoked or initiated attacks on Palestinian Arabs, including in such areas as the Qatamon and Shaykh Jarrah quarters of Jerusalem, the cities of Jaffa and Haifa, the village of Dayr Yasin, and scores of other communities.[21] If Palestinian Arabs responded in defense, Zionist forces retaliated with indiscriminate and overwhelming lethal force.

Haganah and IZL military orders indicate that provoking civilian flight was in fact a key and explicit goal of offensive attacks. The panic-inducing pressure continued even after a community began to evacuate. Zionist forces would intimidate already panicked Arab civilians into further flight by pursuing them as they sought safety, as was witnessed in Haifa, Jaffa, and numerous towns and villages. By designating a sole escape route during a three-pronged attack, particularly in villages, Zionist forces drove villagers through an exit chute away from their homes, robbing, harassing, and humiliating the Arabs while expelling them.

Incorporating the voices of the dislocated into the historical record helps to confirm that intimidation tactics drove the exodus. The refugees' accounts typically contradict Morris's assertion that deteriorating living conditions in the villages and urban areas, and the Zionists' capture of nearby locales, were primary reasons Arabs evacuated. No significant evidence supports the argument that the Palestinian leadership or the Arab states intentionally encouraged a mass exodus. Ample evidence does show that they tried to stop it. In only a few cases in the civil war period did Arab commanders order inhabitants of certain villages to vacate for strategic or safety reasons.

Desertion by Arab military commanders and civil leaders before and during critical battles was also not a direct cause of Palestinian Arab flight. Refugees rarely if ever cited it as a major factor in their evacuation. By contrast, they consistently cited the violence of direct military attack, the trauma of civilian deaths in their communities from attacks, a rational fear of rape and massacre, threats of these or other atrocities, and ordered expulsion.

Even as major cities fell to Zionist forces, agrarian villagers maintained high morale, due to their relative economic self-sufficiency and because the war had not yet reached them. The Palestinian Arab peasantry simply could not conceive of indefinite dislocation. Their visceral bond to the land was underpinned by economic necessity: the land was their life; they knew

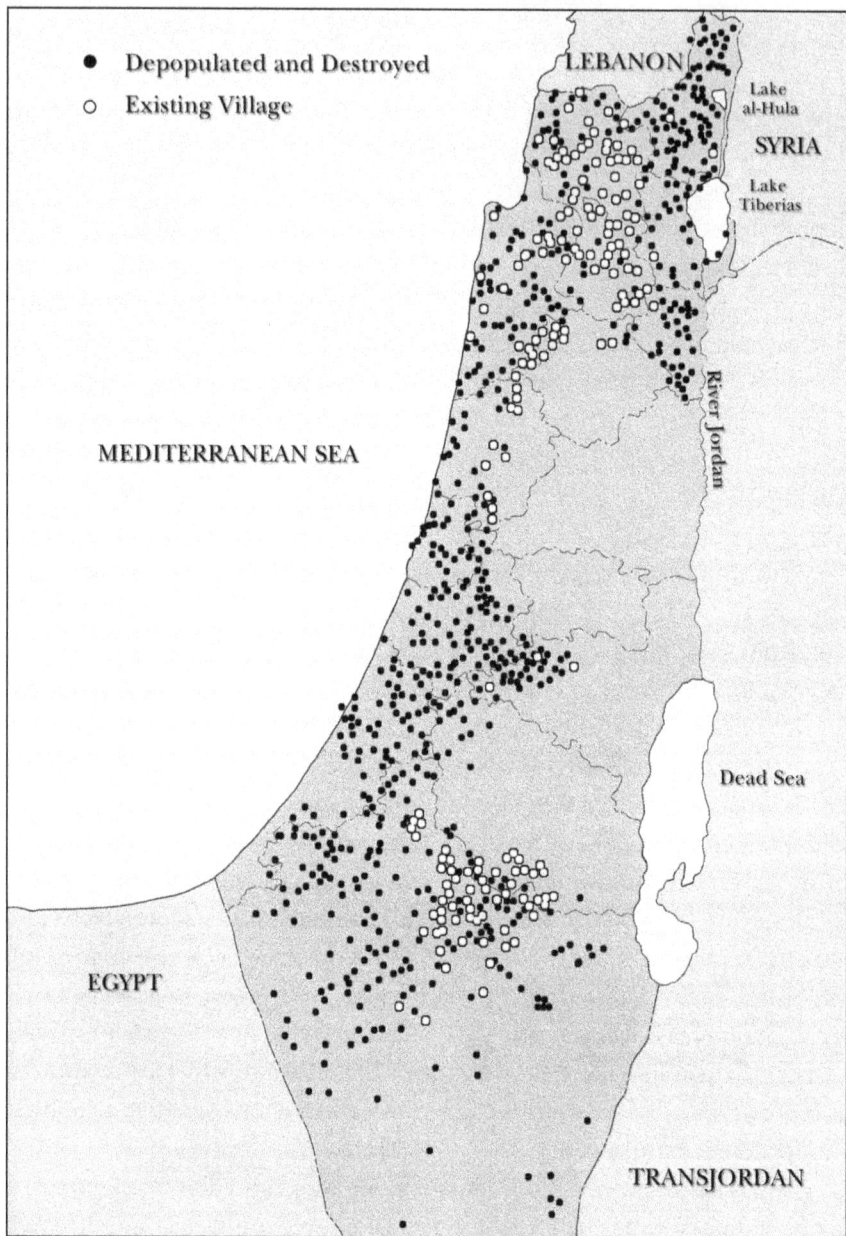

THE 531 DEPOPULATED PALESTINIAN TOWNS AND VILLAGES, 1947–49

no other. Ayoub Talhami, from the Arab village of Shafr ʿAmr, explained that in the course of daily life, "people came to say goodbye when you went to the next village. Going somewhere unknown was unthinkable."[22]

Palestinian Arabs often attempted to defend their towns and villages with a meager supply of rifles, ammunition, and inexperienced fighters, until they realized they were unable to withstand a military onslaught. This brought a realistic fear of further violence after defeat, based on implicit or explicit threats, observed abuse and atrocities during the takeover of the community, and credible reports of harm to life and "honor" from Zionist actions elsewhere. They also believed that they had to withstand Zionist attacks only until May 15, when the Arab armies, as repeatedly promised, would come to their rescue and foil the Zionist plan to form a Jewish state in Palestine. This contributed to the perception that evacuation—in the face of death—was a short-term risk.

The climate of terror was greatly accentuated by the two most critical events of the civil war: the Dayr Yasin massacre in early April and by the fall of Haifa two weeks later. Both clearly illustrated British forces' inability and unwillingness to protect Arab civilians. The Dayr Yasin massacre particularly motivated villagers to depart just before, during, and after a Zionist attack. Palestinian Arabs were terrified and demoralized by the reported size and brutality of the massacre, and particularly horrified by the accounts of rape and mutilation. In Arab tradition, honor is paramount and female purity is a central measure of family honor. "The whole world revolved around this," said Hamdi Muhammad Matar from Qalunyia near Jerusalem. "People fled in order to safeguard their honor."[23] Palestinians were terrified that they would be left defenseless to the depredations of the Zionist army and terrorist militias. Arab villagers feared the "Jews would come and do to us what they had done at Dayr Yasin. If we had stayed, we would have been killed," said Matar.[24] Fatima Husayn al-Jawabri, of Haifa, said that "when people saw three or four killed, they became afraid. People feared for their daughters. They preferred to protect their honor instead of their lands."[25]

Fearing slaughter and rape, villagers often evacuated women, children, and elderly to areas perceived as safer. Refugee testimony bears out, however, that in the overwhelming majority of cases, Palestinian Arabs did not abandon their villages en masse, or leave Palestine's borders, until they felt directly intimidated by an actual or reasonably expected Zionist attack, or experienced threats through psychological warfare.

Strong evidence indicates that Zionists planned to displace the Arabs. The historical literature attests to a well-established intention to "transfer" Arabs out of Palestine. The Zionists' political motive for forced "transfer" was to create a Jewish state with few non-Jews. The Haganah's Plan D explicitly articulated a policy of driving out Arab communities and destroying their villages, obliterating traces of Arab society. Its implementation during the civil war resulted in the expulsion of more than 400,000 civilian Palestinian Arabs from some 225 rural locales and urban centers.

Ninety-four percent of the Palestinian Arab population displaced during this period was driven out by direct Zionist attacks or psychological warfare. Only 2 percent of the Arabs left their homes before they were directly intimidated or attacked.[26] Appendix 1 details the decisive causes for the fall of each Arab population locale, based on documentary sources and oral testimony of Palestinians' direct experience during the civil war.

After the declaration of the State of Israel on May 14, the Israeli Defense Forces (IDF) continued to implement the policy of "population transfer." By January 1949, approximately 400,000 more Palestinian Arabs would be expelled from their homes and the IDF would destroy more than 306 additional Palestinian Arab towns and villages. Overall, during both the civil war and multistate periods of the 1948 war, Zionist forces expelled over 80 percent of the Arabs from the conquered areas, depopulating about 531 villages, towns, Bedouin areas, and cities, the overwhelming number by violent intimidation. Most of these locales were physically destroyed during or after the war.[27]

An Enduring International Problem

In large part, the intractability of the enduring "Palestinian refugee problem" centers emotionally, if not legally and economically, on questions of responsibility. Each party can clearly be assigned a share of the historical blame. The member states of the United Nations, under significant political pressure from the United States, adopted the flawed partition resolution, which did not uphold the principles of self-determination and the preservation of international peace and security mandated by the U.N. Charter. Great Britain bears fundamental responsibility for abdicating its duties to maintain law and order during the mandate's final six months. The Arab states and their rhetoric fanned the flames of the destructive conflict, especially by introducing armed bands that provoked a superior enemy force but failed to defend the Arab population. Palestinian Arabs and their leadership contributed to the violence by responding emotionally and without a clear vision to a complex political problem. The political and psychological consequences of the expulsion have fueled regional violence and stymied Middle East peacemaking ever since.

In the final analysis, however, the Jewish Agency and dissident Zionist groups, and now the State of Israel, bear the major responsibility for intentionally creating the Palestinian refugees during the civil war and throughout the first multistate Arab-Israeli war. Lieutenant General Sir John Glubb Pasha, commander of the Transjordan Arab Legion, observed a certain irony in the Zionists' determined drive to create a Jewish state in Palestine through conquest. "For 2,000 years," he wrote, the Jews "have claimed that might conveys no right. . . . Driven from country to country as refugees, they have suffered everywhere from the persecution of military powers, and have everywhere denounced their persecutors and looked forward to an age when justice will replace armed power. But now, placed for the first time in a position to persecute others, they suddenly announce that military conquest is the true basis for settlement between nations."[28]

The British, for their part, learned that the presence of a third party in the dispute was a hindrance to any solution, let alone one based on justice. The British chiefs of staff concluded on their withdrawal from Palestine that "an agreement [to the Arab-Israeli dispute] will not come so long as one side or the other believes that it can use the strength of a great power to achieve domination over its opponent."[29]

Attempts to resolve the conflict will likely turn at some point to the question of causation. Comprehensive awareness of past events is important to understanding the present situation. To achieve and sustain peace, the causes of war must be examined. The irrefutable factors that led to the displacement of the Palestinian Arabs were the shirking of responsibility by the British government and the escalation of conflict by Arab leaders, both of which created the opportunity for Zionist leaders to establish a majority Jewish state. They achieved this aim by using superior military force to terrorize and expel the indigenous Palestinian Arabs under the cover of war. Resolving the Arab-Israeli conflict will require righting the wrongs of 1948, which continue to be inflicted on a largely civilian population to this day.

༄༅

1. The percentage of Palestinian Arabs displaced during the civil war period is based on the populations and locales depopulated before May 15, 1948, identified by this study.
2. Braun, "Memoirs of an Anti-Zionist Jew."
3. Zerubavel Gilad, *Palmach Book*, vol. 2, 924–25; cited in Pappé, *Ethnic Cleansing of Palestine*, 88n5.
4. MacMillan report, appendix.
5. TNA CAB 21/2494, Cabinet Official Committee on Palestine, Composition, and Terms of Reference, 1947–49, April 8, 1948.
6. LCP, Emile al-Ghoury interview.
7. CP III/1/23, Cunningham to Creech Jones, no. 113, January 24, 1948; Wilson, *Cordon and Search*, 156.
8. FBIS, European section, Near and Middle East and North African transmitters, Radio Damascus in Arabic to Syria and the Near East, December 7, 1947.
9. CP III/4/152, Cunningham to Creech Jones, no. 1211, April 30, 1948.
10. 'Arif al-'Arif, *Al-Nakba, 1947–1952*, vol. 1 (Beirut and Sidon: al-Maktaba al-'Asriyya, 1956–60), 15; cited in John, *Palestine Diary*, 281.
11. CP III/5/52, Cairo to Cunningham, no. 77, report of conversation with Egyptian Minister for Foreign Affairs Khasaba Pasha.
12. Ibid.
13. Edward Marroum, interviewed by author in Alexandria, Va., September 22, 2002.
14. *Al-Difa'a, Filastin, al-Wahda*, July 17, 1947; quoted in Levenberg, *Military Preparations of the Arab Community*, 47.
15. LCP, David Ben-Gurion interview.
16. NACP 84/350/63/11/5–6, Pinkerton to Marshall, no. 160, May 3, 1948.
17. LCP, David Ben-Gurion interview.
18. Ibid.
19. Morris, *Birth*, 289.
20. "Memories of Palestine," interview with Amina Rifai from Jerusalem, *Guardian*, May 15, 1976.
21. CP III/5/11, Creech Jones to Cunningham, no. 1760, May 1, 1948.
22. Stories from Exile, Ayoub Talhami interview.
23. Hamdi Muhammad Matar, interviewed by author at Amman, Jordan, August 1, 2001.
24. Nazzal, "The Flight of the Palestinian Arabs from Galilee," Muhammad Ibrahim Diyab interview, 470.
25. Haifa, Fatima Husayn al-Jawabri, interviewed by author at Baq'a Camp, Jordan, July 19, 2001.
26. See appendix 1.
27. *Palestine 1948*, in Abu-Sitta, *Palestinian Nakba*; Abu-Lughod, *Transformation of Palestine*, 153-61.
28. GLP, box 211, Suggested Partition Frontiers in Palestine [n.d.].
29. TNA DEFE 4/13 COS (48), 71st meeting, 25/5/48, annex 1.

We have promised to continue fighting and struggling against Israel for our land. They expelled us with their weapons and by frightening us with terrorism.

Na'isa Khalid, Dayr Tarif village

PALMACH COMMANDO, 1948

Causes for Palestinian Arab Flight
November 29, 1947 to May 15, 1948

By including Palestinian testimony, as well as British, Zionist, and other documentary sources, the decisive causes for the Arab population's evacuation can be more accurately determined. These detailed categories describe the reported experiences that caused the Palestinian Arab exodus from their cities, towns, and villages during the civil war. The range of causes is organized in descending order by intensity of violent intimidation.

The cities, towns, and villages are listed alphabetically in their respective subdistrict, followed by the date of depopulation. In the next column, I list the reasons for flight, followed by Morris's assigned causes. The final column indicates the estimated population for each locale in 1948.

1 On-site massacre, atrocities, rape, expulsion by Zionist forces
2 Expulsion orders or transported out by Zionists
3 Direct mortar attacks on civilians, siege, shooting at fleeing Arabs
4 Terror raids, house demolitions, sniping, hostage-taking, looting, destruction of crops and livestock
5 Psychological warfare to promote Arab evacuation: verbal threats of violence, threatening broadcasts, loudspeakers, leaflets, etc.
6 Attack or atrocity in neighboring village or community
7 Fear of impending attack, or fall of neighboring town or village
8 Victims' or witnesses' reports of atrocities, attack, and expulsion
9 Evacuation on Arab orders

Morris assigned the causes for the Palestinian Arabs' abandonment of towns and villages to the following categories.

E Expulsion by Jewish forces
A Abandonment on Arab orders
F Fear of Jewish attack or of being caught up in the fighting
M Military assault on the settlement by Jewish troops
W Haganah/IDF "whispering" campaigns (i.e., psychological warfare geared to obtaining an Arab evacuation)
C Influence of fall of, or exodus from, neighboring town

PALESTINIAN CITIES, TOWNS, AND VILLAGES
DEPOPULATED BY MAY 15, 1948

LOCALE	DATE	CAUSE	MORRIS	POP. 1948
Acre Subdistrict				
1 Acre	5/5-17/1948	1, 3, 5, 6	M	14,280
2 Al-Bassa	5/14/1948	1, 2, 3, 4	M, E	3,422
3 Al-Manshiyya	5/14/1948	3, 4	M	940
4 Al-Sumayriyya	5/14/1948	1, 3, 4, 8	M	882
5 Al-Zib	5/14/1948	1, 2, 3, 4	M	2,216
Baysan Subdistrict				
6 Al-Ashrafiyya	5/12/1948	3, 4	C	267
7 Baysan	5/12/1948	1, 2, 3, 6	M, C, E	6,009
8 Farwana	5/11/1948	3, 4	M	383
9 Al-Fatur	5/12/1948	1, 3	-	128
10 Al-Hamidiyya	5/12/1948	3	C	255
11 Kafr Misr	5/14/1948	4, 5	-	213
12 Khirbat al-Taqa	5/15/1948			868
13 Qumya	3/26/1948	3, 4, 7	F	510
14 Al-Sakhina	5/12/1948		-	615
15 Sirin	4/6/1948	2, 7	A	940
16 Tall al-Shawk	5/12/1948		C	139
17 Al-Tira	4/15/1948	5	W	174
18 Zab'a	5/12/1948		-	197
Beersheba Subdistrict				
19 Al-'Imara	5/13/1948	2, 3, 4	-	46
Gaza Subdistrict				
20 'Arab Suqrir	5/10/1948	3, 4	M	440
21 Barqa	5/13/1948	3	M	1,032
22 Al-Batani al-Gharbi	5/13/1948	3	M	1,137
23 Al-Batani al-Sharqi	5/13/1948	1, 3	M	754
24 Bayt 'Affa	1/10/1948	4		812
25 Bayt Daras	5/1/1948	1, 3, 4	M	3,190
26 Burayr	5/12/1948	1, 3, 4	M	3,178
27 Hulayqat	5/12/1948	6, 7	C	487
28 Kawkaba	5/12/1948	3	C	789
29 Najd	5/13/1948	1, 3, 4	E	719
30 Al-Sawafir al-Gharbiyya	5/10/1948	2, 3, 4		1,195
31 Al-Sawafir al-Shamaliyya	5/10/1948	2, 3, 4		789

| 32 | Al-Sawafir al-Sharqiyya | 5/10/1948 | 2, 3, 4 | F | 1,125 |
| 33 | Simsim | 5/13/1948 | 1, 3, 4 | E | 1,496 |

Haifa Subdistrict

34	Abu Shusha	4/9/1948	1, 2, 3, 4	M	835
35	Abu Zurayq	4/12/1948	1, 2, 3, 4	M, E	638
36	'Arab al-Fuqara'	4/10/1948	1	E	360
37	'Arab al-Ghawarina (Jidru)	4/15/1948	3, 5	W, M	719
38	'Arab al-Nufay'at	4/10/1948	1, 3	E	951
39	'Arab Zahrat al-Dumayri	4/10/1948	1, 3	-	719
40	'Atlit	5/15/1948	1, 3	-	174
41	Balad al-Shaykh	4/25/1948	1, 3, 4	M, C	4,779
42	Barrat Qisarya	5/15/1948	1, 2, 3, 4	F, E	na
43	Bayt Laham	4/17/1948	2, 3	M	429
44	Burayka	5/5/1948	3, 7	C	336
45	Khirbat al-Burj	2/15/1948	1, 2, 4	-	na
46	Al-Butaymat	5/1/1948	3	F	128
47	Daliyat al-Rawha'	3/1/1948	2, 5	W, M	325
48	Khirbat al-Damun	4/30/1948	1, 3	F, M	394
49	Al-Dumayri	4/10/1948	1	E	na
50	Al-Ghubayya al-Fauqa	4/8/1948	3, 8	M	na
51	Al-Ghubayya al-Tahta	4/8/1948	3, 8	M	na
52	Haifa (Arab)	4/21/1948	1, 2, 3, 4	M, A	72,848
53	Hawsha	4/15/1948	1, 3, 4	F	464
54	Al-Jalama	5/1/1948	1	-	na
55	Kabara	4/30/1948	1	M, C	139
56	Al-Kafrayn	4/12/1948	3, 4	M	1,067
57	Khirbat al-Kasayir	4/16/1948	3	M	na
58	Khubbayza	5/12/1948	3	M	336
59	Khirbat Lid (Lid al-'Awadin)	4/9/1948	1, 3	-	742
60	Khirbat al-Manara	3/1/1948	3	M	na
61	Al-Mansi ('Arab Baniha)	4/12/1948	3, 5	M	1,392
62	Khirbat al-Mansura	4/28/1948	1	-	223
63	Al-Naghnaghiyya	4/12/1948	3, 4	M	1,311
64	Qannir	4/25/1948	3, 4	C, F	870
65	Qira wa Qamun	3/1/1948	1	W	476
66	Qisarya (Caesarea)	2/15/1948	1, 2, 3, 4	E	1,114
67	Khirbat Qumbaza	5/15/1948	3	-	na
68	Khirbat Ras 'Ali	4/1/1948	3	-	na
69	Al-Rihaniyya	4/30/1948	1, 2, 3	-	278
70	Sabbarin	5/12/1948	1, 3, 8	M	1,972
71	Khirbat al-Sarkas	4/15/1948	1	E	751
72	Khirbat Sa'sa'	4/28/1948	1, 2, 3	-	151
73	Khirbat al-Shuna	3/15/1948	1	-	na
74	Al-Sindiyana	5/12/1948	2, 3	M	1,450
75	Umm al-Shawf	5/12/1948	1, 3	M	557
76	Umm al-Zinat	5/15/1948	1, 3, 4, 7	-	1,705

77	Wa'arat al-Sarris	April 1948	1	-	220
78	Wadi 'Ara	2/27/1948	1	F	267
79	Waldheim (Umm al-'Amad)	4/17/1948	2, 3	M	302
80	Yajur	4/25/1948	1, 3, 5, 7, 8	M, C	708

Jaffa Subdistrict

81	Al-'Abbasiyya (Al-Yahudiyya)	5/4/1948	1, 3	M	6,554
82	Abu Kishk	3/30/1948	7	F, C	2,204
83	Bayt Dajan	4/25/1948	1, 3	C	4,454
84	Biyar 'Adas	4/12/1948	1, 3, 4	M	348
85	Fajja	5/15/1948	3, 4, 7	W	1,392
86	Al-Haram (Sayyiduna 'Ali)	2/3/1948	1	F	603
87	Ijlil al-Qibliyya (Jalil al-Qibliyya)	4/3/1948		F	545
88	Ijlil al-Shamaliyya	4/3/1948		F	220
89	Jaffa	4/26/1948	3, 4, 5	M	76,920
90	Al-Jammasin al-Gharbi	3/17/1948	3	F	1,253
91	Al-Jammasin al-Sharqi	3/17/1948	3	F	847
92	Jarisha	5/1/1948	1, 4	-	220
93	Kafr 'Ana	4/25/1948	1, 3	M	3,248
94	Al-Khayriyya	4/25/1948	1, 3	M	1,647
95	Al-Mas'udiyya (Summayl)	12/25/1947	1, 3	F	986
96	Al-Mirr (Al-Mahmudiyya)	2/1/1948	3	F	197
97	Al-Muwaylih	12/31/1947	3	-	418
98	Rantiyya	4/28/1948	3	M	684
99	Salama	4/25/1948	3, 4	M	7,807
100	Saqiya	4/25/1948	3	M	1,276
101	Sarona	5/15/1948	3	-	na
102	Al-Sawalima	3/30/1948	4, 5	F, C	928
103	Al-Shaykh Muwannis	3/30/1948	3, 4	M, F	2,239
104	Yazur	5/1/1948	1, 3, 4	C, M	4,675

Jerusalem Subdistrict

105	Bayt Mahsir	5/10/1948	1, 3, 4	M	2,784
106	Bayt Naqquba	4/1/1948	3, 4	M	278
107	Bayt Thul	4/1/1948	4	-	302
108	Dayr Yasin	4/9/1948	1, 2, 3, 4	M, E	708
109	Jerusalem-Qatamon quarter	4/28/1948	3, 4, 5, 8		69,693
110	Lifta	1/1/1948	1, 3, 4, 8	M	2,958
111	Al-Maliha	4/21/1948	3, 4, 8	C, M	2,250
112	Nitaf	4/15/1948	4	-	46
113	Qalunya	4/3/1948	1, 2, 3, 4	M	1,056
114	Al-Qastal	4/3/1948	1, 3, 4	M	104
115	Saris	4/16/1948	1, 3, 8	M	650

Jinin Subdistrict

116 'Ayn al-Mansi	4/12/1948	3	M	104
117 Khirbat al-Jawfa (Mazra'at al-Jawfa)	5/12/1948		C	na
118 Al-Lajjun	4/16/1948	3, 4	M	1,279

Nazareth Subdistrict

119 'Arab al-Subeih	4/19/1948	1, 3	C	na

Al-Ramla Subdistrict

120 Abu al-Fadl ('Arab al-Satariyya)	5/9/1948		C	592
121 Abu Shusha	5/14/1948	1, 3, 4, 8	M	1,009
122 'Aqir	5/6/1948	1, 2, 3, 4	M	2,877
123 Bashshit	5/13/1948	3, 4	M	1,879
124 Khirbat Bayt Far	4/7/1948		-	348
125 Bayt Nabala	5/13/48; 7/48	3, 8	A	2,680
126 Bayt Susin	4/15/1948	3	M	237
127 Bir Salim	5/9/1948	3	M	476
128 Dayr Ayyub	3/6/1948	2, 3, 4, 6, 8	M	371
129 Dayr Muhaysin	4/6/1948	1, 3	M	534
130 Khulda	4/6/1948	3, 4	M	325
131 Al-Maghar	5/15/1948	1, 3, 4	M	1,740
132 Al-Mansura	4/20/1948	3	M	104
133 Al-Mukhayzin	4/30/1948	1, 3	M	232
134 Al-Na'ani	5/14/1948	3, 4, 7	F	1,705
135 Qatra	5/6/1948	1, 3, 4	M, E	1,404
136 Al-Qubab	5/15/1948	3	M	2,297
137 Sarafand al-'Amar	5/20/1948	7	-	2,262
138 Sarafand al-Kharab	4/20/1948	7	F	1,206
139 Saydun	4/6/1948	3	-	244
140 Shahma	5/14/1948	1, 3	C	325
141 Umm Kalkha	4/7/1948		-	70
142 Wadi Hunayn	4/17/1948	3	C	1,879

Safad Subdistrcit

143 Abil al-Qamh	5/10/1948	6, 7	F, C	383
144 'Akbara	5/9/1948	3, 6, 8	-	302
145 'Arab al-Shamalina	5/4/1948	1, 3	M, E	754
146 'Arab Zubayd	4/20/1948	6, 7	F	na
147 'Ayn al-Zaytun	5/2/1948	1, 3, 4	M	951
148 Biriyya	5/2/1948	3, 4	M	278
149 Al-Butayha	5/4/1948	1, 4	-	754
150 Buwayziyya (includes Meis)	5/11/1948	7	C	592

151 Dallata	5/10/1948	3, 4	-	418
152 Al-Dirbashiyya	5/1/1948	3	-	360
153 Al-Dirdara (Mazari' al-Daraja)	4/30/1948	3	-	116
154 Fir'im	5/1/1948	3, 6	M	858
155 Al-Hamra'	5/1/1948	3	F, M	na
156 Hunin (Hula and Udeisa)	5/3/1948	1, 3	F, E	1,879
157 Al-Husayniyya	4/21/1948	1, 3, 4	C	394
158 Jahula	5/1/1948	3	-	487
159 Al-Ja'una	5/9/1948	1, 6, 7	C	1,334
160 Jubb Yusuf ('Arab al-Suyyad)	5/4/1948	1, 3	M, E	197
161 Khirbat Karraza	5/4/1948	3	-	na
162 Al-Khalisa	5/11/1948	3, 7	C,W	2,134
163 Khiyam al-Walid	5/1/1948	6, 7	F	325
164 Kirad al-Baqqara	4/22/1948	1	C	418
165 Kirad al-Ghannama	4/22/1948	1	C	406
166 Madahil	4/30/1948	6, 7	F	na
167 Mansurat al-Khayt	1/18/1948	1, 3, 4	M	232
168 Mirun	5/10/1948		C	336
169 Mughr al-Khayt	5/2/1948	3	M	568
170 Al-Na'ima	5/14/1948		C	1,195
171 Qabba'a	5/4/1948	3	M	480
172 Qaditta	5/11/1948	6, 7	C	278
173 Al-Qudayriyya	5/4/1948	1, 3	M, E	452
174 Safad (Arab)	5/11/1948	1, 2, 3, 7, 8	M	11,055
175 Al-Sammu'i	5/12/1948		C	360
176 Al-Sanbariyya	5/1/1948	3	-	151
177 Al-Shawka al-Tahta	5/14/1948		F	232
178 Taytaba	5/1/1948	3, 6, 7	F	615
179 Tulayl	4/28/1948	3	-	394
180 Al-'Ulmaniyya	4/20/1948	3	M	302
181 Al-'Urayfiyya	4/1/1948	3	-	na
182 Al-Wayziyya	5/1/1948	3	-	116
183 Yarda	4/1/1948	3	-	23
184 Al-Zahiriyya al-Tahta	5/10/1948	6, 7, 8	C	406
185 Al-Zanghariyya (Zuhluq)	5/4/1948	1, 3	M, E	974
186 Al-Zuq al-Tahtani	5/11/1948		C	1,218

Tiberias Subdistrict

187 'Awlam ('Ulam)	5/12/1948	3	A	835
188 Al-Dalhamiyya	4/15/1948	2	-	476
189 Ghuwayr Abu Shusha	4/21/1948	2, 3, 4	M, C	1,438
190 Hadatha	5/12/1948	1, 3, 5	A	603
191 Kafr Sabt	4/22/1948	3	C	557
192 Ma'dhar	5/12/1948	5, 8	A	557
193 Al-Majdal	4/22/1948	3	M, C	418
194 Al-Manara ('Arab al-Manara)	3/1/1948	1, 3, 5	M	568
195 Al-Manshiyya (Manshiyyat Samakh)	3/3/1948	1, 3	-	na

196 Al-Mansura	5/10/1948	3	-	2,482
197 Nasir al-Din	4/12/1948	1, 3	M, C, F	104
198 Al-Nuqayb (al-Naqib)	5/14/1948	1, 3	E	371
199 Samakh	4/28/1948	3, 7, 8	M	4,014
200 Al-Samakiyya	5/4/1948	1, 3	-	441
201 Al-Samra	4/21/1948	3	C	336
202 Al-Shajara	5/6/1948	3	M	893
203 Al-Tabigha (Tall al-Hunud)	5/4/1948	1, 3, 4	-	383
204 Tiberias (Arab)	4/18/1948	1, 3, 5, 7, 8	M	6,160
205 Al-'Ubaydiyya	3/3/1948	1, 3	F	1,009
206 Wadi al-Hamam	4/22/1948		-	na
207 Al-Wa'ra al-Sawda' (Arab al-Mawas)	4/18/1948	1, 3	-	2,169
208 Yaquq	5/1/1948	7	-	244

Tulkarm Subdistrict

209 Khirbat Bayt Lid	4/5/1948	2, 7, 8	F	534
210 Bayyarat Hannun	3/31/1948	1	-	na
211 Birket Ramadan (Wakf Khirbat Rahman)	4/20/1948		-	na
212 Fardisya	4/1/1948	1	-	23
213 Ghabat Kafr Sur	5/15/1948	3	-	858
214 Khirbat al-Jalama	3/1/1948	1	-	81
215 Kafr Saba	5/15/1948	3	M	1,473
216 Khirbat al-Majdal	3/1/1948		-	na
217 Khirbat al-Manshiyya	4/15/1948	1, 3, 4, 5	F	302
218 Miska	4/20/1948	2 , 3	E	1,021
219 Raml Zayta (Khirbat Qazaza)	3/15/1948	1, 3	-	162
220 Tabsur (Khirbat 'Azzun)	4/3/1948	2	F, E	na
221 Umm Khalid	3/20/1948	3, 4	-	1,125
222 Wadi al-Hawarith	3/15/1948	3, 5	M, F	2,552
223 Wadi Qabbani	3/1/1948	1	-	371
224 Khirbat Zababida	5/15/1948	1	-	na
225 Khirbat Zalafa	4/15/1948	5, 7	F	244
				441,961

Research Methodology and Primary Sources

The research methodology used for this book was "from the ground up." I approached the subject mostly from the perspective of ordinary participants and eyewitnesses rather than from that of decision makers. I used several types of primary sources. Among the most important sources for the final mandate period are British military records and recollections. British field forces deployed across Palestine prepared periodic reports. Those I reviewed include the quarterly historical reports of Middle East Land Forces and British Troops Headquarters located in Haifa, Jaffa, Tel Aviv, and Sarafand-Lydda. I also consulted British command and garrison records, including those of the Gaza Subdistrict, Sixth Airborne Division, and North and South Palestine, as well as reports by brigades that served in Palestine.[1] These underutilized War Office records contain up-to-the-minute situation reports, intelligence assessments, and daily incident reports crucial for a ground-level understanding of events.

Several unpublished British primary sources of high-level military officials provided insight into their decision making. These included the private papers and recorded interviews of General Harold Pyman, chief of staff of Middle East Land Forces (MELF), Lieutenant General Gordon H. MacMillan, general officer commanding (GOC) in Palestine, and Major General Hugh C. Stockwell, GOC Sixth Airborne Division in Haifa. Despite these British commanders' presence and participation in civil war events, their extensive observations have been neglected. I also reviewed British narrations found in archival records and mandate government officials' memoirs, interviews, and private papers held in the National Archives in Kew[2] as well as in various British libraries and research institutes.

Contemporary Zionist and Palestinian Arab narratives and history are drawn from a variety of sources. Zionist perspectives are found in published Israeli archival documents dating to prestate activities. I also used memoirs, oral histories, and secondary works, particularly those of the Israeli "new historians." Palestinian perspectives and experiences came from original and geographically extensive oral-history interviews with Palestinian refugees of 1948 that I collected. I supplemented these with existing published oral testimonies, as well as published research of Arab historians, primarily Palestinian.

These perspectives and related sources are further complemented and supported by documents and visual sources from U.S. and U.N. archives as well as the documentary record of other organizations involved in humanitarian relief work during the 1948 war. These include the Red Cross and the American Friends Service Committee. I also consulted the personal papers of the author Larry Collins, held at Georgetown University. These contain extensive interviews with primary participants from all relevant backgrounds as well as related research material collated for the popular history *O Jerusalem!*, which Collins coauthored with fellow journalist Dominique Lapierre. Additional sources include news photographs and newsreels from the U.S. Archives and the Library of Congress, along with audio tapes and films produced by journalists and independent filmmakers.

Oral History Interviews: Method and Selection

Palestinian documentation from the civil war period is scarce, making Palestinian oral history necessary for a more complete narrative of events. In the summer and fall of 2001, I traveled to Jordan and Lebanon to conduct interviews with Palestinian Arabs displaced from their homes and lands during the 1948 civil war. This research was sponsored by the Council of American Overseas Research Centers (CAORC). The region was especially tense due to the uprising raging in the West Bank and Gaza since September 2000, which became known as the al-Aqsa Intifada. Due to the fighting, I had to cancel planned research in the occupied West Bank and Gaza, as well as in Israel. Also, the later phase of research occurred in the wake of the September 11, 2001 terrorist attacks on the United States. The prevailing political climate presented challenges to conducting research in the Middle East. I nevertheless was able to contact Palestinians from a great number of villages and towns who had detailed memories of 1948.

The actual interview process as well as the initial groundwork to record interviews was time-consuming. Written permission was required from Jordan's Department of Palestinian Affairs for research work inside the Palestinian refugee camps. Meeting this challenge and others were facilitated by three institutions in Amman and many individuals: the Council of American Overseas Research Centers, the Centre d'Etudes et de Recherches sur le Moyen-Orient Contemporain (CERMOC), and the Jordanian Women's Union. Palestinian sociologist Afaf al-Jabiri was an invaluable assistant in this field research. Her training, experience, and knowledge of the refugee camps, particularly Baq'a Camp, where she was raised, facilitated navigation of the expansive camps and gave me greater credibility and acceptance.

The criteria established for selecting interviewees were as follows: the individual had to have resided within the borders of mandate Palestine at a locale depopulated during the civil war, that is, before May 15, 1948 (see appendix 1 for the list of locales). The interviewee had to have been old enough to be aware of events, and preferably an adult. In most cases, the interviewee was employed or married with children during the war. Some Palestinians interviewed were children in 1948. It became apparent in comparing interviews that even children had vivid and detailed recollections, albeit occasionally confusing the chronology of events, as did some of the adults.

Interview candidates were not so much chosen as found. Local inhabitants of a refugee camp or neighborhood were questioned about the village and town origins of those living in the immediate surroundings. When a prospective interviewee was identified through this process, the two-person interview team, composed of my assistant and me, appeared unannounced at the home (and sometimes workplace), explained the research, and asked for an interview and permission to record the session.

The interviews usually evolved into intimate personal dialogues between the interviewee and the interviewer. Emotional reactions to the subject matter varied by individual. Sometimes narratives were delivered in a surprisingly straightforward and matter-of-fact tone, even while the interviewee recounted having personally witnessed atrocities. At other times, recollections were delivered emotionally with tears and breaks in the narrative.

To allow the informant to be evaluated with the few other studies of Palestinian displacement that incorporated oral histories, I developed a standard list of questions on the war and the exodus. These were based on a review of the documentary record, as well as Nafez Nazzal's 1978 study *The Palestinian Exodus from Galilee, 1948,* and Peter Dodd and Halim Barakat's 1968 book *River without Bridges: A Study of the Exodus of the 1967 Palestinian Arab Refugees.* Both of these works employed questionnaires to obtain oral testimony from Palestinian refugees concerning the primary factors for their displacement during the 1948 and 1967 wars, respectively. More specific and detailed questions for certain locales were added when the documentary record suggested special circumstances. The guiding questionnaire can be found in appendix 3.

Of the approximately 225 known locales that fell to Zionist forces before May 15, 1948, I conducted interviews with Palestinian Arabs from 75. These Palestinians were living dispersed in more than ten refugee camps throughout Jordan, as well as several "unofficial" camps, and in numerous neighborhoods of Amman and other Jordanian cities. It was frequently impossible to conduct interviews with more than one eyewitness from each depopulated village or town, typically because of the breadth of dispersion and the declining numbers of the 1948 refugee generation. In Lebanon, I also conducted interviews in two camps: Mar Elias in Beirut and 'Ayn al-Hilwa in Sidon. Refugees living in these camps generally were originally from the Galilee, the northern part of Palestine. Interviews using the same methodology as that employed in Jordan were recorded in these camps. Oroub El-Abed, a Jordanian-Palestinian researcher, and Ibtisam al-Khalil, a Palestinian employee with the National Institute of Social Care and Vocational Training, located in 'Ayn al-Hilwa camp, assisted with the interviews in Lebanon. In total, I recorded approximately 135 original interviews.

Oral History as a Necessary Methodology

Palestinian oral history is an essential source of this book due to a number of factors, not least of which is the prevailing illiteracy of the old community. For illiterate and less-developed societies, oral history may be the only choice for preserving a full history. Indeed, not using oral narratives may represent a decision not to record history at all.[3] Sixty-six percent of the Palestinian Arab population in 1944 was agrarian, with a literacy rate of only 15 percent when last officially estimated in 1937.[4] On this basis alone, oral history is necessary to obtain a direct Palestinian perspective of that period's events.

Oral history also helps redress biases in recorded history. Rashid Khalidi has suggested that the modern history of Palestine has been complicated by "inherent historical biases." He argues with considerable logic that "the views and exploits of those able to read and write are perhaps naturally more frequently recorded by historians, with their tendency to favor written records, than those of the illiterate."[5]

There are other causes for the relative rarity of Palestinian documentary history aside from endemic illiteracy. The Palestinian Arabs never secured their own government and therefore had no state papers in 1948. Contemporary Palestinian Arab documentary sources are thus not extensive, and few organized and methodical studies based on Palestinian Arab eyewitnesses exist. Arab Higher Committee (AHC) reports were destroyed during the war, except for a small fraction that were captured and are held in the Israel state archives.[6] In addition, the archives of Arab governments involved in the 1948 war remain closed to researchers. Most letters, diaries, and contemporary Palestinian Arab personal papers were destroyed or seized during the war, or they were left behind and lost by fleeing refugees. Some Palestinian Arab newspapers ceased to operate in mid-1948, and Palestinian Arab documentation that does exist is scattered widely among the diaspora population.

The political instability and repression faced by the dispersed Palestinian communities since 1948 have also hindered research and studies. "The unsettled situation of the Palestinian people since 1948," writes Khalidi, "whether under occupation or in the diaspora, has meant that when Palestinian archives, research institutions and universities could be created, they were often denied the stability, continuity, and possibilities for long-term planning necessary to provide the requisite support for sustained research and scholarship."[7] The Palestine Liberation Organization's (PLO) Research Center and the Institute for Palestine Studies (IPS), founded in Beirut in the mid-1960s, nevertheless assembled substantial documentary collections. (Israeli occupying forces seized the PLO Center's archives during the 1982 invasion of Lebanon. Although the Israelis returned the archives in 1983, some remain inaccessible to researchers.)[8] Nevertheless, given the limitations engendered by Palestinian Arab society and history, it is doubtful that what documentation exists could fill the historical gaps. Therefore, in the absence of a rich and systematically available source of contemporary Palestinian documentary records, oral interviews with the waning population of 1948 refugees remain a natural and critical source for constructing a more comprehensive narrative of the war.

Evidentiary Value of Oral History

Oral history is defined as "primary source material obtained by recording the spoken words . . . of persons deemed to harbor hitherto unavailable information worth preserving."[9] Increasingly, oral history has gained acceptance as a respected method to record history, and it is afforded substantial weight as an evidentiary tool. Oral tradition among underdeveloped societies is a well-established and time-honored means of preserving and transmitting historical knowledge from one generation to another.[10] Oral-history interviews additionally provide access to the history of "people on the margins: workers, women, indigenous peoples, ethnic minorities, and members of other oppressed or marginalized groups," notes historian Alistair Thomson.[11]

The intrinsic value of oral history is in fact also recognized and sought to contribute to the preservation of epic and complex events, even in cases that are otherwise well-documented. The U.S. Congress, for example, enacted a law requiring the Library of Congress to collect and preserve oral histories from the nation's veterans. Oral history is of such importance in the collection and memorialization of the Holocaust that the U.S. Holocaust Memorial Museum has a separate Department of Oral History dedicated solely to preserving Holocaust testimonies as primary sources.[12]

The validity of oral history is not undermined by the logical or inherent weaknesses in accuracy due to time and bias. Oral historians generally acknowledge certain limitations arising from the use of oral history in research. Louis Starr notes that "memory is fallible, ego distorts and contradictions sometimes go unresolved." Nevertheless, Starr compellingly answers critics of oral history that "problems of evaluation are not markedly different from those inherent in the use of letters, diaries, and other primary sources. . . . the scholar must test the evidence in an oral history memoir for internal consistency and, whenever possible, by corroboration from other sources, often including the oral history memoirs of others on the same topic."[13]

The evidentiary value of interviews with Palestinian refugees who were eyewitnesses to the events of the civil war period is borne out by the mutually supportive consistency of their recollections. The similarity in individual narratives, by Palestinian Arabs from the same locales, proved striking. The Palestinian collective memory recalls similar descriptive details regarding Zionist military actions that were experienced. The credibility and reliability of these recollections is further strengthened by the fact that the testimonies reflect a great deal of cross-consistency, despite a lack of contact between villagers or townsmen due to their vast geographic dispersal.

It is also significant that the oral histories hold up well against the documentary record. The collected Palestinian narratives correlate frequently with available Israeli, U.S., U.N. and British documentary records, including official government accounts and contemporary news sources not widely available to the refugees. In addition, these recently obtained oral-history accounts are consistent with others—repeating broadly the same information as oral interviews conducted more than 30 years ago by other historians and researchers.

Benny Morris cites the issue of accuracy as a reason for not using such interviews in his 1987 study, *The Birth of the Palestinian Refugee Problem, 1947–1949*. But he implicitly concedes a measure of the accuracy and usefulness of oral history—despite his expressed lack of confidence in interviews—by repeatedly relying on Nafez Nazzal's oral interviews with Arab refugees from the Galilee.[14] In fact, regarding certain refugee recollections, Morris acknowledges that "taken as a whole, they probably give a good idea of the reality."[15] Even though Morris accepts that refugee recollections can reflect reality, he nonetheless famously concludes—based on a heavy reliance of declassified Israeli documents and meager acknowledgement of the refugees' experience—that the Palestinian refugees were "born of war, not by design."[16] This book has shown, however, that when Palestinian testimony is introduced into a critical examination of civil war events, Morris's conclusion of an "accidental" genesis of the refugees is not supported by his own evidence and is definitively refuted by Palestinian Arab oral testimony.

Primary and Secondary Sources

Throughout this book, I have compared data from the Palestinian interviews I collected, in conjunction with broad archival research, to the findings in Morris's study and with data from Nafez Nazzal's doctoral dissertation, "The Flight of the Palestinian Arabs from Galilee." Other secondary sources consulted for comparison and factual background were Walid Khalidi's *All That Remains: The Palestinian Villages Occupied and Depopulated by Israel in 1948*, which incorporates and compares the above-cited works, and also reviews other primary sources, including the *New York Times, Filastin* (the leading Palestinian Arabic daily), *Sefer Toldot Hahaganah* (*The History of the Haganah*), and 'Arif al-'Arif's *Al-Nakba* (*The Catastrophe*).[17] These latter works I in turn compared with Salman Abu-Sitta's *The Palestinian Nakba, 1948: The Register of Depopulated Localities and Towns*, which compares the above-mentioned sources, along with original research.

The analysis of all these sources confirms that in numerous cases, the reasons that Palestinian Arabs gave for fleeing their homes differ significantly from what Morris concluded in his study. When viewed in light of other sources (including, at times, Morris's own data), Palestinian Arab testimony is supported, if not wholly corroborated, by other sources. A comparison of my conclusions with those of Morris detailing the causes for the depopulation of each Arab population locale during the civil war period is provided in appendix 1.

The Palestinian Arabs' expulsion during the 1948 civil war was experienced under differing local conditions by a largely illiterate community in the throes of social breakdown. With little or no Palestinian documentary record for this time period, oral history is the sole means of reconstructing the community's history. Palestinian oral interviews in the aggregate are supported by a wealth of independent sources, are internally and externally consistent, and provide a credible means of contributing to the reconstruction of events. These recollections not only withstand critical analysis but can be augmented and subjected to cross-examination as long as Palestinians from the 1948 generation remain and we are willing to seek out their narratives. Whether or not such efforts continue to be undertaken, this study's newly collected evidence contributes to a more precise understanding of the relatively undocumented experience of the Palestinian refugees forcibly displaced during the civil war period, and refines the prevailing historical record of the roots of a major regional conflict.

⚬

1. Quarterly historical reports, record group TNA WO 261, replaced official war diaries in 1946.
2. The Public Record Office (PRO) and the Historical Manuscripts Commission (HMC) joined to form the National Archives of the United Kingdom (TNA) on April 2, 2003.
3. Ellen Fleischmann, "Crossing the Boundaries of History: Exploring Oral History in Researching Palestinian Women in the Mandate Period," *Women's History Review* 5.3 (1996): 1.
4. *Survey of Palestine*, 697. See also A. L. Tibawai, *Arab Education in Mandatory Palestine: A Study of Three Decades of British Administration* (London: Luzac, 1956), 225. The Palestine Department of Education conducted no literacy tests after 1932 (222). The estimate of Arab literacy was prepared for the 1937 Royal Commission.
5. Rashid Khalidi, *Palestinian Identity: The Construction of Modern National Consciousness* (New York: Columbia University Press, 1997), 89. See also Fleischmann, "Crossing the Boundaries of History," 1; and Swedenburg, *Memories of Revolt.*
6. Levenberg, *Military Preparations of the Arab Community in Palestine*, x.

7. Khalidi, *Palestinian Identity*, 89. Nazzal, "The Flight of the Palestinian Arabs from Galilee." Nazzal consulted the PLO and IPS archives in Beirut for his dissertation research prior to the 1982 war in Lebanon.

8. Khalidi, *Palestinian Identity*, 90.

9. Louis Starr, "Oral History," in *Oral History: An Interdisciplinary Anthology*, ed. David K. Dunaway and Willa K. Baum (Nashville, Tenn.: American Association for State and Local History, 1984), 4.

10. Anthony Seldon and Joanna Pappworth, *By Word of Mouth: Elite Oral History* (London: Methuen, 1983), 49–50; Gary Okihiro, "Oral History and the Writing of Ethnic History," in Dunaway, *Oral History*, 206.

11. Alistair Thomson, "Fifty Years On: An International Perspective on Oral History," *Journal of American History* 85.2 (1998): 584.

12. *Department of Oral History Staff, Oral History Interview Guidelines* (Washington, D.C.: United States Holocaust Memorial Museum, 1998), ii.

13. Starr, *Oral History*, 5.

14. Nafez Nazzal, "Flight of the Palestinian Arabs."

15. Morris, *Birth*, 2, 304n13.

16. Ibid., 286.

17. Khalidi, *All That Remains*, xiii.

Interview Questions

The 1948 War

1. How did you get news in the village?
2. What did you hear about the war?
3. What was your response?
4. Did you expect the war to come to your village?
5. What happened in your village during the war? Was it disrupted, occupied, bombed, strafed? What date, time and for how long?
6. Do you know of anyone killed or wounded in your village during the war? Were they relatives?
7. Did you see the Zionists (soldiers or civilians) in your village? If not, what did you hear about them and from whom? If yes, where did you see them?
8. How many were they? How did they come to your village? Which direction and what means of transportation? Were you surprised? Why?
9. What did they do in your village?
10. What preparations did your village make for the war? (arms, supplies, food).
11. Did you have any arms or military training? Where did you obtain them?
12. Do you know of anyone in your village who had arms or military training? Where did they get them?
13. Who was responsible for your protection? Were they members of the Arab Liberation Army? Where were they stationed? How many were they? What arms did they have?
14. Did anyone give you instructions about what to do if attacked?
15. Did you hear of any instructions?

THE EXODUS

16. When did you leave? What date and what time?
17. Was this the first time you had left your home?
18. Did you leave alone? Who left with you?
19. Did you leave any of your relatives behind?
20. Did any of your relatives leave before you? Why?
21. Did others leave a member of their family behind?
22. Did anyone in the village leave before you? Why?
23. Do you know of anyone who left the village after you did?
24. Do you know of anyone who remained in the village permanently?
25. Why did you leave?
26. What did you take with you when you left? Why?
27. What did others take? Why?
28. Where did you go? Why did you choose that place?
29. How far was it? How long did it take you to get there?
30. Where and how long did you stay? Why?
31. What did you do there?
32. Did you go back to your village? How long did you stay there?
    What did you do there?
33. Why didn't you stay in the village?
34. What did you do next?

BIOGRAPHICAL NOTES

Allon (Paicovitch) Yigal (1918–80), b. Kfar Tavor, Palestine. Palmach commander 1945–48, OC Operation Yiftah, April–May 1948.

Al-'Arif, 'Arif (1892–1973), b. Palestine. Chief secretary to King Abdullah.

Attlee, Clement Richard (1883–1967). Labor MP, 1922–55. Leader of the Labor Party, 1935–55. British prime minister, 1945–51.

Azzam, Pasha, 'Abd al-Rahman (1893–1976). Secretary general of the Arab League.

Ben-Gurion (Gruen), David (1886–1973), b. Poland. Secretary general of the Histradut, 1921–35; Mapai leader; chairman, Jewish Agency Executive, 1935–48; prime minister of Israel and minister of defense, 1948–53 and 1955–63.

Bevin, Ernest (1881–1951). General secretary of transport and General Workers Union, 1921–40; Labor MP, 1940–51; minister of Labor and National Service, 1940–45; foreign secretary, 1945–51.

Cadogan, Sir Alexander George Montagu (1884–1968). Permanent undersecretary of the Foreign Office, 1938–46; permanent U.N. representative, 1946–50.

Carmel (Zalizky), Moshe (1911–2002), b. Minsk Mazowiecki, Poland. OC Haganah's Haifa District, 1947; OC Carmeli Brigade, April–May 1948.

Clayton, Brigadier Sir Iltyd Nicholl (1886–1955). Arab affairs adviser to the minister of state, Cairo, 1943–45; head of the British Middle East Office (BMEO), 1945–48.

Cohen, Aharon (1910–80) b. Bessarabia. Director of Mapam and member of Mapam political committee, 1948–49.

Cunningham, General Sir Alan Gordon (1887–1983). GOC Eighth Army in North Africa, World War II; high commissioner of Palestine and Transjordan, November 1945 until May 14, 1948.

Danin, Ezra (1903–85), b. Jaffa. Shai Arab section founder, 1940; Arab affairs advisor to the Jewish Agency's political department, 1940–48.

D'Arcy, Lieutenant General John Conyers (1894–1966). GOC Palestine, 1944–46.

Dawson, Air Chief Marshal Sir Walter Lloyd (1902–1994). Air officer commanding, Levant, 1946–48.

Elath (Epstein), Eliahu (1903–90). b. Ukraine. Jewish Agency U.S. representative, 1945–48.

Glubb, Lieutenant General Sir John Bagot (1897–1986). Posted to the Arab Legion in Transjordan, 1930; Arab Legion commander, 1939.

Gurney, Sir Henry Lovell Goldsworthy (1898–1951). Chief secretary, Palestine government, 1946–48.

Al-Khalidi, Dr. Husayn Fakhri (1894–1962), b. Jerusalem, Palestine. Mayor of Jerusalem 1934–37; member of Arab Higher Committee 1936–37, 1946–48.

Ibn al-Husayn, Abdullah (1882–1951), b. Makkah. Emir (1921–1946) and king (1946–1951) of Transjordan.

Al-Husayni, 'Abd al-Qadir (1907–1948), b. Jerusalem, Palestine. Led Arab irregular militias during 1947–48. Killed during the April 1948 battle for al-Qastal.

Al-Husayni, Haj Amin (c. 1895/1897–1970), b. Jerusalem, Palestine. Mufti of Jerusalem, 1921; Supreme Muslim Council president, 1922–37; president, Arab Higher Committee from 1936.

Jones, Arthur Creech (1891–1964). Labor MP, 1935–50; parliamentary undersecretary, Colonial Office, August 1945 to October 1946; colonial secretary 1946–50.

Kirkbride, Sir Alec Seath (1897–1978). District commissioner, Acre and Galilee District, Palestine, 1937–38; British resident, Amman, 1939–46; minister, Transjordan, 1946–51.

Lippincott, Aubrey. U.S. consul general in Haifa.

Macatee, Robert B. U.S. consul general in Jerusalem.

MacMillan, General Sir Gordon Holmes Alexander (1897–1986). GOC Palestine, 1947–48.

Mardam, Jamil (1894–1960). Prime minister of Syria, December 1946–48.

Meir (Meyerson), Golda (1898–1978), b. Russia. Head of the Histradut's political department, 1936–46; director Jewish Agency's Political Department in Jerusalem, 1948.

Montgomery of Alamein, First Viscount Field Marshal Sir Bernard Law (1887–1977). Chief of the Imperial General Staff, 1946–48.

Murray, General Sir Horatius (1903–?). First Infantry Division 1947–50, Palestine.

Nelson, Major General (Eustace) **Sir John** (Blois) (1912–93). Commander First Guards Parachute Battalion, Palestine, 1946–48.

Pinkerton, Lowell. U.S. consul in Lebanon.

Pyman, General Sir Harold English (1908–71). Chief of staff, general headquarters, Middle East Land Forces, December 1946 to July 1949.

Al-Quwatly, Shukri (1891–1967). President of Syria, 1943 to March 1949.

Al-Qawuqji, Fawzi (1890–1977). Commander of the Arab Liberation Army.

Sasson, (Eliahu) Elias (1902–78), b. Syria. Director of the Jewish Agency's Arab section of the political department, 1939–48.

Sharett (Shertok), Moshe (1894–1965), b. Russia. Head of the Jewish Agency's political department, 1933–48; foreign minister of Israel, 1948–56; prime minister, 1954–55.

Shiloah (Zaslani), Reuven (1909–59), b. Jerusalem. Assistant head of the Histradut's Arab section, 1933–36; intelligence officer in the Jewish Agency's political department and liaison officer with the British forces in Palestine, 1936–48. Held peace talks with King Abdullah, 1948–51.

Shinwell, Baron Emanuel (1884–1986). British secretary of state for war, 1947–50.

Shimoni, Yaacov (1915–97), b. Berlin. Served with Shai, 1941–45. Member of the Jewish Agency's political department's Arab section, 1945–48.

Stockwell, General Sir Hugh Charles (1903–1986). Commander, Sixth Airborne Division Palestine, 1947–48 based in Haifa.

Wasson, Thomas C. (1897–1948). U.S. consul general in Jerusalem.

Weitz, Joseph (1890–1972) b. Poland. Director of Jewish National Fund (JNF) Lands Department/Development (1890-1972), Division, 1932–67; Member of Arab Affairs Committee of National Institutions, 1940s; JNF representative to the committee of directorates of the National Institutions, 1940s; chairman of the first and second Transfer Committees, 1948–49; chairman Negev committee, 1948.

Weizmann, Chaim (1874–1952), b. Russia. Negotiated the Balfour Declaration, 1917; member of Zionist Commission to Palestine, 1918; signatory of the Faisal-Weizmann Agreement, 1919; president of the World Zionist Organization, 1920–31 and 1935–46; first president of Israel, 1949–52.

Wingate, Major General Orde Charles (1903–44). Palestine and Transjordan, 1936–39. Trainer of Haganah night patrols during the Arab Revolt.

Yadin (Sukenik), Yigael (1917–85), b. Jerusalem. OC Haganah operations, 1944 and 1947 to May 1948.

Zisling, Aharon (1901–64), b. Russia. Ahdut Ha'avodah leader; minister of agriculture (Mapam), 1948–49.

PERMISSIONS

The front and back cover photographs and photograph 15 are from the Library of Congress Prints and Photographs Division. The Institute of Palestine Studies, Beirut, granted permission to reprint photographs 2 and 4 from *Before Their Diaspora: A Photographic History of the Palestinians, 1876–1948*, by Walid Khalidi, © 1991, The Institute for Palestine Studies. All other photographs are from the U.S. National Archives, College Park, Maryland, Still Pictures Unit.

The English translation of the stanza from Badir Shakir al-Sayyab's poem "Caravan of the Wretched," on page viii, is from Khalid Abdullah Sulaiman Mohammad, "The Influence of the Political Situation in Palestine on Arabic Poetry from 1917–1973," PhD diss., University of London, School of Oriental and African Studies, 1982.

The maps are composites based on U.S., U.K., and U.N. archival maps and my research. They were created by graphic artist Alex McDonald.

I also acknowledge the *Arab World Geographer* and *Holy Land Studies* journals, which previously published sections of two chapters.

Every effort was made to contact copyright holders. The publisher will correct in future editions any errors or omissions.

BIBLIOGRAPHY

PRIMARY SOURCES

ENGLAND

Friends Service Committee, London
Imperial War Museum, London. Private Papers:
    Lieutenant Colonel C. R. W. Norman (NP)
Liddell Hart Centre for Military Archives, Kings College, University of London
Private Papers:
    Major General Charles Whish Dunbar
    Captain Sir Basil Henry Liddell Hart
    Major General Sir John Nelson
    General Sir Harold English Pyman (PP)
    Colonel Robert Colin Russell Stevenson
    Lieutenant General Sir Hugh Charles Stockwell Papers (SP)
The National Archives of the United Kingdom (TNA), Kew. Record Groups:
    Air Ministry (AIR)
    Cabinet (CAB)
    Colonial Office (CO)
    Ministry of Defence (DEFE)
    Foreign Office (FO)
    Prime Minister Office (PREM)
    War Office (WO)

St. Antony's College, Oxford, Middle East Centre Archives (MECA),
Private Papers:
    Sir Alan Cunningham Papers (CP)
    Susanna Emery, English High School, Haifa (EP)
    Sir John Fletcher-Cooke
    W. V. Fuller, District Commissioner Lydda (FP)
    Sir John Glubb Pasha (GLP)
    Sir Henry Gurney (GP)
    Jerusalem and East Mission Papers (JEM)
    Sir Donald MacGillivray
    Brigadier General Angus McNeil
    Elizabeth Monroe (EMP)
    Miss Dorothy Blanche Morgan (MP)
    Thames Television (TT), Interview transcripts with 1948 war participants for
        a documentary series on the Palestine Mandate, 1976.

UNITED STATES

American Friends Service Committee Archive (AFSC), Philadelphia
Georgetown University, Special Collections
    Larry Collins Papers (LCP)
    Foreign Service Oral History Collection
U.N. Archives (UN), New York.
    DAG 13.3.1.0:1, Missions and Commissions, U.N. Palestine Commission
    DAG 13.3.3.0:12, Missions and Commissions, Ralph Bunche Papers
    S 0157, Executive Office Secretary General, Missions and Commissions
    S 0158, Executive Assistant to the Secretary General, U.N. Mediator for
        Palestine
    S 0453-003, U.N. Palestine Commission, Advance Party Communications
    S 0453-0013, Refugees
    S 0455-0058, Arab Losses in Palestine
U.S. National Archives, College Park, Maryland (NACP)
    Military Records:
    RG 38 Records of the Office of the Chief of Naval Operations,
        Naval Intelligence
    RG 218 Records of the U.S. Joint Chiefs of Staff, Chairman's, Geographic
    RG 319 Army Staff Plans and Operations Division, G2 Intelligence
    Civilian Records:
    RG 43 United States Participation in International Conferences
    RG 59 General Records of the Department of State
    RG 84 Foreign Service, Department of State: Amman, Cairo, Damascus,
        Haifa, Jerusalem, London
    RG 306 NT *New York Times* Photos, Paris Bureau

CORRESPONDENCE WITH AUTHOR
Palestine Police, e-correspondence 1999–2001
Royal Marines, e-correspondence 2001
Dallata, Qassim Muhammad Hamid, 2001

INTERVIEWS WITH AUTHOR
Jordan
Matar Saqir, UNRWA, Public Information Officer, Amman, July 12, 2001

Baysan Subdistrict
Baysan, Ma'susih 'Abd al-Rahman al-Naqqash, Hashmiyya, Zarka, August 8, 2001
Qumya, Ayshi Mahmud Khalid, Irbid Camp, September 24, 2001
Sirin, Fatma al-Mahir, Irbid Camp, September 24, 2001

Beersheba Subdistrict
Beersheba, Halimi Abu Jabir, Baq'a Camp, July 26, 2001
Sar'a, Fatma Hasan Safi, Baq'a Camp, July 26, 2001
Al-'Imara, Muhammad Abu Susin, Jarash Camp, September 3, 2001

Gaza Subdistrict
Bayt 'Affa, Musallam 'Ajid Wishah, Baq'a Camp, July 23, 2001
Yasur, 'Ali Hasan al-Muhtasib, Baq'a Camp, July 23, 2001
Hirbiya, Samid Khaddura Mustafa al-Khatib, Jabal Taj, Amman, August 1, 2001
Najd, Abu Muhammad, Hittin Camp, August 5, 2001
Najd, Umm Muhammad, Hittin Camp, August 5, 2001
Hulayqat, Ibrahim Salim, Hittin Camp, August 7, 2001
Kawkaba, Jamila 'Abd al-Qadir Ahmad, Hittin Camp, Jordan, August 7, 2001
Burayr, 'Abd al-Rahman al-'Alawi, Hittin Camp, August 8, 2001
Al-Batani al-Gharbi, Umm Khalid, Jabal al-Amir Faysal, Zarka, August 9, 2001
Al-Sawafir al-Sharqiyya, Ramadan 'Abdullah al-Bahsi, Hittin Camp, August 11, 2001
Bayt Daras, Muhammad, Hittin Camp, August 11, 2001
Al-Batani al-Sharqi, Muhammad 'Ali 'Abd al-Qadir Muslih, Jarash Camp, September 3, 2001
Bayt Daras, Muhammad Sa'id Muhammad Jabir, Jarash Camp, September 3, 2001
Al-Sawafir al-Shamaliyya, Shaykh Ramadan, Jarash Camp, September 3, 2001

Haifa Subdistrict
Al-Mansi ('Arab Baniha), Umm Basim, Baq'a Camp, July 19, 2001
Haifa, Fatima Husayn al-Jawabri, Baq'a Camp, July 19, 2001
Sabbarin, Jamila Hatib, Hittin Camp, August 5, 2001
Umm al-Zinat, Rafik 'Urabi Mahmud Hamdan Fahmawi, al-Risafi, Zarka, August 6, 2001

Al-Kafrayn, Yusif Muhammad Husayn al-Jammal, al-Risafi, Zarka, August 8, 2001

Al-Rihaniyya, Asad Nimir Dib Sidik, al-Risafi, Zarka, August 8, 2001

Burayka, Mustafa Sa'id, Hittin Camp, August 8, 2001

Khirbat al-Sarkas, Hittin Camp, August 18, 2001

Umm al-Zinat, Amina Ahmad Dabbur, Baq'a Camp, August 27, 2001

Al-Ghubayya al-Fauqa, Jamil 'Abd al-Rahman Muhsin, Baq'a Camp, Jordan, August 22, 2001

Qisarya, Abu Hakim, Baq'a Camp, September 17, 2001

Al-Kafrayn, Souf Camp, September 19, 2001

Al-Sindiyana, Ahmad 'Abdullah al-Sawalma, Souf Camp, September 19, 2001

Khirbat Lid (Lid al-'Awadin), Souf Camp, September 19, 2001

Daliyat al-Rawha', 'Alya Muhammad Hasan, Irbid Camp, September 20, 2001

Hadatha, Ahmad, Irbid Camp, September 20, 2001

Yajur, 'Alya 'Ali 'Abdullah, Irbid Camp, September 24, 2001

Yajur, Ayshi Muhammad Husayn Abu Shtaya, Irbid Camp, September 24, 2001

Jaffa Subdistrict

Al-'Abbasiyya, Fatma Muhammad 'Abd al-Hamid, Amman, July 19, 2001

Al-'Abbasiyya (al-Yahudiyya), Nijma Shawarib, Baq'a Camp, July 19, 2001

Al-'Abbasiyya, Shakir al-Musa, Amman, July 19, 2001

Kafr 'Ana, Muhammad Abu al-'Aziz Khayr, al-Wihdat Camp, Jordan, July 21, 2001

Kafr 'Ana, Rasmi Mahmud, al-Wihdat Camp, Jordan, July 21, 2001

Yazur, 'Uthman Yusif Abu Nabus, Baq'a Camp, July 23, 2001

Bayt Dajan, Umm Amal, Baq'a Camp, July 26, 2001

Abu Kishk, Hamdi Abu Hattab, Hittin Camp, July 29, 2001

Al-Shaykh Muwannis, Muhammad Hamad Haddad, Hittin Camp, July 29, 2001

Salama, 'Abd al-'Aziz Kamal al-Minawi, Hittin Camp, July 29, 2001

Bayt Dajan, anonymous elder woman, Hittin Camp, August 4, 2001

Fajja, Amina 'Umran Zahra, Hittin Camp, August 5, 2001

Yazur, Ra'ida Amman, August 7, 2001

Al-Mas'udiyya (Summayl), Yusra Ibrahim, Hittin Camp, August 11, 2001

Al-Jammasin al-Gharbi, Abu Sami, al-Husayn Camp, August 12, 2001

Al-Khayriyya, Khadra Muhammad Mustafa Abu al-Rus, Amman, Jordan, August 15, 2001

Saqiya, Abu Muhammad, Baq'a Camp, August 15, 2001

Bayt Dajan, Mahatta Camp, August 21, 2001

Fajja, Ahmad 'Abdullah al-Swalma, al-Husayn Camp, Jordan, September 11, 2001

Jaffa, Fatima Matar, Jabal Taj, September 12, 2001

Saqiya, Abu Muhammad, Hirshi, Amman, September 12, 2001

Jaffa, 'Abd al-Ghani Nasi, Zarka Camp, September 22, 2001

Jerusalem Subdistrict
Bayt Mahsir, Fatima 'Ubayd al-Ababdah, Baq'a Camp, July 23, 2001
Bayt Mahsir, 'Aysha 'Ali Mahmud Tayim, Manara, Amman, July 24, 2001
Saris, Mahmud Ziyad, al-Nasr, Amman, July 24, 2001
Abu Ghosh, Fatma, Baq'a Camp, July 25, 2001
Al-Maliha, Wadha Yusif 'Ammar, Jabal Taj, Amman, August 1, 2001
Qalunya, Hamdi Muhammad Matar, Jabal Amman, August 1, 2001
Lifta, 'Ali Mahmud Abu Ta'ih, Naz'ah, Amman, August 12, 2001
Dayr Yasin, Hilwi Muhammad 'Atallah, Mahatta Camp, August 21, 2001
Dayr Yasin, Umm Bassam, Mahatta Camp, August 21, 2001
Dayr Yasin, Khadija, Jabal Taj, Amman, August 29, 2001
Dayr Yasin, Muhammad Isma'il 'Id, Jabal Taj, Amman, August 29, 2001
'Ayn Karam, Khadija, Hashmi, Amman, September 2, 2001
'Ayn Karam, Umm Salim, Amman, August 30, 2001
'Ayn Karam, Shaykh Mahmud, Hashmi, Amman, September 2, 2001
'Ayn Karam, Sulayman, Hashmi, Amman, September 2, 2001
Jerusalem, (Shaykh Jarrah) Hazem Nuseibeh, Amman, September 30, 2001

Nablus Subdistrict
Summeil, Hittin Camp, August 5, 2001

Nazareth Subdistrict
'Arab al-Subeih, Sa'da al-Subeih, Irbid Camp, September 20, 2001

Al-Ramla Subdistrict
Al-Tira (Dindan), Umm 'Isa, al-Wihdat Camp, July 21, 2001
Dayr Tarif, Na'isa Khalid, al-Wihdat Camp, July 21, 2001
Sarafand al-'Amar, Amina 'Abd al-Qadir Hammad, Baq'a Camp, Jordan, July 23, 2001
Sarafand al-'Amar, Fatima Mahmud 'Ali, Baq'a Camp, July 23, 2001
Sarafand al-'Amar, Hasan Khalid Tarahan, Baq'a Camp, July 23, 2001
Abu Shusha, 'Abd al-Rahman Salih Abu Shraykh, Baq'a Camp, July 23, 2001
Al-Qubab, Aziza Mahmud Nababti, Baq'a Camp, July 23, 2001
Al-Ramla, Maysar 'Umar Abu Sahab, al-Husayn Camp, July 24, 2001
Al-Ramla, Muhibba al-Shami, Jabal Husayn, Amman, July 25, 2001
Saydun, Musa Muhammad Mansur, Baq'a Camp, July 26, 2001
Bayt Nabala, Hasan al-'Ashawi, Hittin Camp, July 28, 2001
'Aqir, 'Abd al-Fattah al-Asmar, Hittin Camp, July 29, 2001
Khulda, Ahmad Rashid Mizhir, al-Nasr, Amman, August 1, 2001
Bayt Jiz, Muhammad 'Abd al-Rahim, Hittin Camp, August 5, 2001
Al-Maghar, Tahsin Shihadi, Jabal al-Amir Faysal, August 9, 2001
Qatra, Yusuf Khalil Abu Sa'lan, Jabal al-Amir Faysal, August 9, 2001
Sarafand al-Kharab, Zaynab Hasan 'Anbar, Hittin Camp, August 11, 2001
Al-Na'ani, Muhammad Khamis Muhammad Hasanayn, Hittin Camp, August 18, 2001
Al-Haditha, Tababur, Amman, August 19, 2001

Al-Mukhayzin, Ziyad 'Abdullah al-Wihdat, Baq'a Camp, August 26, 2001
Bashshit, Latifa Muhammad Hamdan, Baq'a Camp, August 26, 2001
Bayt Susin, Wardi, Baq'a Camp, August 26, 2001
Shahma, Thurayya Shahin, Baq'a Camp, August 26, 2001
Al-Qubab, Iskan al-Hashimi, Amman, August 30, 2001
Dayr Ayyub, Fatma Muhammad 'Ali 'Ammar, Nuzha, Amman, August 30, 2001
Dayr Ayyub, Fatima Muhammad 'Ali, Hashmi, September 2, 2001
Bayt Nabala, Zahra Zaki, Mahatta Camp, September 9, 2001
Nahalin, Halima Sa'id 'Abdullah, Mahatta Camp, September 9, 2001
Abu Shusha, 'Abd al-Rahman Salih Abu Shraykh, al-Husayn Camp, September
    11, 2001
Al-Qubab, Halima Idris, Manara, Amman, September 12, 2001
Idnabba, Hirshi, September 12, 2001
Al-Lid, Darwish Mahmud Darwish, al-Husayn Camp, September 16, 2001

Tiberias Subdistrict
Ghuwayr Abu Shusha, Salih Ramadan Shatawi Hamudi, Hittin Camp,
    July 28, 2001
'Awlam, Isma'il Salih al-Ta'ib, Hittin Camp, August 18, 2001
Hadatha, 'Abd al-Salam Abu al-Hayja, al-Wihdat Camp, August 28, 2001
Ma'dhar, Salah Ahmad Gharib, Irbid Camp, September 24, 2001

Tulkarm Subdistrict
Wadi al-Hawarith, Abu Muhammad, Baq'a Camp, July 26, 2001
Wadi al-Hawarith, Baq'a Camp, July 26, 2001
Raml Zayta, Zakiyya Abu Hammad, Hittin Camp, July 28, 2001
Khirbat Bayt Lid, Husni 'Abd al-Latif 'Atawat, Zarka, August 8, 2001
Umm Khalid, Ahmad, 'Ayn Basha, Amman, August 27, 2001
Kafr Saba, 'Uthman Ahmad, Baq'a, September 17, 2001
Ghabat Kafr Sur (Bastat al-Falaq), Salim Abu Sayf, Souf Camp, September 18,
    2001

LEBANON INTERVIEWS
Manshiyya (Acre), Maryam 'Ali Wardi, 'Ayn al-Hilwa Camp, August 16, 2001
Qaddita (Safad), Ahmad Dakkur, 'Ayn al-Hilwa Camp, August 16, 2001
Safsaf (Safad), Abu Kamal, 'Ayn al-Hilwa Camp, August 16, 2001

Suhayl Natur, Democratic Front for the Liberation of Palestine, Mar Elias Camp,
    August 12, 2001
Mu'taz al-Dajani, Beirut, Arab Resource Center for Popular Culture (ARCPA),
    August 13, 2001

U.S. INTERVIEWS
Haifa, Masud 'Ali Masud, telephone interview (Chicago), September 11, 1998
Jerusalem, Edward Marroum, Alexandria, Va., September 22, 2002
Issa Nakhleh, telephone interview (New York), February 15, 2003

UNPUBLISHED MANUSCRIPTS

Mohammad, Khalid Abdullah Sulaiman. "The Influence of the Political Situation in Palestine on Arabic Poetry from 1917-1973." PhD diss. University of London, School of Oriental and African Studies, 1982.

Nazzal, Nafez. "The Flight of the Palestinian Arabs from Galilee: A Historical Analysis." PhD diss. Georgetown University: Washington, D.C., 1974.

Soukarieh, Maysson Fadel. "For the Sake of Remembrance: A Reader in English for Ninth Graders in the Palestinian Camps in Lebanon." MA thesis, American University of Beirut, February 2000. Interviews: Acre, Matti Bouri; Haifa, Khalid al-Khatib.

DOCUMENTARY FILMS

Collecting Stories from Exile: Chicago Palestinians Remember 1948. Chicago: American Friends Service Committee, 1999. Ayoub Talhami, Masud 'Ali Masud interviews.

NEWSPAPERS

Al-Ahram
Al-Dustour
Filastin
Guardian
Ha'aretz
Jerusalem Post
New York Times
Palestine Post
Times (London)

GOVERNMENT DOCUMENTS

Foreign Broadcast Intelligence Service (FBIS), European Section, Near and Middle East—North African Transmitters.

Foreign Relations of the United States: The Paris Peace Conference, 1919. Vol. 12. Washington, D.C.: U.S. Government Printing Office, 1947.

Foreign Relations of the United States, 1947: The Near East, South Asia, and Africa, part 2. Washington, D.C.: U.S. Government Printing Office, 1971.

Foreign Relations of the United States, 1948. Vol. 5, The Near East, South Asia, and Africa, part 1. Washington, D.C.: U.S. Government Printing Office, 1975.

Foreign Relations of the United States, 1948. Vol. 5, The Near East, South Asia, and Africa, part 2. Washington, D.C.: U.S. Government Printing Office, 1976.

Haycraft Report, Commission of Inquiry, Cmd. 1540, October 21, 1921.

Israeli Ministry of Defense, *Toldot Milchemet ha-Qomemiyyut* (The History of the War of Independence). Tel Aviv: Ma'arachot, 1959.

Israel State Archives (ISA). *Te'udot mediniyot ve-diplomatiyot, Detsember*

1947–Mai 1948 (Political and Diplomatic Documents, State of Israel, December 1947–May 1948), ed. Gedalia Yogev, Jerusalem 1979.

Palestine Royal Commission Report, Presented by the Secretary of State for the Colonies to Parliament by Command of His Majesty. London: His Majesty's Stationery Office, July 1937.

The Political History of Palestine under British Administration: Memorandum by His Britannic Majesty's Government, Presented in 1947 to the United Nations Special Committee on Palestine. Jerusalem, 1947. Reprinted by British Information Services, an Agency of the British Government. New York.

Report by His Majesty's Government in the United Kingdom of Great Britain and Northern Ireland to the Council of the League of Nations on the Administration of Palestine and Transjordan, 1937.

Survey of Palestine: Prepared in December 1945 and January 1946 for the Information of the Anglo-American Committee of Inquiry. Palestine: Government Printer, 1946. Reprinted by the Institute of Palestine Studies. Washington, D.C., 1991.

U.N. Information Center, London. "United Nations Relief for Palestine Refugees," no. iii, 13. February 4, 1949.

Books

Abu Eishe, Anwar. *Mémoires palestiniennes: La Terre dans la tête.* Paris: Clancier-Guénaud, 1982.

Abu-Lughod, Ibrahim, ed. *The Transformation of Palestine: Essays on the Origin and Development of the Arab-Israeli Conflict.* Evanston, Ill.: Northwestern University Press, 1971.

Abu Nowar, Maan. *The Jordanian-Israeli War, 1948–1951: A History of the Hashemite Kingdom of Jordan.* Reading, U.K.: Ithaca, 2002.

Abu-Sitta, Salman H. *The Palestinian Nakba, 1948: The Register of Depopulated Localities in Palestine.* London: Palestine Return Centre, 1998.

—. *From Refugees to Citizens at Home.* London: Palestine Land Society, 2001.

Antonius, George. *The Arab Awakening: The Story of the Arab National Movement.* New York: Capricorn, 1965.

The Arab Refugee Problem: How It Can Be Solved. Proposals, Submitted to the General Assembly of the United Nations, December 1951.

Al-'Arif, 'Arif, *Al-Nakba* (The Disaster). 6 vols. Beirut and Sidon: Al-Maktaba al-'Asriyya, 1956–60.

Avigur, Shaul, Yitzhak Ben-Zvi, Elazar Galili, Yehuda Slutzky, Ben-Zion Denur, and Gershon Rivlin, eds. *Sefer Toldot Hahaganah* (History of the Haganah). 3 vols. Tel Aviv: Am Oved, 1954–73.

Avizohar, Meir. *Paamei Medina.* Tel Aviv, 1994.

Ayalon, Avraham, ed. *Havitat Givati Bemilhemet Hakomemiut* (The Givati Brigade in the War of Independence), Tel Aviv: Ma'arachot, 1959.

Azcárate, Pablo de. *Mission in Palestine, 1948–1952.* Washington, D.C.: Middle East Institute, 1966.

Banks, Lynne Reid. *Torn Country: An Oral History of the Israeli War of Independence.* New York: Franklin Watts, 1982.

Bar-Zohar, Michael. *Ben-Gurion: The Armed Prophet.* Englewood Cliffs, N.J.: Prentice-Hall, 1966.

—. *Ben-Gurion: A Political Biography.* Vol. 1. Tel Aviv: Am Oved, 1975.

—. *Ben-Gurion: A Political Biography.* Vol. 2. Tel Aviv: Am Oved, 1977.

Begin, Menachem. *The Revolt.* Los Angeles: Nash, 1972.

Bell-Fialkoff, Andrew. *Ethnic Cleansing.* New York: St. Martin's, 1996.

Ben-Gurion, David. *Be-hilahem Yisrael* (As Israel Fights). Tel Aviv: Mapai, 1952.

—, ed. and trans. Mordekhai Nurock: *Rebirth and Destiny of Israel.* New York: Philosophical Library, 1954.

—. *Memoirs.* Vol. 2. Tel Aviv: Am Oved, 1974.

—. *The War Diary, 1948–1949.* 3 vols., Ed. Gershon Rivlin and Elhannan Orren. Tel Aviv: Israel Defense Ministry Press, 1982.

Bethell, Nicholas. *The Palestine Triangle.* New York: G. P. Putnam's Sons, 1979.

Bierman, John, and Colin Smith. *Fire in the Night: Wingate of Burma, Ethiopia, and Zion.* New York: Random House, 1999.

Black, Ian, and Benny Morris. *Israel's Secret Wars.* New York: Grove Weidenfeld, 1991.

Carmel, Moshe. *Ma'arachot Tzafon* (Northern Battles). Tel Aviv: IDF-Ma'arachot, 1949.

Cohen, Eliot A. *Supreme Command.* New York: Anchor, 2002.

Collins, Larry, and Dominique Lapierre. *O Jerusalem!* London: Pan, 1972.

Department of Oral History Staff. *Oral History Interview Guidelines.* Washington, D.C.: United States Holocaust Memorial Museum, 1998.

Dodd, Peter, and Halim Barakat. *River without Bridges: A Study of the Exodus of the 1967 Palestinian Arab Refugees.* Monograph Series no. 10. Beirut: Institute of Palestine Studies, 1968.

Dunaway, David K., and Willa K. Baum, eds. *Oral History: An Interdisciplinary Anthology.* Nashville, Tenn.: American Association for State and Local History, 1984.

Finkelstein, Norman, G. *Image and Reality of the Israel-Palestine Conflict.* London: Verso, 1995.

Flapan, Simha. *The Future of Palestine.* With a preface by Musa Alami. Beirut: Hermon, 1970.

—. *The Birth of Israel: Myths and Realities.* New York: Pantheon, 1987.

—. *Zionism and the Palestinians.* London: Croom Helm, 1979.

Gabbay, Rony. *A Political Study of the Arab-Jewish Conflict: The Arab Refugee Problem (A Case Study).* Geneva: E. Droz; Paris, Minard, 1959.

García Granados, Jorge. *The Birth of Israel: The Drama as I Saw It.* New York: Alfred A. Knopf, 1948.

Giv'ati, Moshe. *In the Path of Desert and Fire: The History of the Ninth Armored Battalion, 1948–1984* (Hebrew). Tel Aviv: Ma'arachot/Defense Ministry Press, 1994.

Grossman, Dave. *On Killing: The Psychological Cost of Learning to Kill in War and Society.* Boston: Little Brown, 1995.

Gutman, Roy, David Rieff, and Anthony Dworkin, eds. *Crimes of War: The Book,* New York: W. W. Norton, 1999.

Hadawi, Sami. *Bitter Harvest: Palestine between 1914–1967.* New York: New World, 1967.

—. *Palestinian Rights and Losses in 1948: A Comprehensive Study.* London: Saqi, 1988.

Herman, Judith. *Trauma and Recovery: The Aftermath of Violence—from Domestic Abuse to Political Terror.* New York: Basic, 1997.

Hurewitz, J. C. *The Struggle for Palestine.* New York: W. W. Norton, 1950.

Ilan, Amitzur. *The Origin of the Arab-Israeli Arms Race: Arms, Embargo, Military Power and Decision in the 1948 Palestine War.* New York: New York University Press, 1996.

John, Robert, and Sami Hadawi. *The Palestine Diary.* Vol. 1, 1914–1945; Vol. 2: 1945–1948. New York: New World, 1970.

Jones, Christina. *The Untempered Wind: Forty Years in Palestine.* London: Longman, 1975.

Jones, Philip. *Britain and Palestine, 1914–1948: Archival Sources for the History of the British Mandate.* Oxford: Oxford University Press, 1979.

Joseph, Dov. *The Faithful City: The Siege of Jerusalem.* New York: Simon and Schuster, 1960.

Kanaan, Sharif, and Nihad Zitawi. *Deir Yassin.* Monograph no. 4, Destroyed Palestinian Villages Documentation Project. Bir Zeit University, 1987.

Karmi, Ghada, and Eugene Cotran, eds. *The Palestinian Exodus, 1948–1998.* Reading, U.K.: Ithaca, 1999.

Karsh, Ephraim. *Fabricating Israeli History: The "New Historians."* London: Frank Cass, 1997.

Katz, Yossi. *Partner to Partition: The Jewish Agency's Partition Plan in the Mandate Era.* London: Frank Cass, 1998.

Keesing's Contemporary Archives. London: Keesing's, 1987.

Khalidi, Walid, ed. *From Haven to Conquest: Readings in Zionism and the Palestine Problem until 1948.* Beirut: Institute for Palestine Studies, 1971.

—. *Before Their Diaspora: A Photographic History of the Palestinians, 1876–1948.* Washington, D.C.: Institute for Palestine Studies, 1991.

—. *All That Remains: The Palestinian Villages Occupied and Depopulated by Israel in 1948.* Washington, D.C.: Institute of Palestine Studies, 1992.

—. *Deir Yassin: 9 April 1948.* Beirut: Institute for Palestine Studies, 2000.

Khalidi, Rashid. *Palestinian Identity: The Construction of Modern National Consciousness.* New York: Columbia University Press, 1997.

Khoury, Philip S. *Syria and the French Mandate: The Politics of Arab Nationalism, 1920–1945.* Princeton, N.J.: Princeton University Press, 1987.

Khuri, Musa, ed. *Tension, Terror and Blood in the Holy Land.* Damascus: Palestine Arab Refugees Institution, 1955.

Kirkbride, Alec. *From the Wings: Amman Memoirs, 1947–51*. London: Frank Cass, 1976.

Klieman, Aaron S. *Foundations of British Policy in the Arab World: The Cairo Conference of 1921*. Baltimore: Johns Hopkins University Press, 1970.

Kohn, Hans, ed. *Nationalism and the Jewish Ethic*. New York: Schocken, 1962.

Kurtzman, Dan. *Genesis 1948: The First Arab-Israeli War*. New York: World, 1970.

Levy (Levitza), Yitzhak. *Jerusalem in the War of Independence* (Hebrew). Tel Aviv: Ma'arachot (Israel Defense Army Press), 1986.

—. *Nine Measures* (Hebrew). Tel Aviv: Ma'arachot (Israel Defense Army Press), 1986.

Levenberg, Haim. *The Military Preparations of the Arab Community in Palestine, 1945–1948*. London: Frank Cass, 1993.

Lorch, Netanel. *The Edge of the Sword: Israel's War of Independence, 1947–1949*. New York: G. P. Putnam's Sons, 1961.

Louis, William Roger, and Robert W. Stookey, eds. *The End of the Palestine Mandate*. Austin: University of Texas Press, 1986.

Lynd, Staughton, Sam Bahour, and Alice Lynd, eds. *Homeland: Oral Histories of Palestine and Palestinians*. New York: Olive Branch, 1994.

Masalha, Nur. *The Expulsion of the Palestinians: The Concept of "Transfer" in Zionist Political Thought, 1882–1948*. Washington, D.C.: Institute for Palestine Studies, 1992.

McGowan, Daniel A., and Marc H. Ellis, eds. *Remembering Deir Yassin: The Future of Israel and Palestine*. New York: Olive Branch, 1998.

—, and Matthew C. Hogan. *The Saga of Deir Yassin: Massacre, Revisionism and Reality*. Geneva, N.Y.: Deir Yassin Remembered, 1999.

Meir, Golda. *My Life*. New York: G. P. Putnam's Sons, 1975.

Menuhin, Moshe. *The Decadence of Judaism*. New York: Exposition, 1965.

Miller, Ylana N. *Government and Society in Rural Palestine, 1920–48*. Austin: University of Texas, 1985.

Milstein, Uri. *History of Israel's War of Independence*. Vol. 1, *A Nation Girds for War*. Trans. and ed. Alan Sacks. Lanham, Md.: University Press of America, 1996.

—. *History of Israel's War of Independence*. Vol. 2, *The First Month*. Trans. and ed. Alan Sacks. Lanham, Md.: University Press of America, 1997.

—. *History of Israel's War of Independence*. Vol. 3, *The First Invasion*. Trans. and ed. Alan Sacks. Lanham, Md.: University Press of America, 1998.

—. *History of Israel's War of Independence*. Vol. 4, *Out of Decision Came Crisis*. Trans. and ed. Alan Sacks. Lanham, Md.: University Press of America, 1998.

Monroe, Elizabeth. *Britain's Moment in the Middle East, 1914–1956*. Baltimore: Johns Hopkins University Press, 1963.

Moore, John Norton, ed. *The Arab-Israeli Conflict: Readings and Documents*. Vol. 1. Princeton, N.J.: Princeton University Press, 1974.

Morris, Benny. *The Birth of the Palestinian Refugee Problem, 1947–1949*. Cambridge: Cambridge University Press, 1987.

—. *1948 and After: Israel and the Palestinians.* Oxford, U.K.: Clarendon, 1990.

—. *The Birth of the Palestinian Refugee Problem Revisited.* Cambridge: Cambridge University Press, 2004.

Naimark, Norman M. *Fires of Hatred: Ethnic Cleansing in Twentieth-Century Europe.* Cambridge, Mass.: Harvard University Press, 2001.

Nakhleh, Issa. *Encyclopedia of the Palestine Problem.* Vols. 1 and 2. New York: Intercontinental, 1991.

Nazzal, Nafez. *The Palestinian Exodus from Galilee, 1948.* Beirut: Institute for Palestine Studies, 1978.

Nijim, Basheer K., ed., and Bishara Muammar, researcher. *Toward the De-Arabization of Palestine/Israel, 1945–1977.* Dubuque, Iowa: Kendall Hunt, 1984.

Palumbo, Michael. *The Palestinian Catastrophe: The 1948 Expulsion of a People from Their Homeland.* London: Quartet, 1989.

Papp, Richard, ed. *As I Saw It: By Dean Rusk as told to Richard Rusk.* New York: W. W. Norton, 1990.

Pappé, Ilan. *Britain and the Arab-Israeli Conflict, 1947–51.* London: MacMillan, 1988.

—. *The Making of the Arab-Israeli Conflict, 1947–51.* London: I. B. Tauris, 1992.

—. *The Ethnic Cleansing of Palestine.* Oxford, U.K.: Oneworld, 2006.

Rogan, Eugene L., and Avi Shlaim. *The War for Palestine: Rewriting the History of 1948.* Cambridge: Cambridge University Press, 2001.

Sabbagh, Hasib. *From Palestinian Refugee to Citizen of the World.* Ed. Mary-Jane Deeb and Mary E. King. Washington, D.C.: Middle East Institute, 1996.

Sakakini, Hala. *Jerusalem and I: A Personal Record.* Amman: Economic, 1990.

Sayegh, Fayez A. *The Palestine Refugees.* Washington, D.C.: Amara, 1952.

Schechtman, Joseph B. *European Population Transfers, 1939–1945.* New York: Oxford University Press, 1947.

—. *The Arab Refugee Problem.* New York: Philosophical Library, 1952.

Segev, Tom. *1949: The First Israelis.* New York: Owl, 1998.

Seldon, Anthony, and Joanna Pappworth. *By Word of Mouth: Elite Oral History.* London: Methuen, 1983.

Shapira, Anita. *Land and Power: The Zionist Resort to Force, 1881–1948.* Oxford: Oxford University Press, 1992.

Shavit, Yaakov, ed. *Havlaga o teguva* (Self-Restraint or Response?). Tel Aviv, 1983.

Shlaim, Avi. *Collusion Across the Jordan: King Abdullah, the Zionist Movement, and the Partition of Palestine.* New York: Columbia University Press, 1988.

Silberstein, Laurence J. *New Perspectives on Israeli History: The Early Years of the State.* New York: New York University Press, 1991.

Simons, Chaim. *International Proposals to Transfer Arabs from Palestine, 1895–1947: A Historical Survey.* Hoboken, N.J.: Ktav, 1988.

Steward, Desmond. *Theodor Herzl: Artist and Politician.* London: Hamish Hamilton, 1974.

St. John, Robert. *Ben-Gurion.* New York: Doubleday, 1959.

Sugrue, Thomas. *Watch for the Morning: The Story of Palestine's Jewish Pioneers and Their Battle for the Birth of Israel.* New York: Harper and Brothers, 1950.

Swedenburg, Ted. *Memories of Revolt: The 1936–1939 Rebellion and the Palestinian National Past.* Minneapolis: University of Minnesota Press, 1995.

Talmi, Ephraim. *Lexicon Melhemit ha-Itzmaout* (A Lexicon of the War of Independence). Tel Aviv: Davar, 1970.

Tamari, Salim, ed. *Jerusalem 1948: The Arab Neighbourhoods and their Fate in the War.* Jerusalem: Institute of Jerusalem Studies and Badil Resource Center, 1999.

Tannous, Izzat. *The Palestinians: Eyewitness History of Palestine under British Mandate.* New York: IGT, 1988.

Teveth, Shabtai. *Moshe Dayan: The Soldier, the Man, the Legend.* Trans. Leah Zinder and David Zinder. Boston: Houghton Mifflin, 1973.

—. *Ben-Gurion and the Palestinian Arabs from Peace to War.* New York: Oxford University Press, 1985.

Thicknesse, S. G. *Arab Refugees: A Survey of Resettlement Possibilities.* London: Royal Institute of International Affairs, 1949.

Thompson, Paul. *The Voice of the Past: Oral History.* Oxford: Oxford University Press, 1988.

Tibawai, A. L. *Arab Education in Mandatory Palestine: A Study of Three Decades of British Administration.* London: Luzac, 1956.

Truman, Harry. *Years of Trial and Hope.* Vol. 2. Garden City, N.Y.: Doubleday, 1956.

Tzur, Zeev. *From the Partition Dispute to the Allon Plan* (Hebrew). Tel Aviv, 1982.

Ulizki, Yossef. *From Events to a War* (Hebrew). Tel Aviv: Haganah Publication of Documents, 1951.

Urquhart, Brian. *Ralph Bunche: An American Life.* New York: W. W. Norton, 1993.

Weizmann, Chaim. *Trial and Error.* London: East and West, 1950.

Wilson, Major R. D. *Cordon and Search: With Sixth Airborne Division in Palestine.* Aldershot, U.K.: Gale and Polden, 1949.

Wilson, Mary. *King Abdullah, Britain and the Making of Jordan.* Cambridge: Cambridge University Press, 1987.

Wolpert, Stanley. *Shameful Flight: The Last Years of the British Empire in India.* Oxford: Oxford University Press, 2006.

Yahav, Dan. *Purity of Arms: Ethos, Myth and Reality, 1936–1956* (Hebrew). Tel Aviv: Tamuz, 2002.

Zurayk, Constantine K. *The Meaning of the Disaster.* Trans. R. Bayly Winder. Beirut: Khayat, 1956.

ARTICLES

Abbasi, Mustafa. "The Battle for Safad in the War of 1948: A Revised Study." *International Journal of Middle East Studies* 36 (2004): 21–47.

Al-Qawauqji, Fawzi. "Memoirs 1948, Part 1." *Journal of Palestine Studies* 1.4 (1972): 27–57.

—. "Memoirs 1948, Part 2." *Journal of Palestine Studies* 2.4 (1972): 3–33.

Ashkar, Ahmad. Abu Salim Khawalid interview, the National Committee for the Defence of the Rights of the Uprooted in Israel. Minority Rights Group International. n.d.

Braun, Hanna. "Memoirs of an Anti-Zionist Jew." *Olive Stone,* Autumn 1994: 3–4.

Budeiri, Musa. "A Chronicle of a Defeat Foretold: The Battle for Jerusalem in the Memoirs of Anwar Nuseibeh." *Jerusalem Quarterly File,* nos. 11–12 (2001), www.jqf-jerusalem.org/ journal/2001/jqf11-12/anwar.html.

Childers, Erskine. "The Other Exodus." *Spectator,* May 12, 1961, 672–75.

Cohen, Avner. "Israel and Chemical/Biological Weapons: History, Deterrence, and Arms Control." *Nonproliferation Review* 8 (Fall–Winter 2001): 29–30.

Cunningham, Alan. "Palestine—The Last Days of the Mandate." *International Affairs* 24.4 (1948): 481-90.

Fleischmann, Ellen. "Crossing the Boundaries of History: Exploring Oral History in Researching Palestinian Women in the Mandate Period." *Women's History Review* 5.3 (1996): 351–371.

Gilmour, David. "The Unregarded Prophet: Lord Curzon and the Palestine Question." *Journal of Palestine Studies* 25.3 (1996): 60–68.

Hogan, Matthew C. "The 1948 Massacre at Deir Yassin Revisited." *Historian* 63.2 (2001): 309–33.

Karmi, Ghada. "The 1948 Exodus: A Family Story." *Journal of Palestine Studies* 33.2 (1994): 31–40.

Khalidi, Walid. "The Fall of Haifa." *Middle East Forum,* December 1959, 22–32.

—. "Why Did the Palestinians Leave?" *Middle East Forum,* July 1959, 21–24.

—. "Plan Dalet: Master Plan for the Conquest of Palestine." *Journal of Palestine Studies* 18.69 (1988): 22–28.

—. "Selected Documents on the 1948 Palestine War." *Journal of Palestine Studies* 27.3 (1998): 60–105.

Masalha, Nur. "From Propaganda to Scholarship: Dr. Joseph Schechtman and the Origins of Israeli Polemics on the Palestinian Refugees." *Holy Land Studies: A Multidisciplinary Journal* 2.2 (2004): 188–97.

Morris, Benny. "The Causes and Character of the Arab Exodus from Palestine: The Israel Defence Forces Intelligence Branch Analysis of June 1948." *Middle Eastern Studies* 22.1 (1986): 5–19.

—. "Yosef Weitz and the Transfer Committees, 1948–49." *Middle Eastern Studies* 22.4 (October 1986): 522–61.

—. "The Eel and History: A Reply to Shabtai Teveth." *Tikkun* 5.1 (1989): 27–9.

—. "The Historiography of Deir Yassin." *Journal of Israeli History* 24.1 (2005): 79–107.

Shlaim, Avi, "The Debate about 1948." *International Journal of Middle East Studies* 27.3 (1995): 288–304.

Shoufani, Elias. "The Fall of a Village." *Journal of Palestine Studies* 1.4 (1972): 108–21.

St. Aubin, W. de "Peace and Refugees in the Middle East." *Middle East Journal* 3.3 (1949): 249–59.

Stauffer, Thomas R. "The Cost of Conflict in the Middle East: What the U.S. Has Spent." *Middle East Policy* 10.1 (2003): 45–102.

Tal, David. "The Forgotten War: Jewish-Palestinian Strife in Mandatory Palestine, December 1947–May 1948." *Israeli Affairs* 6.3 (2000): 3–21.

—. "Between Intuition and Professionalism: Israeli Military Leadership during the 1948 Palestine War." *Journal of Military History* 68 (2004): 885–909.

Teveth, Shabtai. "The Palestine Arab Refugee Problem and Its Origins." *Middle Eastern Studies* 26.2 (1990): 220–26.

Thomson, Alistair. "Fifty Years On: An International Perspective on Oral History," *Journal of American History* 85.2 (1998): 581–595.

Weizmann, Chaim. "Palestine's Role in the Solution of the Jewish Problem." *Foreign Affairs* 20.2 (1942): 337–38.

INTERNET WEBSITES

Britain's Small Wars, www.britains-smallwars.com.

Crimes of War: the Book, www.crimesofwar.org/thebook/arab-israeli-war.html.

Isseroff, Ami. Peace Middle East Dialog Group. www.ariga.com/peacewatch/dy/dycg.htm.

Jerusalemites, www.jerusalemites.org, Ahmad Tell, "The Battle of Old Jerusalem in 1948."

Palestine Remembered. www.allthatremains.com.

Shahak, Israel, "The New Israeli Historians and 1948," 12 February 1995. www.soci.niu.edu/~phildept/Kabitan/Morris/html.

MAPS

Abu-Sitta, Salman H. *Palestine 1948: 50 Years after Al-Nakba—The Towns and Villages Depopulated by the Zionist Invasion of 1948.* London: Palestine Return Centre, 1998.

—. *Palestine 1948: Commemoration of Al-Nakba. The Towns and Villages Depopulated by the Zionist Invasion of 1948,* 2001.

Palestine, Boundaries in Majority Plan. Research Dept., Foreign Office, September 1947, TNA PREM 8 859.

Palestine, Civil and Military Administrative Boundaries. GS1 HQ Palestine (1943, 1944, 1947), 19 Field Survey Regiment, R.E., June 1948.

Palestine, Evacuation of Formations and Units. Period 1 December 1947–1 April 1948, Geographical Section, General Staff, W.O. 1945.

Palestine, Index to Villages and Settlements, Land in Jewish Possession 31 December 1944, Survey of Palestine, April 1946.

Palestine, Survey of Palestine, April 1946.

INDEX

* Page numbers in italics indicate maps or photographs

171n130, 175, 219n11, 405
Maccabi (Operation), 208
MacMillan, Sir Gordon Holmes Alexander
  biographical information, 405
  on British withdrawal from Palestine, 120,
    123, 128, 129, 134, 135
  on de-Arabization of Haifa and Jaffa, 256,
    257, 264, 281, 282, 285
  on early part of civil war (through Feb. 1948),
    143, 148, 153, 157
  on end of mandate, 335, 352
  on escalation of civil war (March-April 1948),
    177, 192, 193, 200, 201, 202, 203, 204, 207
  nonintervention policy of, 372
  on prelude to civil war, 65, 69, 71
MacMillan Report, 75n44, 143, 153, 202, 282
Madahil, *327*, 391
Ma'dhar, *210*, 215–17, 225n223, 291
al-Maghar, *298*, 300, 302–3, 305, 390
al-Mahir, Fatima, 340
Mahmud, Abu, 187
Mahmud, Rasmih, 293
Mahmud, Shaykh, 189–90
al-Mahmudiyya (al-Mirr), *290*, 389
al-Majdal, *210*, 295, 308–10, 391
Maklef, Mordechai, 227
al-Maliha, 189, 195, *206*, 207, 209, 211, 389
al-Manara ('Arab al-Manara), *210*, 211, 214, 216,
  335, 391
mandate Palestine. *See also* specific towns,
  villages, and subdistricts
  administrative boundaries, civil and
    military, *118*
  allotment to Britain after WWI, 53
  Arab rebellion of 1936–39, 55–57, 82, 84
  British in. *See* British in Palestine
  British withdrawal from. *See* British
    withdrawal from Palestine
  civil war period in. *See* civil war
  depopulated towns and villages
    list of, 387–92
    map of, *380*
  end of, 350–53
  organized immigration by Jews to, 27, 51–56,
    59, 102, 133, 161
  roads and railways
    civil war battles for control of, 182–84, 233,
      276, 341
    map of, *140*
  subdistricts and capitals, 30
  in World War I and postwar years, 51–55
  Zionist insurgency, pre-civil war, 61–66
  Zionist preparation for war and expulsion of
    Arabs (1930s-40s), 58–61, *60*
al-Manshiyya (Acre), *346*, 347, 387

al-Manshiyya (Jaffa quarter), 272, 276, 287
al-Manshiyya (Manshiyyat Samakh), 210, 211,
  212, 216, 346, 390, 391
al-Mansi ('Arab Baniha), *196*, 197, *259*, 390
al-Mansura (al-Ramla), *298*, 390
al-Mansura (Tiberias), *210*, 392
Mansurat al-Khayt, *327*, 365n157, 391
Mapai (Labor Party), 54, 86, 315
Mapam, 199, 339, 354, 357, 365n145
Marchal, F., 213
Mardam, Jamil, 114n87, 405
Marriott, Cyril, 255
Marshall, George C., 360
Masalha, Nur, 37, 41–43, 81
massacres
  al-Husayniyya, 329
  'Arab al-Subeih, 349
  'Ayn al-Zaytun, 332, 337, 356
  al-Dawayima, 357
  Dayr Yasin, 185–92. *See also* Dayr Yasin
  Hawsha, 261, 356
  Kafr 'Ana, 293–95
  al-Maghar, 302–3, 305
  Mount Scopus, 203–5
  Nasir al-Din, 212–14, 216, 286, 348, 356, 392
  numbers and sites of, 356, 365n157
  oil refinery massacre, Haifa, and reprisal,
    230–32
  Tantura, 261, 263, 269n180
  Zionist use of, 356–59
Masud, Masud 'Ali, 191
al-Mas'udiyya (Summayl), *290*, 295, 314, 389
Matar, Hamdi Muhammad, iv, 103, 183–84,
  223n129, 381
Mazra'at al-Jawfa (Khirbat al-Jawfa), *196*, 390
Mazari' al-Daraja (al-Dirdara), *326*, 391
McMahon-Hussein correspondence, 52
Meade, Stephen J., 185, 220n53, 223n133
Medhurst, Sir Charles, 91
Meir (Meyerson), Golda
  biographical information, 405
  in early part of civil war (through Feb. 1948),
    149
  in escalation of civil war (March-April 1948),
    187, 190, 220n65, 221n83
  in final days of mandate (April-May 1948),
    339, 350
  Haifa campaign, 254
  in prelude to civil war, 65
  "transfer" of Arab populations, support for,
    86, 112n42
Menuhin, Moshe, 80–81
Meuron, Maximilian de, 343
Middle East Land Forces (MELF), 70, 75n49, 120,
  136n46, 137n64, 393